THE
YOUNG
OFFENDERS
ACT
ANNOTATED

by

Nicholas Bala and Heino Lilles
Faculty of Law, Queen's University
Kingston, Ontario

Published by

Richard De Boo Publishers in cooperation with
The Solicitor General Canada and the
Canadian Government Publishing Centre,
Supply and Services Canada.

These materials were submitted in November, 1982, in fulfillment of a contract between the Ministry of the Solicitor General of Canada and the authors. Published by the Policy Branch, under the authority of the Hon. Bob Kaplan, P.C., M.P., Solicitor General of Canada, and produced by the Communication Division, Solicitor General Canada. The views expressed in this report do not necessarily reflect the views or policies of the Solicitor General of Canada.

Published and distributed by

 **Richard De Boo Publishers**

81 Curlew Drive
Don Mills, Ontario
M3A 3P7
(416) 445-4940

Canadian Cataloguing in Publication Data

Bala, Nicholas C.
The Young Offenders Act Annotated
Includes index.
ISBN 0-88820-184-2
1. Canada. Young Offenders Act.   2. Children — Legal status, laws, etc. — Canada.
3. Juvenile delinquency — Canada.   I. Lilles, Heino.   II. Canada. Young Offenders Act.
III. Title.
KE9445.A315B34   1984   345.71'03   C84-098882-6

FOREWORD

Passage of the *Young Offenders Act* marked the end of a critical phase in the lengthy process of reform of the Canadian Juvenile Justice System. The next phase, however, involving as it does the application of the law, is no less critical. Although I am of the view that the *Young Offenders Act* is basically sound and realistic legislation, it cannot in itself realize the goals of reform for, like any other system of law, it is highly dependent for its success on those who administer it. Thus, the roles to be played by the judges, police, prosecutors, defence counsel, law enforcement officers, court clerks, probation officers and other correctional and social service personnel, in implementing the Act, are vital. I am conficent that they will meet this challenge with commitment and resolve.

I would like to express my sincere appreciation to the authors of *The Young Offenders Act Annotated*, Professor Nicholas Bala and Professor Heino Lilles, for their untiring efforts in its realization. The high calibre of this work is a reflection of their dedication and expertise. I expect that this manual will be an invaluable tool for those who will be entrusted with the responsibility of applying this new law. In making the manual available, it is hoped that my Ministry will further contribute to the smooth and uniform implementation of the *Young Offenders Act* throughout Canada.

Bob Kaplan, P.C., M.P.
Solicitor General of Canada

PREFACE

The *Young Offenders Act* is innovative legislation which will create a new way of dealing with young persons who violate the criminal law in Canada. The basic principles and philosophies, the procedures, the rights and responsibilities are all markedly changed from those now in effect under the *Juvenile Delinquents Act*. The *Young Offenders Act* is an important piece of legislation; it will mark the beginning of a new era of juvenile justice in this country.

The Y.O.A. is a complex piece of legislation and these materials are intended to serve as a guide for those who will be implementing and interpreting the Act. Each section of the Act is set out and then followed by a commentary. The discussion explains the meaning of each section and its significance in relation to other sections of the Act, provisions of the *Criminal Code* and other legislation; where appropriate, the implications of the common law and the *Canadian Charter of Rights and Freedoms* are also explained. These materials do not attempt to take a critical policy perspective but rather, provide an explanation of the policy rationale for the enactment of the provisions of the Y.O.A. In addition, the novel features of the Act are contrasted to the law and practice under the *Juvenile Delinquents Act*.

The *Young Offenders Act Annotated* is written for an experienced professional audience: judges, Crown attorneys, defence counsel, court clerks, probation officers and other correctional and social service personnel. This is not an introductory text. It is assumed that readers are familiar with the fundamental principles of the Canadian criminal justice system and will, for example, have ready access to a copy of the *Criminal Code*.

It is possible to read this volume from beginning to end. It is also intended that readers should be able to use this as a reference work and refer to the discussion of a single section of the Act, recognizing that many of the provisions of the Y.O.A. are interrelated. For the legal researcher, this volume may serve as a useful tool; there are many references to existing jurisprudence and such secondary sources as articles and textbooks. It is not intended, however, that this volume should serve as a comprehensive research text.

As these materials were completed in November 1982 and deal with legislation which was not yet proclaimed in force, they inevitably have a speculative quality. An attempt has been made to provide some certainty and guidance for those who must interpret and implement the Act. It is, however ultimately they who must decide what the Act means and how its provisions are to be put into effect. The approaches taken with respect to a number of issues were significantly influenced by our discussions with Judge J.R. Omer Archambault, Director of Policy (Young Offenders), Policy Branch, Ministry of the Solicitor General, but it must bestressed that the views expressed herein do not necessarily reflect the views or policies of the Solicitor General of Canada.

For ease of exposition, the general practice of using masculine pronouns and adjectives in situations where the person referred to may be male or female has been adopted. It goes without saying that judges, lawyers, probation officers, young persons and others come in both sexes.

Nicholas Bala
Heino Lilles
of the Faculty of Law
Queen's University

ACKNOWLEDGEMENTS

These materials could not have been prepared without the efforts of our research assistants: Janet Drysdale, a recent graduate of the Faculty of Law at Queen's University, and two third-year law students at Queen's, Vincent Westwick and Tom Brigham. We thank them for their diligence, intelligence and enthusiasm.

We thank the secretaries and staff at the Faculty of Law at Queen's University, and in particular Tricia McIlveen who, with grace and good humour, did the bulk of typing of the numerous drafts of these materials. We also thank Angela Mangiacasale for her painstaking work as a proofreader, and John Scheulderman for his assistance with the index.

We also express our gratitude to Judge J.R. Omer Archambault, Judge Frederick W. Coward, Mary-Anne Kirvan, Maureen Shea-DesRosiers and the staff of the Young Offenders Policy Division of the Ministry of the Solicitor General of Canada for their assistance, advice, support and patience.

The Faculty of Law at Queen's University provided us with a place to work and materials to work with, and for this we are grateful. A number of colleagues made helpful suggestions, in particular Professor Allan Manson was of great assistance.

Finally, we must thank our families, and especially our wives, Martha and Sheila. They provided the support and advice we have come to expect, but always continue to appreciate.

Nicholas Bala
Heino Lilles

TABLE OF CONTENTS

JURISDICTION: SECTIONS 5 AND 6

DETENTION PRIOR TO DISPOSITION:
SECTIONS 7 AND 8

NOTICES TO PARENTS: SECTIONS 9 AND 10

RIGHT TO COUNSEL: SECTION 11

APPEARANCE: SECTION 12

MEDICAL AND PSYCHOLOGICAL REPORTS: SECTION 13

PRE-DISPOSITION REPORT: SECTION 14

TRANSFER OF JURISDICTION: SECTION 18

ADJUDICATION: SECTION 19

DISPOSITIONS: SECTIONS 20 TO 26

APPEALS: SECTION 27

REVIEW OF DISPOSITIONS: SECTIONS 28 TO 34

TEMPORARY RELEASE FROM CUSTODY: SECTION 35

MAINTENANCE AND USE OF RECORDS:
SECTIONS 40 TO 46

CONTEMPT OF COURT: SECTION 47

FORFEITURE OF RECOGNIZANCES: SECTIONS 48 AND 49

INTERFERENCE WITH DISPOSITIONS: SECTION 50

APPLICATION OF THE CRIMINAL CODE: SECTION 51

PROCEDURE: SECTIONS 52 TO 55

EVIDENCE: SECTIONS 56 TO 63

FORMS, REGULATIONS AND RULES OF COURT: SECTIONS 66 TO 68

YOUTH JUSTICE COMMITTEES: SECTION 69

AGREEMENTS WITH PROVINCES: SECTION 70

CONSEQUENTIAL AMENDMENTS: SECTIONS 71 TO 78

TABLE OF FORMS
under
THE YOUNG OFFENDERS ACT

TABLE OF CASES

SHORT TITLE
(Section 1)

SECTION 1

1. *Short title.*—This Act may be cited as the *Young Offenders* Act.

Title: section 1

The short title of the Act is the *Young Offenders Act*. A previous draft model Act to replace the *Juvenile Delinquents Act* was entitled the *Young Persons in Conflict with the Law Act*. The title of the new Act denotes a young person in conflict with the law, as distinct from any involvement with child welfare or child protection legislation.

The term "young offender" means a young person who has violated any federal statute, rule or regulation. It also reflects the narrower offence jurisdiction of the Y.O.A., and emphasizes that young persons are responsible for their illegal behaviour.

The legislative citation is S.C. 1980-81-82-83, c. 110.

INTERPRETATION
(Section 2)

Introduction

The definition section, explaining words and expressions used in the *Young Offenders Act*, is found in s. 2. The Y.O.A. uses a number of terms that are different from the *Juvenile Delinquents Act*, thus some explanation is warranted. Moreover, the terminology used at present with respect to delivery of services may vary from province to province, making the common frame of reference found in s. 2 helpful. According to s-s. 2(4) of the Y.O.A., the definitions in the *Criminal Code* apply in the case of words and expressions not defined in the Y.O.A. Only terms that are likely to cause difficulty are discussed below.

SECTION 2

2. (1) *Definitions.*—In this Act,

"adult" means a person who is neither a young person nor a child;

"alternative measures" means measures other than judicial proceedings under this Act used to deal with a young person alleged to have committed an offence;

"child" means a person who is or, in the absence of evidence to the contrary, appears to be under the age of twelve years;

"disposition" means a disposition made under section 20 or sections 28 to 33 and includes a confirmation or a variation of a disposition;

"offence" means an offence created by an Act of Parliament or by any regulation, rule, order, by-law or ordinance made thereunder other than an ordinance of the Yukon Territory or the Northwest Territories;

"ordinary court" means the court that would, but for this Act, have jurisdiction in respect of an offence alleged to have been committed;

"parent" includes, in respect of another person, any person who is under a legal duty to provide for that other person or any person who has, in law or in fact, the custody or control of that other person;

"predisposition report" means a report on the personal and family history and present environment of a young person made in accordance with section 14;

"progress report" means a report made in accordance with section 28 on the performance of a young person against whom a disposition has been made;

"provincial director" means a person, a group or class of persons or a body appointed or designated by or pursuant to an Act of the legislature of a province or by the Lieutenant Governor in Council of a province or his delegate to perform in that province, either generally or in a specific case, any of the duties or functions of a provincial director under this Act;

"review board" means a review board established or designated by a province for the purposes of section 30;

"young person" means a person who is or, in the absence of evidence to the contrary, appears to be

(a) twelve years of age or more, but

(b) under eighteen years of age or, in a province in respect of which a proclamation has been issued under subsection (2) prior to April 1, 1985, under sixteen or seventeen years, whichever age is specified by the proclamation,

and, where the context requires, includes any person who is charged under this Act with having committed an offence while he was a young person or is found guilty of an offence under this Act;

"youth court" means a court established or designated by or under an Act of the legislature of a province, or designated by the Governor in Council or the Lieutenant Governor in Council of a province, as a youth court for the purposes of this Act;

"youth court judge" means a person appointed to be a judge of a youth court;

"youth worker" means a person appointed or designated, whether by title of youth worker or probation officer or by any other title, by or pursuant to an Act of the legislature of a province or by the Lieutenant Governor in Council of a province or his delegate, to perform, either generally or in a specific case, in that province any of the duties or functions of a youth worker under this Act.

(2) *Proclamation changing definition of "young person".*—The Governor in Council may, at any time prior to April 1, 1985, by proclamation

(a) direct that in any province "young person", for the purposes of this Act, means a person who is or, in the absence of evidence to the contrary, appears to be twelve years of age or more, but under sixteen or under seventeen years of age, as the case may be; and

(b) revoke any direction made under paragraph (a).

(3) *Limitation.*—Any direction made under paragraph (2)(a) shall cease to have effect on April 1, 1985.

(4) *Words and expressions.*—Unless otherwise provided, words and expressions used in this Act have the same meaning as in the *Criminal Code.*

"Adult"

Under s-s. 2(1), "adult" is defined to mean a person who is "neither a young person nor a child". After April 1, 1985, in all provinces an adult will be a person aged 18 years or over. Until that date, however, a province may, with the approval of the Governor in Council (the federal Cabinet), determine that a young person becomes an adult for the purposes of the Y.O.A. at the age of 16 or 17. The provisions of s-s. 2(2) authorize the Governor in Council to make a proclamation directing the lowering of the maximum age limit for young persons to 16 or 17, prior to April 1, 1985; obviously this would only be done on the basis of a provincial request.

Jurisdiction of the youth court depends on age. A line of cases decided under the *J.D.A.* holds that age is an essential element of the prosecution's case, and that a proper finding as to age must be made in order to establish the jursidcition of the court: see *R. v. P.* (1979), 48 C.C.C. (2d) 390 (Ont. Prov. Ct.) and *R. v. L.* (1981), 59 C.C.C. (2d) 160 (Ont. Prov. Ct.). While some judges have taken the view that it was the court's responsibility to establish age because it goes to jurisdiction, others have held that the onus falls on the Crown and that failure to do so will result in a dismissal. For example, in *R. v. L., supra,* the court stated: "The finding of age should be part of the trial process in which the trial judge should stand impartial" (at p. 162). While it would be desirable for the prosecutor to deal with the issue as part of his case, or to obtain an admission of age (see s. 58 of the Y.O.A.), the definition of "young person" has been changed from the corresponding definition of "child" in the *J.D.A.*, with the intention of providing that a youth court judge must, at least in the absence of evidence to the contrary, address the question whether an inference of age can be drawn, and where feasible, make a finding of age based on appearance.

Both the J.D.A. and the Y.O.A. permit findings as to age based on actual or apparent age. The Y.O.A. places primary emphasis on actual age. A finding may be made based on appearance, where there is no evidence of actual age, or in corroboration of other evidence specified in s-s. 57(3). Thus, where a person appears to be a young person, in the absence of evidence that he is actually a child or an adult, the court must find that he is a young person. A youth court will have no jurisdiction to deal with an adult, except for purposes of contempt against itself.

The significant date in determining whether an accused is a "young person", for the purposes of the Act, is the date of the commission of the offence rather than the age of the individual when he is arrested or brought to trial. This is expressly stated in the definition of "young person", which "includes any person who is charged under thie Act with having committed an offence *while he was a young person . . .*".

The issue of age on the day of a person's birthday has been resolved by the repeal of s-s. 3(1) of the Code by An Act to amend the Criminal Code in relation to sexual and other offences against the person, S.C. 1980-81-82-83, c. 125, which received Royal Assent October 27, 1982 and was proclaimed in force January 4, 1983. Until the repeal of s-s. 3(1), which provided that a person is deemed not to reach a given age until the commencement of the day following his birthday, cases from three different provinces had held that s-s. 3(1) of the Code was the operative provision (R. v. R.N.B. (1980), 55 C.C.C. (2d) 43 (B.C.S.C.); R. v. Lanteigne (1980), 31 O.R. (2d) 239, 56 C.C.C. (2d) 95, 118 D.L.R. (3d) 520, 3 Fam. L. Rev. 13 (C.A.); and Re Regina and Allan (1981), 58 C.C.C. (2d) 282 (Man. C.A.)) rather than s-s. 25(9) of the Interpretation Act, which deems a person to have attained a specific number of years only upon the commencement of the anniversary of his birth. The Interpretation Act will now govern. Thus, the youth court has exclusive jurisdiction over any offence committed by a young person prior to the commencement of a young person's birthday.

Age may be proved under the Y.O.A. by a variety of means, including production of a birth certificate or other documentary evidence of age, and testimony of a parent. As well, the Act provides that inferences may be drawn from the young person's appearance or testimony. Proof of age is discussed in more details in the comments under s. 57.

"Alternative measures"

"Alternative measures" is defined in s-s. 2(1) of the Y.O.A. to mean "measures other than judicial proceedings under this Act, used to deal with a young person alleged to have committed an offence". Alternative measures programs authorized by the provincial Attorney General may be set up in accordance with the provisions of s. 4 of the Y.O.A. Section 4 outlines criteria setting minimum standards to be adhered to in the application of non-judicial modes of intervention. These minimum standards are designed primarily to safeguard the young person's rights, including his right to insist upon court proceedings.

The term "alternative measures" is used in the Y.O.A. rather than the term "diversion". "Diversion" is currently used to denote both structured diversion programs and unstructured methods of diverting young persons from the courts. For example, "diversion" may include informal "police screening", which is regularly employed to divert a significant proportion of potential cases away from the courts, simply on the basis of a decision on the part of the police not to lay charges. The term "diversion" is also used to describe certain innovative sentencing programs. The term "alternative measures" has been selected to distinguish the structured and formalized type of diversion program from these other, broader uses of the word "diversion". Furthermore, the objective of such programs is to provide more flexibility and alternative options for dealing with young offenders and is not *per se* a substitute for court proceedings. To put it another way, the objective is not so much to "divert from the judicial process", but to seek alternative solutions which will be effective in dealing with young offenders.

"Child"

A "child" under the Y.O.A. is "a person who is or, in the absence of evidence to the contrary, appears to be under the age of twelve years". As mentioned in the discussion of the term "adult", above, age is an essential element of jurisdiction under the Y.O.A., as it is under the J.D.A.: see *R. v. P.* (1979), 48 C.C.C. (2d) 390 (Ont. Prov. Ct.) and *R. v. L.* (1981), 59 C.C.C. (2d) 160 (Ont. Prov. Ct.). The youth court has no jurisdiction to deal with any person accused of an offence under the Y.O.A. unless a finding is made that the accused is a young person, based on actual or apparent age. Thus, it is important to consider two further matters regarding the issue of age: how the issue is brought before the court, and how age is proven. In *R. v. L.*, the court held that the onus is on the Crown to raise the issue; James, Prov. Ct. J. held: "The finding of age should be part of the trial process in which the trial Judge should stand impartial" (at p. 162). It is suggested by *R. v. L.* that the judge has no authority to raise the issue on his own. While it would be desirable for the prosecutor to deal with the issue as part of his case or to obtain an admission of age (see s. 58 of Y.O.A.), the definition of "young person" has been changed from the corresponding definition of child in the *J.D.A.*, with the intention of providing that a youth court judge must, at least in the absence of evidence to the contrary, address the question as to whether or not an inference can be drawn, and where feasible, make a finding of age based on appearance.

Age may be proven in a number of ways. The Y.O.A., like the J.D.A., allows for findings of either actual or apparent age. The primary test under the Y.O.A., however, is actual age. Where no finding of actual age has been made and where there is no evidence to the contrary, a finding of age may be based upon apparent age. A finding of apparent age may be based on a consideration of the person's size, demeanor and general appearance, including dress.

Section 57 of the Y.O.A. governs proof of age. It provides for the tendering of documentary evidence such as a birth certificate as well as permitting testimony by a parent to prove age. Section 57 also allows the drawing of inferences as to age from testimony given by the young person or from appearance. See the comments following s. 57 for further discussion of proof of age.

The significant date in determining whether an accused is a "child" or a "young person" for the purposes of the Act, is the date of the commission of the offence, rather than the age when the individual is arrested or brought to trial. This is expressly stated in the definition of "young person", which "includes any person who is charged under this Act with having committed an offence *while he was a young person.*"

The issue of age on the day of a person's birthday has been resolved by the repeal of s-s. 3(1) of the *Code* by *An Act to amend the Criminal Code in relation to sexual and other offences against the person*, which received Royal Assent October 27, 1982 and was proclaimed in force January 4, 1983. Until the repeal of s-s. 3(1), which provided that a person is deemed not to reach a given age until the commencement of the day following his birthday, cases from three different provinces had held that s-s. 3(1) of the *Code* was the operative provision (*R. v. R.N.B.* (1980), 55 C.C.C. (2d) 43 (B.C.S.C.); *R. v. Lanteigne* (1980), 31 O.R. (2d) 239, 56 C.C.C. (2d) 95, 118 D.L.R. (3d) 520, 3 Fam. L. Rev. 13 (C.A.); and *Re Regina and Allan* (1981), 58 C.C.C. (2d) 282 (Man. C.A.)) rather than s-s. 25(9) of the *Interpretation Act*, R.S.C. 1970, c. I-23, which deems a person to have attained a specific number of years only upon the commencement of the anniversary of his birth. The *Interpretation Act* will now govern. Thus, a child who commits an offence on his twelfth birthday may be prosecuted under the Y.O.A.

The jurisdiction of the youth court under the Y.O.A. is narrower than that of the juvenile court under the *J.D.A.* in a number of respects. The age jurisdiction of the youth court, at the lower end of the range, is restricted. Under the *J.D.A.*, the minimum age of criminal responsibility is seven (s. 12 of *Criminal Code*). A juvenile between seven and fourteen can only be convicted under the *J.D.A.* if it is proven that "he was competent to know the nature and consequences of his conduct and to appreciate that it was wrong" (s. 13 of the *Criminal Code*). The Y.O.A. raises the minimum age of criminal responsibility to 12, while repealing ss. 12 and 13 of the *Code* (s. 72 of the Y.O.A.). It is felt that children under the age of 12 should not be held criminally responsible for their acts, and are not to be dealt with under federal criminal legislation. Provincial legislation may be enacted to deal with offences committed by children under the age of 12. It is likely that such children will be dealt with under some form of child welfare legislation, enacted by the provinces pursuant to their general power to legislate in the area of property and civil rights, under s-s. 92(14) of the *Constitution Act, 1867*.

"Offence"

The jurisdictional basis of the Y.O.A. is considerably narrower than that found in the J.D.A. The definition of "juvenile delinquent", found in s-s. 2(1) of the J.D.A. is:

> any child who violates any provision of the *Criminal Code* or any federal or provincial statute, or any by-law or ordinance of any municipality, or who is guilty of sexual immorality or any similar form of vice, or who is liable by reason of any other act to be committed to an industrial school or juvenile reformatory under any federal or provincial statute.

The Y.O.A. is restricted to dealing with violations of federal law. The definition of "offence" in s-s. 2(1) of the Y.O.A. is:

> an offence created by an Act of Parliament or by any regulation, rule, order, by-law or ordinance made thereunder other than an ordinance of the Yukon Territory or the Northwest Territories.

The narrower offence jurisdiction of the Y.O.A. excludes violations of provincial and municipal laws, and such "status offences" as "sexual immorality". This will permit attention to be focussed more on serious criminal offences. The restricted definition of "offence" also obviates any jurisdictional disputes between the federal and provincial governments. In any event, it has been suggested that pursuant to the J.D.A., young persons are unnecessarily subjected to criminal proceedings for non-criminal offences, such as provincial and municipal offences, which can be dealt with effectively by provincial law. Federal regulatory offences are included in the definition of "offence" in the Y.O.A. for reasons of expedience and practicality, although their nature is not truly criminal.

The narrower offence jurisdiction of the Y.O.A. ensures that young persons are not held more responsible than adults for their conduct. Furthermore, the exclusion of such "status offences" as "sexual immorality" will afford young persons the same element of certainty as adults now enjoy in regard to knowing whether their conduct violates the criminal law.

Provincial legislation will have to be enacted to deal with offences against any law within the legislative purview of the provinces. Further, provinces may wish to enact child welfare legislation to deal with juveniles presently dealt with under the status offence provisions of the J.D.A. In fact, in a number of provinces, the existing child welfare legislation may already be broad enough to deal with such cases.

"Parent"

The definition of a "parent" is very broad: It "includes, in respect of another person, any person who is under a legal duty to provide for that other person or any person who has, in law or in fact, the custody or control of that other person." This broad definition was chosen to ensure that anyone acting in the place of a "parent" is included, so that the benefits flowing from the provisions for notice to parents and the parents' right to make representations and to seek review will be extended to as many young persons as possible.

The definition of parent clearly includes the biological parents, a person such as a guardian who is under a legal duty to provide for the young person, and persons with custody. A child protection agency with custody of the young person under child welfare legislation is also included.

Although not intended to include a spouse, the definition of "parent" appears to be sufficiently broad to include a spouse of a young person, at least where a spouse is liable under provincial law to "provide for" the support of the other. However, it is clear that such an interpretation was not intended. The principle of parental responsibility which is articulated in para. 3(1)(h) is inconsistent with such an interpretation. In addition, in s. 9 of the Y.O.A., dealing with notices to parents, there is specific provision in s-s. 9(4) for giving notice to a spouse "instead of a parent"; this suggests that the terms "spouse" and "parent" are mutually exclusive.

"Provincial director"

The "provincial director" is defined in the Act to mean "a person, a group or class of persons or a body" appointed or designated by a provincial government "to perform in that province, either generally or in a specific case, any of the duties or functions of a provincial director under this Act." This definition deliberately allows a class of persons to be apppointed provincial directors, for example, a class of employees of the Department of Social Services or the Department of Northern Affairs.

Since the provincial director is an important provincial administrative position, the definition has been made very flexible to accommodate the needs of different provinces and territories.

"Young person"

A young person is "a person who is or, in the absence of evidence to the contrary, appears to be (a) twelve years of age or more, but (b) under eighteen years of age ...". Until April 1, 1985, any province may request the Governor in Council to provide for a lower maximum age of under 16 or under 17 years. The provisions of s-s. 2(2) authorize the Governor in Council to make proclamations in this regard. In deciding whether an accused is a young person for the purposes of the Act, one must consider the date of the commission of the offence, rather than the age of the individual when he is arrested or brought to trial. This is specifically provided for in the definition; young person "includes any person who is charged under this Act with having committed an offence *while he was a young person.*"

The minimum age of criminal responsibility under the Y.O.A. has been set at 12. A minimum age has been chosen to promote certainty, because it is felt that a young person must know at what age responsibility for illegal activity will be presumed. The age level at which capacity is presumed to exist must be specifically established and must be uniform across Canada.

The decision to adopt a uniform maximum age was in part based on considerations of fairness and uniformity, and also because any age disparity could result in this legislation being ruled unconstitutional under the *Canadian Charter of Rights and Freedoms*. Section 15 of the *Charter*, which guarantees "equal protection and equal benefit of the law" would be the likely basis of any challenge; this particular section will not come into force until April of 1985. Therefore, until April 1, 1985, the provinces may opt under the Y.O.A. for a lower maximum age of either under 16 or under 17. This provision for a flexible age limit gives the provinces that have not already been using a maximum age of under 18 time to prepare facilities, programs and staff for the necessary changes.

While recognizing that there were inherent difficulties associated with choosing a particular age, on February 9, 1982, the Solicitor General of Canada gave the following reasons in support of a maximum uniform age of under 18:

1. The fact that growth into full maturity is not, as a general rule, achieved until age 18 or later, particularly in current times because of the prolonged period of dependency that is required of young persons.

2. The desirability of protecting young persons for as long a period as possible from entry into correctional institutions where they will be exposed to older, more experienced offenders.

3. Having moved to a rights and responsibility model of juvenile justice, it is felt that the benefits of the system should be extended to the largest number of young persons possible who have not yet attained full maturity. This extension of benefits holds out the most promise of preventing a young person's further involvement in illegal activity. The full benefit of the resources of the juvenile justice system with its greater emphasis on individual needs than that adult system should be extended to young persons up to 18 because they are, until then, generally speaking, still in their formative years and at an age level where they can be favourably influenced by positive action and guidance. The law must be particularly sensitive to the special needs and requirements of young persons and provide them with every opportunity for reformation in order to prevent them from graduating into adult offenders.

4. Given sufficient protective safeguards for society which, it is believed, the new Act contains, it is preferable to set the age at a higher rather than a lower level. This is especially desirable in view of the retention of the transfer provision to adult court which provides the system with a "safety valve" mechanism for such difficult cases as the "mature" criminal who is under 18, or the offender who has committed an extremely serious offence.

5. This age level is consistent with the treatment of young persons under civil law including the age of majority. The fact that no province in Canada has its age of civil majority below the level of 18 years bears testimony to the general recognition that young persons under age 18 have not yet attained full maturity and are not considered to have reached adulthood.

6. The age 18 level better accords with international standards and is consistent with the situation prevailing in most European and Western democracies, and most common law jursidictions including a high proportion of States in the U.S.

For a discussion in respect of a finding of age, see pp. 4-8.

DECLARATION OF PRINCIPLE
(Section 3)

Introduction

The Declaration of Principle set out in s-s. 3(1) of the Y.O.A. is to serve as a guide to the interpretation and application of the Act. Rather than simply having oa Preamble, as some pieces of legislation have, to assist in explaining their purpose, a policy section is included in the body of the Y.O.A.; such a section is an integral part of the Act, while a Preamble is not. The section containing the Declaration of Principle will govern the interpretation of the whole Act; s-s. 3(2) adds that the Act "shall be liberally construed to the end that young persons will be dealt with in accordance with the principles set out in subsection (1)."

The years from 1908 to the present have exposed many problems with the welfare approach of the *J.D.A.*, and the federal Parliament has sought to strike a reasonable and acceptable balance in the Y.O.A. between the needs of young persons and the interests of society. To achieve this balance, the Y.O.A. recognizes that young persons must bear responsibility for their acts and that while society has the responsibility to take reasonable measures to prevent crime, it must be protected against illegal behaviour. The Act stipulates, however, that young persons should not always be held as accountable for their behaviour as adults and that they have special needs and require guidance and assistance.

The principles underlying the Y.O.A. can be contrasted with those underlying the *J.D.A.*, enacted in 1908. The *J.D.A.* takes a social welfare approach to juvenile delinquency; the courts exercise a *parens patriae* ("father of the country") jurisdiction, dealing with young persons as a strict, watchful but loving parent. Under the *J.D.A.*, s. 38 requires that "every juvenile delinquent . . . be treated, not as [an offender], but as a misdirected and misguided child . . .". Subsection 17(2) of the *J.D.A.* provides: "No adjudication or other action of a juvenile court . . . shall be quashed or set aside because of any informality or irregularity where it appears that the disposition of the case was in the best interests of the child." Thus, the emphasis in the *J.D.A.* is upon treatment, rehabilitation and informality.

The special parent-child relationship is recognized as well: young persons are only to be removed from parental control when measures that provide for continuing parental supervision are inappropriate.

There is also much more emphasis on the legal rights of young persons. If a young person is to be held responsible and accountable for his actions, he is to be afforded all of the protections an adult receives in our criminal justice system. In particular, the Act guarantees to young persons the right to be informed of their rights and the right to the least possible interference with freedom consistent with society's protection. The informality prevalent in some jurisdictions under the *J.D.A.* will not, for the most part, be allowed under the *Y.O.A.*

SECTION 3

3. (1) *Policy for Canada with respect to young offenders.*—It is hereby recognized and declared that

(a) while young persons should not in all instances be held accountable in the same manner and suffer the same consequences for the behaviour as adults, young persons who commit offences should nonetheless bear responsibility for their contraventions;

(b) society must, although it has the responsibility to take reasonable measures to prevent criminal conduct by young persons, be afforded the necessary protection from illegal behaviour;

(c) young persons who commit offences require supervision, discipline and control, but, because of their state of dependency and level of development and maturity, they also have special needs and require guidance and assistance;

(d) where it is not inconsistent with the protection of society, taking no measures or taking measures other than judicial proceedings under this Act should be considered for dealing with young persons who have committed offences;

(e) young persons have rights and freedoms in their own right, including those stated in the *Canadian Charter of Rights and Freedoms* or in the *Canadian Bill of Rights,* and in particular a right to be heard in the course of, and to participate in, the processes that lead to decisions that affect them, and young persons should have special guarantees of their rights and freedoms;

(f) in the application of this Act, the rights and freedoms of young persons include a right to the least possible interference with freedom that is consistent with the protection of society, having regard to the needs of young persons and the interests of their families;

(g) young persons have the right, in every instance where they have rights and freedoms that may be affected by this Act, to be informed as to what those rights and freedoms are; and

(h) parents have responsibility for the care and supervision of their children, and, for that reason, young persons should be removed from parental supervision either partly or entirely only when measures that provide for continuing parental supervision are inappropriate.

(2) *Act to be liberally construed.*—This Act shall be liberally construed to the end that young persons will be deals with in accordance with the principles set out in subsection (1).

Responsibility, accountability and the protection of society: paragraphs 3(1)(a) and (b)

Three of the fundamental principles upon which the Y.O.A. is based are: responsibility, accountability and the protection of society. Society must be protected from the illegal behaviour of young persons, and thus they are to be held responsible for their acts; in view of their level of development, however, young persons will not in all instances be held as accountable for their behaviour as adults.

Two of the major principles of the Y.O.A. are found in para. 3(1)(a). The first of these is the proposition that young persons should "bear responsibility for their contraventions". The degree of responsibility young persons must bear is not to be the same as an adult would face as the second major principle establishes that "young persons should not in all instances be held accountable in the same manner or suffer the same consequences for their behaviour as adults". An example of the lesser degree of accountability young persons are held to is reflected in the dispositions available under the Act, which are generally less severe than those an adult might face. Moreover, a young peron may never receive a harsher disposition for an offence than that to which an adult is liable.

An essential part of the Y.O.A. and a third fundamental principle of the Act is the recognition of the need to protect society from illegal behaviour. The fact that para. 3(1)(b) is separate from the two other fundamental principles emphasizes the importance of this principle to the Y.O.A.: "society must ... be afforded the necessary protection from illegal behaviour." The manner in which we treat young offenders is, in part, decided in accordance with the right of society to be protected.

Special needs: paragraph 3(1)(c)

The recognition given under the Y.O.A. to the special needs of the young person illustrates a fundamental distinction between the aims and priorities of the juvenile justice system and the adult criminal justice system. Although both the J.D.A. and the Y.O.A. accept the premise that young persons are more amenable to rehabilitation than are adults, the J.D.A.'s approach is to treat the young person as "a misguided child" and to offer him "aid, encouragement, help and assistance", while the Y.O.A. puts more emphasis on the goals of responsibility and protection of society. The Y.O.A. does not focus exclusively upon the young person's special needs as the primary reason for intervention, as the J.D.A. does. Nevertheless, the Y.O.A. expressly recognizes that young persons have special needs arising out of their "state of dependency and level of development and maturity", and the Act recognizes that young persons "require guidance and assistance" as well as "supervision, discipline and control".

Special provisions to meet the young person's needs come into effect at disposition. There is a considerable amount of flexibility in the Act to assist the young person, particularly through the use of alternative measures or through the wide range of dispositional alternatives. Adequate assessment of the young person's needs is crucial in order to give the young person special help. The youth court may order a medical examination or a psychiatric or psychological assessment in circumstances outlined in s. 13 of the Y.O.A. Pre-disposition reports are also available to ensure that as much pertinent information as possible is before the court prior to disposition. Pre-disposition reports are mandatory before a custodial disposition is ordered for the young person.

The Y.O.A. also provides for parental involvement to promote parents' participation in the court proceedings and their assistance to their child throughout the process and following disposition. It is hoped that involving parents in the judicial proceedings against their child may alert them to his problems, giving the parents a chance to offer guidance and support. Parental involvement may also ensure that a young person's legal rights are protected.

Alternative measures: paragraph 3(1)(d)

The Y.O.A. includes provisions for the establishment of programs of alternative measures by individual provinces and territories, in accordance with s. 4. Alternative measures are mentioned expressly in the Declaration of Principle to signify the importance to be attached to and the use to be made of such procedures. As the provisions of s. 4 of the Y.O.A. include guidelines to provide minimum safeguards for the protection of young persons' rights, the use of alternative measures in lieu of judicial proceedings may be encouraged wherever alternative measures are consistent with the principle of the protection of society. The establishment of standardized parameters within which alternative measures programs operate, with adequate safeguards for the protection of young persons who participate in them, is an important development in diversion.

It has been suggested that a number of benefits result from the use of alternative measures. It is generally recognized that the criminal law need not be invoked in all instances when a law is violated, and that some young persons are being unnecessarily brought before the juvenile court. The benefits of alternative measures range from reducing delays in handling young persons to the increased scope for flexibility, especially in procedures and in the manner of dealing with young persons. The use of alternative measures frees court facilities, allowing the youth court to be reserved for the more serious cases. The range of dispositional options that may be used in alternative measures programs includes special education and counselling for behavioural problems or drug or alcohol related problems. Alternative measures programs can be adaptable to the particular needs of the communities in which they are set up, whether the community is rural, urban, native, etc. One aim of such programs is to involve the community in dealing with the problems of the illegal behaviour of young persons; this is often achieved through the use of community participants at all levels of the alternative measures program, through the involvement of the victim and the employment of innovative forms of disposition.

Rights of young persons: paragraph 3(1)(e)

Paragraph 3(1)(e) provides that "young persons have rights and freedoms in their own right, including those stated in the *Canadian Charter of Rights and Freedoms* or in the *Canadian Bill of Rights*"; young persons also have "a right to be heard ... and to participate, in the processes that lead to decisions that affect them." Further, in view of their usually limited economic resources, and the state of their emotional and intellectual development, young persons "should have special guarantees of their rights and freedoms." The inclusion of the above-mentioned provisions in the Declaration of Principle is a clear statement that the Y.O.A. has adopted a "due process" model of juvenile justice. Under the social welfare approach of the *J.D.A.*, proceedings were intentionally informal, and the rules of criminal procedure and evidence were often not enforced. By way of contrast, the Y.O.A. expressly recognizes that young persons have the same rights to "due process" of law as adults. There are many provisions in the Y.O.A. concerning the legal rights of young persons and these establish "due process" requirements and procedural regularity from the time of initiation of proceedings (by arrest or summons), through adjudication, disposition, appeal and review of disposition.

In addition to legal protections afforded adults in criminal proceedings, such as those contained in the *Charter of Rights*, the Y.O.A. recognizes that because of the level of their emotional and intellectual development, young persons require special legal safeguards. For example, s. 10 of the *Charter* guarantees everyone the right to "retain and instruct counsel" upon arrest or detention. Section 11 of the Y.O.A. goes beyond this, and guarantees every young person being dealt with under the Act by way of trial, hearing or review, who wishes to obtain counsel but is unable to do so, the right to have counsel appointed and paid for by the state. A number of other provisions of the Y.O.A. afford young persons special guarantees of their rights and freedoms.

Right to the least possible interference: paragraph 3(1)(f)

In para. 3(1)(f) of the Y.O.A., it is recognized that a young person has the right "to the least possible interference with freedom that is consistent with the protection of society, having regard to the needs of young persons and the interests of their families." The principle of minimal interference represents a shift away from the treatment-oriented philosophy of the J.D.A. Intervention in the life of the young person is justifiable under the Y.O.A. primarily for the protection of society although the Act continues to recognize that young persons have special needs and require guidance and assistance. It is this philosophy which will distinguish the juvenile justice system from the adult justice system. If intervention is justifiable to protect society, it should be to the least extent possible, and in determining its nature and scope, regard should be had for the needs of the young person and the interests of his family. The principle of minimal interference should serve as a guide at each stage of the proceedings, including alternative measures, pre-trial detention, disposition, and disposition review. Serious restraint measures, such as custodial dispositions, should be used only as last resort remedies.

Right to be informed: paragraph 3(1)(g)

Young persons have the right to be informed of their rights, in every instance where their rights may be affected by the Act. Police, judges, youth workers, counsel and other persons who are part of the juvenile justice system have the primary responsibility for the enforcement of this right. Owing to their age and inexperience, young persons, in many instances, may not be aware of their rights and therefore, a number of specific provisions provide that they shall be so informed. Sections 11 and 12 of the Y.O.A. ensure that a young person must be informed upon his arrest, at court appearances, and on court documents of his right to be represented by counsel. Section 56 requires that police officers take special steps to inform a young person of his rights prior to taking a statement.

Parental responsibility: paragraph 3(1)(h)

The Act recognizes in para. 3(1)(h) that "parents have responsibility for the care and supervision of their children, and, for that reason, young persons should be removed from parental supervision . . . only when measures that provide for continuing parental supervision are inappropriate." This special status, for example, entitles parents to receive notice of any proceedings commenced against their child, to receive copies of reports prepared for the youth court, and to make representations at a transfer hearing and at disposition. They also have a right to initiate and participate in disposition review proceedings. Under s. 10, a judge is empowered to make an order requiring a parent's attendance at proceedings against his child.

This principle recognizes that parents are responsible for the care and supervision of their children; however, this concept does not extend to vicarious liability. Pursuant to s. 22 of the J.D.A., a parent, under certain circumstances, can be ordered to pay a fine, damages, or costs when his child is found guilty of an offence. As well, a parent may be ordered to pay for the support of his delinquent child pursuant to s-s. 20(2) of the J.D.A.; the Y.O.A. does not have similar provisions. A parent has a right to participate in proceedings, but is under no obligation to assume financial responsibility for the young person's misdeeds.

The decision a youth court makes in regard to such matters as pre-disposition detention, disposition and disposition review should always be based on a recognition of parental responsibility. To the greatest extent possible, young persons should be dealt with in their community and family environment. Notwithstanding the principle of parental responsibility, it must also be recognized that some young persons, particularly those who are 16 or 17, may have withdrawn from parental control. In such circumstances, in view of the principle of least interference and in consideration of the needs of a young person, it may not be appropriate to force a young person to resume a relationship with his parents.

ALTERNATIVE MEASURES
(Section 4)

Introduction

The Y.O.A. provides legislative authority for the use of voluntary "alternative measures" other than judicial proceedings under this Act. The Act defines alternative measures in s-s. 2(1) as "measures other than judicial proceedings under this Act used to deal with a young person alleged to have committed an offence". Alternatives to the juvenile justice system have been commonly been known as "diversion" and as the Law Reform Commission of Canada has noted, many types of diversion, formal and informal, are described by this one term. Pre-trial diversion programs involving the handling of cases outside of the juvenile court by settlement or mediation procedures, have been implemented in a number of locations across the country. The Y.O.A. sanctions the use of such programs and, by adopting the designation "alternative measures", avoids the imprecision of "diversion" and encourages flexibility as to the kinds of programs which may be developed in the future.

Another type of diversion, commonly known as "police screening", refers to the police practice of not charging all young people with whom they deal. The police often choose to give the young person a warning and then send him home for appropriate parental disciplinary measures. This kind of diversion has not been formalized, although it will continue as an important method of dealing with young people without resorting to formal alternative measures programs or the courts.

Although the J.D.A. does not specifically refer to diversion, informal diversion programs grew out of dissatisfaction with the traditional juvenile justice system and concern for its possible harmful effects on young people, especially the consequences of a criminal record. As a rule, court proceedings are formal, time-consuming, difficult for a young person to understand and its dispositions are limited by those established by legislation. Many sociologists propound a "labelling theory" that a young person dealt with in juvenile court might come to perceive himself as an "offender", and hence the imposition of stigmatizing labels was, in itself, a secondary cause of law-breaking behaviour. Concern about stigmatization was heightened because of the danger of the young person's susceptibility to labelling. It was felt that removing the young person from the formal court system would prevent labelling and would offer protection from the other harmful aspects of the court process.

Two aims of alternative measures are to prevent the continuation of criminal behaviour and to lessen the stigma of proceedings. Another goal is to promote community involvement and to foster community awareness, partly through participation in alternative measures programs and partly as a result of putting greater emphasis on restitution and victim involvement. Alternative measures also permit the use of effective means of intervention other than by formal court proceedings, where they appear appropriate and adequate to deal with the young offender. In addition, as a by-product, alternative measures should bring some relief to crowded court calendars by dealing with young people out of court. This would leave the court with its limited resources, free to deal with the more serious cases which come before it.

As well as accepting alternative measures as a method of dealing with young people, the Y.O.A. also adopts the closely-related concept of non-intervention. Paragraph 3(1)(d) of the Y.O.A. states that "where it is not inconsistent with the protection of society, taking no measures or taking measures other than judicial proceedings under this Act should be considered". Paragraph 3(1)(f) guarantees the young person "a right to the least possible interference with freedom that is consistent with the protection of society." Although non-intervention must be balanced against the protection of society, these principles emphasize the need to consider non-judicial means of resolving conflicts between the young offender and the State.

Under the Y.O.A., each province is free to set up and administer alternative measures programs. If the provincial programs follow the most common model of present diversion programs, a decision will be made prior to the first court appearance to determine whether the young person will be offered an opportunity to participate in the program. If the young person agrees, a meeting will be held to discuss the alleged offence and the choice of alternative measures available. The young person must acknowledge responsibility for the act, as a minimum prerequisite to participation. If he is not prepared to accept responsibility, the young person should be dealt with in youth court. If alternative measures are felt suitable, the legislation does not specify the conditions which may be imposed. Normally, they might include measures such as writing an essay, restitution, community service work, participation in a recreation program, involvement with Big Brothers/Big Sisters, or some form of counselling. There will be no formal record of a conviction as a result of participation in alternative measures. A record of participation in alternative measures will likely be kept pursuant to s. 43, though access to this record will be limited.

The Y.O.A. incorporates a number of safeguards to ensure that the rights of the young person are not abused. Among these are the fact that the young person must acknowledge responsibility, the requirement of full and free consent and the right to consult counsel before participating in alternative measures. The Y.O.A. legislates minimum standards and rights for the protection of the young person while at the same time it seeks to preserve the public's right to protection.

SECTION 4

4. (1) *Alternative measures.*—Alternative measures may be used to deal with a young person alleged to have committed an offence instead of judicial proceedings under this Act only if

(a) the measures are part of a program of alternative measures authorized by the Attorney General or his delegate or authorized by a person, or a person within a class of persons, designated by the Lieutenant Governor in Council of a province;

(b) the person who is considering whether to use such measures is satisfied that they would be appropriate, having regard to the needs of the young person and the interests of society;

(c) the young person, having been informed of the alternative measures, fully and freely consents to participate therein;

(d) the young person has, before consenting to participate in the alternative measures, been advised of his right to be represented by counsel and been given a reasonable opportunity to consult with counsel;

(e) the young person accepts responsibility for the act or omission that forms the basis of the offence that he is alleged to have committed;

(f) there is, in the opinion of the Attorney General or his agent, sufficient evidence to proceed with the prosecution of the offence; and

(g) the prosecution of the offence is not in any way barred at law.

(2) *Restriction on use.*—Alternative measures shall not be used to deal with a young person alleged to have committed an offence if the young person

(a) denies his participation or involvement in the commission of the offence; or

(b) expresses his wish to have any charge against him dealt with by the youth court.

(3) *Admissions not admissible in evidence.*—No admission, confession or statement accepting responsibility for a given act or omission made by a young person alleged to have committed an offence as a condition of his being dealt with by alternative measures shall be admissible in evidence against him in any civil or criminal proceedings.

(4) *No bar to proceedings.*—The use of alternative measures in respect of a young person alleged to have committed an offence is not a bar to proceedings against him under this Act, but

(a) where the youth court is satisfied on a balance of probabilities that the young person has totally complied with the terms and conditions of the alternative measures, the youth court shall dismiss any charge against him; and

(b) where the youth court is satisfied on a balance of probabilities that the young person has partially complied with the terms and conditions of the alternative measures, the youth court may dismiss any charge against him if, in the opinion of the court, the prosecution of the charge would, having regard to the circumstances, be unfair, and the youth court may consider the young person's performance with respect to the alternative measures before making a disposition under this Act.

(5) *Laying of information, etc.*—Subject to subsection (4), nothing in this section shall be construed to prevent any person from laying an information, obtaining the issue or confirmation of any process or proceeding with the prosecution of any offence in accordance with law.

When alternative measures may be used: subsection 4(1)

Subsection 4(1) outlines the situations in which alternative measures are appropriate. Alternative measures may be used to deal with a young person "alleged to have committed an offence". Since the word "alleged" is broader than "charged with", it is not necessary for an information to be sworn as a precondition to utilizing alternative measures. It should be noted that alternative measures may be used either before or after the laying of an information. Subsection 2(1) of the Y.O.A. defines "offence" as an offence created by or under an Act of Parliament and therefore s. 4 of the Y.O.A. may only be used to sanction diversion in the case of alleged "federal" offences.

Authorized programs: paragraph 4(1)(a)

Alternative measures must be part of an authorized program. The Act does not set out guidelines for establishing the programs; it merely provides legislative authority for them and legislates minimum standards to safeguard the young person's rights. The Act permits each province to determine whether it wishes to implement alternative measures programs, and provides flexibility for the development of different types of programs in response to local needs, interests and resources. Programs may be local or province-wide. Each program must be authorized by the provincial Attorney General or his delegate, or by a person or class of persons designated by the Lieutenant Governor in Council (Cabinet) of a province. Further, it would seem to be *intra vires* a province to enact complementary legislation governing the administration, staffing and funding of alternative measures programs, as long as such legislation does not conflict with the Y.O.A.

"Needs of young person and interests of society": paragraph 4(1)(b)

The Act specifies that alternative measures should only be used where the person who is authorized to decide whether they should be used is satisfied that they would be "appropriate, having regard to the needs of the young person and the interests of society". The authorized person will be the one designated in any program approved pursuant to para. 4(1)(a). The consideration of these two factors is required in other provisions of the Y.O.A.:

see for example s-s. 28(17) governing review of dispositions. Although in some cases the needs of the young person and the interests of society may be quite consistent, in other situations they may be inconsistent and some balancing will be required.

The needs of the young person may in many situations be advanced if alternative measures are employed. The youth will not be burdened or stigmatized by a formal offence record, and the labelling effect of involvement in the juvenile justice system may be minimized. These needs are recognized in the Declaration of Principle in paras. 3(1)(d) and (f), which recognize the advantages of minimal intervention in a young person's life. Furthermore, a particular program available under alternative measures may be best suited to a young person's needs. On the other hand, in some circumstances it may be felt that the needs of a young person will be best served if he is impressed with the serious consequences of his acts, and is held accountable through the court process: see para. 3(1)(b). Further, if the appropriate response to an offence is a form of treatment available only by way of a formal disposition under s. 20, alternative measures would not be suitable.

The interests of society require protection from illegal behaviour: see para. 3(1)(b). In the case of more serious offences, it may be that the more onerous consequences attached to a court appearance will best ensure the protection of society and deter future offences. On the other hand, society may also benefit if a young offender is dealt with by alternative measures, as this may minimize the possibility of a repetition of criminal behaviour and promote the rehabilitation of the offender.

In each case, the person deciding whether to employ alternative measures will have to consider the offender, the offence, the type of alternative measures which might be employed and the resources of the juvenile justice system.

Consent of the young person: paragraph 4(1)(c)

Alternative measures can be used only if the young person "fully and freely consents"; this requirement protects against possible coercion from parents or other individuals in authority. Before consenting, the young person must be informed of the specific measures to be used. The requirement that a young person must consent with knowledge of the specific form that the alternative measures will take is one method of safeguarding the young person from unsuitable or overly burdensome measures.

Right to counsel: paragraph 4(1)(d)

The young person must be informed of his right to counsel before giving his consent to participate in alternative measures. Without a reasonable opportunity to consult with counsel, it is possible that the young person's consent may not be "fully and freely" given.

The requirements of para. 4(1)(d) are that a young person be informed of his right to consult counsel and be given a "reasonable opportunity to consult with counsel." The use of the term "opportunity" would seem to suggest that a young person be given enough time to consult with counsel, but would not seem to make it mandatory that he be provided with counsel. Thus, if a young person could not afford counsel or obtain some form of legal aid, he might not actually obtain legal advice before consenting to or participating in a program of alternative measures. The provisions of para. 4(1)(c) should be contrasted with s. 11, which creates a scheme for ensuring that each young person involved in judicial proceedings in youth court actually has representation by counsel, provided he wants it and is unable to obtain same. Although the provision of legal counsel is not mandatory pursuant to para. 4(1)(c), in certain circumstances there may be some doubt as to whether the consent was an informed one and was freely given if legal counsel has not been made available. Legal aid officials or administrators of programs of alternative measures may choose to ensure that counsel is actually provided to young people before they participate in alternative measures.

Acknowledging responsibility: paragraph 4(1)(e)

The young person must accept "responsibility for the act or omission that forms the basis of the offence". Intervention and imposition of alternative measures can only be justified where a young person is prepared to acknowledge responsibility as a minimum basis for the application of such voluntary measures. It appears that accepting responsibility is something less than indicating an intention to plead guilty if charged in youth court. The wording of para. 4(1)(e) requires acknowledgement of responsibility for the act that forms the basis of the offence, rather than responsibility for the offence *per se*, which would require acknowledgement of responsibility for all elements of the offence, both mental and physical. A young person might "accept responsibility" by acknowledging that he is a party or accessory to the offence, rather than admitting full criminal responsibility. On the other hand, a mere acknowledgement by a young person that he was present at the scene while another person committed a criminal act, would undoubtedly not suffice.

A young person may acknowledge responsibility either orally or in writing. Subsection 4(3) provides that no statement made for the purposes of para. 4(1)(e) may be used in subsequent proceedings.

Sufficient evidence: paragraph 4(1)(f)

Alternative measures are only permitted if there is "sufficient evidence to proceed with the prosecution of the offence". This provision acts as a safeguard against "widening the net"; it militates against using alternative measures for weak cases which would not otherwise proceed to court, thus ensuring that alternative measures are truly alternative, and not in addition to, prosecution.

The question of whether there is sufficient evidence must be addressed by the Attorney General or his agent. An "agent" must be someone qualified to pass on the sufficiency of the evidence, from which can be inferred the requirement that the agent be trained in law.

Barred at law: paragraph 4(1)(g)

Alternative measures may only be used when prosecution of the offence is "not in any way barred at law". Where a legal bar exists which would prevent prosecution through the normal court process, intervention of any other kind would be unjustifiable. Thus, for example, alternative measures may not be used after a limitations period has passed. By virtue of s. 51 of the Y.O.A., the six months' limitation period for summary conviction offences set out in s-s. 721(2) of the *Criminal Code* applies to all summary conviction offences under the Y.O.A. Another example of a situation where use of alternative measures is prohibited is one in which a young person was previously acquitted or convicted of an offence in youth court. Owing to the principle of *res judicata* and the special pleas of *autrefois acquit* and *autrefois convict*, further prosecutions would be barred for the offence and thus alternative measures should not be employed. The need for independent legal counsel is again emphasized, as the recognition of the availability of these legal defences can be a complex matter.

Consequences of breach of paragraphs 4(1)(c) to (g)

The Y.O.A. does not specify any consequences for a failure to comply with paras. 4(1)(c) to (g). If, for example, alternative measures are used without a young person having been advised of his right to representation by counsel or without having given a full and free consent. It would seem that no program should be authorized under para. 4(1)(a) unless it is clear that paras. 4(1)(c) to (g) will be satisfied. If any one of these conditions are not satisfied, then it would seem that no adverse use should be made of the fact of participation in subsequent youth court proceedings: see subpara. 14(2)(c)(iv) which ordinarily allows reference to be made in a pre-disposition report to "the history of alternative measures used to deal with the young person". Similarly, the young person should not be adversely affected by a failure to satisfy the conditions of paras. 4(1)(c) to (g). On the other hand, he should be able to rely on para. 4(4)(a) or (b) if he has totally or partially complied with the terms of the alternative measures, regardless of whether paras. 4(1)(c) to (g) have been complied with or not.

Restrictions on use of alternative measures: subsection 4(2)

The voluntary nature of a young person's participation in alternative measures programs is emphasized in s-s. 4(2). If the young person "denies his participation or involvement in the commission of the offence" (para. 4(2)(a)), he may not be proceeded with except through the youth court. This follows from the presumption of innocence, until guilt is acknowledged or proven. Since the minimum prerequisite for the imposition of alternative measures is acknowledgement of responsibility, this minimum is absent if the young person denies involvement in the offence.

Paragraph 4(2)(b) provides that the young person may choose to have any charge dealt with by the youth court. It is possible that a young person could receive a more onerous disposition as a result of alternative measures than he would receive in youth court. In this situation, the young person could see the youth court as the more favourable forum. Moreover, the young person has the choice at all times to have available the procedural and substantive protections of the youth court. The choice is the young person's — not his parents' or another adult's.

Admissions not to be received in evidence: subsection 4(3)

Subsection 4(3) renders the young person's "admission, confession or statement accepting responsibility . . . made . . . as a condition of his being dealt with by alternative measures" inadmissible in subsequent civil or criminal proceedings. This provision is intentionally narrow and excludes statements which were not made as a condition of being dealt with by alternative measures. An admission relating to an offence, other than the offence which has been the subject of altertnative measures, could presumably be used subsequently. Similarly, an admission made prior to alternative measures being considered would be admissible, as would any physical or other evidence obtained as a result of any admission. The prohibition would seem to cover certain admissions made at the alternative measures hearing, but an admission made after the conclusion of such a hearing would likely be admissible subject to s. 56.

The fact of participation in alternative measures may be noted in subsequent proceedings for the purpose of determining the appropriate disposition. Subparagraph 14(2)(c)(iv) of the Y.O.A. specifically requires the inclusion of the history of alternative measures, where applicable, in a pre-disposition report. See R. v. Drew, [1979] 1 W.W.R. 530, 45 C.C.C. (2d) 212, 7 C.R. (3d) S-21 (B.C.C.A.) for a discussion of the extent to which a judge should take into account previous participation in alternative measures in sentencing on a subsequent charge.

The Canadian Charter of Rights and Freedoms, s-s. 24(2), allows a court to exclude "evidence . . . obtained in a manner that infringed or denied any rights or freedoms guaranteed by this Charter . . . if . . . the admission of it in the proceedings would bring the administration of justice into disrepute." This provision may be a further safeguard for the young person, for example, if he was denied the opportunity to consult counsel.

Further proceedings: paragraph 4(4)(a)

Paragraph 4(4)(a) provides that if a young person "has totally complied with the terms and conditions of alternative measures", the youth court shall dismiss any charge which formed the basis of the invocation of alternative measures. The youth court is to be satisfied on a balance of probabilities that the terms of the alternative measures have been completed. The use of the civil standard of proof to make this determination should be noted. Once the court is satisfied that the alternative measures have been completed, there is no discretion to do other than dismiss the charge. This provision requires the court to prevent an abuse where there has been total compliance with alternative measures.

Further proceedings: paragraph 4(4)(b)

Paragraph 4(4)(b) provides that where a young person has only partially complied with the terms of alternative measures, he may be dealt with in youth court on a charge based on the original offence. If the judge is satisfied on the balance of probabilities (the civil standard of proof), that the young person has partially complied with the terms of the alternative measures, he may dismiss the charge under para. 4(4)(b). If he is satisfied there has been total compliance, he must dismiss the charge under para. 4(4)(a). Where there has been no compliance at all, there is no discretion to dismiss the charge.

In deciding whether to dismiss a charge the judge must form an opinion, having regard to the circumstances, whether prosecution of the charge would be "unfair". The court is thus empowered to consider, for example, why the alternative measures were not completed. For example, if restitution were required as a term of alternative measures, and a victim chose to forego further restitution or moved away, it might be unfair to allow a prosecution. Similarly, where there had been substantial compliance with the voluntary measures, prosecution might be unwarranted. In such cases, para. 4(4)(b) permits the judge to prevent an abuse of process, preserving the fairness of the judicial system.

Paragraph 4(4)(b) also provides that where the court has allowed the charge to proceed, and a conviction results, it may consider the young person's performance in alternative measures before making a disposition under the Y.O.A. The Act does not specify how the performance is to be taken into account, and the court has flexibility in considering this factor. In making a disposition, a court might decide merely to require the completion of the terms of alternative measures, or in some other way take into account the partial completion of alternative measures to lessen the severity of disposition. Or the court might simply consider the young person's difficulties with the particular alternative measures imposed, and select a different type of disposition. In any event, it is for the court to take into account all of the circumstances in deciding how to consider the young person's performance in alternative measures.

Double jeopardy

Both paras. 4(4)(a) and (b) protect the young person against double jeopardy. Since alternative measures are not equivalent to proceedings in court, it would seem that the prohibition against double jeopardy found in para. 11(h) of the *Canadian Charter of Rights and Freedoms* is not violated.

Private prosecutions: subsection 4(5)

Section 455 of the *Criminal Code* permits private prosecutions. Subsection 4(5) of the Y.O.A. confirms that the private citizen has the right to lay an information under the Y.O.A. "in accordance with law". This right is subject to the provisions of s-s. 4(4), which protect the young person who has completed alternative measures from further prosecution in court. Subsection 4(5) follows the approach of the Supreme Court of Canada in *A.-G. Que. v. Lechasseur* (1981), 128 D.L.R. (3d) 739, 25 R.F.L. (2d) 1, 63 C.C.C. (2d) 301, 28 C.R. (3d) 44, 38 N.R. 516, where it was held that citizens should not be deprived of access to the courts and should have the right to commence a private prosecution instead of having a young person dealt with by way of alternative measures. Though the Crown may stay a private prosecution pursuant to s. 732.1 of the *Code*, in view of s-s. 4(5) of the Y.O.A., it would not seem appropriate for the Crown to routinely stay proceedings with the intention of stopping a private prosecution in order to invoke alternative measures; there may be, however, special circumstances which would justify such an action.

JURISDICTION
(Sections 5 and 6)

Introduction

The Y.O.A. gives exclusive jurisdiction to a youth court for any offence alleged to have been committed by a young person. The two exceptions to this general rule are:

(1) where a young person is subject to the *National Defence Act*; or

(2) where a young person is transferred to ordinary court under s. 16.

Exclusive jurisdiction of the youth court ensures that the guiding principles and entrenched rights and safeguards, found in the Y.O.A. extend to all young persons.

SECTION 5

5. (1) *Exclusive jurisdiction of youth court.*—Notwithstanding any other Act of Parliament but subject to the *National Defence Act* and section 16, a youth court has exclusive jurisdiction in respect of any offence alleged to have been committed by a person while he was a young person and any such person shall be dealt with as provided in this Act.

(2) *Period of limitation.*—No proceedings in respect of an offence shall be commenced under this Act after the expiration of the time limit set out in any other Act of Parliament or any regulation made thereunder for the institution of proceedings in respect of that offence.

(3) *Proceedings continued when adult.*—Proceedings commenced under this Act against a young person may be continued, after he becomes an adult, in all respects as if he remained a young person.

(4) *Powers of youth court judge.*—A youth court judge, for the purpose of carrying out the provisions of this Act, is a justice and a magistrate and has the jurisdiction and powers of a summary conviction court under the *Criminal Code*.

(5) *Court of record.*—A youth court is a court of record.

Youth court: subsection 5(1)

Youth court is defined in s-s. 2(1) of the Y.O.A. Each jurisdiction is to designate a particular court as the "youth court". In some jurisdictions it is likely this will be a provincial court, but in others it may be a county or superior court. The Y.O.A. contemplates that there may be variation in the level of court designated: see for example s-s. 16(11).

"Exclusive jurisdiction" of youth court: subsection 5(1)

The Y.O.A. requires that unless dealt with by alternative measures under s. 4, a young person who commits an offence will be dealt with, at least initially, by the youth court with its special expertise, experience and facilities for dealing with young persons. It is generally expected that all aspects of a case involving a young person will occur in this specially designated court. Adjudication, disposition and review of disposition are all to be decided by the youth court. Also such issues as pre-trial detention (ss. 7 and 8), service of notice of the hearing (s. 9), parental presence at a hearing (s. 10), custody for medical or psychological examination (s. 13) and access to records arising out of charges under the Y.O.A. (ss. 40 to 44), are to be dealt with in youth court. There are, however, provisions to allow another judicial official to decide matters such as pre-trial detention, which should be resolved expeditiously, where "having regard to the circumstances, a youth court judge is not reasonably available" (s-s. 8(1)).

Provision is also made for appeals to the higher levels of the ordinary (adult) courts if a litigant is dissatisfied with a decision in youth court: see for example s-ss. 8(6) and (9), pre-trial detention; s-ss. 16(9), (10) and (11), transfer; and s. 27, a general appeal provision governing adjudication and disposition.

On the other hand, adults who commit offences involving young people are to be dealt with by the ordinary courts. The J.D.A., s. 33 creates the offence of "contributing to delinquency", under which adults are dealt with by the juvenile court. There is no equivalent to s. 33 of the J.D.A. in the Y.O.A. Adults who unlawfully interfere with young people will be dealt with under the Criminal Code in ordinary court; amendments to the Code, for example s-s. 246.1(2), have effectively replaced the offence of "contributing to delinquency". The Y.O.A. specifically creates certain offences for failure to abide by the statutory protections afforded young people; for example, it is an offence under s-s. 38(2) of the Y.O.A. to publish a report identifying a young person charged with an offence under the Act. These offences will be dealt with by the ordinary courts, unless of course the offender is a young person.

Exceptions to youth court jurisdiction: subsection 5(1)

Subsection 5(1) creates two exceptions to the exclusive jurisdiction of the youth court to deal with young persons alleged to have violated the criminal law.

A person who is 17 years old may, with parental consent, become a member of the Canadian Armed Forces. As a result of s-s. 5(1) of the Y.O.A., young persons who are members of the Armed Forces will usually not be dealt with under the Y.O.A., but rather will be subject to the Code of Service Discipline and the jurisdiction of the Courts Martial pursuant to the *National Defence Act*, R.S.C. 1970, c. N-4. It is generally desirable to deal with all those who choose to enter the services, with the special demands and discipline entailed, in the military judicial system. However, s-s. 61(1) of the *National Defence Act* states:

> 61. (1) Nothing in the Code of Service Discipline affects the jurisdiction of any civil court to try a person for any offence triable by that court.

This provision allows a prosecuter to choose to proceed in youth court rather than in the military courts with a charge against a young person who is a member of the Forces. Thus, a provincial Crown Attorney or other prosecutor may decide to charge a young person in the Forces in youth court in regard to offences not directly related to military discipline, or may choose to leave the matter to military courts: see s-ss. 61(2) and (3) of the *National Defence Act* and paras. 11(h) and (i) of the *Canadian Charter of Rights and Freedoms* for provisions concerning situations of double jeopardy. It should be noted that young persons who commit offences on military installations but who are not members of the Armed Forces are within the jurisdiction of youth court; thus, children of servicemen who live on military bases are not to be dealt with by military courts.

Subsection 5(1) provides for another exception to the exclusive jurisdiction of the youth court based on s. 16 of the Y.O.A. Section 16 provides that where a young person is charged with a serious offence, a youth court may decide that his case should be transferred to the ordinary courts for trial and sentencing, which could result in confinement of the young person in an adult correctional facility. Even after transfer to ordinary court under s. 16, it is possible under s. 75 of the Y.O.A. that, at the discretion of the correction authorities, a young person may be placed in custody in a juvenile facility.

It would also seem that s-s. 47(3) creates a further exception to the rule that young persons are dealt with in youth court. Subsection 47(3) provides that if a young person commits contempt in the face of a court, other than a youth court, both the youth court and the other court have jurisdiction to deal with the matter. Subsection 47(4) provides that regardless of which court deals with contempt, if the young person is found guilty of contempt, the court can only impose one of the dispositions found in s. 20 of the Y.O.A.

"While he was a young person": subsections 5(1) and (3)

The relevant date for determining the jurisdiction of the youth court is the date of the occurrence of the offence or alleged offence. Subsection 5(3) is clear in providing that if a young person becomes an adult after the date of the offence or alleged offence, he will continue to be dealt with under the Y.O.A. There is provision in s-s. 24(14) of the Y.O.A. for confinement in a provincial correctional facility for adults of a person committed to custody under the Y.O.A.; this transfer is to occur only after a young person reaches the age of 18, requires a judicial order made at a youth court hearing, and leaves the individual subject to the Y.O.A.

"Young person" is defined in s-s. 2(1) of the Y.O.A. and "proof of age" is dealt with in s. 57.

Period of limitation: subsection 5(2)

Subsection 5(2) stipulates that the time limitations for commencing proceedings are to be determined by the statute creating the offence. By virtue of s-s. 721(2) of the *Criminal Code*, this means the limitation period for summary conviction offences is six months. Few indictable offences have specific limitations and therefore the general common law rule *nullum tempus occurrit regi* (time does not run against the Crown) applies to indictable offences committed by young persons. By virtue of s. 27 of the *Interpretation Act*, hybrid offences, which are summary or indictable at Crown election, are deemed indictable unless the Crown otherwise elects.

Powers of youth court judge: subsection 5(4)

Subsection 5(4) provides that a youth court judge "is a justice and a magistrate and has the jurisdiction and powers of a summary conviction court under the *Criminal Code*." The terms "justice" and "magistrate" are defined in s. 2 of the *Code*, while "summary conviction court" is defined in s. 720.

By virtue of s-s. 52(1) of the Y.O.A., the procedure to be followed in youth court is generally that of a summary proceeding under the *Criminal Code*, whether the offence itself is summary or indictable. The combined effect of s-ss. 5(4) and 52(1) is to cloak the youth court judge with sufficient authority to conduct proceedings under the Y.O.A. The powers vested in a youth court judge include the authority:

— to conduct a trial (s. 733 of *Code*);
— to preserve order in the court (s. 440 of *Code*; also s. 47 of Y.O.A.);
— to issue a summons of warrant for arrest (ss. 455 to 456.3 of *Code*);
— to deal with pre-trial detention of young person (ss. 7 and 8 of Y.O.A. and ss. 457 to 458 of *Code*);
— to arraign the accused and accept plea (s. 736 of *Code* and s. 12 of Y.O.A.);
— to make a finding of insanity at time offence or at time of trial (ss. 542 and 543 of *Code*);
— to issue a subpoena or warrant for a witness (s. 728 of *Code*; also s. 54 of Y.O.A.);
— to adjourn proceedings (ss. 725 and 738 of *Code*);

— to require a young person to enter into a recognizance to keep the peace and be of good behaviour ("peace bond", s. 745 of *Code*).

In addition, youth court judges are expressly given certain powers in the Y.O.A., for example in s. 47 dealing with contempt, and ss. 48 and 49 governing forfeiture of recognizances, and s. 54 concerning the issue of a subpoena.

"Court of record": subsection 5(5)

The term "court of record" is not defined in the Y.O.A. or *Criminal Code*, but the import of s-s. 5(5) of the Y.O.A. is the same as that of s-s. 489(1) of the *Code*.

Stephen's Commentaries, vol. 3, p. 372 as quoted in *Dixon v. MacKay* (1903), 21 Man. R. 762, at p. 765, defines "court of record" as: " 'One whereof the acts and judicial proceedings are enrolled for a perpetual memorial and testimony; which rolls are called the records of the Court, and are of such high and supereminent authority that their truth is not to be called in question.' " Thus, there is an obligation upon the youth court to maintain a record of its orders; further certified copies of its orders are self-authenticating and do not require a witness to vouch for their authenticity. Section 40 of the Y.O.A. deals in considerable detail with the youth court record: see that section and the comments following.

As a "court of record", a youth court also has an inherent jurisdiction to deal with contempt in the face of the court: see *R. v. Dunning* (1979), 50 C.C.C. (2d) 296 (Ont. C.A.). Practically, the fact that a youth court is a "court of record" has little significance in regard to contempt jurisdiction, as s. 47 of the Y.O.A. gives the youth court a broad contempt jurisdiction.

Proceedings before a justice: section 6

SECTION 6

6. *Certain proceedings may be taken before justices.*—Subject to section 8, any proceeding that may be carried out before a justice under the *Criminal Code*, other than a plea, a trial or an adjudication, may be carried out before such justice in respect of an offence alleged to have been committed by a young person, and

any process that may be issued by a justice under the *Criminal Code* may be issued by such justice in respect of an offence alleged to have been committed by a young person.

Section 5 of the Y.O.A. establishes the powers and authority of a youth court judge. It is clear from s. 5, as well as other specific provisions, that the Act contemplates that most of the important judicial functions in respect of a young person will be performed exclusively by a youth court judge.

However, s. 6 of the Y.O.A. provides that certain functions in respect of a young person may be performed by a "justice", where authority is given to a justice by the *Code* to perform these functions. "Justice" is defined in s. 2 of the *Criminal Code* to mean a justice of the peace or a magistrate.

Section 6 of the Y.O.A. generally permits a justice to preside over the same proceedings and issue the same processes under the Y.O.A. that he would be able to preside over or issue under the *Criminal Code*, with certain important exceptions as discussed below. Section 6 allows a justice to carry out certain preliminary or peripheral functions in regard to proceedings under the Y.O.A., such as:

— issuing a summons or warrant for arrest (ss. 455 to 456.3 of *Code*);

— issuing a subpoena or warrant for a witness (s. 728 of *Code*);

— taking an information (s. 723 of *Code*);

— adjournment of proceedings (s. 725 of *Code*);

— dealing with judicial interim release, where "having regard to the circumstances" a youth court judge is "not reasonably available" (ss. 7 and 8 of Y.O.A., ss. 457 to 458 of *Code*).

DETENTION PRIOR TO DISPOSITION
(Sections 7 and 8)

Introduction

Section 7 deals with the arrest and pre-disposition detention of a young person, and establishes procedures for making decisions as to the place where a young person is to be detained, or if he is to be released, to whom and under what circumstances. Section 8 provides that the youth court is to have a central position in the making of decisions about pre-trial detention, and provides a mechanism for the review of these decisions.

The Y.O.A. incorporates the basic philosophy of the J.D.A. in regard to pre-disposition detention; young persons held in custody are not to be confined with adults, unless absolutely necessary. The Y.O.A. does introduce some new practices, and clarifies some of the confusion concerning pre-disposition detention under the J.D.A. Most significantly, it makes clear that the liberal provisions of the *Bail Reform Act* (found in Part XIV of the *Criminal Code*) are to be applied to young people as well as adults.

Some of the significant features of the scheme set out in the J.D.A. which will remain essentially unchanged in the Y.O.A. include:

— detention of young people in places separate from adults, Y.O.A., s-s. 7(1) (J.D.A., s-s. 13(1));

— exceptions to separate detention if juvenile facilities not reasonably available or safety problems exist, Y.O.A., s-s. 7(3) (J.D.A., s-s. 13(4));

— release of young person into care of responsible person, Y.O.A., s-s. 7(4) (J.D.A., s-s. 14(2));

— offence established for those who fail to ensure separate pre-disposition detention of young people, Y.O.A., s-s. 7(7) (J.D.A., s-s. 13(2)).

The Y.O.A. presents certain significant new features:

— clarification that provisions of *Criminal Code* governing detention prior to disposition apply to young people, Y.O.A., ss. 8, 51 and 52;

— introduction of scheme of judicial review of decisions concerning pre-disposition, Y.O.A., s. 8;

— opportunity for consultation with counsel after arrest and for provision of counsel at detention hearings, Y.O.A., ss. 11 and 56;

— notification of parents as soon as possible if young person is detained in custody, Y.O.A., s-s. 9(1).

By virtue of ss. 51 and 52 of the Y.O.A., the substantive features of Part XIV of the *Criminal Code*, governing arrest, release and pre-disposition detention are applicable to offences involving young people. Section 7 of the Y.O.A. qualifies the provisions of the *Code* by ensuring that young persons are generally to be detained separate from adults, and s. 8 provides that decisions regarding the detention of young persons are generally to be decided by a youth court judge.

Therefore the Y.O.A. provides for the application of the general provisions of the criminal law with respect to arrest, and pre-disposition detention and release, but with modification to allow the juvenile justice system to accommodate the special needs and problems of young offenders.

SECTION 7

7. (1) *Designated place of temporary detention.*—**A young person who is arrested and detained prior to the making of a disposition in respect of the young person under section 20 shall, subject to subsection (2), be detained in a place of temporary detention designated as such by the Lieutenant Governor in Council of the appropriate province or his delegate or in a place within a class of such places so designated.**

(2) *Exception.*—**Subsection (1) does not apply in respect of the arrest of a young person or in respect of any temporary restraint of a young person in the hands of a peace officer after the arrest of the young person but prior to his detention in custody.**

(3) *Detention separate from adults.*—No young person who has been arrested shall be detained prior to the making of a disposition in respect of the young person under section 20 in any part of a place in which an adult who has been charged with or convicted of an offence against any law of Canada or a province is detained or held in custody unless a youth court judge or, where a youth court judge is, having regard to the circumstances, not reasonably available, a justice authorizes the detention, being satisfied that

(a) the young person cannot, having regard to his own safety or the safety of others, be detained in a place of detention for young persons; or

(b) no place of detention for young persons is available within a reasonable distance.

(4) *Placement of young person in care of responsible person.*—Where a youth court judge or a justice is satisfied that

(a) a responsible person is willing and able to take care of and exercise control over a young person who has been arrested, and

(b) the young person is willing to be placed in the care of that person,

and where that person undertakes in writing to take care of and to be responsible for the attendance of the young person in court when required, the young person may be placed in the care of that person instead of being detained in custody.

(5) *Authorization of provincial authority for detention.*—In any province for which the Lieutenant Governor in Council has designated a person or a group of persons whose authorization is required before a young person who has been arrested may be detained prior to his appearance before a youth court judge or a justice, no young person shall be so detained unless such authorization is first obtained.

(6) *Transfer by provincial director.*—A young person who is detained in custody in accordance with this section may, during the period of detention, be transferred by the provincial director or his delegate from one place of temporary detention to another.

(7) *Offence and punishment.*—Any person who fails to comply with subsection (1), (3) or (5) is guilty of an offence punishable on summary conviction.

Arrest

The provisions of the *Criminal Code* dealing with arrest are made applicable to the arrest of young persons by virtue of ss. 51 and 52 of the Y.O.A. and the retention in the Y.O.A. of the distinction between indictable and summary conviction offences (s. 52).

By virtue of s. 449 of the *Criminal Code*, a young person may be arrested without warrant by any person where:

— the young person is found committing an indictable offence;

— the young person is believed on reasonable and probable grounds to have committed a criminal offence and is being freshly pursued;

— the young person is found committing a criminal offence in relation to property, he may be arrested by the owner or person in lawful possession of the property.

A peace officer acting on the authority of s. 450 of the *Criminal Code* has authority, in addition to s. 449, to arrest a young person without warrant where:

— the young person is found committing a criminal offence;

— the peace officer believes on reasonable and probable grounds that the young person has committed or is about to commit an indictable offence;

— the peace officer believes on reasonable and probable grounds that a warrant is in force for the young person.

The authority for arrest without warrant by a peace officer is limited by s-s. 450(2) of the *Code*. It provides that, for certain less serious offences, the peace officer shall not arrest without a warrant unless it is in the public interest to do so (for example, to establish the identity of the person) or if the peace officer has a reasonable belief that the young person will fail to attend court.

In situations where the peace officer does not arrest, for offences specified in s-s. 450(2) of the *Code*, the peace officer may issue to the young person an appearance notice under the authority of s. 451 of the *Criminal Code*.

If the young person is arrested without warrant under s. 449 of the *Code*, or with warrant under s. 456.3 of the *Criminal Code*, the Y.O.A. provides that the police

(1) *must* detain the young person separate from adult offenders, subject to the exception in s-ss. 7(2) and (3);

(2) *must* forthwith advise the young person of his right to be represented by counsel and give him an opportunity to obtain counsel, s-s. 11(2);

(3) *must not* fingerprint or photograph the young person unless permitted by the *Identification of Criminals Act*, s. 44;

(4) *must* give notice to the young person's parents as required by s-ss. 9(1) and (2);

(5) *must* comply with requirements of s. 56 if statement to be taken from young person (notification of rights, reasonable opportunity to consult counsel, parent or other adult, and reasonable opportunity to make statement in presence of such a person).

These requirements of the Y.O.A. are in addition to those found in the *Canadian Charter of Rights and Freedoms*, s. 10 which provides:

10. Everyone has the right on arrest or detention

(a) to be informed promptly of the reasons therefor;

(b) to retain and instruct counsel without delay and to be informed of that right; and

(c) to have the validity of the detention determined by way of *habeas corpus* and to be released if the detention is not lawful.

If a young person is arrested for one of the less serious offences listed in s-s. 450(2) of the *Code*, and if the public interest has been satisfied and there no longer exists a reasonable belief that the young person will fail to attend court, then the young person shall be released, either by the arresting officer or by the officer in charge under ss. 452 and 453 of the *Criminal Code*. In either case, the young person can be compelled to attend court by an appearance notice or summons. The officer in charge also has authority to release a young person arrested for an indictable offence where the maximum punishment for an adult is five years or less; the officer in charge also has authority to require a young person to give his promise to appear or enter into a cognizance to secure his release.

Where the arresting officer or the officer in charge releases a young person under s. 452 or 453 of the *Criminal Code*, notice must be given to the parent of the young person pursuant to s-s. 9(2) of the Y.O.A..

Judicial interim release

Sections 457 to 459 of the *Criminal Code* deal with "judicial interim release": the judicial decision to release an arrested person rather than having him detained in custody pending ultimate resolution of his case. Sections 51 and 52 of the Y.O.A. make these provisions of the *Code* applicable.

Where a young person has been arrested, but not released pursuant to s. 452 or 453 of the *Code*, then s. 454 requires that a young person be brought for a decision on judicial interim release before a youth court judge, or where one is not immediately available, as soon as possible thereafter. Subsection 8(1) of the Y.O.A. provides that where a youth court judge is "having regard to the circumstances. . . not reasonably available", the young person shall be brought before a justice for judicial interim release. The Y.O.A. thus ensures that the sensitive issue of pre-disposition detention will normally be dealt with by the youth court, with its special expertise and understanding. Subsection 8(1) provides an exception to ensure that a young person is not unduly detained on account of the unavailability of a youth court judge.

The substantive features of the *Code* provisions governing judicial interim release also apply to the pre-disposition detention of young persons. Thus, as a rule the onus will be on the prosecutor to "show cause why the detention of the accused in custody is justified." However, in the more serious circumstances listed in s-s. 457(5.1) or paras. 457.7(2)(b) to (d.1) of the *Code*, the youth court will order the young person detained unless he can show cause why his detention is not justified. Subsection 457(7) of the *Code* provides that the detention of an accused person is only justified if it is necessary to ensure his attendance in court, or if it is "necessary in the public interest or for the protection or safety of the public, having regard to all the circumstances including any substantial likelihood that the accused will, if he is released from custody, commit a criminal offence or an interference with the administration of justice". Thus it will clearly not be appropriate for a young person to be detained pending judicial resolution of his case because he may be in need of protection, or lacks a place to stay, or "needs to be taught a lesson." Subsection 13(3) of the Y.O.A., however, allows a young person to be detained in custody to permit preparation of a medical or psychological report.

Sections 457.2 and 457.3 of the *Code* govern the conduct of a hearing to determine judicial interim release. Generally, the hearings are relatively informal; the court may receive and base its decision upon "evidence considered credible or trustworthy" in the circumstances. Thus the prosecutor often presents all his evidence by means of his own submissions, rather than providing oral testimony. The scope of the hearings is broad; the court may learn of the record of previous convictions, any outstanding charges, and the "circumstances of the alleged offence". Provision is also made for a ban on publication of the details of the hearing.

The court may decide to detain the accused young person, or to release him upon conditions specified in s-ss. 457(2) and (4) of the *Code*, including that the accused:

— enter into a recognizance, with or without sureties and with or without the requirement of a deposit of a sum of money or other valuable security;
— report to a peace officer or other designated person at times specified, and notify such person of a change in address, employment or occupation;
— remain in a specified territorial jurisdiction;
— abstain from communicating with any witness or other designated person;
— deposit his passport, where he has one;
— comply with such "other reasonable conditions specified".

The statutory provisions of the *Code* governing judicial interim release and the jurisprudence interpreting these provisions are complex. The presention here merely summarizes the *Code* and case law. For a further discussion, see Roger Salhany, *Canadian Criminal Procedure*, 3rd ed. (Aurora, Canada Law Book, 1978), chapter 4; John Scollin, *The Bail Reform Act* (Toronto, Carswell, 1972); John Scollin, *Pre-Trial Release* (Toronto, Carswell, 1977).

"Place of temporary detention": subsections 7(1) and (3)

Section 7 of the Y.O.A. provides that where a decision is made to detain a young person prior to disposition, this will be in a "place of temporary detention". Places of temporary detention will continue under the Y.O.A. to be a provincial responsibility, and are to be designated by the Lieutenant Governor in Council (provincial Cabinet). It is likely that existing facilities will continue to be used, but there will probably need to be some new facilities designated in provinces where 16 and 17 year olds are currently dealt with in the adult system.

Subsection 7(3) of the Y.O.A. provides that, unless otherwise ordered by a youth court, "no young person . . . shall be detained prior to the making of a disposition . . . in *any part* of a place in which an adult . . . is detained" (emphasis added). Ideally, young persons should be detained in completely separate facilities, but this may not always be feasible, especially in remote areas. Although s-s. 7(3) is perhaps slightly ambiguous, the apparent Parliamentary intent is to allow young persons and adults to be detained in separate parts of the same place, as long as they are not detained in the same part of a place. This intent is revealed by contrasting s-s. 7(3) of the Y.O.A. with s. 13 of the J.D.A.; the latter provision simply provided that a juvenile was not to be detained pending disposition in a "gaol or other place in which adults" are or may be imprisoned. Subsection 7(3) of the Y.O.A. provides that detention of young persons in a particular part of a place with adults is prohibited, but implicitly allows detention of young persons in different parts of the same place.

Thus, young persons and adults may be kept in separate facilities, or different parts of the same facility. For example, young persons may be detained in a separate wing of a facility in which adults are detained. It would, however, seem that all aspects of the detention must be separate, and hence if young persons are detained in separate parts of a facility in which there are adults, provision must be made for separate use of such areas as exercise yards, recreation areas, and food service areas.

The provisions of s. 7 regarding pre-disposition detention may be contrasted with those found in s-s. 13(3) which allow a young person to be remanded in "custody" for a medical or psychological assessment; this may involve confinement with adults, for example, in a psychiatric facility.

"Temporary restraint": subsection 7(2)

Subsection 7(2) gives a police officer arresting a young person some leeway. A young person may be kept in "temporary restraint" immediately upon arrest and before the commencement of formal "detention", and during this time the young person need not be kept in a separate designated "place of temporary detention". "Temporary restraint" is not statutorily defined, but it would seem that a young person is in "temporary restraint" until a decision is made to detain the young person and bring him before a youth court judge or a justice for consideration of judicial interim release. Such a decision will normally be made by the officer in charge, pursuant to s. 453 of the *Code*. If the young person is arrested on a serious charge, for which he can only be released by judicial decision, "temporary restraint" would appear to end when he is placed in a cell, room or other place designed to detain him pending judicial hearing. Situations of "temporary restraint" would include:

— the young person is taken to the station in a police vehicle;
— the young person is being "booked" or processed through at the police station, including, where appropriate under s. 44, fingerprinted and photographed;
— the police are taking a statement from the young person prior to taking the young person before a youth court judge pursuant to s. 434 of the *Code*;
— the arresting peace officer or officer in charge is taking appropriate steps to satisfy the public interest by ensuring the young person's attendance at court, prior to releasing the young person under s. 452 or 453 of the *Criminal Code*.

Subsection 7(2) gives the police some flexibility in restraining a young person and in dealing with the young person after his initial arrest; it allows some time for a decision as to whether a charge should be laid and if so, whether the young person should be released. If this provision is abused, however, those responsible face possible criminal prosecution under s-s. 7(7), for violating s-ss. 7(1), (3) or (5).

Detention with adults: subsection 7(3)

As a general rule, young persons are to be detained separate and apart from adults, but s-s. 7(3) provides two exceptions:

(1) where the safety of the young person or of others requires it (para. 7(3)(a)); or

(2) where no place of detention for a young person is available within a reasonable distance (para. 7(3)(b)).

The first exception refers to situations where the young person may be in physical danger as a result of detention with other young persons. This exception also encompasses the danger which the young person may present to other inmates or staff; a repeat offender aged 17 may be a serious threat to younger and less experienced young persons. In *R. v. P.*, [1979] 2 W.W.R. 262 at p. 266, 8 R.F.L. (2d) 277 (Man. Q.B.) Wilson J. commented on s-s. 13(4) of the *J.D.A.* which provides that where a child over the age of 14 "cannot safely be confined" with others his age, he may be detained with adults:

> In my view, the phrase "safely be confined" relates to all the circumstances of the intended confinement — safety to the accused himself, the accused delinquent; safety to other persons sharing that confinement with him and safety to persons charged with supervision of the alleged delinquent and his associates in that area of confinement. I think the word "safely" has to be given a wide meaning.

These words would seem equally applicable to the provisions of para. 7(3)(a) of the Y.O.A., and indeed, the subsection appears to have been explicitly worded to comply with this interpretation.

Paragraph 7(3)(b) allows detention with adults when no designated place of detention is available "within a reasonable distance". This provision allows the court to balance the ill-effects of detention with adults against the benefits of family and local community support which may be sacrificed if the young person is detained in a distant facility for young persons. The court will have to consider the distance involved, the likely length of detention, the nature of the adult facility and the type of adults contained therein, the age and maturity of the young person, and the nature of the family relationship. It may be appropriate in some circumstances for a court to consider placing the young person with a responsible person pursuant to s-s. 7(4), rather than detaining him in an adult facility under para. 7(3)(b).

Authorization for detention in an adult facility under s-s. 7(3) must be obtained from a youth court judge and only where a youth court judge is not reasonably available may a justice authorize it. This requirement serves as a further protection for the young person for it ensures that whenever possible the specialized experience and competence of a youth court judge will be applied to these important decisions.

Placement with a "responsible person": subsection 7(4)

Subsection 7(4) allows the court to place a young person in the care of a "responsible person" rather than detaining the young person in custody. This provision is not intended to be an alternative to release; rather only following a finding by the youth court that the criteria for detention as set out in the Code have been met should a court consider placing a young person in the care of a responsible person as an alternative to actual custody.

This provision recognizes the right of a young person to the least possible interference with his freedom (para. 3(1)(f)) and offers the court an alternative to actual detention where the court is satisfied that public safety can reasonably be protected.

It would appear that "responsible person" is not restricted to a parent or even necessarily an adult; presumably a young person could be placed in the care of a spouse who is a minor, or a corporation such as the Children's Aid Society. The person must be "willing" and "able" to take care of and exercise control over the young person; although no specific form is identified under the Y.O.A., the person must undertake in writing to take care of and ensure the attendance in court of the young person. The Act provides no consequences for breach of this undertaking although arguably wilful deceit by the person making such an undertaking may fall within contempt of court (see s. 47 of the Y.O.A.).

In a strictly technical sense it might seem less onerous for a "responsible person" to undertake to take care of a young person and be responsible for his attendance in court under s-s. 7(4) of the Y.O.A. than for the same person to act as a surety for the young person's own recognizance under paras. 457(2)(c) or (d) of the *Code*. A surety under the *Code* may incur financial liability if the young person fails to attend while the "responsible person" under the Y.O.A. will not. It is generally appropriate for a surety to be required under the *Code* if a decision is made to release the young person, and it is felt the young person lacks sufficient financial resources for him to enter into a meaningful "pledge" to guarantee his attendance; the surety is in effect a financial guarantor. Subsection 7(4) of the Y.O.A. should be used where a decision is made to detain the young person in custody unless some responsible person personally agrees to take care of the young person and be responsible for his attendance in court; the person undertaking this responsibility assumes a broader obligation than one undertaken by a surety.

Paragraph 7(4)(b) requires the youth court to satisfy itself that "the young person is willing to be placed in the care of that person". This indicates that the young person must be committed to this plan, and agree to stay in the care of the responsible person.

Additional authorization for detention: subsection 7(5)

Subsection 7(5) is a permissive provision allowing a province to designate a person or persons other than the police to authorize detention of a young person prior to his appearance in court. This authority, if so designated, would operate only in the narrow class of situations between temporary restraint in the hands of the police under s-s. 7(2) and the young person's appearance before a youth court pursuant to s. 454 of the *Criminal Code*.

Transfer by provincial director: subsection 7(6)

The provincial director, as defined in s-s. 2(1) of the Y.O.A., is given discretion under s-s. 7(6) to transfer a young person detained in accordance with the Act from one facility to another. Presumably such a transfer would be based on a consideration of the level of security required for the young person, his needs and the facilities available.

Offence: subsection 7(7)

In order to encourage compliance with these provisions concerning pre-trial detention, the Act sets out an offence punishable on summary conviction for a failure to comply with s-ss. 7(1), (3) and (5).

SECTION 8

8. (1) *Order respecting detention or release.*—No order may be made under section 457 of the *Criminal Code* by a court, judge or justice, other than a youth court judge, for the release from or the detention in custody of a young person against whom proceedings have been taken under this Act unless, having regard to the circumstances, a youth court judge is not reasonably available.

(2) *Application to youth court.*—Where an order is made under section 457 of the *Criminal Code* in respect of a young person by a justice who is not a youth court judge, an application may, at any time after the order is made, be made to a youth court for the release from or detention in custody of the young person, as the case may be, and the youth court shall hear the matter as an original application.

(3) *Notice to prosecutor.*—An application under subsection (2) for release from custody shall not be heard unless the young person has given the prosecutor at least two clear days notice in writing of the application.

(4) *Notice to young person.*—An application under subsection (2) for detention in custody shall not be heard unless the prosecutor has given the young person at least two clear days notice in writing of the application.

(5) *Waiver of notice.*—The requirement for a notice under subsection (3) or (4) may be waived by the prosecutor or by the young person or his counsel, as the case may be.

(6) *Application for review under section 457.5 or 457.6 of Criminal Code.*—An application under section 457.5 or 457.6 of the *Criminal Code* for a review of an order made in respect of a young person by a youth court judge who is a judge of a superior, county or district court shall be made to a judge of the court of appeal.

(7) *Idem.*—No application may be made under section 457.5 or 457.6 of the *Criminal Code* for a review of an order made in respect of a young person by a justice who is not a youth court judge.

(8) *Interim release by youth court judge only.*—Where a young person against whom proceedings have been taken under this

Act is charged with an offence referred to in section 457.7 of the *Criminal Code*, a youth court judge, but no other court, judge or justice, may release the young person from custody under that section.

(9) *Review by court of appeal.*—A decision made by a youth court judge under subsection (8) may be reviewed in accordance with section 608.1 of the *Criminal Code* and that section applies, with such modifications as the circumstances require, to any decision so made.

Orders respecting detention or release: section 8

Section 8 modifies the provisions of the *Criminal Code* concerning judicial interim release by requiring all orders regarding pre-disposition, detention or release of a young person to be made by a youth court judge. Where a youth court judge is "not reasonably available", s-s. 8(1) allows these issues to be decided by any justice. The justice will have to decide whether a youth court judge is not reasonably available before dealing with the matter. In deciding the issue of judicial interim release, the youth court judge or justice will generally apply the principles of ss. 457 to 459 of the *Criminal Code* and the jurisprudence thereunder, except as procedurally modified by the Y.O.A. Thus the same guiding principles as are applicable to judicial interim release for adults apply to young persons. (See discussion above under s. 7.)

If the issue of detention or release of a young person should be decided by a justice, as a youth court judge is not available, then s-s. 8(2) provides that the prosecutor or young person can subsequently apply to a youth court judge to hear the matter again. In this situation, the youth court judge will not simply be reviewing the original decision, but "shall hear the matter as an original application"; there will be a hearing *de novo*. If an application is made to a youth court judge to rehear the matter, s-ss. 8(3) and (4) require two clear days' written notice of the application, though s-s. 8(5) allows the notice requirement to be waived.

Section 8 thus ensures that decisions regarding detention and release of young persons will be made by a judge with special expertise and sensitivity, while allowing some flexibility by recognizing that youth court judges may not always be immediately available.

Review of youth court orders: subsections 8(6) and (7)

Sections 457.5 and 457.6 of the *Criminal Code* allow for a review by a judge of orders made by a justice regarding detention and release. There is conflicting jurisprudence as to whether this review is a *de novo* hearing with the judge having the authority to substitute his own discretion, or whether this is rather an appeal in which the judge should only reverse the original decision if there has been a demonstrable error: for example, contrast *R. v. Thompson* (1972), 7 C.C.C. (2d) 70, 18 C.R.N.S. 102, [1972] 3 W.W.R. 729 (B.C.S.C.) and *R. v. O'Neill* (1973), 11 C.C.C. (2d) 240, 21 C.R.N.S. 107, 6 N.B.R. (2d) 735 (S.C.).

The decision of a youth court judge regarding detention or release of a young person may be reviewed pursuant to ss. 457.5 and 457.6 of the *Code*. Normally the review is by a superior, county or district court judge. Subsection 8(6) of Y.O.A. provides that if a province designates that its youth court is to be the superior, county or district court, then the review under ss. 457.5 and 457.6 is to be made by a judge of the court of appeal.

Subsection 8(7) of the Y.O.A. provides that if an initial order regarding detention or release was made by a justice as a youth court judge was not reasonably available, then review of that order is to be by a youth court judge under s-s. 8(2), and not under s. 457.5 or 457.6 of the *Code*. Of course, under the s-s. 8(2) rehearing the youth court judge's decision is subject to review under the *Code* provisions.

Offences referred to in section 457.7 of the Criminal Code: subsections 8(8) and (9)

Section 457.7 of the *Code* provides that where a person is accused of one of the serious offences specified, then he is to be released pending trial only by a judge of the superior court of criminal jurisdiction. Subsection 8(8) of the Y.O.A. ensures that where a young person is charged with such an offence, only a youth court judge may release him.

Subsection 8(9) of the Y.O.A. provides that a decision of a youth court judge, made pursuant to s-s. 8(8), dealing with a young person, charged with one of the serious offences listed in s. 457.7 of the *Code*, is reviewable only by the court of appeal. Such a review is to be in accordance with s. 608.1 of the *Criminal Code*.

NOTICES TO PARENTS
(Sections 9 and 10)

Introduction

In the Y.O.A.'s Declaration of Principle, it is recognized that primary responsibility for the care and supervision of a young person lies with his parents (para. 3(1)(h)). In keeping with the principle of parental responsibility and to ensure that parents may be available to protect the rights and interests of their children, provision is made in s. 9 of the Y.O.A. to notify the parents of a young person about proceedings under the Act. Further, under s. 10 the youth court can in certain circumstances compel the attendance of a parent if his child is being prosecuted under the Y.O.A. Parents who attend proceedings under the Y.O.A. are not parties to the proceedings, but at certain stages they are assured an opportunity to participate (s. 16 transfer; s. 20 disposition; ss. 28 to 33 dispositional review).

The *J.D.A.* includes a provision for parental notice of the court proceedings, but not for compelling the attendance of parents. Section 9 of the Y.O.A. expands these notice requirements, in particular, by requiring notice to parents as soon as possible if a young person is detained after arrest. The Y.O.A. also clarifies some matters concerning notice, including: service of other adults if parents are unavailable, methods of service, dispensing with notice, contents of the notice, and the effect of a failure to give notice.

Notice to parents: section 9

SECTION 9

9. (1) *Notice to parent in case of arrest.*—**Subject to subsections (3) and (4), where a young person is arrested and detained in custody pending his appearance in court, the officer in charge at the time the young person is detained shall, as soon as possible, give or cause to be given, orally or in writing, to a parent of the young person notice of the arrest stating the place of detention and the reason for the arrest.**

(2) *Notice to parent in case of summons or appearance notice.*—Subject to subsections (3) and (4) where a summons or an appearance notice is issued in respect of a young person, the person who issued the summons or appearance notice, or, where a young person is released on giving his promise to appear or entering into a recognizance, the officer in charge, shall, as soon as possible, give or cause to be given, in writing, to a parent of the young person notice of the summons, appearance notice, promise to appear or recognizance.

(3) *Notice to relative or other adult.*—Where the whereabouts of the parents of a young person

(a) who is arrested and detained in custody,

(b) in respect of whom a summons or an appearance notice is issued, or

(c) who is released on giving his promise to appear or entering into a recognizance

are not known or it appears that no parent is available, a notice under this section may be given to an adult relative of the young person who is known to the young person and is likely to assist him or, if no such adult relative is available, to such other adult who is known to the young person and is likely to assist him as the person giving the notice considers appropriate.

(4) *Notice to spouse.*—Where a young person described in paragraph 3(a), (b) or (c) is married, a notice under this section may be given to the spouse of the young person instead of a parent.

(5) *Notice on direction of youth court judge or justice.*—Where doubt exists as to the person to whom a notice under this section should be given, a youth court judge or, where a youth court judge is, having regard to the circumstances, not reasonably available, a justice may give directions as to the person to whom the notice should be given, and a notice given in accordance with such directions is sufficient notice for the purposes of this section.

(6) *Contents of notice.*—Any notice under this section shall, in addition to any other requirements under this section, include

(a) the name of the young person in respect of whom it is given;

(b) the charge against the young person and the time and place of appearance; and

(c) a statement that the young person has the right to be represented by counsel.

(7) *Service of notice.*—Subject to subsection (10), a notice under this section given in writing may be served personally or may be sent by mail.

(8) *Proceedings not invalid.*—Subject to subsection (9), failure to give notice in accordance with this section does not affect the validity of proceedings under this Act.

(9) *Exception.*—Failure to give notice in accordance with subsection (2) in any case renders invalid any subsequent proceedings under this Act relating to the case unless

(a) a parent of the young person against whom proceedings are held attends court with the young person; or

(b) notice has been dispensed with pursuant to paragraph (10)(b).

(10) *Where a notice not served.*—Where there has been a failure to give a notice in accordance with this section and none of the persons to whom such notice may be given attends court with a young person, a youth court judge or a justice before whom proceedings are held against the young person may

(a) adjourn the proceedings and order that the notice be given in such manner and to such person as he directs; or

(b) dispense with the notice where, in his opinion, having regard to the circumstances, notice may be dispensed with.

(11) *Form of notices.*—A notice under subsection (1) or (2) may be in Form 1 and a notice under subsection (3) may be in Form 2.

A "parent": section 9

"Parent" is broadly defined in s-s. 2(1) of the Y.O.A. The definition "includes, in respect of another person, any person who is under a legal duty to provide for that other person or any person who has, in law or in fact, the custody or control of that other person." An agency with custody of the young person, for example, a Children's Aid Society, would be included as a parent according to this definition. The spouse of the young person, if he is married, might also be included as a person who is under a legal duty to provide for the young person.

Section 9 requires notice to "*a* parent" only. Although the provision does not require notice to be given to everyone who is a "parent", notice may be given to more than one parent. Subsection 26(7) of the *Interpretation Act*, R.S.C. 1970, c. I-23 states :

"Words in the singular include the plural, and words in the plural include the singular." If the biological parents are separated it would seem to be good practice to give notice to the custodial parent.

If there is some doubt about who is a "parent", or who should be given notice, direction may be sought from the court pursuant to s-s. 9(5). It is suggested that, as a matter of practice and in order to avoid later delays, directions should be sought whenever there is any doubt as to who should be served.

Notice where young person in custody: subsection 9(1)

Where a young person is arrested and detained in custody pending his appearance in court, the officer "in charge" is responsible for seeing that notice is given to a parent of the young person "as soon as possible". The notice provisions are in keeping with the recognition in the Y.O.A. of the primary responsibility of parents for the care and supervision of their child. Assumption of this responsibility is predicated upon parents being promptly informed of their child's involvement with the law; notification may allow parents to become involved and ensure that the rights and interests of their child are protected. See also s-s. 56(2) of the Y.O.A. which guarantees a young person the right to a reasonable opportunity to consult with a parent prior to making a statement to the police, and after consulation to have a reasonable opportunity to have his parent present when a statement is made; the young person must be informed of these rights and may choose to consult with counsel instead of a parent. Notice to parents is additional to the *Criminal Code* provisions for notice to the accused and any information that must be given to the young person under s. 10 of the *Canadian Charter of Rights and Freedoms*.

The officer in charge has the responsibility of giving or causing notice to be given. The definition of "officer in charge" in s. 448 of the *Criminal Code* includes "the officer . . . responsible for the . . . place to which an accused is taken after arrest or a peace officer designated by him . . . who is in charge of such place at the time an accused is taken to that place to be detained in custody." The officer in charge is also responsible under Part XIV of the *Code* for release of an accused from custody, upon issuing an appearance notice, a promise to appear, a summons, an undertaking or a recognizance to the accused.

Notice pursuant to s-s. 9(1) must state the place of detention and the reason for the arrest. Subsection 9(6) further specifies the contents of notice to a parent. Notice under s-s. 9(1) may be in Form 1 (see sample form at end of discussion of s. 9).

Under s-s. 9(1), notice of detention must be given to a parent "as soon as possible". To facilitate quick notification, it may be oral or in writing; this contrasts with s-s. 9(2) dealing with the issuance of a summons or appearance notice, which requires notice to the parent to be in writing. If oral notice is given, the person giving it must ensure that all of the requirements of s-s. 9(6) concerning the contents of the notice are satisfied. Although s-s. 9(7) permits service of written notice personally or by mail, it would seem that personal notification, perhaps by a telephone call, would generally seem to be appropriate under s-s. 9(1).

Notice where young person not in custody: subsection 9(2)

Subsection 9(2) applies where the young person is not detained in custody. In cases "where a summons or an appearance notice is issued" to the young person, or "where the young person has been released on giving his promise to appear or entering into a recognizance", notice must be given to a parent. A notice given pursuant to s-s. 9(2) must contain the information required by s-s. 9(6) and must be in writing. As the young person is not being detained in custody, service by mail is sufficient, although personal service is equally acceptable under s-s. 9(7). Notice under s-s. 9(2) may be in Form 2.

Whereabouts of parent unknown: subsection 9(3)

If the whereabouts of the young person's parents are unknown or if no parent is available, s-s. 9(3) permits a notice to be served under s-ss. 9(1) or (2) on an adult relative of the young person "who is known to the young person and is likely to assist him". If no such adult relative is available, notice may be given to "such other adult who is known to the young person and is likely to assist him as the person giving the notice considers appropriate". A neighbour or friend of the family of the young person might come within the definition of "appropriate adult", provided they are known to the young person and likely to assist him. Generally it would seem necessary to consult with the young person to discover whether an adult is known to the young person and is likely to assist him.

The decision as to which relative to serve or as to whether another adult is appropriate is to be made by the "person giving the notice", usually the police. If there is doubt about the person to whom notice should be given, judicial direction may be sought under s-s. 9(5).

Subsection 9(11) provides that notice under s-s. 9(3) may be in Form 2 (see sample form at end of discussion of s. 9).

Where young person is married: subsection 9(4)

Notice "may be given to a spouse of the young person instead of a parent" where the young person is married; the spouse need not be an adult. Although it is sufficient to notify only the spouse, s-s. 9(4) does not rule out notifying the parents of a young person who is married. This provision illustrates an acceptance of the view that while marriage brings with it a legal independence from one's parents, parents continue to have a continuing interest in the welfare of their children.

Since it may be expected that a young person who is married will look for assistance more to his spouse than to his parents, it may be preferable to give notice to the spouse rather than to the parents. Alternatively, there may be a situation where notice to two or more parties is appropriate. Even if notice is given initially only to the spouse, an order may be made under s. 10 to require the presence of the parents, in appropriate cases.

Notice on direction of the youth court: subsection 9(5)

An application may be made to a youth court judge for directions "as to the person to whom the notice should be given". No principles have been set out to clarify to whom service of notice is appropriate. It is likely that each case will have to be decided on the basis of its particular circumstances. The court may have to determine who is a "parent"; consideration may have to be given to the relationship of different adults to the young person. Notice may be served on more than one parent; as a rule, a custodial parent should get notice, even though notice to another parent would satisfy the Act's requirements. See also s-s. 9(10) which gives the court discretion to dispense with parental notice altogether.

A justice may give directions under s-s. 9(5), where a youth court judge is "having regard to the circumstances, not reasonably available". In deciding whether a youth court judge is not reasonably available, a justice will probably consider the length of time which will elapse before a judge could be available, the distance a judge would have to travel, and the circumstances of the young person. For example, in regard to a notice to be given under s-s. 9(1) where the young person is being detained, a delay of even a few hours until a youth court judge was available might not be justified.

Contents of notice: subsection 9(6)

In order to satisfy the requirements of s-s. 9(6), the following must be included in a notice given a parent: the name of the young person, the charge and the time and place of appearance, and a statement that the young person has the right to be represented by counsel. Subsection 9(6) applies to oral and written notice. See Forms 1 and 2 at end of discussion of s. 9 (see sample forms).

Service of notice: subsection 9(7)

Subsection 9(7) allows a written notice to be served on a parent personally or sent by mail; presumably pre-paid, first-class mail will be sufficient. Subsections 9(1) and (2) refer to service of notices "as soon as possible"; where a young person is being detained, this would suggest that a s-s. 9(1) notice should be given orally or served personally at the earliest opportunity. Subsection 9(10) gives a court flexibility to adjourn proceedings and order notice in a "manner directed", where there has been a failure to give notice and no parent or other appropriate person attends court with the young person.

Effect on validity of proceedings: subsections 9(8) and (9)

Where there has been failure to give notice according to s. 9, the validity of proceedings under the Y.O.A. is preserved by s-s.

9(8), subject to s-s. 9(9). The validity of the proceedings will not be affected if a parent attends court with the young person or if notice is dispensed with pursuant to para. 9(10)(b). If there has been a failure to give notice in accordance with s-s. 9(2), however, and no parent attends with the young person and no order is made dispensing with notice under s-s. 9(10), then any subsequent proceedings under the Y.O.A. are rendered invalid by s-s. 9(9). Where a young person is detained in custody and the notice to a parent required by s-s. 9(1) is not given, the failure to give such a notice to the parents does not invalidate the proceedings or the pre-disposition detention.

The approach of s-ss. 9(8) and (9) of the Y.O.A. marks a change from that taken to this issue under the J.D.A. Subsection 10(1) of the J.D.A. states that "due notice of the hearing of any charge of delinquency shall be served on the parent or parents ...". The courts held that compliance with s. 10 of the J.D.A. was a condition precedent to a Juvenile Court acquiring jurisdiction to proceed: *Smith v. The Queen*, [1959] S.C.R. 638, 124 C.C.C. 71, 22 D.L.R. (2d) 129, 30 C.R. 230. In *R. v. Cote* (1976), 31 C.C.C. (2d) 414, 35 C.R.N.S. 347 (Sask. Q.B.) it was held that even the presence of the parents at the hearing was not sufficient where it was not proven they had been served with written notices. In *R. v. L.* (1981), 59 C.C.C. (2d) 160 (Ont. Prov. Ct.) it was suggested that the judge himself might take responsibility for ensuring compliance with s-s. 10(1) of the J.D.A. James, Prov. Ct. J. stated at p. 161:

> Having stated that it is not improper for a Judge to bring a defect in due notice to the attention of the Crown and defence counsel, and that a Judge has a duty to ensure compliance with s. 10, it does not follow that a Judge should conduct the inquiry as to the sufficiency of notice ... The onus rests with the Crown to satisfy the Judge that there has been due notice ...

If the approach of James, Prov. Ct. J. is followed under the Y.O.A., youth court judges may initiate inquiries as to compliance with the notice provisions of s. 9, though there may still be an onus upon the prosecutor to show that proper notice has been served.

Proof of service

The Y.O.A. provides in s-s. 62(1) that service of a notice required by s. 9 may be proved in either of two ways. Oral

evidence given under oath by "the person claiming to have personally served it or sent it by mail" is sufficient, as is an affidavit
or statutory declaration of that person. Subsection 62(2) states
that where proof of service "is offered by affidavit or statutory
declaration, it is not necessary to prove the signature or official
character of the person making or taking the affidavit or declaration, if the official character of that person appears on the face
thereof." Technically, if service of a notice is by mail, it is sufficient to prove it was posted; it is not necessary to prove receipt.
Similarly if substituted service is ordered under para. 9(10)(a), it
must be proved that the service was effected as ordered, not that
notice was actually received.

Court order regarding notice: subsection 9(10)

If a young person appears in court, and no parent attends and
no parent or other adult has been served with notice under s. 9,
then the youth court judge or justice before whom proceedings
are held may deal with the issue of notice under s-s. 9(10).

Under para. 9(10)(a) the judge or justice may adjourn the
proceedings and order that notice be given in such manner and to
such person as directed. Alternatively "having regard to the circumstances", the judge or justice may dispense with notice under
para. 9(10)(b).

In deciding what type of order to make under s-s. 9(10), the
general principle which should govern is that parents are responsible for their children and hence should have notice of proceedings involving them (para. 3(1)(h)). Nevertheless, the circumstances may support ordering some form of substituted service,
such as serving notice upon a relative or friend of a parent under
para. 9(10)(a), or dispensing with notice altogether. The *Canadian Charter of Rights and Freedoms*, para. 11(b) guarantees a right
to trial "within a reasonable time"; a lengthy delay in order to
notify a parent or obtain adult assistance may be unwarranted,
especially if the charge is not serious. In determining what type of
order to make under s-s. 9(10), consideration should be given to
a number of factors, including: the age of the young person, the
degree of independence he has achieved from his parents, the
seriousness of the offence, and the likely difficulty of effecting
notice. Generally, a justice, who can only adjourn a proceeding
and deal with pre-disposition detention, should be reluctant to

dispense with notice altogether under para. 9(10)(b); it would be preferable for a justice to order notice under para. 9(10)(a) during an adjournment, as this should not further delay the proceedings.

Form of notices: subsection 9(11)

A notice to a parent under s-s. 9(1) or (2) may be in Form 1, and a notice to a relative or other adult under s-s. 9(3) may be in Form 2. (See following samples.)

SAMPLE FORM

FORM 1
THE YOUNG OFFENDERS ACT
IN THE YOUTH COURT FOR ONTARIO

NOTICE TO PARENT

Canada
Province of Ontario
County of Queens

To John Smith of 25 First Ave., Anytown, Ontario.

Whereas it is alleged that you are a parent of, a person under a legal duty to provide for or a person who has in law or in fact the custody or control of David Smith of 25 First Ave., Anytown, Ontario a young person within the meaning of the *Young Offenders Act*;

This is therefore to notify you that an information has been received in the Youth Court wherein it is alleged that:

David Smith on the second day of June 1982 did steal two hundred and fifty dollars from The Corner Milk Store, 2 West Street, Anytown, Ontario, and at the same time thereat did use threats of violence contrary to section 303 of the *Criminal Code of Canada*;

and that David Smith has been arrested in respect of the said offence and detained in The Anytown Youth Detention Centre and is to appear before the Youth Court at 100 Main Street, Anytown, Ontario on the 6th day of June 19 82 at 10:00 o'clock in the fore noon, to answer to the information and to be dealt with according to the *Young Offenders Act*;

And this is also to notify you that David Smith has the right to be represented by counsel;

And this is also to notify you that you or any person who is a parent of, is under a legal duty to provide for or has in law or in fact the custody or control of David Smith may attend with him at the time and place mentioned above.

Dated this 3rd day of June 19 82, at Anytown in the Province of Ontario.

"Thomas Brown"

. . . .

A Judge of the Youth Court

NOTE: Destruction of records

Section 45 provides for the destruction of records where a young person is charged with an offence and acquitted or the charge is withdrawn or stayed or where a young person who is found guilty of an offence has not been charged with or found guilty of a further offence for a period of five years after all dispositions have been completed in the case of an indictable offence or two years in the case of a summary conviction offence.

SAMPLE FORM

FORM 2
THE YOUNG OFFENDERS ACT
IN THE YOUTH COURT FOR ONTARIO

NOTICE TO RELATIVE OR FRIEND

Canada
Province of Ontario
County of Queens

To Peter Martin of 48 Centre Street, Anytown, Ontario :

Whereas it is alleged that you are a relative of David Smith ,
being a maternal uncle of David Smith , a young person within
the meaning of the *Young Offenders Act*;

This is therefore to notify you that an information has been
received in the Youth Court wherein it is alleged that

David Smith, on the second day of June 1982 did steal
two hundred and fifty dollars from The Corner Milk
Store, 2 West Street, Anytown, Ontario and at the time
thereat did use threats of violence contrary to section
303 of the *Criminal Code of Canada*;

and David Smith has been arrested in respect of the said offence
and detained in The Anytown Youth Centre and David
Smith is to appear before the Youth Court at 100 Main Street,
Anytown, Ontario on the 6th day of June 19 82 at 10.00
o'clock in the fore noon, to answer to the information and to be
dealt with according to the *Young Offenders Act*;

And this is also to notify you that David Smith has the right
to be represented by counsel;

And this is also to notify you that you may, if you wish to do
so, attend with David Smith at the time and place mentioned
above.

Dated this 3rd day of June 19 82 , at Anytown in the
Province of Ontario.

"Thomas Brown"
....
A Judge of the Youth Court

Attendance of parent: section 10

SECTION 10

10. (1) *Order requiring attendance of parent.*—Where a parent does not attend proceedings before a youth court in respect of a young person, the court may, if in its opinion the presence of the parent is necessary or in the best interest of the young person, by order in writing require the parent to attend at any stage of the proceedings.

(2) *Form and service of order.*—An order made under subsection (1) may be in Form 3 and a copy of the order shall be served by a peace officer or by a person designated by a youth court by delivering it personally to the parent to whom it is directed, unless the youth court authorizes service by registered mail.

(3) *Failure to attend.*—A parent who is ordered to attend a youth court pursuant to subsection (1) and who fails without reasonable excuse, the proof of which lies on that parent, to comply with the order

(a) is guilty of contempt of court;

(b) may be dealt with summarily by the court; and

(c) is liable to the punishment provided for in the *Criminal Code* for a summary conviction offence.

(4) *Appeal.*—Section 9 of the *Criminal Code* applies where a person is convicted of contempt of court under subsection (3).

(5) *Warrant to arrest parent.*—If a parent who is ordered to attend a youth court pursuant to subsection (1) does not attend at the time and place named in the order or fails to remain in attendance as required and it is proved that a copy of the order was served on the parent, a youth court may issue a warrant to compel the attendance of the parent.

(6) *Form of warrant.*—A warrant issued under subsection (5) may be in Form 4.

Order requiring attendance of parent: subsection 10(1)

A parent who receives notice of proceedings pursuant to s-s. 9(2) is not normally obliged to attend. Subsection 10(1) of the Y.O.A., however, allows a youth court judge to order that a parent attend. Such an order may be made at any stage of the proceedings, for example at a pre-disposition hearing, at the adjudication stage, or at disposition.

The Act does not specify who may seek such an order, and it would seem open to either the prosecutor or the young person to request the order. It would also seem acceptable for the judge to make the order on his own motion, providing the parties have an opportunity to address the issue.

The court should only order a parent to attend if this is "necessary" or "in the best interest of the young person". The presence of a parent might be necessary to provide information about a young person's background at a disposition hearing. In some circumstances it might be in the best interest of a young person that his parent attend a disposition hearing to learn more about the young person's problems.

Normally, one would expect the court to order parental attendance only if a parent fails to attend voluntarily after receiving notice of the hearing.

If a party is seeking an order for parental attendance simply so that the parent can be called as a witness, the proper procedure would be for the party to issue a subpoena in the ordinary way. The court should not make an order under s. 10 to require a parent to give testimony at the adjudicative stage.

Form and service of order: subsection 10(2)

An order requiring the presence of a parent may be in Form 3 (see sample at end of discussion of s. 10). Personal service is required unless service by registered mail has been authorized. If the order is to be served personally, this may be done by a peace officer or by a person designated by a youth court. Personal service is preferred here because a parent may be penalized for failure to attend, and the court should be sure that the order was in fact received.

Failure to attend: subsection 10(3)

Failure to attend pursuant to an order made under s-s. 10(1) can result in a parent being found guilty of contempt of court, unless the parent proves he had a reasonable excuse for failing to comply. The onus is on the parent to show "reasonable excuse", for example, non-service or, possibly, physical incapacity. If the parent fails to attend, the contempt of court can be dealt with summarily by the court and he is liable to the punishment for a summary conviction offence provided for in s. 722 of the *Criminal Code*; currently the maximum punishment is six months in jail, or a fine of up to $500 or both.

Appeal from contempt conviction: subsection 10(4)

Subsection 10(4) of the Y.O.A. provides that if a parent is convicted of contempt of court under s-s. 10(3), the parent may appeal the conviction or sentence in the manner provided in s. 9 of the *Criminal Code*.

Warrant may issue for failure to attend: subsection 10(5)

In addition to the contempt power set out in s-s. 10(3), the youth court may issue a warrant to require the police to compel the attendance of the parent. The youth court judge may choose between making a contempt order or issuing a warrant or he may do both. A warrant will only issue after an order has been made compelling parental attendance under s-s. 10(1). Appropriate service of an order under s-s. 10(1) must be proved before a warrant is issued.

Form of warrant: subsection 10(6)

A warrant may be in Form 4. See sample on page 72.

SAMPLE FORM

FORM 3
THE YOUNG OFFENDERS ACT
IN THE YOUTH COURT FOR ONTARIO

ORDER FOR ATTENDANCE OF PARENT

Canada
Province of Ontario
County of Queens

To John Smith of 25 First Ave, Anytown, Ontario:

Whereas David Smith of 25 First Ave., Anytown, Ontario, a young person within the meaning of the *Young Offenders Act*, has been charged with the following offence:

robbery: to wit on the second day of June, 1982 did steal two hundred and fifty dollars from The Corner Milk Store, 2 West Street, Anytown, Ontario, and at the same time thereat did use threats of violence contrary to section 303 of the *Criminal Code of Canada*;

And whereas it is alleged that you are a parent of, a person under a legal duty to provide for or a person who has in law or in fact the custody or control of David Smith ;

And whereas it has been made to appear that your presence at the proceedings against David Smith is necessary or in the best interest of David Smith ;

This is therefore to command you to attend before the Youth Court at 100 Main Street, Anytown, Ontario on the 6th day of June 19 82 at 10.00 o'clock in the fore noon, and to remain in attendance, unless excused by the Youth Court, during the conduct of proceedings against David Smith , and your failure without reasonable excuse to appear may constitute contempt of court and be punishable by the penalty provided for in the *Criminal Code* for a summary conviction offence;

And further take notice that if you do not attend at the time and place stated herein a warrant may be issued to compel your attendance.

Dated this 3rd day of June 19 82, at Anytown in the Province of Ontario.

"Thomas Brown"
. . . .
A Judge of the Youth Court

SAMPLE FORM

FORM 4
THE YOUNG OFFENDERS ACT
IN THE YOUTH COURT FOR ONTARIO

WARRANT TO COMPEL ATTENDANCE OF PARENT

Canada
Province of Ontario
County of Queens

To the peace officers in the County of Queens :

Whereas it is alleged that John Smith of 25 First Ave., Anytown, Ontario is a parent of, a person under a legal duty to provide for or a person who has in law or in fact the custody or control of David Smith of 25 First Ave., Anytown, Ontario, a young person within the meaning of the *Young Offenders Act*;

And whereas David Smith has been charged with the following offence:

> robbery: to wit on the second day of June 1982 did steal two hundred and fifty dollars from The Corner Milk Store, 2 West Street, Anytown, Ontario, and at the same time thereat did use threats of violence contrary to section 303 of the *Criminal Code of Canada*;

And whereas it has been made to appear that the presence of John Smith at the proceedings against David Smith is necessary or in the best interest of David Smith ;

And whereas John Smith has been duly served with an Order for Attendance of Parent and has neglected or failed to attend at the time and place appointed therein.

This is therefore to command you forthwith to arrest John Smith and bring him before the Youth Court at 100 Main Street, Anytown, Ontario to be dealt with in accordance with the *Young Offenders Act*.

Dated this 15th day of June 19 82 at Anytown in the Province of Ontario.

"Thomas Brown"
....
A Judge of the Youth Court

RIGHT TO COUNSEL
(Section 11)

Introduction

The principles and provisions of the *Young Offenders Act* with respect to rights and safeguards reflect a fundamental shift in philosophy and approach from that adopted in the *Juvenile Delinquents Act*. Under the welfare approach of the *J.D.A.*, juvenile offenders are treated as informally as possible, with the result that a juvenile may not be afforded all the elements of due process of law, notwithstanding that his liberty may be at stake. Historically, this meant that in proceedings under the *J.D.A.*, young persons were often not represented by counsel and that judges often did not follow the rules of evidence or procedure applicable to trials in adult court.

In recent years, there has been more emphasis on due process in the juvenile courts. In the United States, *In Re Gault*, 387 U.S. 1, 87 S. Ct. 1428 (1967) established that juvenile courts must comply with constitutional requirements of due process, and in particular that a young person charged in such proceedings must be advised of his right to counsel, and if his liberty is threatened, the State must provide counsel if he is unable to afford representation. In Canada, in recent years, there has been a continuous trend towards greater recognition of due process and more legal representation in the juvenile court (for example, *R. v. Moore* (1974), 22 C.C.C. (2d) 189 (B.C.S.C.); *R. v. M.* (1975), 7 O.R. (2d) 490, 22 C.C.C. (2d) 344 (H.C.)).

The Y.O.A. marks a shift from the welfare approach of the J.D.A. to one recognizing accountability of young persons for their offences and accepting the need for society to be protected from illegal behaviour. The Y.O.A. also places more emphasis on due process, in part reflecting previous trends in this direction, and in part representing a recognition that an emphasis on accountability and the protection of society must be accompanied by appropriate protections for the young person accused of violating the criminal law. Paragraph 3(1)(e) of the Y.O.A. declares that "young persons have rights and freedoms in their own right, including those stated in the *Canadian Charter of Rights and Freedoms* or in the *Canadian Bill of Rights*, and in particular a right to be heard in the course of, and to participate in, the processes that lead to decisions that affect them, and young persons should have special guarantees of their rights and freedoms."

One of the most significant rights provided for in the Y.O.A. is the right to counsel, found principally in s. 11. The provision of counsel will help ensure that all of the other rights guaranteed by the Y.O.A., the *Charter* and the *Bill of Rights* will be adequately protected.

The principal features of the Y.O.A., which provide for the right to counsel include:

— the right of young persons to retain and instruct counsel at any stage of proceedings, s-s. 11(1);

— the obligation on the authorities to advise the young person of the right to counsel at the most important stages of the process including:

— upon arrest, s-s. 11(2),

— before making a statement to police, s-ss. 56(2) and (3),

— upon first appearance in court, para. 12(1)(b),

— at most appearances in court (detention, release, transfer and review hearings and at trial), s-s. 11(3),

— before participating in alternative measures, para. 4(1)(d);

— the right to be given a reasonable opportunity to obtain counsel, s-s. 11(3) and para. 56(2)(c);

— the obligation on the court to direct that a young person who wishes to obtain counsel but is unable to do so be represented by counsel, s-ss. 11(4), (5) and (6);

— the requirement that various court documents include a statement that the young person has a right to be represented by counsel, s-s. 11(9).

The rights to counsel afforded a young person under the Y.O.A. are considerably broader than the minimum guarantees of the *Charter of Rights*, s. 10, which simply ensures the "right on arrest or detention ... to retain and instruct counsel without delay and to be informed of that right". The mere "right to retain counsel" may not have much effect if the accused lacks resources to retain counsel on his own and is unable to obtain any form of legal aid. Thus, it is most significant that the Y.O.A. effectively ensures that a young person actually has the right to *have* counsel, with the State providing counsel if the young person is unable to do so. These special rights afforded young persons in regard to counsel recognize that because of their limited intellectual and emotional development, and their usually limited economic resources, special steps must be taken to guarantee the rights and freedoms of young persons in criminal proceedings.

SECTION 11

11.(1) *Right to retain counsel.*—**A young person has the right to retain and instruct counsel without delay at any stage of proceedings against him and prior to and during any consideration of whether, instead of commencing or continuing judicial proceedings against him under this Act, to use alternative measures to deal with him.**

(2) *Arresting officer to advise young person of right to counsel.*—**Every young person who is arrested or detained shall, forthwith on his arrest or detention, be advised by the arresting officer or the officer in charge, as the case may be, of his right to be represented by counsel and shall be given an opportunity to obtain counsel.**

(3) *Justice, youth court or review board to advise young person of right to counsel.*—**Where a young person is not represented by counsel**

(a) at a hearing at which it will be determined whether to release the young person or detain him in custody prior to disposition of his case,

(b) at a hearing held pursuant to section 16,

(c) at his trial, or

(d) at a review of a disposition held before a youth court or a review board under this Act,

the justice before whom, or the youth court or the review board before which, the hearing, trial or review is held shall advise the young person of his right to be represented by counsel and shall give the young person a reasonable opportunity to obtain counsel.

(4) *Trial, hearing or review before youth court or review board.*—**Where a young person at his trial or at a hearing or review**

referred to in subsection (3) wishes to obtain counsel but is unable to do so, the youth court before which the hearing, trial or review is held or the review board before which the review is held

(a) shall, where there is a legal aid or assistance program available in the province where the hearing, trial or review is held, refer the young person to that program for the appointment of counsel; or

(b) where no legal aid or assistance program is available or the young person is unable to obtain counsel through such program, may, and on the request of the young person shall, direct that the young person be represented by counsel.

(5) *Appointment of counsel.*—Where a direction is made under paragraph (4)(b) in respect of a young person, the Attorney General of the province in which the direction is made shall appoint counsel, or cause counsel to be appointed, to represent the young person.

(6) *Release hearing before justice.*—Where a young person at a hearing before a justice who is not a youth court judge at which it will be determined whether to release the young person or detain him in custody prior to disposition of his case wishes to obtain counsel but is unable to do so, the justice shall

(a) where there is a legal aid or assistance program available in the province where the hearing is held,

(i) refer the young person to that program for the appointment of counsel, or

(ii) refer the matter to a youth court to be dealt with in accordance with paragraph (4)(a) or (b); or

(b) where no legal aid or assistance program is available or the young person is unable to obtain counsel through such program, refer the matter to a youth court to be dealt with in accordance with paragraph (4)(b).

(7) *Young person may be assisted by adult.*—Where a young person is not represented by counsel at his trial or at a hearing or review referred to in subsection (3), the justice before whom or the youth court or review board before which the proceedings are held may, on the request of the young person, allow the young person to be assisted by an adult whom the justice, court or review board considers to be suitable.

(8) *Counsel independent of parents.*—In any case where it appears to a youth court judge or a justice that the interests of a

young person and his parents are in conflict or that it would be in the best interest of the young person to be represented by his own counsel, the judge or justice shall ensure that the young person is represented by counsel independent of his parents.

(9) *Statement of right to counsel.*—A statement that a young person has the right to be represented by counsel shall be included in any appearance notice or summons issued to the young person, any warrant to arrest the young person, any promise to appear given by the young person, any recognizance entered into before an officer in charge by the young person or any notice of a review of a disposition given to the young person.

Right to retain counsel: subsection 11(1)

Subsection 11(1) sets out the right of a young person to "retain and instruct" counsel without delay. By providing that the right exists at "any stage of proceedings", and also prior to and during any considerations of the use of alternative measures, the Y.O.A. has covered virtually every instance where the young person may be subject to the Act.

"Without delay" suggests the right to counsel must be a direct and available right. The wording of the subsection is such that the right to counsel is a right which will survive any previous waiver of the right. Thus for example, a young person might waive the right to counsel when making a statement to police (s-s. 56(4)), or at a pre-trial detention hearing, but still assert the right at trial.

Subsection 11(1) provides the young person with the right to "retain and instruct" counsel. These words should be interpreted broadly as the intention of s. 11 is to guarantee the young person a right to counsel, and to ensure that at all times the young person has a reasonable opportunity to consult counsel, and that counsel has a reasonable opportunity to meet with his client and prepare for any proceedings.

Subsection 11(1) assures the young person of a right to retain counsel at any stage of Y.O.A. proceedings: s-ss. 11(2), 56(2) and (3) ensure such a right upon arrest and prior to making a statement. Subsection 11(1) and para. 4(1)(d) ensure that a young person has a right to retain and consult counsel when considering whether to participate in alternative measures under s. 4. A young person must freely consent to participation in alternative measures (para. 4(1)(c), and consultation with counsel may help ensure the voluntariness of this consent, but it must be noted that unlike the situation in regard to proceedings in youth court (s-ss. 11(4), (5) and (6)), there are no statutory obligations upon those administering the program of alternative measures to ensure that a young person has counsel, nor is there any obligation to provide counsel if he is unable to obtain counsel on his own.

Role of counsel in youth court

There has been considerable controversy and confusion over the appropriate role for counsel in proceedings under the *Juvenile Deliquents Act*. Difficult issues have arisen in regard to the capacity of a juvenile to instruct counsel, whether privilege attaches to all statements made by a juvenile to his lawyer, and whether the lawyer should be promoting the juvenile's "best interests".

One Manitoba juvenile court judge wrote (Roy St. George Stubbs, "The Role of the Lawyer in Juvenile Court" (1974), 6 Manitoba Law Journal 65, at p. 70):

> I would like, however, to qualify the statement that the presence of lawyers in juvenile courts will provide better justice, by adding the rider that these lawyers should be lawyers who understand what the juvenile court system is trying to do, who are in harmony with its basic philosophy, who take a socio-legal, and not a strict legal, approach to the problems of children.
>
> When a lawyer comes into a juvenile court, throws his brief case down on the counsel table and announces to the court: "I represent this accused. He is pleading not guilty", the presiding judge knows at once that the lawyer thinks that he is in a criminal court for children, that he does not know what it is all about . . .

On the other hand, a Sub-Committee of the Professional Conduct Committee of the Law Society of Upper Canada, in its *Report on the Representation of Children* (1981), wrote that:

> . . . in criminal proceedings, which juvenile delinquency proceedings effectively are, it is the understanding of the Sub-Committee that the traditional solicitor and client role is presently adopted by most counsel. In our opinion, that is the appropriate role.
>
> Even where a child may lack capacity to properly instruct counsel, in our view there is no place in a quasi-criminal proceeding for counsel representing a child to argue which is in his opinion in the

best interests of the child. Counsel should not be deciding whether training school would be "good" for the child.

The *Young Offenders Act* does not expressly address the issue of the role of counsel, and indeed, any express directions in this regard might be considered improper. The thrust of the Y.O.A., however, makes it considerably easier to define an appropriate role for a lawyer. This Act is clearly criminal legislation, with an emphasis on holding young persons accountable for their contraventions of the law and protecting society from illegal behaviour (see paras. 3(1)(a) and (b)). It is submitted that a lawyer representing a young person charged under the Y.O.A. has the same obligation to his client that counsel for an adult has. The lawyer has a duty to advise his client and be certain that his client understands the nature and consequence of the proceedings, but ultimately counsel must follow his client's instructions and advocate the position his client chooses to adopt. If a young person instructs counsel to enter a not guilty plea, counsel must raise all legal defences, even those which rest on "technicalities". At disposition, counsel must continue to follow the instructions of his client. Although the youth court must consider the "special needs" of the young person (para. 3(1)(b)), it is submitted that at disposition, counsel for the young person should continue in his advocate's role, and follow his client's instructions, which will often involve advocating a disposition involving the least possible interference with the freedom of the young person. Counsel should be actively involved in the dispositional proceeding, challenging witnesses, calling his own evidence, addressing the needs of the young person, and perhaps putting forward a plan for disposition, but this activity should be based on instructions from the young person, and not on counsel's unilateral assessment of the young person's "best interests". There are others participating in the disposition process who will focus on the child's needs and interests, including parents, youth workers, psychologists, psychiatrists and other experts, the prosecutor and the judge himself. Counsel for the young person is there to advocate the wishes of his client.

Even with these views in mind, it must be recognized that in proceedings under the Y.O.A. counsel may often face difficult ethical issues, and in some cases may have difficulty in receiving instructions from a client, particularly if he is young. It is submitted that if a young person does not give adequate instructions, counsel should use all reasonable efforts to secure an acquittal, and if the young person is convicted, should seek a disposition consistent with the least possible intervention with the freedom of the young person. This approach would be consistent with Y.O.A. proceedings being adversarial and criminal in nature, with the onus on the State to justify any intervention in the life of the young person.

It should be emphasized that counsel representing a young person in proceedings under the Y.O.A. is representing that young person, and *not* the parents or family or society as a whole. It will often be appropriate for counsel for the young person to interview parents, family, friends, social workers and others involved in the young person's life, but counsel must only, in the final analysis, take instructions from his client — the young person; this will require interviewing his client alone at some point.

For a further discussion of the issues raised in this discussion, see J. S. Leon, "Recent Developments in Legal Representation of Children: A Growing Concern with the Concept of Capacity" (1978), 1 Canadian Journal of Family Law 375; K. N. Komar, "The Criminal Domestication of the Juvenile Delinquents Act: The Lawyer's Role in Juvenile Court" (1979), 2 Canadian Journal of Family Law 90; F. Maczko, "Some Problems with Acting for Children" (1979), 2 Canadian Journal of Family Law 267; and G. Thomson, N. Bala and H. Lilles, *Canadian Children's Law: Cases, Notes and Materials* (Toronto: Butterworths, 1982), Chapter 12. See also A. S. Manson, "Observations from an Ethical Perspective on Fitness, Insanity and Confidentiality" (1982), 27 McGill Law Journal 196, which discusses the ethical difficulties which arise in taking instructions from a client who lacks mental capacity.

Counsel upon arrest or detention: subsection 11(2)

Where a young person is arrested or detained, s-s. 11(2) requires the arresting officer or the officer in charge to comply with a two-fold duty in respect of the right to counsel:

(1) the young person must be advised of his right to be represented by counsel; and

(2) the young person must be given an opportunity to obtain counsel.

By requiring the police to advise the young person of his right to counsel "forthwith" on arrest or detention, the Y.O.A. ensures that the young person will be apprised of his rights at the time of initial involvement with the justice system. It would seem that upon arrest the young person must be advised of his rights by the arresting officer, and if detained must be advised by the officer in charge; this might result in the advice being given more than once, although it is not obligatory upon detention if it was given on arrest.

The Y.O.A. does not require the young person to be advised of his right to counsel under s-s. 11(2) in any particular manner or by using any specific words (contrast s. 56 which is quite specific, and requires any waiver of the right to counsel to be in writing). It would seem, however, that the advice must be meaningful, and hence in language appropriate to the age and understanding of the young person. A. B. Ferguson and A. C. Douglas in "A Study of Juvenile Waiver" (1970), 7 San Diego Law Review 39 reports a study of juveniles given "*Miranda* warnings" (advised of the right under the American constitution to remain silent and have court appointed counsel). The authors concluded (at p. 54) that only "a small percentage of juveniles is capable of knowingly and intelligently waiving *Miranda* rights. The great majority should be advised and counseled carefully if they are to understand their rights competently."

If a young person who has been arrested or detained decides to obtain counsel, he must be given an opportunity to do so. An onus lies upon the police to provide assistance in this regard, to make the "opportunity" meaningful; this might, for example, require the police to provide access to a phone and a list of lawyers' names and phone numbers. As Laskin J. (as he then was) stated in *Brownridge v. The Queen*, [1972] S.C.R. 926 at pp. 952-53, 18 C.R.N.S. 308, 7 C.C.C. (2d) 417, 28 D.L.R. (3d) 1:

> The right to retain and instruct counsel without delay can only have meaning to an arrested or detained person if it is taken as raising a correlative obligation upon the police authorities to facilitate to reach counsel . . .

In *R. v. Giesbrecht*, [1979] 5 W.W.R. 630 (Man. Co. Ct.) it was held that *Brownridge* meant that an accused should be allowed as many phone calls as required over a reasonable length of time.

It is reasonably clear that if a young person requests that he consult counsel in private, this request must be granted: see *R. v. Penner*, [1973] 6 W.W.R. 94, 39 D.L.R. (3d) 246, 12 C.C.C. (2d) 468, 22 C.R.N.S. 35 (Man. C.A.); and *R. v. Paterson* (1978), 39 C.C.C. (2d) 355 (Ont. H.C.). However, *Jumaga v. The Queen*, [1977] 1 S.C.R. 486, 29 C.C.C. (2d) 269, 68 D.L.R. (3d) 639, [1976] 3 W.W.R. 637, 34 C.R.N.S. 172, suggests that if there is no objection to a lack of privacy, the fact that communication with counsel is not private does not constitute a deprivation of the right to counsel.

Subsection 11(3) of the Y.O.A. provides that a young person unrepresented in youth court is to be given a "reasonable opportunity" to obtain counsel, while s-s. 11(2) provides that upon arrest or detention, the young person shall "forthwith be given an opportunity to obtain counsel". The requirement of s-s. 11(2) must, however, be interpreted in light of the circumstances. For example, while an arresting officer should advise the young person of his right to counsel immediately upon arrest, if the young person is being taken straight to the station without any questioning at the scene of arrest, it would seem sufficient to give the young person an opportunity to consult counsel at the police station. On the other hand, if police questioning is undertaken at the scene of arrest, s-ss. 11(2) and 56(2) and (3) require that the young person be given an opportunity to consult counsel at that place.

The obligation under s-s. 11(2) to advise a young person of his right to be represented by counsel is in addition to other statutory requirements that a young person must be so advised (e.g. before making a statement, s-ss. 56(2) and (3); upon first appearance in court, s-s. 12(1); at other appearances in court, s-s. 11(3)). The repetition of this advice is to ensure that a young person truly understands his rights, and has ample opportunity to change his mind and obtain counsel, and even change his mind if he has initially waived the right to consult counsel.

Advice of right to counsel: subsection 11(3)

In keeping with the philosophy of the Y.O.A., s-s. 11(3) provides for a young person who is not represented by counsel to be advised of his right to be represented by counsel and to have a reasonable opportunity to obtain counsel at every significant proceeding under the Act including:

— at a pre-trial detention hearing (s. 8 of Y.O.A. and ss. 457 to 457.7 of the *Criminal Code*);

— at a transfer hearing pursuant to s. 16 of Y.O.A.;

— at trial; and

— at a review of disposition before a youth court or review board pursuant to ss. 28 to 33 of Y.O.A.

Paragraph 11(3)(c) refers to a young person being advised of the right to counsel and having a reasonable opportunity to obtain counsel "at his trial". The word "trial" has a broad meaning. Citing *Morin v. The Queen* (1890), 18 S.C.R. 407, *The Encyclopedia of Words and Phrases: Legal Maxims (Canada)*, 3rd ed., Vol. 4, p. 328, states:

> The word "trial" . . . embraces all proceedings before the judge presiding at the trial, whether those proceedings are preliminary to the investigation by the jury, or, as in the instance of a prisoner pleading guilty, result in a conviction without the intervention of a jury; or relate to the evidence or the directions or ruling of the judge, or to the reception or recording of the verdict; or arise after the conviction, as, for example, with regard to the appropriateness of the sentence or to the punishment assigned by law to the offence; and whether any such questions are actually mooted while the trial is in progress or have not suggested themselves until the trial is over, the prisoner convicted and sentence passed upon him.

"Trial" as used in para. 11(3)(c) of the Y.O.A. thus includes arraignment, plea, and disposition hearings. Therefore since first appearances are similarly covered in s-s. 12(1), the young person must be informed of his right to counsel at virtually every important stage of proceedings in court, provided he is not represented. In an appearance in court by the young person, not technically covered by either s-s. 11(3) or 12(1), such as an appearance to set a date for trial, good practice would indicate that the youth court judge should inform the young person of his right to counsel.

Once an unrepresented young person has been informed of his right to be represented by counsel, he must be given a reasonable opportunity to obtain counsel; this gives substance to the right to counsel guaranteed by s. 11. "Reasonable opportunity" will depend upon circumstances. In determining the duration of any adjournment to be granted to provide an opportunity to obtain counsel, consideration should be given to:

— any indicated desire by the young person to obtain counsel,

— whether the young person has previously sought adjourn-ments to obtain counsel,

— the availability of counsel experienced in dealing with the matters being decided,

— the nature of the proceedings and issues to be resolved, and

— the degree of inconvenience to the prosecutor, witnesses, and others involved.

Although a reasonable opportunity must be given to the young person to obtain counsel, the right granted under s-s. 11(3) does not entitle a young person to indefinitely seek adjournments and unreasonably delay proceedings on the pretext of seeking counsel.

"Represented by counsel": subsections 11(2), (3) and (4)

The phrase "right to be represented by counsel" is used in s-ss. 11(2), (3) and (4), although the term is not defined in the Act. The substantive right provided for in s-s. 11(1) is "the right to retain and instruct counsel without delay" which is the same wording as subpara. 2(c)(ii) of the *Canadian Bill of Rights* and para. 10(b) of the *Canadian Charter of Rights and Freedoms*.

In defining the extent of this right under the Y.O.A., the courts may refer to existing jurisprudence under the *Bill of Rights* and will refer to decisions under the *Charter*. See for example, *Brown-ridge v. The Queen*, [1972] S.C.R. 926, 7 C.C.C. (2d) 417, 28 D.L.R. (3d) 1, 18 C.R.N.S. 281; *Jumaga v. The Queen*, [1977] 1 S.C.R. 486, 29 C.C.C. (2d) 269, 68 D.L.R. (3d) 639, [1976] 3 W.W.R. 637, 34 C.R.N.S. 172; *R. v. Penner* (1973), 12 C.C.C. (2d) 468, 22 C.R.N.S. 35 (Man. C.A.); and *R. v. Hogan* (1979), 48 C.C.C. (2d) 149, 11 C.R. (3d) 328 (N.S.C.A.).

It would seem that the minimum requirement under the Y.O.A. for a young person who is arrested or detained is to have reasonable assistance from the police in securing counsel (see comments under s-s. 11(2)) and having obtained counsel the young person is entitled to consultation with counsel in private, if requested, and consultation for a reasonable length of time unless being used for the purpose of delay.

Subsections 11(3) to (6) provide for representation by counsel before a youth court, justice or review board. Some Canadian jurisdictions presently have "duty counsel" available in juvenile courts. These are lawyers who are at the court, available to provide assistance to those who are not represented; such duty counsel only meet the juveniles at court, and have little or no time to prepare: see Ministry of the Attorney General of Ontario, "Report on Representation of Children in Provincial Court (Family Division)" (1977), 29 R.F.L. 134. Jurisprudence in the United States suggests that in some circumstances representation by duty counsel may not constitute adequate "representation by counsel". For example, in *West v. State of Louisiana*, 478 F. 2d 1026 (5th Cir. 1973), Wisdom Cir.Ct.J. stated at pp. 1033-34:

> We hold the applicable standard should be that stated in MacKenna v. Ellis, 5 Cir. 1960, 280 F. 2d 592, 599:
>
> > "We interpret the right to counsel as the right to effective counsel. We interpret counsel to mean not errorless counsel, and not counsel judged ineffective by hindsight, but counsel likely to render *and rendering* reasonably effectively assistance." (Emphasis by the Court.)
>
> To "administer justice without respect to persons, and do equal right to the poor and to the rich" we must apply the same standard, whether counsel be court-appointed or privately retained. From the facts of the case it is plain that West's lawyer fell far short of this standard. West might just as well have had no lawyer. By his own admission West's attorney conferred with West no more than an hour prior to trial, and perhaps for little more than five minutes. He conducted no investigation. At the trial he called no witnesses for the defense. After the prosecution presented its case, the defense moved for a directed verdict. When the court denied this motion, the defense immediately rested. We hold that ... West's legal representation was so inadequate as to deny his constitutional rights [to legal representation].

In *West v. Louisiana*, the conviction which resulted was quashed, and the accused was ordered retried or released.

It is clear that duty counsel can perform a valuable function in youth court, for example at pre-trial detention hearings, on adjournments, and in making representations in regard to dispositions on minor offences. However, there are many situations in which "representation by counsel" will require that counsel have an adequate opportunity to interview the young person, to carry out any necessary investigations and to prepare for trial. Unless he is able to perform these functions adequately, representation by duty counsel may not meet the requirement of "representation by counsel".

The term "counsel" is defined in s. 2 of the *Criminal Code* to mean a barrister or solicitor, and hence an articling student or law student would not satisfy the Y.O.A.'s provisions regarding "representation by counsel". Such students might, however, be able to serve as suitable adults, assisting a young person under s-s. 11(7).

Appointment of counsel: subsections 11(4) and (5)

Subsections 11(4) and (5) of the Y.O.A. create a scheme under which a young person who is being dealt with under the Y.O.A. is provided with legal representation, if he wishes to obtain counsel but is unable to do so. These provisions extend beyond s-s. 11(3) of the Y.O.A. and s. 10 of the *Canadian Charter of Rights and Freedoms*; the young person is not merely to be advised of his right to obtain counsel on his own and given an opportunity to do so; counsel will be provided.

Under s-s. 11(4), if a young person appears in youth court at his trial (including plea, adjudication and disposition) or at a hearing referred to in s-s. 11(3) (pre-trial detention, transfer under s. 16, disposition review) or if he appears before a review board for disposition review, and the young person "wishes to obtain counsel but is unable to do so", the court or board must ensure that he is represented. First the young person must be referred to any legal aid or assistance program available. If no such program is available, or if the young person is "unable to obtain counsel through such program", the youth court or review board *shall* "direct that the young person be represented by counsel". This provision is not discretionary — if the young person wishes counsel, but is unable to obtain counsel, "upon the request of the young person", the direction for representation must be made. The reference to "the request" of the young person serves to indicate that the appointment of counsel through s-s. 11(5) should not be made against the wishes of the young person. Paragraph 3(1)(g) of the Y.O.A. requires that the young person be advised of his right to make this request.

Before making a direction under para. 11(4)(b) that a young person be represented, the court or board must be satisfied that the young person is "unable" to obtain counsel. The inability to obtain counsel might result from immaturity or inexperience, but most likely will result from financial inability to retain counsel. The court or board may inquire as to the ability of the parents of a young person under the age of 16 to pay for counsel; such parents may be under a duty to provide a young person with such "necessaries" as legal services. The court or board, however, should be reluctant to force unwilling or hostile parents to pay for counsel, particularly in view of s-s. 11(8) which provides that where the interests of the young person and his parents are in conflict or it would be in the best interests of the young person, the court shall ensure that the young person is represented by counsel independent of his parents. Further, if a young person lacks financial means and his parents simply refuse to pay for his counsel, this constitutes "inability" to obtain counsel. It is submitted that in view of the importance of counsel and the general scheme of the Y.O.A., a court or board should normally make a direction that counsel be appointed where the young person claims inability to obtain counsel.

Under para. 11(4)(b), the court or board makes a direction that counsel be appointed; when such a direction is made, s-s. 11(5) requires the provincial Attorney General to appoint counsel, or cause counsel to be appointed. There is no direct appointment and this avoids any apprehension of bias and any difficulties which could result from a judge or board being required to select specific counsel. Further, s-s. 11(5) gives the province control over the method of delivery of legal services to young offenders. There may be a "judicare" scheme (private counsel paid by the province), "public defender" (staff counsel directly employed by the province or an agency of the province) or some combination of these schemes.

Direction by justice: subsection 11(6)

Subsection 8(1) of the Y.O.A. provides that where, having regard to the circumstances, a youth court judge is "not reasonably available", a justice may deal with the issue of pre-trial detention. Subsection 11(6) provides for the appointment of counsel where a young person appears before a justice for a hearing to determine whether he will be detained or released prior to disposition of his case pursuant to s-s. 8(1). If a young person wishes to be legally represented, but is unable to obtain counsel, the matter will be adjourned so counsel may be provided. The justice may refer the young person to a legal aid or assistance program to obtain counsel. The justice may choose to refer the matter to a youth court judge to deal with the issue of representation, and he must do so if no legal aid or assistance program is available or if the young person is unable to obtain counsel through such program.

Assistance by an adult: subsection 11(7)

The youth court, justice or review board has discretion to allow a young person, on request, to be assisted by an adult whom the court or board considers suitable. Such a request may occur where the young person is not represented by counsel but wishes some assistance at a trial, hearing, or review referred to in s-s. 11(3).

A youth court, justice or review board has the authority to refuse a request under s-s. 11(7) in a situation where the court or board considers that it would not be in the best interests of the young person to be assisted by the adult or where the court or board believes the adult may frustrate the proceedings.

Subsection 2(1) of the Y.O.A. defines an "adult" as a person who is neither a young person nor a child, and therefore the person requested to assist under s-s. 11(7) must be over 18 years. This means that a spouse under 18 years would not be considered suitable to assist a young person. In addition to age, the youth court, justice or board, in considering suitability, should refer to the following:

— relationship of the adult to the young person;
— the abilities of the adult;
— the adult's undertaking and appreciation of his role in assisting the young person and of the issues involved;
— nature and complexity of issues being dealt with; and
— circumstances surrounding the appearance.

The court or review board should be sensitive to the fact that a young person may prefer to be assisted by a known and trusted adult, rather than professional counsel, no matter how competent the lawyer may be. For example, on a guilty plea on a minor charge, it might be quite appropriate for a parent, relative, social worker or other suitable adult to assist the young person. This assistance might include making a statement, examining and cross-examining witnesses, filing documents and so on. On the other hand, a lay adviser may not appreciate the complexity or seriousness of the matter and the court or board, under such circumstances, may refuse to permit an adult to assist the young person, and might well at that time remind the young person of his right to obtain counsel.

Under appropriate circumstances, a law student or articling student may be a suitable adult under s-s. 11(7), though such a student does not satisfy the requirements of s. 11 for representation by counsel.

Although s. 11 of the Y.O.A. provides for advising the young person of his right to counsel and for appointment of counsel, there is no authority aside from s-s. 543(3) of the *Criminal Code* (insanity at time of trial) to force counsel upon a young person who does not wish to be represented. The intention of the Y.O.A. is to ensure that young persons are aware of their rights in respect of counsel, and to encourage them to employ counsel where needed and desired, but the Act does not presume that every young person will be represented by counsel.

Counsel independent of parents: subsection 11(8)

If a young person becomes involved in the juvenile justice system, there may be considerable family strain and emotional upheaval; the young person and his parents may be in a position of conflict. Subsection 11(8) of the Y.O.A. requires a youth court judge or justice to ensure that a young person is "represented by counsel independent of his parents" where it appears that "the interests of a young person and of his parents are in conflict" or that it would be in the "best interests" of the young person to be represented by his own counsel.

Although the subsection does not specify the options open to the court, it is clear that a conflict between the interests of the young person and his parents would be cause for a direction to appoint counsel pursuant to para. 11(4)(b). The court should ensure that counsel is "independent" of the parents, and where he is being paid by them, is not acting on their instructions.

The wording of s-s. 11(8) does not require the court to operate only upon a request of the young person, but requires the court to act on its own initiative where it recognizes conflict. Presumably this mandate would entitle the judge to direct questions to the parents, the young person, the Crown or to counsel concerning the independence of the representation. A youth court judge or justice may act to ensure the independence of representation at any stage of a proceeding, but it seems most likely a conflict may arise at disposition.

Statement of right to counsel: subsection 11(9)

In order to ensure that a young person who has not been arrested is advised of his right to counsel prior to appearance in court, any appearance notice or summons issued to a young person must contain a statement concerning the right to be represented by counsel. Further, to ensure that a young person understands and remembers the advice given at the time of arrest or detention, pursuant to s-s. 11(2), such advice must appear on any warrant to arrest the young person, and any recognizance entered into before an officer in charge by the young person. The statement must also appear on any notice of review.

These statements not only ensure that a young person has knowledge of his right to representation, but also may facilitate consultation with counsel prior to appearance. Paragraph 9(6)(c) requires that notices given to parents or other adults in connection with proceedings under the Y.O.A. contain similar statements; this should also help to ensure that these objectives are secured.

The Y.O.A. does not specify the exact words which are to be employed, however, see Forms 1, 11, 12, 16 and 17. It might be appropriate for a statement under s-s. 11(9) to include reference to legal aid or assistance programs which may be available, and to the possibility of appointment of counsel under s-s. 11(4).

The requirements of s-s. 11(9) may necessitate police officers using special summonses, appearance notices, warrants, promises to appear and recognizances for young persons. Alternatively, such documents may be amended for use in regard to adults or young persons, with special statements directed only at young persons: for example, see Forms 11 and 17. A properly worded statement on such documents might be applicable to both adults and young persons; adults also have the right to representation by counsel, though there are no equivalent guarantees for the provisions of counsel like those found in s-ss. 11(4) to (6) of the Y.O.A.

Consequence of failure to comply with section 11

The Y.O.A. does not specify the consequences of a failure to advise a young person of his rights to representation, or a failure to provide him with counsel as required under s-ss. 11(4) to (6). If a proceeding is completed without adequate provision for counsel, this would doubtless be a ground for appeal.

A statement of a young person obtained by police without adequate advice of the right to and opportunity to consult counsel, is inadmissible under s-s. 56(2) of the Y.O.A. Other evidence obtained in violation of rights to counsel guaranteed by para. 10(b) of the *Charter of Rights* might be excluded in subsequent proceedings under s. 24 of the *Charter*.

Under certain circumstances, violation of s. 11 of the Y.O.A. might give rise to civil remedies, or even a charge under s. 115 of the *Criminal Code* (disobeying a statute).

APPEARANCE
(Section 12)

Introduction

Section 12 sets out the responsibilities of a youth court judge or justice before whom a young person charged under the Y.O.A. first appears, and the further responsibilities of a judge in regard to taking a plea from a young person.

Subsection 12(1) provides that on first appearance the judge or justice shall cause the information to be read to the young person, thereby informing the young person of the reason he is before the court; if the young person is not represented by counsel, the judge or justice must inform him of his right to be so represented. Subsection 12(3) requires that before a plea is accepted from a young person who is unrepresented, the youth court judge must satisfy himself that the young person understands the charge and must explain to the young person that he may plead guilty or not guilty. Subsection 12(4) provides that if the judge is not satisfied that the young person understands the charge, a not guilty plea is to be entered.

Section 12 of the Y.O.A. should be read in conjunction with s. 19 of the Act, which requires a youth court judge to satisfy himself that a plea of guilty by the young person is supported by the facts.

The purpose of s. 12 is to ensure that a young person understands the proceedings and his rights under the Y.O.A.; additional safeguards are provided for the young person who is not represented.

SECTION 12

12. (1) *Where young person appears.*—Where a young person against whom an information is laid first appears before a youth court judge or a justice, the judge or justice shall

(a) cause the information to be read to him; and

(b) where the young person is not represented by counsel, inform him of his right to be so represented.

(2) *Waiver.*—A young person may waive the requirement under paragraph (1)(a) where the young person is represented by counsel.

(3) *Where young person not represented by counsel.*—Where a young person is not represented in youth court by counsel, the youth court shall, before accepting a plea,

(a) satisfy itself that the young person understands the charge against him; and

(b) explain to the young person that he may plead guilty or not guilty to the charge.

(4) *Where youth court not satisfied.*—Where the youth court is not satisfied that a young person understands the charge against him, as required under paragraph (3)(a), the court shall enter a plea of not guilty on behalf of the young person and shall proceed with the trial in accordance with subsection 19(2).

First appearance: subsections 12(1) and (2)

Paragraph 12(1)(a) requires that the youth court judge or justice, before whom the young person first appears when charged under the Y.O.A., must cause the information to be read to the young person. This ensures that the young person is aware of the charge which he must face and his reason for being in court. Where the young person's rights are protected by the presence of counsel, the requirement of para. 12(1)(a) may be waived to expedite the proceedings.

Paragraph 12(1)(b) also requires the judge or justice presiding at a young person's first appearance to inform him of his right to be represented by counsel, if he is not so represented. In many jurisdictions, a lawyer (often called "duty counsel") will be available in the court-house to provide information and preliminary legal assistance to accused persons who are without their own lawyers. The functions of duty counsel should include explaining the charge to the young person and assisting him to obtain appropriate representation for subsequent appearances. Owing to the obligations of the court with respect to the appointment of counsel pursuant to s-s. 11(4), the young person should be made aware of his rights to counsel under s. 11 of the Y.O.A. at the earliest opportunity. This will ensure that steps can be taken to obtain appropriate representation so as to avoid unnecessary adjournments.

Plea by young person: subsections 12(3) and (4)

The *Criminal Code* and Y.O.A. (in particular s-ss. 12(3) and (4) of the Y.O.A.) establish a procedure which a youth court must follow when taking a plea from a young person concerning a charge under the Y.O.A. The procedure is as follows:

— the information shall be read to the young person and he shall be asked to enter a plea, s. 736 of the *Code* deals with arraignment, also para. 12(1)(a) of Y.O.A.;

— where the young person is *not* represented by counsel, the youth court judge *must*:

> (i) advise the young person of his right to be represented by counsel, s-s. 11(3) and para. 12(1)(b) of Y.O.A.;
>
> (ii) satisfy himself that the young person understands the charge against him, para. 12(3)(a) of Y.O.A.; and
>
> (iii) explain to the young person that he may plead guilty or not guilty, para. 12(3)(b) of Y.O.A.;

— where the young person is *not* represented by counsel, and the judge is not satisfied that the young person understands the charge, he must enter a plea of not guilty and proceed with a trial, s-s. 12(4) of the Y.O.A.;

— the usual pleas will be guilty or not guilty, but the young person may also enter a "special plea" as provided in the *Criminal Code*, such as *autrefois acquit, autrefois convict,* pardon, and justification for a defamatory libel, *Criminal Code* ss. 534 to 541 (applicable to Y.O.A., see R. *v. Riddle,* [1980] 1 S.C.R. 380, [1980] 1 W.W.R. 592, 48 C.C.C. (2d) 365, 100 D.L.R. (3d) 577); or may enter a plea of guilty to an included or other offence pursuant to s-s. 534(4) of the *Code.* The Y.O.A. does not, however, require the judge to advise the young person regarding these special pleas;

— if the young person refuses to plead or does not answer directly, the court shall enter a plea of not guilty and proceed to trial, *Criminal Code,* s-s. 534(2);

— where a plea of guilty is entered by the young person, whether or not he is represented by counsel, the youth court judge must be satisfied that the facts support the charge, s-s. 19(1) of the Y.O.A.;

— where the judge is satisfied that the facts support the charge, the court shall find the young person guilty of the offence and proceed to disposition, s-s. 19(1) of the Y.O.A.;

— where the young person pleads guilty but the judge is *not* satisfied that the facts support the charge, the judge shall proceed with the trial, s-s. 19(2) of the Y.O.A.; and

— where the young person enters a plea of not guilty, the court shall proceed with the trial, s-s. 19(2) of the Y.O.A.

The effect of these provisions, in particular ss. 12 and 19 of the Y.O.A., is to ensure that a young person understands the charges against him and has every reasonable opportunity to give a full and considered answer to the charges he faces.

Judicial inquiry and explanation concerning plea: subsection 12(3)

A number of reported cases have stressed the obligation upon a judge to ensure that an accused in a criminal trial, whether adult or juvenile, understands and appreciates the full significance of a guilty plea. In *Brosseau v. The Queen*, [1969] S.C.R. 181 at pp. 188-89, [1969] 3 C.C.C. 129, 5 C.R.N.S. 31, 65 W.W.R. 751, 2 D.L.R. (3d) 139, Cartwright C.J. stated:

> No doubt when a plea of guilty is offered and there is no reason to doubt the accused understands what he is doing, the judge or magistrate will make inquiry to ascertain whether he does so and the extent of the inquiry will vary with the seriousness of the charge to which the accused is pleading.

In the context of a juvenile trial, in *Smith v. The Queen*, [1959] S.C.R. 638 at p. 649, 30 C.R. 230, 124 C.C.C. 71, 22 D.L.R. (2d) 129, Locke J. stated:

> It is unlikely that a boy of fourteen would understand what an "information" was or appreciate the gravity of the offence . . . with which he is charged. These are matters which should have been explained to him before he was permitted to plead.

Essentially, s-s. 12(3) of the Y.O.A. requires a youth court judge to offer the type of explanation suggested in *Smith*. Where a young person appears without counsel, a youth court judge, before accepting a plea, must "satisfy" himself that the young person understands the charge against him, and must explain to the young person that he may plead guilty or not guilty. If the judge is not "satisfied" that the young person understands the charge, s-s. 12(4) provides that the judge must enter a plea of not guilty and proceed to trial.

The Y.O.A. does not specify the nature of the inquiry which a judge must conduct to "satisfy" himself that the young person understands the charge, nor does it specify the kind of explanation which must be offered concerning a plea of guilty or not guilty.

Citing R. v. Anderson (1912), 5 W.W.R. 1052, 22 C.C.C. 455, 16 D.L.R. 203, 7 Alta. L.R. 102 (C.A.), the Encyclopedia of Words and Phrases: Legal Maxims (Canada), 3rd ed. (1979), Vol. 4, p. 121, defines "satisfy" to mean: "to free from uncertainty, doubt or anxiety, to set at rest the mind." This suggests that the judge should have a high level of assurance that the young person understands the charge against him. If the judge has any real doubt or uncertainty about whether the young person understands the charge against him, the judge is not "satisfied" in this regard.

In conducting an inquiry into the understanding of the young person, the judge will have to consider all of the circumstances, including the age of the young person, his apparent degree of intelligence, the nature of the charge, and whether he is receiving assistance from an adult other than counsel under s-s. 11(7). The judge should be cautious about simply accepting the assurance of the young person that he "understands the charge" and should never simply rely on the assurance of a parent or other adult. In some situations, a young person may state that he understands, when in fact he does not. This may be done out of sheer naiveté, a desire to expedite the process and quickly resolve the matter, or as a result of peer or parental pressure; it may also be done out of a desire not to appear "stupid", or in an attempt to appear cooperative.

To "satisfy" himself that a young person understands, the judge may engage the young person in conversation, perhaps attempting to explain the charge or clarify any uncertainty. A judge should be cautious when explaining or paraphrasing a complicated charge, however, because of the danger of giving it a slightly different meaning. A good device to ascertain understanding of the charge may be to ask the young person to explain in his own words the nature and ramifications of the charge. Clearly, "understanding" of the charges requires appreciation of their nature, and of the consequences of conviction.

Under para. 12(3)(b), a youth court judge has an obligation to explain to the young person that he may plead guilty or not guilty. This explanation should be in language appropriate to the age and understanding of the young person. The judge should not, however, attempt to advise the young person about the appropriate plea, and if there is any doubt about how the young person wishes to plead, the matter should be adjourned to allow the young person to obtain the advice of counsel.

Cases like *Brousseau v. The Queen*, [1969] S.C.R. 181, [1969] 3 C.C.C. 129, 5 C.R.N.S. 31, 65 W.W.R. 751, 2 D.L.R. (3d) 139, indicate that the judge must ascertain that the young person comprehends the distinction between guilty and not guilty. If the young person does not appear to understand, the judge may consider adjourning the matter to allow the young person time to obtain counsel. A lack of comprehension, due to immaturity, concerning the meaning of a plea will often constitute a lack of "understanding of the charges", and hence the court shall, pursuant to s-s. 12(4), enter a plea of not guilty and proceed to trial. If there appears to be a lack of competence to understand because of mental illness, or the young person otherwise appears incapable on account of insanity of conducting his defence, the issue of fitness to stand trial may be raised pursuant to s-ss. 13(7) and (8) of the Y.O.A. and s. 543 of the *Criminal Code*: see the discussion of s. 13. If the young person simply refuses to plead, the court should enter a plea of not guilty, and proceed to trial (see s-s. 534(2) of the *Code* and Salhany, *Canadian Criminal Procedure*, 3rd ed. (1978), p. 248).

Where young person does not understand: subsection 12(4)

Subsection 12(4) of the Y.O.A. provides that where a youth court judge is "not satisfied that a young person understands the charge against him", as required under para. 12(3)(a), the judge shall enter a plea of not guilty and proceed with the trial in accordance with s-s. 19(2); this requires the prosecutor to adduce evidence and prove all the elements of the offence beyond a reasonable doubt.

If the young person wishes to obtain counsel, but is unable to obtain counsel on his own or through a legal aid or assistance plan, the judge must make a direction under s-s. 11(4) that counsel be appointed. It is submitted that if a trial is to be held after a judge has entered a not guilty plea pursuant to s-s. 12(4), the judge should strongly urge the young person to avail himself of the services of counsel.

Where a young person is not represented by counsel and the judge is not satisfied that the young person understands the charges against him, the judge may, instead of entering a plea of not guilty pursuant to s-s. 12(4), consider an adjournment to allow the young person an opportunity to obtain counsel. Counsel could then ensure that the young person understands the charge and could assist him in making a decision about plea.

If the young person appears to lack the competence to understand the charges because of mental illness, or otherwise appears incapable of conducting his defence on account of insanity, the issue of fitness to stand trial may be raised pursuant to s-ss. 13(7) and (8) of the Y.O.A. and s. 543 of the *Criminal Code*; see also the discussion above, and of s. 13 of the Y.O.A.

MEDICAL AND PSYCHOLOGICAL REPORTS
(Section 13)

Introduction

To give effect to the principles of the Y.O.A. which recognize the special needs and circumstances of young persons and which stipulate that young persons are to remain under parental supervision whenever possible, it is essential that an accurate assessment of a young person's condition be available to the youth court. Section 13 of the Y.O.A. deals with the preparation of reports by experts, i.e., a doctor, psychiatrist, psychologist or other qualified person, to assist the court in a number of matters. These include an application for transfer to ordinary court (s. 16 of Y.O.A.), the making or reviewing of a disposition (s. 20 and ss. 28 to 34 of the Y.O.A.), and determining whether to direct that there be a judicial inquiry into whether a young person is unfit to stand trial on account of insanity (s. 543 of the Code). Section 14 of the Y.O.A. governs the preparation of "predisposition reports", which may also provide a youth court with valuable background information about a young person; it is anticipated that these s. 14 reports will most often be prepared by youth court workers.

In proceedings under the J.D.A., many courts have made use of medical and psychological reports. Section 13 of the Y.O.A. encourages this procedure in appropriate cases, facilitates the preparation of such reports, and provides for a variety of protections for those involved. The principal features of s. 13 of the Y.O.A. include provisions governing:

— circumstances in which reports can be ordered, s-s. 13(1);

— detention of young person to facilitate examination, s-s. 13(3);

— disclosure of the report, including requirements that certain persons receive a copy of the report, and under limited circumstances allowing for withholding of a report from the young person, his parents or a private prosecutor, s-ss. 13(4), (6) and (10);

— right to cross-examine the maker of the report by the prosecutor, the young person and his counsel (even if the
report is withheld from the young person, his counsel must
always receive a copy of the report and has the right to
cross-examine), s-ss. 13(4) and (5);

— trial of the issue of whether the young person is unfit on
account of insanity to stand trial (provisions of *Criminal
Code*, s. 543 generally apply), s-ss. 13(2), (7) and (8).

SECTION

13. (1) *Medical or psychological examination.*—For the purpose of

(a) considering an application under section 16,

(b) determining whether to direct that an issue be tried
whether a young person is, on account of insanity, unfit to
stand trial, or

(c) making or reviewing a disposition under this Act,

a youth court may, at any stage of proceedings against a young
person,

(d) with the consent of the young person and the prosecutor,
or

(e) on its own motion or on the application of either the
young person or the prosecutor, where the court has reasonable grounds to believe that the young person may be suffering from a physical or mental illness or disorder, a psychological disorder, an emotional disturbance, a learning disability or
mental retardation and where the court believes a medical,
psychological or psychiatric report in respect of the young
person might be helpful in making any decision pursuant to
this Act,

by order require that the young person be examined by a qualified person and that the person who conducts the examination
report the results thereof in writing to the court.

(2) *Examination for fitness to stand trial.*—Where a youth
court makes an order for an examination under subsection (1)
for the purpose of determining whether to direct that an issue be
tried whether a young person is, on account of insanity, unfit to
stand trial, the examination shall be carried out by a qualified
medical practitioner.

(3) *Custody for examination.*—For the purpose of an examination under this section, a youth court may remand the young

person who is to be examined to such custody as it directs for a period not exceeding eight days or, where it is satisfied that observation is required for a longer period to complete an examination or assessment and its opinion is supported by the evidence of, or a report in writing of, at least one qualified person, for a longer period not exceeding thirty days.

(4) *Disclosure of report.*—Where a youth court receives a report made in respect of a young person pursuant to subsection (1),

(a) the court shall, subject to subsection (6), cause a copy of the report to be given to

(i) the young person,

(ii) a parent of the young person, if the parent is in attendance at the proceeding against the young person,

(iii) counsel, if any, representing the young person, and

(iv) the prosecutor; and

(b) the court may cause a copy of the report to be given to a parent of the young person not in attendance at the proceedings against the young person if the parent is, in the opinion of the court, taking an active interest in the proceedings.

(5) *Cross-examination.*—Where a report is made in respect of a young person pursuant to subsection (1), the young person, his counsel or the adult assisting him pursuant to subsection 11(7) and the prosecutor shall, subject to subsection (6), on application of the youth court, be given an opportunity to cross-examine the person who made the report.

(6) *Report may be withheld from young person, parents or prosecutor.*—A youth court may withhold the whole or any part of a report made in respect of a young person pursuant to subsection (1) from

(a) a private prosecutor where disclosure of the report or part thereof, in the opinion of the court, is not necessary for the prosecution of the case and might be prejudicial to the young person; or

(b) the young person, his parents or a private prosecutor where the person who made the report states in writing that disclosure of the report or any part thereof would be likely to be detrimental to the treatment or recovery of the young person or would be likely to result in bodily harm to, or be detrimental to the mental condition of, a third party.

(7) *Insanity at time of proceedings.*—A youth court may, at any time before the adjudication in respect of a young person charged with an offence, where it appears that there is sufficient reason to doubt that the young person is, on account of insanity, capable of conducting his defence, direct that an issue be tried as to whether the young person is then on account of insanity unfit to stand trial.

(8) *Section 543 of Criminal Code to apply.*—Where a youth court directs the trial of an issue under subsection (7), it shall proceed in accordance with section 543 of the *Criminal Code* in so far as that section may be applied.

(9) *Report to be part of record.*—A report made pursuant to subsection (1) shall form part of the record of the case in respect of which it was requested.

(10) *Disclosure by qualified person.*—Notwithstanding any other provision of this Act, a qualified person who is of the opinion that a young person held in detention or committed to custody is likely to endanger his own life or safety or to endanger the life of, or cause bodily harm to, another person may immediately so advise any person who has the care and custody of the young person whether or not the same information is contained in a report made pursuant to subsection (1).

(11) *Definition of "qualified person".*—In this section, "qualified person" means a person duly qualified by a provincial law to practice medicine or psychiatry or to carry out psychological examinations or assessments, as the circumstances require, or, where no such law exists, a person who is, in the opinion of the youth court, so qualified, and includes a person or a person within a class of persons designated by the Lieutenant Governor in Council of a province or his delegate.

(12) *Form of order.*—An order under subsection (1) may be in Form 5.

Medical or psychological report: subsections 13(1) and (11)

Subsection 13(1) provides that a youth court may order an examination of a young person by a "qualified person", who will present the results of the examination to the court in the form of a written report. The court may only make the order for an examination for the purpose of:

(a) considering an application pursuant to s. 16 of the Y.O.A. for transfer of the young person to ordinary (adult) court, para. 13(1)(a);

(b) determining whether to direct that there be a judicial hearing on whether the young person is, on account of insanity, unfit to stand trial, para. 13(1)(b); or

(c) making a disposition under the Y.O.A. s. 20, or reviewing a disposition under ss. 28 to 34, para. 13(1)(c).

The court may make the order for an examination and report on the consent of the prosecutor and the young person. Alternatively, the court may make the order on its own motion or the application of either party, if the court believes a medical, psychological or psychiatric report "*might* be helpful" in making one of the decisions listed above, *and* the court has "reasonable grounds to believe" that the young person may be suffering from:

— a physical illness or disorder;

— a mental illness or disorder;

— a psychological disorder;

— an emotional disturbance;

— a learning disability; or

— mental retardation.

Whether a judge orders a medical, psychiatric or psychological report will depend on the apparent condition of the young person. Provided the conditions stipulated above are satisfied, a youth court may make an order at any stage of the proceedings.

It is suggested that when ordering under s. 13, the youth court should specify the purpose of the report in the order. Thus, a court should specify whether the report is sought in connection with para. 13(1)(a), (b) or (c); further the nature of the court's concerns might be generally described, perhaps using the very broad terminology of para. 13(1)(e) of the Y.O.A. As the Law Reform Commission of Canada, *Report on Mental Disorder in the Criminal Process* (1976), notes (at pp. 33-34):

> The ... order by the court should be specifically linked to the nature of the psychiatric expertise sought and this intent should be clearly communicated to the psychiatrist. Because of the difference in the kinds of information the court is seeking from psychiatrists, it is important that the *purpose* of the report be clearly communicated to the psychiatrist. ...

. . . . .

... the judge must decide what information he needs and then clearly communicate this to the mental health expert. ...

All psychiatric reports are not the same. Different issues arise at different stages of the process. It follows that the form and content of reports will vary. ... [Emphasis added.]

Where an order is made under s-s. 13(1), there must be an examination by a "qualified person", who must report the results thereof in writing to the youth court. Although the court has a discretion as to whether to make the order, it is mandatory that a report be submitted before a disposition is made ordering the detention of a young person for treatment in a hospital pursuant to para. 20(1)(i) of the Y.O.A.

Subsection 13(11) provides that a "qualified person" includes a person or member of a class of persons designated by the Lieutenant Governor in Council (provincial Cabinet) or his delegate. It also includes a medical doctor, a psychiatrist, or a person qualified by provincial law to conduct psychological examinations or assessments. If no provincial laws govern qualification for admission to one of the professions, a youth court judge will have to rule as to whether or not a person is duly qualified. The judge must decide on the qualifications of the person, taking into account the apparent condition of the young person. Subsection 13(2) requires that where the youth court orders an examination under s-s. 13(1) for the purpose of determining whether to direct that there be an inquiry into whether the accused is unfit to stand trial on account of insanity, this examination must be carried out by a "qualified medical practitioner"; the *Criminal Code* has the same requirement when this issue arises in adult proceedings.

Fitness to stand trial: subsections 13(2), (7) and (8)

The *Criminal Code* recognizes two distinct ways in which mental illness may affect criminal responsibility: the defence of insanity at the time of the offence; and lack of fitness to stand trial on account of insanity.

(1) *Defence of Insanity:* By virtue of s. 51 of the Y.O.A., the provisions of the *Criminal Code* governing the defence of insanity, and in particular ss. 16 and 542, and 545 to 547 of the *Code* are applicable. Subsections 16(1) and (2) of the *Code* provide:

16. (1) No person shall be convicted of an offence in respect of an act or omission on his part while he was insane.

(2) For the purposes of this section a person is insane when he is in a state of natural imbecility or has disease of the mind to an extent that renders him incapable of appreciating the nature and quality of an act or omission or of knowing that an act or omission is wrong.

Subsection 542(1) of the *Code* provides that if the evidence at trial reveals that the accused was insane, as defined in s-s. 16(2) of the *Code*, at the time of the commission of an indictable offence, he shall be found not guilty on account of insanity. Pursuant to s-s. 16(4) of the *Code*, a person is presumed to be and to have been sane until the contrary is proven. Accordingly, there is an onus on the accused to establish his insanity on the balance of probabilities: see *Smyth v. The King*, [1941] S.C.R. 17, 74 C.C.C. 273, [1941] 1 D.L.R. 497. If a young person is acquitted on account of insanity, s-s. 542(2) of the *Code* provides that he be held in custody indefinitely at the pleasure of the Lieutenant Governor. This means that a young person in this circumstance would be confined in a mental health facility until released. Release is technically a matter of discretion, but practically is usually governed by a review board process established pursuant to s. 547 of the *Code*. A review board is required under s-s. 547(5) to recommend release only where it is satisfied a person has "recovered" and it is in the "interest of the public" to release him. A young person found not guilty by reason of insanity may thus be detained indefinitely — the limitations governing the maximum duration of any disposition under s. 20 of the Y.O.A. do *not* apply. The young person will be detained until it is considered safe to release him. The detention may be in an adolescent mental health facility or an adult mental health facility, perhaps for the criminally insane.

Where a young person has been acquitted on account of insanity in connection with a summary conviction offence, there appears to be no authority under the *Code* or the Y.O.A. to detain him (see *Re B. and M.* (1975), 33 C.R.N.S. 362 (Ont. Prov. Ct.)). Provincial mental health legislation, however, may be invoked in these circumstances.

(2) *Unfit to Stand Trial on Account of Insanity*: Subsection 543(1) of the *Code* provides that a person is unfit to stand trial if

he is "on account of insanity" incapable of conducting a defence. The concept of fitness to stand trial is distinct from insanity at the time of the commission of the offence. The defence of insanity involves mental disability that operates when the offence is committed and is an issue going directly to criminal responsibility. Lack of fitness, however, relates to mental disability at the time of trial, which affects the accused's ability to participate meaningfully in the trial. Lack of fitness is not a matter of criminal responsibility, but is premised on the rationale that an accused must have a full and fair opportunity to answer allegations and present a defence.

While s. 543 links lack of fitness with "insanity", it is clear that insanity in s. 543 refers to mental disabilities which are very different from those described in s. 16 of the *Code*. To be fit to stand trial, a young person must be "intellectually, linguistically and communicatively present and be able to partake to the best of his natural ability in his full answer and defence to the charge against him": see *R. v. Roberts* (1975), 24 C.C.C. (2d) 539 at p. 545, [1975] 3 W.W.R. 742 (B.C.C.A.); application for leave to appeal to S.C.C. dismissed 24 C.C.C. (2d) 539*n* (S.C.C.). Generally, the young person must be capable of understanding the nature of the proceedings and able to instruct his counsel.

Subsection 13(8) of the Y.O.A. provides that s. 543 of the *Code*, which generally governs the issue of lack of fitness on account of insanity at the time of trial, is applicable to proceedings in youth court, subject to the modifications contained in s-ss. 13(1), (2), (3) and (7) of the Y.O.A..

Thus, where at any time prior to adjudication the youth court judge has doubt about whether a young person has the mental capacity to stand trial, he may order an examination and report under s-s. 13(1). By s-s. 13(2) this examination and report must be carried out by a qualified medical practitioner (doctor or psychiatrist). Subsection 13(3) allows the young person to be remanded in custody for the purpose of an examination for a period of up to 30 days: see discussion of s-s. 13(3) below.

Upon receipt and consideration of the report, if it appears to the youth court judge that "there is sufficient reason to doubt that the young person is, on account of insanity, capable of conducting his defence", he must direct pursuant to s-s. 13(7) that there be a "trial" as to whether the young person is on account of insanity unfit to stand trial. Technically, the judge may make an order for a trial of the issue even without the report, if, for example, from the conduct of the young person in the courtroom, it is apparent that this is appropriate. There is no obligation upon any particular party to raise the issue of fitness to stand trial, and once the judge is satisfied there is "sufficient reason" to doubt the capacity of the young person, it is mandatory that a "trial" of the issue be directed; the issue may be raised by either party or by the judge himself.

A "trial" on the issue of a young person's mental capacity to conduct his defence has been characterized as a non-adversarial inquiry into the mental status of the accused: see R. v. Roberts, [1975] 3 W.W.R. 742, 24 C.C.C. (2d) 539 (B.C.C.A.); and R. v. Budic (No. 2) (1977), 35 C.C.C. (2d) 272, 5 A.R. 37 (C.A.)). It is generally accepted that the accused, the prosecutor or the court itself is entitled to raise the issue of fitness and, if the accused is to stand trial, the onus lies on the prosecutor, where the issue is directed at his instance, to establish to the "reasonable satisfaction" of the trier of fact that the accused is fit. Canadian courts appear to have rejected the application of the presumption of sanity found in s. 16 of the Code when fitness to stand trial is the issue: see R. v. Budic, supra (contra, R. v. Podola, [1959] 3 All E.R. 418 (C.A.) which was relied upon in R. v. Hughes (1978), 43 C.C.C. (2d) 97 (Alta. S.C.) to support the conclusion that when the defence raises lack of fitness, "the onus is on the defence to establish by preponderance of evidence that the accused is unfit for trial").

It should be noted that occasionally the issue of fitness arises in a purely adversarial fashion in that one party asserts that the accused is unfit to stand trial while the other party vigorously disputes the assertion. In such instances, it is not clearly resolved where the burden of proof lies, and the extent of the burden (see the English Court of Appeal decision in R. v. Robertson, [1968] 3 All E.R. 557; R. v. Hughes, supra; see generally A. Manson, "Fit to be Tried: Unravelling the Knots" (1982), 7 Queen's Law Journal 305).

Subsection 543(3) of the Code requires a youth court judge to assign counsel to represent a young person without counsel where "it appears there is sufficient reason to doubt" the capacity of the young person to conduct his defence. Subsections 543(4) and (8) allow a judge to postpone the trial of the issue of capacity until after the prosecution has closed its case, to allow the young person to secure an acquittal, rather than be found unfit to stand trial. Paragraph 577(2)(c) allows the judge to order that the young person be excluded from the court during the trial of the issue of fitness where the failure to do so "might have an adverse effect on the mental health of the accused".

If a young person is found fit to stand trial, the case proceeds as normal. If the young person is found unfit to stand trial, he is detained "at the pleasure of the Lieutenant Governor". This may result in indefinite detention in a mental health facility, either for adolescents or adults. In practice, there may be ultimate release following a recommendation by a review board, depending on relevant provincial legislation; in such a case, however, the prosecutor may again put the accused on trial or choose to drop the charges. Under s-s. 547(5) of the *Code*, when deciding to recommend that a person previously found unfit to stand trial be released from custody and permitted to stand trial, the review board is only to consider whether the "person has recovered sufficiently to stand trial". In making a recommendation concerning the release of a person found not guilty by reason of insanity, who would not be subject to further prosecution, the board must consider both recovery *and* the public interest. Due to s-s. 13(7) of the Y.O.A. and s-s. 738(8) of the *Code*, the issue of fitness to stand trial may be raised in regard to summary conviction offences, as well as for indictable offences.

For a fuller discussion of some of the complex issues which arise in regard to insanity and fitness to stand trial, see A. S. Manson, "Observations from an Ethical Perspective on Fitness, Insanity and Confidentiality" (1982), 27 McGill L.J. 196; S. Verdun-Jones, "The Doctrine of Fitness to Stand Trial in Canada: The Forked Tongue of Social Control" (1981), 4 International Journal of Law and Psychiatry 363; H. Savage, "The Relevance of the Fitness to Stand Trial Provisions to Persons with a Mental Handicap" (1981), 59 Canadian Bar Review 319; and D. R. Stuart, *Canadian Criminal Law: A Treatise* (Toronto, Carswell, 1982), Chapter 7: "Incapacity".

Custody for examination: subsection 13(3)

Where necessary, a youth court judge may remand a young person to "such custody as it directs", for a specified period for an examination or assessment under s. 13.

It is important to note that it is not necessary for the young person to be in custody in order for this type of examination to be performed. However, where it is felt necessary, pursuant to s-s. 13(3), a youth court may, on its own authority, remand the young person to custody for examination for a period not exceeding eight days. Alternatively, the youth court may remand the young person in custody for a period not exceeding 30 days, where the court is satisfied that observation is required for a longer period than eight days, and this opinion is supported by the oral testimony or written report of at least one "qualified person".

It should be noted that an order for detention under s-s. 13(3) should only be made if necessary for examination or assessment. These considerations are quite distinct from those normally applicable at a bail hearing — s-s. 457(7) of the *Criminal Code* normally requires a youth court to detain an accused to ensure his attendance, or if this is necessary in the public interest or to protect the public. A youth court may consider that detention is necessary under the criteria of both s-s. 457(7) of the *Code* and s-s. 13(3) of the Y.O.A.

The youth court may remand the young person under s-s. 13(3) "to such custody as it directs". Even though this appears to give a youth court complete flexibility in designating the place or type of custody, it might be argued that the detention is subject to s-s. 7(3) of the Y.O.A. However, it is submitted that the clear wording of s-s. 13(3) and the fact that this subsection provides a specific power of remand for the purposes of an examination only, are such that the general rule found in s-s. 7(3), governing pre-disposition detention, is not applicable (*expressio unius est exclusio alterius* — expression of one thing is the exclusion of another). Nevertheless, it is suggested that where feasible, when ordering a remand under s-s. 13(3) the youth court should respect the desirability of detaining young persons separate and apart from adults.

If, however, it is held that s-s. 7(3) applies to s-s. 13(3) remands, the flexibility of the court is considerably constrained. Subsection 7(3) provides:

> 7(3) No young person ... shall be detained prior to the making of a disposition ... in any part of a place in which an adult who has been charged with or convicted of an offence ... is detained or held in custody unless a youth court judge ... authorizes the detention, being satisfied that
>
> (a) the young person cannot, having regard to his own safety or the safety of others, be detained in a place of detention for young persons; or
>
> (b) no place of detention for young persons is available within a reasonable distance.

Thus if a young person is to be detained in a part of a place in which adults charged with or convicted of an offence are detained, including a part of a facility in which pre-trial assessments are conducted on adults, the judge must consider the factors set out in s-s. 7(3). For the purpose of a custody order under s-s. 13(3), para. 7(3)(b) would mean no place of detention suitable for examination or assessment is available within a reasonable distance. While s-s. 7(3) restricts the placement of a young person in the *same* part of a place as an adult, a young person may be detained in a *separate* part of the same place. Thus a young person might be detained for assessment in a wing of a psychiatric hospital separate from wings where adults charged with or convicted of offences are detained. This is satisfactory as long as there is no contact between young persons and adults.

To summarize, when a youth court judge makes an order under s-s. 13(1) for an examination or assessment, he has the following options:

(1) not to remand the young person in custody;

(2) remand the young person to a facility or part of a facility for the examination and detention of young persons, or to such other custody as is deemed necessary to carry out an order for examination; or

(3) if s-s. 7(3) *is* held to apply, and the young person is remanded to a facility or part thereof where adults charged with or convicted of offences are detained, the judge must satisfy himself that the conditions of s-s. 7(3) are met.

In the case where a young person is not in custody, and whether or not he is placed in the care of a responsible person, failure to comply with the court order for examination would be contempt of the youth court, and the young person would be liable to the consequences arising therefrom (see s. 47 of the Y.O.A.). Further, where a young person not in custody fails to comply with an order for examination or assessment, the youth court could subsequently remand the young person in custody pursuant to s-s. 13(3).

Disclosure of the report: subsections 13(4) and (6)

Subsection 13(4) provides that the court shall cause a copy of the written medical or psychological report prepared under s-s. 13(1) to be given to the following persons:

— the young person, subject to the report being withheld under s-s. 13(6);

— counsel representing a young person, who is always entitled to a complete copy of the report;

— a parent of a young person in attendance at the proceedings, subject to s-s. 13(6); a youth court may also direct under para. 13(4)(b) that a parent who has been taking an active interest in the proceedings, but who is not in attendance, shall be given a copy of the report;

— a Crown prosecutor who is always entitled to a complete copy of the report; a private prosecutor may receive a copy of the report, subject to s-s. 13(6).

When a medical or psychological report prepared pursuant to s-s. 13(1) is received by the youth court, the court shall cause a copy of the report to be given to all those entitled under s-s. 13(4). Good practice would suggest that the report should normally be sent out by the court prior to the hearing at which it is to be presented, to allow those involved sufficient time to digest the report and to decide whether to exercise their right of cross-examination under s-s. 13(5). Of course, if a report, or part of a report, *might* be withheld under s-s. 13(6) by judicial direction, the report should not be sent out to a person from whom it might be withheld, until a judge has made a final decision in this regard. If a report might be withheld from a young person under s-s. 13(6), it should not be given to his counsel, except on an undertaking not to disclose it to his client, or with an interim judicial direction not to disclose it. The difficulties counsel might face when he has a report and it is withheld from his client are considered below.

Subsection 13(6) allows a youth court to withhold *all or part of* a report from some persons otherwise entitled to a copy under s-s. 13(4). Counsel for the young person, if any, and a Crown prosecutor are always entitled to a copy of the entire report.

Under para. 13(6)(a) a youth court may withhold all or part of a report from a *private* prosecutor, where in the opinion of the court the report, or part thereof, is not necessary for the prosecution of the case and disclosure "*might* be prejudicial to the young person". A judge may decide to withhold a report under para. 13(6)(a) without this being requested by any party, and he need not hold a hearing before deciding to do so. The standard the judge should apply is not high, since it is only necessary that the report "might" (as opposed to "would likely") be "prejudicial" (as opposed to "seriously prejudicial"; contrast para. 13(6)(a) to s-s. 39(1).

Withholding a report prepared under s-s. 13(1) from a private prosecutor should never affect his ability to participate in an adjudication, and further is not permissible if the report is "necessary for the prosecution of the case". In view of the broad judicial discretion in para. 13(6)(a) to withhold a report, a copy should not be given to a private prosecutor prior to a hearing without express judicial approval.

Under para. 13(6)(b) a youth court *may* withhold the whole or any part of a report from a young person, his parents or a private prosecutor, where the qualified person who made the report "states in writing that disclosure of the report or part thereof would be likely to be detrimental to the treatment or recovery of the young person or would be likely to result in bodily harm to, or be detrimental to the mental condition of, a third party." A direction under s-s. 13(6) requires a written recommendation by the maker of the report, but it also requires a judicial decision. Upon receipt of the report and the written recommendation, the judge must decide whether to withhold the report, or part of the report. The Y.O.A. does *not* require the judge to hold any sort of hearing before deciding to withhold all, or part of, the report under s-s. 13(6). However, in many circumstances it might be appropriate to hold some kind of an inquiry. If an inquiry into the issue of withholding a report is held, it would seem appropriate to have present any person from whom the report is *not* being withheld (including counsel for the young person and a Crown prosecutor), and to have the maker of the report available to explain his views and be subject to cross-examination. If an inquiry is held to determine whether to make a s-s. 13(6) direction, it would seem to be a necessary implication of s-s. 13(6) that the person from whom the report, or a part of the report is withheld, is to be excluded; otherwise the very purpose of holding the inquiry would be defeated, as the matters to be withheld would be revealed. The issue of the exclusion of the young person and the interrelationship of s-s. 13(6) and s. 39 of the Y.O.A. is considered below in the discussion of s-s. 13(5).

Although as a rule all of those involved in a proceeding should have access to the information upon which a court will base its decision, there may be circumstances in which it is justifiable to withhold some medical or psychological information, even from the accused person or his parents. Some reasons are suggested by N. Dembitz, "Ferment and Experiment in New York: Juvenile Cases in the New York Family Court" (1963), 48 Cornell Law Quarterly 499 at pp. 516-17:

> For a judge to make the grave decision to commit a child to an institution, without allowing the child or his parents any opportunity to correct misinformation or offset the data in the reports, seems dictatorial and unfair. The argument that disclosure will have the effect of drying up sources of information is not too compelling: the ... worker's informants are not undercover agents who must continue to function in secret, as the argument runs in narcotic prosecutions and the like. Further, the practice could be borrowed from internal security cases of a discretionary deletion of names and the informant [is] thus assured of anonymity; the problem here is not confidentiality in the sense of some of the testimonial privileges, where the information itself is intended to be confidential.

> Of more moment than the problem of sources: the child or his parents may well suffer serious psychological damage from confronting a report that categorizes their inadequacies and depicts their images as others see them. It is therapeutic to declare to a parent that his neighbors observe him drinking or that he has been judged of low intelligence or that his claimed affection for his child covers rejecting behavior, or to spell out that a child is

illegitimate or shunned in the neighborhood as a troublemaker is disapproved by his teacher as the least responsible child in the class? ... Might not such unsought and wounding revelations affect the individual's self-confidence and his relationships and block therapy not only immediately but indefinitely?

Social workers with a high sense of professional ethics say they would tailor a report to prevent psychological damage from its disclosure. The result of a disclosure practice may well be reporting on a vague and superficial level. The judge does not need a report in the depth and detail required for psychiatric or social casework. Still, disclosure of background reports will accomplish nothing if they become so general that the judge must either reject them entirely or in effect accept the ... worker's *ipse dixit*. Thus, there must be a measure of flexibility in a disclosure requirement so that psychological damage can be avoided....

In a number of reported cases dealing with adult criminal proceedings, judges have expressed support for the notion of withholding psychologically harmful information from the accused, at certain points in the proceedings, in particular in regard to sentencing. See R. v. Benson and Stevenson (1951), 100 C.C.C. 247, 13 C.R. 1, 3 W.W.R. 29 (B.C.C.A.) and R. v. Dickson (1949), 34 Cr. App. R. 9 at p. 13, [1950] 1 K.B. 394, where Lord Chief Justice Goddard, of the English Court of Appeal, remarked in regard to a pre-sentence report prepared for an adult proceeding:

It is not clear to me or to any of His Majesty's Judges why it is necessary to serve that report on the prisoner. In some cases I think it is very undesirable, because it may sometimes give him ideas about his mental condition which he perhaps should not know.

Despite this apparent willingness to withhold potentially damaging reports from those involved in criminal proceedings, it is submitted that s-s. 13(6) should be used only in rare cases. In particular, para. 13(6)(b), giving a youth court judge authority to make a direction withholding a report, or part thereof, from a young person, is clearly an exceptional procedure. The desire to protect the young person, or third parties from harm, must always be weighed against the injustice of basing a decision about a young person's future on information which is withheld from the young person himself. The standard required by para. 13(6)(b) is a high one and this is clear by comparing paras. 13(6)(a) and (b).

The judge must be satisfied that disclosure *"would be likely"* (not merely *"might"*) to be "detrimental to the treatment or recovery of the young person or would be *likely* to result in bodily harm to, or be detrimental to the mental condition of, a third party." Thus, if a report is being withheld under the first branch of the test, the young person must *actually* be undergoing some form of treatment or suffering from a mental illness or disorder. It is not sufficient for a psychologist or doctor to assert that a mentally healthy young person will (or might) suffer future emotional shock or harm from the release of the information.

If a report, or part of a report, is withheld from the young person, this may place counsel in a difficult position. Subsection 13(9) of the Y.O.A. makes clear that the report forms part of the "record". Subsection 40(4) provides that any part of a report which has been withheld from the young person under s-s. 13(6) shall not be made available to him for inspection. Further, s-s. 46(2) prohibits any person from revealing to the young person, any information learned from a part of a report if that part has been withheld from the young person. Presumably, this applies to a young person's lawyer. Thus, even the young person's counsel is limited in what he may discuss with his client in regard to a report, or portion thereof, which is withheld from the young person. Counsel may discuss the fact that the report, or part of the report, exists and has been withheld, the general purpose of the report and the general reasons why it was withheld. Counsel may also discuss the legal implications of the information. He may not discuss or reveal the actual information.

The fact that counsel has information which his client does not have, may place counsel in a difficult tactical and ethical position. It may not be possible to receive instructions about how to proceed or handle the information. It may also be difficult for counsel to prepare to challenge those parts of the report. In what might be considered analogous circumstances, in the case of *Re Abel and Advisory Review Board* (1980), 31 O.R. (2d) 520, 56 C.C.C. (2d) 153, 119 D.L.R. (3d) 101 (C.A.), it was suggested that in some circumstances, an Advisory Review Board, making a recommendation on release of persons found insane under ss. 542 and 543 of the *Code*, might place limitations on the information disclosed to counsel preparing for a hearing. Arnup J.A. commented at p. 534 O.R.:

While it may place the lawyers in an awkward situation, one can envisage cases where information might be disclosed on terms that it not be disclosed to the client.

Nairn Waterman, "Disclosure of Social and Psychological Reports at Disposition" (1969), 7 Osgoode Hall Law Jounal 213, stated that in 1969 it was the usual practice of Ontario Juvenile Court Judges not to show psychological reports to juveniles; Waterman commented (note 27, at p. 224):

> An interesting qualification (if we do accept the proposition of mandatory disclosure) may be found in Pinder v. Pinder (unreported B.C. decision) which holds that failure to disclose the contents of a welfare report did not result in a miscarriage of justice when defendant's counsel had consented to this use of the report. Therefore, under the present case law, a viable solution may be to have the judge disclose to the offender's counsel and if he is unrepresented to duty counsel or appointing counsel and getting his consent not to completely disclose the report to the child.

In come cases, counsel may not be unduly hindered by a direction to withhold a report, or part thereof, from the young person. If the young person is in fact suffering from mental or emotional disorder, the client may not be a useful source of information and may not be able to give counsel meaningfully instruction. However, it must be recognized that in some cases counsel will be placed in a very difficult position by the direction under s-s. 13(6). Particular problems may arise when the reason for withholding the information relates to a potential for harm to a third party based on a factual allegation of danger; in this case counsel will be precluded from raising the allegation with his client. In any event, as an officer of the court, counsel has an ethical obligation to obey the direction, and s. 46 of the Y.O.A. makes it an offence not to do so.

In view of some of the difficulties which may arise if an order is made under s-s. 13(6), particularly in regard to the young person, it may sometimes be appropriate for those concerned to consider some form of compromise to protect the interests of all concerned. For example, it might be agreed to delete certain parts of a report which are of marginal relevance to the issues facing the court, but of potentially significant detriment; the deleted portions will not be considered by the court for any purpose. Another possibility is to have the person who prepared the report discuss it with the young person, perhaps in the presence of his counsel, rather than simply handing it over to the young person.

It is possible that a challenge may be made under the *Canadian Charter of Rights and Freedoms* to s-s. 13(6) of the Y.O.A., at least as it affects the right of the young person to have access to a report which concerns him. The challenge would be based on s. 7 of the *Charter*, guaranteeing "everyone the right [not to be deprived] of liberty and security of person . . . except in accordance with the principles of fundamental justice." Paragraph 11(d) of the *Charter* which guarantees any person charged with an offence the right to be proven guilty "according to law in a fair and public hearing", may also have some applicability, though clearly not at disposition or review which occur after a finding of guilt. It may well be, however, that the provisions of s-s. 13(6) do not violate the *Charter*, or are acceptable as a "reasonable limitation" of the rights of the *Charter*. All legislation concerning those who are, or may be, suffering from mental or emotional disorders, involves a balancing of notions of liberty with the best interests of the individual and the protection of others. If s-s. 13(6) of the Y.O.A. is subject to challenge, so are such legislative provisions as para. 577(2)(c) of the *Criminal Code*, allowing exclusion of the accused from a trial of the issue of his fitness to stand trial, "where . . . failure to do so might have an adverse effect on the mental health of the accused." Indeed, considerable portions of provincial mental health legislation might be subject to similar challenge.

Cross-examination: subsection 13(5)

Subsection 13(5) of the Y.O.A. provides that where a report is prepared pursuant to s-s. 13(1), the young person, his counsel or the adult assisting him pursuant to s-s. 11(7), and the prosecutor shall normally have the right to cross-examine the person who made the report. This opportunity to cross-examine is to ensure that the information contained in the report can be adequately tested, explained, qualified or refuted. The right to cross-examine is exercised "on application", which requires the person who wishes to cross-examine to give some notice of his intention to allow arrangements to be made to secure the attendance of the maker of the report.

The right of cross-examination granted in s-s. 13(5) is expressly made "subject to subsection (6)." A Crown prosecutor and counsel for the young person have an unfettered right to cross-examine. If a private prosecutor is involved in the case, however, he obviously cannot cross-examine in regard to a report, or portion thereof, which has been withheld from him. The phrase "subject to subsection (6)" obviously recognizes and sanctions this limitation. The same disability applies to a young person who has chosen to represent himself.

An adult assisting a young person under s-s. 11(7), in place of counsel, has no independent right to receive a copy of the report, and must receive the report from the young person, for the purpose of allowing cross-examination. Thus, to the extent that a report is withheld from a young person, cross-examination by an assisting adult is limited. Further, if the assisting adult is a parent, the right to cross-examine may be limited if a report, or portion thereof, has been withheld pursuant to para. 13(6)(b).

A more difficult question in regard to the interrelationship of s-ss. 13(5) and (6), and the meaning of the phrase "subject to subsection (6)" in s-s. 13(5), arises in connection with who may be present during a cross-examination. If a direction is made under s-s. 13(6) withholding a report, or part of a report, from a person, it makes little sense to merely restrict the person's opportunity to cross-examine. The direction will only be effective in withholding information if the person is also excluded from the court when another person is cross-examining in regard to a report, or portion thereof, which has been withheld. A person attending a cross-examination by another party concerning a part of a report which has been withheld from the first person, may well learn as much, or more, damaging information by attending the cross-examination.

In general, attendance at youth court proceedings is governed by s. 39 of the Y.O.A. Thus, if a report, or part thereof, is withheld from a parent under para. 13(6)(b), the parent may also be excluded from the hearing under s-s. 39(1). Similarly, if a report, or part of a report, has been withheld from a private prosecutor under paras. 13(6)(a) or (b), the private prosecutor can be excluded under s-s. 39(1), at least at the dispositional stage.

The real difficulty arises if a report, or part of a report, is withheld from a young person under s-s. 13(6). Subsections 39(2) and (3) would appear, at first glance, to guarantee the young person's right to attend a cross-examination in regard to any part of the report. One clear limitation to this right of attendance arises out of s. 577 of the *Criminal Code*, which is applicable to all youth court proceedings by virtue of s-s. 52(3) of the Y.O.A.

Paragraph 577(2)(c) of the *Code* allows a youth court judge to *cause* an accused person to be removed from the court during a trial of the issue as to whether the young person is, on account of insanity, unfit to stand trial, if the court is satisfied that the failure to do so might have an adverse effect on the mental health of the accused. Under specified circumstances, this provision might apply to exclude a young person from a cross-examination and thereby ensure that he does not learn information otherwise withheld from him under s-s. 13(6).

Similarly, under para. 577(2)(b) a youth court judge may *permit* a young person to be absent during any portion of a proceeding. Thus, if counsel or a parent receives a report, or part of a report, that has been withheld from a young person and shares the concern about the impact of the report on the young person, counsel or the parent may suggest to the young person that he be absent during the cross-examination. The young person must willingly consent and the judge must agree to the absence. Counsel or the parent acting as an adult assisting the young person under s-s. 11(7) would represent the young person in court.

If neither para. 577(2)(b) nor (c) of the *Code* is applicable, it is submitted that a youth court judge has the power to exclude a young person from the cross-examination of the maker of the report, pursuant to s-s. 13(5), to the extent that the cross-examination deals with matters withheld from the young person under s-s. 13(6). It is submitted that it is a necessary implication of s-s. 13(6) that the person be so excluded, and that this is the meaning to be given to the phrase ''subject to subsection (6)'', which appears in s-s. 13(5). Those who are cross-examining under s-s. 13(5), in particular, counsel for a young person from whom information has been withheld under s-s. 13(6), should have a broad right of cross-examination; they should be able to test all aspects of the report, including those withheld by judicial direction under s-s. 13(6). If information is withheld from a person under s-s. 13(6), and that person is present during a cross-examination under s-s. 13(5), which deals with those matters, the direction under s-s. 13(6) may effectively be rendered useless.

It is thus submitted that it is necessary to interpret s-ss. 13(5) and (6) as giving the judge a power to exclude a person from that portion of a cross-examination under s-s. 13(5), dealing with information withheld from that person under s-s.13(6). Although this interpretation appears to narrow the broad words of s. 39, particularly the apparent right of the young person to be present throughout the hearing, it is submitted that this is the most reasonable interpretation of the Y.O.A., and the only one to give effect to the Parliamentary objective of withholding information from some of those involved in youth court proceedings, under certain very limited circumstances. It may be viewed as an application of the Latin maxim: *generalia specialibus non derogant* — "general words to not derogate from special"; the general rights granted under s. 39 do not derogate from the special power of exclusion given unsder s-ss. 13(5) and (6). See *Maxwell on the Interpretation of Statutes*, 12th ed. (1969), pp. 196-198; also E. Dreidger, *The Construction of Statutes* (1974), Chapter 3, "Construction by Object or Purpose".

Part of the record: subsection 13(9)

A report prepared pursuant to s-s. 13(1) becomes part of the youth court record, by virtue of s-s. 13(9). This means that under s-ss. 40(2) and (3), certain specified persons may have access to the record. Subsection 40(4) specifically provides that if a report, or part of a report, has been withheld from a young person, a parent or a private prosecutor under s-s. 13(6), that person shall not have access to that part of the record under s. 40. Section 45 requires ultimate destruction of all copies of the report, provided certain conditions are satisfied. Section 46 makes it an offence to reveal information contained in a report, except as authorized by legislation.

For a further discussion of the significance of a s. 13 report being a part of the youth court record, see comments below under ss. 40, 45 and 46, "Maintenance and use of records".

Disclosure by a qualified person: subsection 13(10)

Subsection 13(10) gives the "qualified person" who prepares a report pursuant to s-s. 13(1) in regard to a young person, a limited right to disclose some of the information contained in the report. If the young person is being held in detention or committed to custody, and the maker of the report "is of the opinion that the young person ... is likely to endanger his own life or safety or to endanger the life of, or cause bodily harm to, another person", the maker of the report may immediately advise any person who has the "care and custody" of the young person of this danger, whether or not this information is contained in the report prepared under s-s. 13(1). A person who has "care and custody" of a young person would, in appropriate circumstances, include a parent.

The effect of s-s. 13(10) is to encourage the sharing of information concerning situations of danger. The maker of the report is freed from any potential liability to prosecution under s. 46 of the Y.O.A. which might otherwise result from a disclosure of such information by the maker of the report. The American decision in *Tarasoff v. The Regents of the University of California,* 551 P. 2d 334, 131 Ca. R. 14, 17 C. 3d 425 (1976 Cal. S.C.) held that there might be civil liability in negligence for a psychiatrist or other professional who fails to warn of the possible danger that a person he has examined may pose to others. However, the authority for disclosure granted by s-s. 13(10) of the Y.O.A. is permissive only, and may be qualified by any provincial legislation and codes of professional conduct governing the professionals who prepare s. 13 reports.

Form of order: subsection 13(12)

An order for an examination under s-s. 13(1) may be in Form 5. See following sample form.

SAMPLE FORM

FORM 5
THE YOUNG OFFENDERS ACT
IN THE YOUTH COURT FOR ONTARIO

ORDER FOR THE EXAMINATION AND REPORT

Canada
Province of Ontario
County of Queens

To Dr. Sidney Freedman, a psychiatrist under the laws of the Province of Ontario , being a qualified person within the meaning of the *Young Offenders Act*:

Whereas David Smith of 25 First Ave., Anytown Ontario a young person within the meaning of the *Young Offenders Act*, has been charged with the following offence:

> robbery: to wit David Smith on the second day of June 1982 did steal two hundred and fifty dollars from the Corner Milk Store, 2 West Street, Anytown, Ontario, and at the same time thereat did use threats of violence contrary to section 303 of the *Criminal Code of Canada.*

And whereas there exists reasonable grounds to believe that David Smith may be suffering from a mental illness ;

And whereas it has been made to appear that a psychiatric report dealing with the issue of whether David is, on account of insanity, unfit to stand trial , would be helpful in the determination of these proceedings;

This is therefore to command you to conduct a psychiatric examination of David Smith and to report the results thereof in writing to the Court;

To the peace officers in the County of Queen's and the person in charge of the hereinafter mentioned place of custody;

You are hereby commanded to take David Smith and convey him safely to the following place, namely Queen's County Psychiatric Hospital and there deliver him to the person in charge thereof, together with the following precept:

And you, the person in charge of the said place, are hereby commanded to receive David Smith into your custody and to detain him safely there until his return to the Youth Court on the 22nd day of June 1982 at 10:00 o'clock in the fore noon and meanwhile to make him available as required for the purposes of the examination of assessment and for so doing, this is sufficient warrant.

Dated this 15th day of June 1982 , at Anytown in the Province of Ontario.

"Thomas Brown"

. . . .

A Judge of the Youth Court

PRE-DISPOSITION REPORT
(Section 14)

Introduction

Section 14 of the Y.O.A. governs the preparation and use of pre-disposition reports by youth courts. These reports are intended to furnish the courts with sufficient information to make the most appropriate decisions in regard to disposition, and certain other matters.

Section 31 of the J.D.A. briefly provides that juvenile probation officers may be required to conduct "such investigation as may be required by the court" and furnish such information as required to the courts. The approach to pre-disposition reports taken by the Y.O.A. is considerably more comprehensive than that of the J.D.A. and reflects the significance which courts have come to place upon such reports.

The principal features of ss. 14 and 15 include provisions governing:

— situations in which a report may be ordered, s-s. 14(1); see also s-ss. 16(3) and 24(11) requiring that a court must consider a pre-disposition report before deciding whether to transfer a young person to adult court or committing a young person to custody;

— minimum contents of the pre-disposition report, s-s. 14(2);

— reporting and disclosure of the report, s-ss. 14(3), (4), (8) and (9);

— right to access to the report and the right to cross-examine the maker of the report, s-ss. 14(5) and (6);

— prohibition against improper use of statements made by young persons in the course of preparation of the report, s-s. 14(10);

— withholding of a report from a private prosecutor, where disclosure is prejudicial to the young person, s-s. 14(7);

— disqualification of a judge from dealing with a case if he has examined a pre-disposition report in regard to an offence prior to an adjudication, for example in the context of a transfer application, with provision for exception to the rule of disqualification if parties and judge consent, s. 15.

The significance of pre-disposition reports lies in the fact that through their presentation in court, the youth court judge has access to a broad range of information about the young person, his family, his personal and criminal history, and about the resources and facilities which are available. The information will be compiled and presented by youth court workers or other competent persons. The reports should save all concerned considerable time and inconvenience, and still allow the court to make the most appropriate disposition. There is provision for cross-examination of the maker of a report and each party has an opportunity to present other information to the court.

SECTION 14

14. (1) *Pre-disposition report.*—**Where a youth court deems it advisable before making a disposition under section 20 in respect of a young person who is found guilty of an offence it may, and where a youth court is required under this Act to consider a pre-disposition report before making an order or a disposition in respect of a young person it shall, require the provincial director to cause to be prepared a pre-disposition report in respect of the young person and to submit the report to the court.**

(2) *Contents of report.*—**A pre-disposition report made in respect of a young person shall, subject to subsection (3), be in writing and shall include**

(a) the results of an interview with the young person and, where reasonably possible, the results of an interview with the parents of the young person;

(b) the results of an interview with the victim in the case, where applicable and where reasonably possible; and

(c) such information as is applicable to the case including, where applicable,

(i) the age, maturity, character, behaviour and attitude of the young person and his willingness to make amends,

(ii) any plans put forward by the young person to change his conduct or to participate in activities or undertake measures to improve himself,

(iii) the history of previous findings of delinquency under the *Juvenile Delinquents Act* or previous findings of guilt under this or any other Act of Parliament or any regulation made thereunder or under a provincial statute or a by-law or ordinance of a municipality, the history of community or other services rendered to the young person with respect to such findings and the response of the young person to previous sentences or dispositions and to services rendered to him,

(iv) the history of alternative measures used to deal with the young person and the response of the young person thereto,

(v) the availability of community services and facilities for young persons and the willingness of the young person to avail himself of such services or facilities,

(vi) the relationship between the young person and his parents and the degree of control and influence of the parents over the young person, and

(vii) the school attendance and performance record and the employment record of the young person.

(3) *Oral report with leave.*—Where a pre-disposition report cannot reasonably be committed to writing, it may, with leave of the youth court, be submitted orally in court.

(4) *Report to form part of record.*—A pre-disposition report shall form part of the record of the case in respect of which it was requested.

(5) *Copies of pre-disposition report.*—Where a pre-disposition report made in respect of a young person is submitted to a youth court in writing, the court

(a) shall, subject to subsection (7), cause a copy of the report to be given to

(i) the young person,

(ii) a parent of the young person, if the parent is in attendance at the proceedings against the young person,

(iii) counsel, if any, representing the young person, and

(iv) the prosecutor; and

(b) may cause a copy of the report to be given to a parent of the young person not in attendance at the proceedings against the young person if the parent is, in the opinion of the court, taking an active interest in the proceedings.

(6) *Cross-examination.*—Where a pre-disposition report made in respect of a young person is submitted to a youth court, the young person, his counsel or the adult assisting him pursuant to subsection 11(7) and the prosecutor shall, subject to subsection (7), on application to the youth court, be given the opportunity to cross-examine the person who made the report.

(7) *Report may be withheld from young person or private prosecutor.*—Where a pre-disposition report made in respect of a young person is submitted to a youth court, the court may, where the prosecutor is a private prosecutor and disclosure of the report or any part thereof to the prosecutor might, in the opinion of the court, be prejudicial to the young person and is not, in the opinion of the court, necessary for the prosecution of the case against the young person,

(a) withhold the report or part thereof from the prosecutor, if the report is submitted in writing; or

(b) exclude the prosecutor from the court during the submission of the report or any part thereof, if the report is submitted orally in court.

(8) *Report disclosed to other persons.*—Where a pre-disposition report made in respect of a young person is submitted to a youth court, the court

(a) shall, on request, cause a copy or a transcript of the report to be supplied to

(i) any court that is dealing with matters relating to the young person, and

(ii) any youth worker to whom the young person's case has been assigned; and

(b) may, on request, cause a copy or a transcript of the report, or a part thereof, to be supplied to any person not otherwise authorized under this section to receive a copy or transcript of the report if, in the opinion of the court, the person has a valid interest in the proceedings.

(9) *Disclosure by the provincial director.*—A provincial director who submits a pre-disposition report made in respect of a young person to a youth court may make the report, or any part thereof, available to any person in whose custody or under whose supervision the young person is placed or to any other person who is directly assisting in the care or treatment of the young person.

(10) *Inadmissibility of statements.*—No statement made by a young person in the course of the preparation of a pre-

disposition report in respect of the young person is admissible in evidence against him in any civil or criminal proceedings except in proceedings under section 16 or 20 or sections 28 to 32.

Ordering a pre-disposition report: subsection 14(1)

Subsection 14(1) provides that where a youth court judge "deems it advisable . . . [he] may require the provincial director . . . cause to be prepared a pre-disposition report" which shall be submitted for consideration to the court. It is suggested that if either party or the parents of the young person request that the court order such a report, the court should accede to the request, unless it is clearly frivolous: see C. F. Domek and M. W. Chitra, "The Pre-sentence Report: An Update" (1981), 23 Criminal Law Quarterly 216 for a discussion of when a report ought to be ordered. But note that cases from adult proceedings are of limited applicability as it is generally more important for a court dealing with a youthful offender to have such information: *R. v. Bates* (1977), 32 C.C.C. (2d) 493 (Ont. C.A.). The judge may also require a report on his own motion. A pre-disposition report must be prepared and submitted to the court when an application to transfer a young person to adult court is being considered, s-s. 16(3), and before a young person is committed to custody, s-s. 24(11).

When a youth court orders a pre-disposition report to be prepared, it is the responsibility of the "provincial director" (defined in s-s. 2(1) of the Y.O.A.) to ensure that this is done. Paragraph 37(d) provides that the preparation and presentation of such reports is one of the functions of "youth court workers", although the provincial director may appoint any person to prepare a report. If the court requires relatively sophisticated information about a young person, it may be appropriate to order a report under s. 13 of the Y.O.A., which will be prepared by a medical doctor, psychiatrist, psychologist or other "qualified person". A court may order either a s. 13 report, a s. 14 report or both, depending upon the circumstances, except where the Y.O.A. requires that a pre-disposition report be prepared (s-ss. 16(3) and 24(11)), at *least* this report must be ordered.

Contents of report: subsection 14(2)

Subsection 14(2) requires a pre-disposition report to be in writing (subject to s-s. 14(3)), and outlines the minimum content for such a report.

The person preparing the pre-disposition report is required to interview the young person who is the subject of the report, and where reasonably possible to interview the parents of the young person, see para. 14(2)(a). The results of the interview are to be reported; this will convey information to the court about the background of the young person and his parents, and any plans they may have for the young person. The interviews will also allow the person making the report to assess the maturity, character and attitude of the young person. Subsection 14(10) ensures that statements made by the young person in the course of the preparation of a report are not used for extraneous purposes.

If there is a known victim, the person making the report shall interview the victim where reasonably possible, and report the results of the interview, para. 14(2)(b). The victim may be asked about whether some form of restitution, compensation or personal service by the offender for the victim is sought and appropriate (see paras. 20(1)(c) to (f)).

In addition to interviewing the young person (and where possible, the parents and victim) the person preparing the report has considerable discretion in regard to the obtaining of information. A person preparing a pre-disposition report would not appear to have an automatic right to disclosure of a young person's youth court record, or police criminal history record, but a youth court should invariably order disclosure of such records under paras. 40(2)(e) or (3)(l); subpara. 14(8)(a)(ii) gives a youth court worker a right to obtain pre-disposition reports on request. The maker of the report may consider it appropriate to consult teachers, a guidance counsellor, family friends or relatives, neighbours, an employer, family doctor, the investigating police officers, or those who may have been involved in supervising previous dispositions or treating the young person. The maker of the report has an obligation to ensure that the contents of the report are adequately substantiated. In R. v. White (1978), 16 Nfld. & P.E.I. R. 46 at p. 49, 42 A.P.R. 46 (Nfld. C.A.), Gushue J.A. stated:

In my view, reports of this nature should be strictly factual. They should not speculate, nor should they reach unwarranted or indeed any conclusions. They are meant to assist the trial Judge, particularly with regard to the antecedents of the accused, where the Judge has before him what he considers to be insufficient information relating to the accused for the purpose of imposing sentence. In the particular report in this case, comments are made relating to the alleged effect of the appellant's actions on other prisoners in relation to a job held by him while in prison; it was mentioned that White manipulates acquaintances and friends; that he became *"well-known"* to the R.C.M.P. Drug Squad within four to five weeks of his last release from prison. These comments are not founded on any facts and, even if they were, would in my view be improper. Further, the probation officer says that White *"is apparently dependent upon the profits of illicit drug trading."* There is no evidence to support this statement and it is totally inappropriate.

R. P. Nadin-Davis, *Sentencing in Canada* (Toronto, Carswell, 1982), comments (at. p. 527):

It is further submitted that persons preparing reports should be scrupulous in identifying sources of negative substantiated information. In the absence of such identification, it may be difficult if not impossible for the accused adequately to contest allegations which may be quite false.

Paragraph 14(2)(c) specifies that a pre-disposition report shall contain such information as is applicable. Subparagraph 14(2)(c)(i) requires information as to the "age, maturity, character, behaviour and attitude of the young person and his willingness to make amends." Assessments of such matters as "maturity, character, behaviour and attitude" are inevitably subjective, and the maker of the report should at least be clear in identifying whether the assessments are his own, or based on the statements of others. Further, while subparas. 14(2)(c)(iii) and (iv) specifically require that a report contain information about the young person's history of involvement with the courts and alternative measures, a report on "behaviour" should not include a statement that the young person is suspected of being involved in criminal activity which has not resulted in a criminal conviction: *R. v. Morelli* (1977), 37 C.C.C. (2d) 392 (Ont. Prov. Ct.) and *R. v. Bartkow* (1978), 1 C.R. (3d) S-36, 35 A.P.R. 518, 24 N.S.R. (2d) 518 (C.A.). Such information may be highly prejudicial and unless it has resulted in a conviction it is not appropriately before the court.

Subparagraph 14(2)(c)(ii) requires information on "any plans put forward by the young person to change his conduct or to participate in activities or undertake measures to improve himself." This suggests that the person preparing the report should raise these matters in his interview with the young person, thus encouraging the young person to take responsibility for his own rehabilitation.

Subparagraph 14(2)(c)(iii) requires the report to include the history of previous findings of guilt under the Y.O.A., the J.D.A. or any provincial or municipal law. The report shall also describe the young person's response to previous dispositions and to community or other services rendered to the young person as a result of his previous involvement with the courts. In *R. v. Tan*, [1975] 2 W.W.R. 747, 22 C.C.C (2d) 184 (B.C.C.A.) it was held in an adult sentencing that a prior discharge ought to be considered by a court contemplating a conditional or absolute discharge, and therefore a notation of a prior discharge should be included in a pre-disposition report. See also para. 36(1)(e) of the Y.O.A. which specifically allows a court to make use of a previous absolute discharge in considering a subsequent disposition. Section 45 of the Y.O.A. requires the destruction of all records concerning a previous conviction under the Y.O.A. or J.D.A. if a young person has had a conviction-free period (two years after completion of disposition of summary conviction offence, five years after completion of disposition on indictable offence). If a destruction of the record is required, the previous convictions are not to be mentioned in the pre-disposition report or considered by the court.

Subparagraph 14(2)(c)(iv) requires the person making the report to include the history of alternative measures and the response of the young person thereto. *R. v. Drew*, [1979] W.W.R. 530, 45 C.C.C. (2d) 212, 7 C.R. (3d) S-21 (B.C.C.A.) stands for the proposition that a court ought to take into account a young person's experience in a diversion program, but that the weight given the consideration should be tempered by the fact that diversion is not a substitute for a previous discharge and does not involve a finding of guilt.

Subparagraph 14(2)(c)(v) requires the report to provide information about the "availability of community services and facilities for young persons and the willingness of the young person to avail himself of such services or facilities." This requires the person making the report to be familiar with the resources of the juvenile correctional system, and to discuss possible dispositions with the young person. It is apparently not an uncommon practice for pre-disposition reports prepared in connection with charges under the *J.D.A.* to include a recommendation as to an appropriate disposition. In the adult courts, this practice has been the subject of adverse judicial comment. There may be a concern that in the absence of a request by the judge for advice, such recommendations may be too influential and infringe upon the judicial function. See *R. v. Bartkow* (1978), 1 C.R. (3d) S-36, 35 A.P.R. 518, 24 N.S.R. (2d) 518 (C.A.); and *R. v. Silk* (1979), 20 Nfld. & P.E.I. R. 465, 53 A.P.R. 465 (Nfld. C.A.), where Furlong C.J.N. said at pp. 467-68):

> Before leaving this case we should also like to repeat what has already been said about pre-sentence reports. These reports should be limited to a recital of facts with regard to the antecedents and background of the accused. In this case the report went further than was strictly necessary and the probation officer included in it the general recommendations as to the form of punishment. Punishment is a matter that lies exclusively within the preserve of the Judge and should remain outside the ambit of any probation officer's report unless his views are sought.

According to this view, it is acceptable for a pre-disposition report to discuss available resources and facilities and the young person's apparent amenability to various dispositions, but unless specifically requested, a recommendation is inappropriate.

Subparagraph 14(2)(c)(vi) of the Y.O.A. requires the report to include information about "the relationship between the young person and his parents and the degree of control and influence of the parents over the young person". The information may come from the assessment of the young person and his parents, or may be based on observations by the maker of the report or others.

Subparagraph 14(2)(c)(vii) provides that where appropriate the report shall include information about school attendance and performance of the young person and about his employment record.

Oral report: subsection 14(3)

While a pre-disposition report shall normally be in writing to give the court and parties an opportunity to study its contents, s-s. 14(3) provides that, with leave of the court, where a report cannot "reasonably be committed to writing" it may be submitted orally in court. Leave to present an oral report might be given when the offence is less serious, or a lack of facilities or time makes it difficult to prepare a report. It is submitted, however, that a court should be reluctant to grant leave for an oral presentation where a severe disposition is being contemplated or where complex issues are involved. An oral report may make it difficult for the parties to prepare for a disposition hearing and participate effectively in the cross-examination of the maker of the report; an oral report may also complicate the court's task. An oral report may not be as well organized and clearly presented as a written report.

Although not expressly provided for in the legislation, it is suggested that where leave is to be sought to present an oral report, the young person, his counsel, the prosecutor and any parent in attendance, where possible, should be informed prior to the court appearance that leave will be sought, and they should be informed of the substance of the report.

Further, where an oral report is being presented and a person entitled under s-s. 14(6) to cross-examine the maker of the report requests an adjournment or recess to allow time to prepare for cross-examination, it is submitted that this request should normally be granted.

A youth court judge may exclude a *private* prosecutor from the oral submission of all, or part, of a report, where disclosure "might . . . be prejudicial" to the young person and the information withheld is not necessary for the prosecution of the case: see s-s. 14(7) and discussion *infra*.

Report part of record: subsection 14(4)

Subsection 14(4) makes clear that a pre-disposition report is a part of the record of the youth court, and therefore subject to the provisions of ss. 40, 45 and 46 in regard to access, disclosure and destruction.

Provision of copies of pre-disposition report: subsection 14(5)

Subsection 14(5) requires that where a pre-disposition report has been prepared, the youth court shall cause copies of the report to be given to:

(i) the young person;

(ii) the young person's parent if present at the proceedings; para. 14(5)(b) allows a youth court to cause a copy of the report to be given to a parent not in attendance at the proceedings, if the parent is "in the opinion of the court, taking an active interest in the proceedings";

(iii) counsel for the young person, if there is one; and

(iv) the prosecutor, subject to having all or part of the report withheld from a *private* prosecutor under s-s. 14(7).

Thus, where a pre-disposition report is completed, it should be submitted to the youth court. The court should then ensure that all of those entitled to the report under s-s. 14(5) receive copies of the report. Normally, as a matter of practice the copies of the report should be given out prior to appearance in court, to allow those involved to consider the report, and decide whether to exercise their right of cross-examination under s-s. 14(6). A copy of the pre-disposition report should not be given to a private prosecutor without express judicial approval, in view of the broad discretion given to a judge under s-s. 14(7) to withhold all or part of such a report.

Cross-examination: subsection 14(6)

On application to the youth court, the young person, his counsel or an adult assisting the young person pursuant to s-s. 11(7) shall be given the opportunity to cross-examine the person who made a pre-disposition report. Similarly, on application the prosecutor will have the opportunity to cross-examine the maker of the report, subject to s-s. 14(7), which may in certain circumstances reduce or even eliminate a private prosecutor's right to cross-examine. As with a medical or psychological report prepared under s. 13 of the Y.O.A., a pre-disposition report is not a part of the case of either party and so both parties should have a right of cross-examination, to allow adequate testing or qualification of its contents.

As noted above in the discussion of s-ss. 14(3) and (5), as a matter of practice, it is usually appropriate to ensure that parties have copies of the report prior to the hearing at which it is submitted, or if the report is to be submitted orally under s-s. 14(3), notice of the substance of the report. Such prior notice of the report may be necessary to give the parties an opportunity to prepare for an effective and proper cross-examination. If a party has not had adequate notice of the report, it is submitted that the court should normally exercise its discretion to grant an adjournment or recess.

Withholding of report from private prosecutor: subsection 14(7)

Subsection 14(7) provides that all, or a part, of a pre-disposition report may be withheld from a *private* prosecutor where "disclosure . . . to the prosecutor *might*, in the opinion of the court, be prejudicial to the young person and is not, in the opinion of the court, necessary for the prosecution of the case". This test for withholding disclosure should be contrasted with s-s. 39(1). Subsection 14(7) adopts a less stringent test with "might" as opposed to "would", and be "prejudicial" as opposed to "seriously prejudicial". Subsection 14(7) might be used to withhold information of an embarrassing nature about background, character or condition. The court may consider the identity of the private prosecutor when deciding whether to direct withholding of information; it may be relevant whether it is a neighbour of the young person or a department store that is prosecuting the case. It should be noted that there is *no* provision for withholding any part of a report from a Crown prosecutor (the Attorney General or his agent).

Paragraph 14(7)(a) allows withholding of a copy of the report from a private prosecutor if it is submitted in writing, while para. 14(7)(b) provides for the exclusion of a private prosecutor from "the court during the submisison of the report or a part thereof, if the report is submitted orally in court."

Subsection 14(6), granting a prosecutor the right to cross-examine the maker of a pre-disposition report, is expressly "subject to subsection (7)." Clearly, s-s. 14(7) may be invoked to prevent a private prosecutor from asking questions. It would also seem that s-s. 14(7) is broad enough to have a private prosecutor excluded from the court during cross-examination by the young person. Paragraph 14(7)(b) allows exclusion of a private prosecutor from the court "during the *submission* of the report, or a part thereof, if the report is submitted orally"; this would seem to cover exclusion during cross-examination. In any event, s-s. 39(3) allows exclusion of a private prosecutor during the disposition stage of a Y.O.A. proceeding if information is "being presented, the knowledge of which [by the private prosecutor] might, in the opinion of the court ... be seriously injurious or prejudicial to the young person." See also discussion of s-ss. 13(5) and (6) regarding exclusion of a private prosecutor from proceedings.

The decision to withhold disclosure from a private prosecutor under s-s. 14(7) rests with the judge, and no hearing need be held before it is made. The judge may act on his own motion, or as a result of written or oral submissions from the young person or the person preparing the report.

If a youth court withholds all or part of a pre-disposition report from a private prosecutor under s-s. 14(7), s-s. 40(4) provides that this part of the youth court record shall not be made available to him for inspection, and s-s. 46(2) prohibits unauthorized disclosure of information from the report to him.

It should be noted that the English marginal note to s-s. 14(7) states "Report may be withheld from young person or private prosecutor". This marginal note is incorrect, and results from a failure to change the note after the subsection was amended between Second and Third Reading of the Y.O.A. The *Interpretation Act*, R.S.C. 1970, c. I-23, s. 13 provides that "[m]arginal notes ... form no part of the enactment, but shall be deemed to have been inserted for convenience of reference only." Therefore, although the marginal note to s-s. 14(7) of the Y.O.A. is incorrect, it in no way affects the substantive provisions contained therein. There is no equivalent error in the French marginal note.

Court disclosure of report to other persons: subsection 14(8)

In addition to those immediately involved in youth court proceedings, and hence entitled to a copy of a pre-disposition report under s-s. 14(5), there may be others who should have access to the report; s-s. 14(8) provides for release of a report to other courts, to youth workers, and to others who have a "valid interest".

Under subpara. 14(8)(a)(i), a copy of a pre-disposition report, or a transcript of the report if it is submitted orally, shall, upon request, be supplied by the youth court to "any court that is dealing with matters relating to the young person". This would appear to include a youth court, a court dealing with the young person under child welfare or youth protection legislation, an ordinary (adult) court dealing with the young person after transfer under s. 16 of the Y.O.A., and a court dealing with the young person after he becomes an adult. This broad reading of subpara. 14(8)(a)(i) is consistent with paras. 40(3)(f) and (g) which give other courts access to youth court records.

Under subpara. 14(8)(a)(ii), a copy of a report or transcript of its oral submission shall, upon request, be supplied by the court to "any youth worker to whom the young person's case has been assigned". A youth worker preparing a pre-disposition report or progress report (for review proceedings under ss. 28 to 34) should find a previously prepared pre-disposition report of great assistance. Similarly, a youth worker assigned to supervise a young person on probation or carry out other duties under s. 37 should find a report to be a valuable source of information to help him better understand the young person.

Paragraph 14(8)(b) allows a youth court to supply a copy or transcript of a report, or part thereof to any person not otherwise entitled under s. 14 access to the report, if, "in the opinion of the court, the person has a valid interest in the proceedings." A court has a broad discretion under para. 14(8)(b) and must weigh any benefits to society or the young person which may result from release of the report against any harm which may result from the release of sensitive and potentially prejudicial information. Examples of persons who might, under certain circumstances, have a "valid interest" in the proceedings are a psychiatrist, psychologist or other therapist treating the young person, or the victim if he has agreed to have the young person perform personal services as a part of his disposition. As a pre-disposition report is a part of the youth court record, a number of persons have a right of access to the report or may at least seek access under s-ss. 40(2) and (3). A youth court judge is not obliged to hold a hearing before deciding to release a report under para. 14(8)(b).

If a copy or transcript of a report is released by a youth court under s-s. 14(8), the privacy of the young person is still protected by s-ss. 40(4) and 46(2). Copies of the report or transcript are not to be released to unauthorized persons, nor is information from the report to be improperly disclosed. Further, all copies and transcripts are subject to the destruction provisions of s. 45.

Disclosure by provincial director: subsection 14(9)

Subsection 14(9) authorizes a provincial director who submits a pre-disposition report to a court to make the report, or a part of the report, available to "any person in whose custody or under whose supervision the young person is placed or to any other person who is directly assisting in the care or treatment of the young person." Access to the report may have an obvious benefit for those dealing with the young person, and further obviates the need for those persons to contact again those who contributed information to the original report (e.g. parents, the victim, employers), sparing them inconvenience and potential embarrassment or unpleasantness.

If a copy of a report is released by a provincial director under s-s. 14(9), the privacy of the young person is still protected by s-ss. 40(4) and 46(2); copies of the report are not to be released to unauthorized persons, nor is information to be improperly disclosed. Further, all copies of the report are subject to the destruction provisions of s. 45.

Inadmissibility of statements: subsection 14(10)

Pursuant to s-s. 14(10) of the Y.O.A., statements made by a young person in the course of the preparation of a pre-disposition report in respect of the young person are not "admissible in evidence against him in any civil or criminal proceedings except in proceedings under section 16 [transfer to ordinary court] or 20 [disposition] or sections 28 to 32 [disposition review]". The purpose of s-s. 14(10) is to ensure that statements made by the young person for the purpose of preparing a report are used for the purposes for which they were intended. For example, if a young person admits complicity in criminal activity not arising out of the charge for which the report is being prepared, such an admission is "privileged" and cannot be used against the young person in other proceedings. As indicated above in the discussion of s-s. 14(2), it is generally considered improper to include such information in a pre-disposition report.

The purpose of s-s. 14(10) is to protect the young person against self-incrimination, and to encourage open communication between the maker of the report and the young person.

DISQUALIFICATION OF JUDGE
(Section 15)

Introduction

Subsection 15(1) of the Y.O.A. provides that as a rule a youth court judge who, prior to an adjudication, examines a pre-disposition report or hears a transfer application under s. 16 of the Y.O.A. shall not continue to deal with the case thereafter. This is to prevent any possibility that a judge may be predisposed by any information he receives, or that there is any *appearance* of such predisposition.

Subsection 15(2) provides an exception to the general rule if the young person and prosecutor both consent *and* the judge is satisfied that he has not been predisposed by any information received.

SECTION 15

15. (1) *Disqualification of judge.*—**Subject to subsection (2), a youth court judge who, prior to an adjudication in respect of a young person charged with an offence, examines a pre-disposition report made in respect of the young person, or hears an application under section 16 in respect of the young person, in connection with that offence shall not in any capacity conduct or continue the trial of the young person for the offence and shall transfer the case to another judge to be dealt with according to law.**

(2) *Exception.*—**A youth court judge may, in the circumstances referred to in subsection (1), with the consent of the young person and the prosecutor, conduct or continue the trial of the young person if the judge is satisfied that he has not been predisposed by information contained in the pre-disposition report or by representations made in respect of the application under section 16.**

Disqualification of judge: subsection 15(1)

Subsection 15(1) provides that, subject to s-s. 15(2), a youth court judge who, prior to an adjudication in respect of an offence,

(1) examines a pre-disposition report made in respect of the young person in connection with *that* offence, or

(2) hears a transfer application under s. 16 of the Y.O.A. in respect of that offence,

shall not "in any capacity conduct or continue the trial of the young person" for that offence, and shall transfer the case to another judge to be dealt with according to law.

The purpose for this general rule is to ensure that a judge is not predisposed in rendering an adjudication in regard to a specific charge, by information received in a pre-disposition report or transfer application, in respect of that charge. This is important not only to ensure that justice is done, but also to ensure that justice appears to be done.

At a transfer hearing under s. 16, a youth court judge may receive evidence of the "seriousness" and "circumstances" of an alleged offence; hearsay and other inadmissible evidence may be received at a transfer hearing. Further, other highly prejudicial information may be revealed at a transfer hearing, for example, concerning a young person's previous convictions. All of this information may be highly relevant to a transfer hearing, but prejudicial and irrelevant to an adjudication.

A pre-disposition report may also contain hearsay evidence and incriminating statements by the accused concerning the circumstances of an offence, and other prejudicial information not relevant to an adjudication. A pre-disposition report will usually be read by a judge in connection with a transfer hearing; s-s. 16(3) requires a judge to read a pre-disposition report in considering a transfer application. There may also be other circumstances in which a judge, through inadvertence or otherwise, reads a pre-disposition report prior to adjudication; this should rarely occur as, apart from a transfer hearing, a pre-disposition report should only be ordered after an adjudication.

Subsection 15(1) requires a disqualified judge to not "in any capacity conduct or continue the trial of the young person for the offence". This means that if the case is not transferred, he is disqualified from dealing with the case in youth court. This also means that if a youth court judge also sits as a judge in ordinary (adult) court and he orders the case transferred to ordinary court, he cannot deal with the case in ordinary court.

It is clear from the wording and punctuation of s-s. 15(1) that a judge who conducts a transfer hearing or reads a pre-disposition report in connection with *one* offence is *not* disqualified from dealing with the young person in connection with another offence. It is quite common for a judge to render an adjudication and disposition in regard to a person who has been convicted by the same judge on other charges. It is only improper for a judge to deal with a case if there is "a reasonable apprehension of bias", and it is clear that mere familiarity with the accused based on previous charges is not in itself sufficient grounds to apprehend bias. In *Barthe v. The Queen*, [1964] 2 C.C.C. 269, 45 D.L.R. (2d) 612, 41 C.R. 47 (Que. C.A.), the accused sought a writ of prohibition to prevent his trial for conspiracy from being heard before a judge who had already tried other members of the same conspiracy; the Quebec Court of Appeal rejected the suggestion of bias. The Court noted that judges often hear inadmissible evidence at a *voir dire*, and they are relied upon to ignore this evidence in disposing of the case. Hyde J. stated (at p. 50, C.R.): "The ability to judge a case only on the legal evidence adduced is an essential part of the judicial process." To the same effect, see *Huziak v. Andrychuk J.M.C.* (1977), 1 C.R. (3d) 132 (Sask. Q.B.).

Exception to disqualification: subsection 15(2)

There is an exception to s-s. 15(1) found in s-s. 15(2) of the Y.O.A. which allows a judge who, prior to an adjudication, has read a pre-disposition report in connection with an offence or heard a transfer application in regard to that offence, to continue to deal with the charge. Under s-s. 15(2) both the young person and the prosecutor *must* consent to the judge continuing or conducting the trial. Further, the judge himself must be "satisfied that he has not been predisposed by information" contained in the pre-disposition report or received in the course of a transfer application.

If the issue of disqualification arises and the young person is not represented by counsel, the judge should be especially concerned that the consent of the young person to his continuing to deal with the case is given freely and with full comprehension of its significance. The judge may wish to encourage the young person to obtain counsel and to exercise his right to have the court direct that counsel be appointed pursuant to s-s. 11(4) of the Y.O.A.

In deciding whether he is satisfied that he is not "predisposed" by information received, the judge will ultimately have to assess his own state of mind. Important factors may include: the nature of the information received; the seriousness of the charge the young person faces; and the nature of the proceedings the judge will be required to conduct, for example conducting a full trial versus accepting a guilty plea. Clearly, if a judge is going to continue to deal with a case, in rendering his adjudication he must not consider any of the information received at the transfer hearing or through the pre-disposition report. As *Barthe* and *Huziak*, cited above, indicate, it is accepted that in rendering an adjudication, members of the judiciary generally have the ability to exclude from their consideration matters not properly before the court.

TRANSFER TO ORDINARY COURT
(Sections 16 and 17)

Introduction

One of the most serious decisions which may affect a young person facing charges under the Y.O.A. is to have his case transferred to ordinary court under s. 16. If a transfer order is made, the young person is thereafter dealt with as an adult; this includes the possibility of incarceration in an adult correctional facility without the time limitations on disposition found in s. 20 of the Y.O.A. In limited circumstances, it is felt that the broader interests of criminal as distinct from juvenile justice must take precedence, that the interests of society must be the governing factor. This procedure provides a safety valve for dealing with difficult cases, particularly where public protection is at issue.

The *Juvenile Delinquents Act* provides for a transfer procedure:

> 9(1) Where the act complained of is, under the provisions of the *Criminal Code* or otherwise, an indictable offence, and the accused child is apparently or actually over the age of fourteen years, the court may, in its discretion, order the child to be proceeded against by indictment in the ordinary courts in accordance with the provisions of the *Criminal Code* in that behalf; but such course shall in no case be followed unless the court is of the opinion that the good of the child and the interest of the community demand it.

This provision of the *J.D.A.* resulted in a considerable amount of jurisprudence, concerning a number of substantive and procedural issues. An oft-quoted passage from Mr. Justice Mac-Kinnon, in *R. v. Mero* (1976), 13 O.R. (2d) 215, 30 C.C.C. (2d) 497 at p. 504, 70 D.L.R. (3d) 551 (C.A.) is representative of judicial pronouncements on the nature of transfer under the *J.D.A.*:

> Parliament has made its intention clear as to the interpretation and application of the Act when, in s. 38 [of the *J.D.A.*] it directs that the Courts should, except in the clearest of cases otherwise, treat the juvenile delinquent not as a criminal but as a misdirected and misguided child who needs aid, encouragement, help and

assistance. To direct that such a child be proceeded against by indictment in the ordinary Courts can only be ordered where the Court is of the opinion that both the good of the child and the interest of the community *demand* it. The Shorter Oxford English Dictionary defines "demand" as: "to ask for peremptorily, imperiously or urgently", and the noun is therein defined as: "an urgent requirement". By this language Parliament has emphasized, it seems to me, that such an order should only be made where the crime is of a most serious nature and the criminal and other record of the child supports no other recourse or solution. The verb "demands" is a powerful one, and with respect, I am of the opinion that the Courts below failed to give it sufficient weight in the context of the legislation, in particular s. 38, and of all the facts of this case.

In practice the actual application of the standard articulated in *Mero* has varied considerably under the *J.D.A.* In some provinces, like Ontario, transfers have been very rare, but in other provinces, such as Manitoba where the *J.D.A.* applies to youths up to the age of 18, transfers have been more common.

The *Young Offenders Act* is intended to ensure more uniformity and a more realistic approach to transfer, and also to resolve certain procedural dilemmas concerning the process. The standard articulated by the Y.O.A. requires the court to consider "the interest of society and having regard to the needs of the young person." This recognizes that the primary concern in a transfer situation is the interests of society; however, the needs of the young person in terms of treatment and the protections afforded him under the Y.O.A. must also be taken into account. The application of the principle that society is to be protected is to be tempered by a consideration of the needs of the young person.

There are a number of provisions in the Y.O.A. which will modify the present practice under the *J.D.A.*, and which should ensure that only appropriate cases are transferred to ordinary court. These include:

— a narrower range of offences than under the *J.D.A.*, s-s. 16(1);

— the young person and his parents have a right to make representations, s-s. 16(1);

— age of the young person is determined at the commission of the offence, s-s. 16(1);

— judicial discretion is more structured than under the J.D.A., with a minimum list of factors to be considered, s-s. 16(2);

— consideration of a pre-disposition report is mandatory, s-s. 16(3);

— the youth court judge must give reasons, s-s. 16(5);

— a statutory right of review exists, s-s. 16(9);

— the young person has a right to counsel, para. 11(3)(b).

SECTION 16

16. (1) *Transfer to ordinary court.*—At any time after an information is laid against a young person alleged to have, after attaining the age of fourteen years, committed an indictable offence other than an offence referred to in section 483 of the *Criminal Code* but prior to adjudication, a youth court may, on application of the young person or his counsel, or the Attorney General or his agent, after affording both parties and the parents of the young person an opportunity to be heard, if the court is of the opinion that, in the interest of society and having regard to the needs of the young person, the young person should be proceeded against in ordinary court, order that the young person be so proceeded against in accordance with the law ordinarily applicable to an adult charged with the offence.

(2) *Considerations by youth court.*—In considering an application under subsection (1) in respect of a young person, a youth court shall take into account

(a) the seriousness of the alleged offence and the circumstances in which it was allegedly committed;

(b) the age, maturity, character and background of the young person and any record or summary of previous findings of delinquency under the *Juvenile Delinquents Act* or previous findings of guilt under this or any other Act of Parliament or any regulation made thereunder;

(c) the adequacy of this Act, and the adequacy of the *Criminal Code* or other Act of Parliament that would apply in respect of the young person if an order were made under subsection (1), to meet the circumstances of the case;

(d) the availability of treatment or correctional resources;

(e) any representations made to the court by or on behalf of the young person or by the Attorney General or his agent; and

(f) any other factors that the court considers relevant.

(3) *Pre-disposition reports.*—In considering an application under subsection (1), a youth court shall consider a pre-disposition report.

(4) *Where young person on transfer status.*—Notwithstanding subsections (1) and (3), where an application is made under subsection (1) by the Attorney General or his agent in respect of an offence alleged to have been committed by a young person while the young person was being proceeded against in ordinary court pursuant to an order previously made under that subsection or serving a sentence as a result of proceedings in ordinary court, the youth court may make a further order under that subsection without a hearing and without considering a pre-disposition report.

(5) *Court to state reasons.*—Where a youth court makes an order or refuses to make an order under subsection (1), it shall state the reasons for its decision and the reasons shall form part of the record of the proceedings of the youth court.

(6) *No further applications for transfer.*—Where a youth court refuses to make an order under subsection (1) in respect of an alleged offence, no further application may be made under this section in respect of that offence.

(7) *Effect of order under subsection (1).*—Where an order is made under subsection (1), proceedings under this Act shall be discontinued and the young person against whom the proceedings are taken shall be taken before the ordinary court.

(8) *Jurisdiction of ordinary court limited.*—Where an order is made under subsection (1) that a young person be proceeded against in ordinary court in respect of an offence, that court has jurisdiction only in respect of that offence or an offence included therein.

(9) *Review of youth court decision.*—Subject to subsection (11), an order made in respect of a young person under subsection (1) or a refusal to make such an order shall, on application of the young person or his counsel or the Attorney General or his agent made within thirty days after the decision of the youth court, be reviewed by the superior court and that court may, in its discretion, confirm or reverse the decision of the youth court.

(10) *Review of superior court decision.*—A decision made in respect of a young person by a superior court under subsection (9) may, on application of the young person or his counsel or the Attorney General or his agent made within thirty days after the decision of the superior court, with the leave of the court of

appeal, be reviewed by that court, and the court of appeal may, in its discretion, confirm or reverse the decision of the superior court.

(11) *Where the youth court is a superior court.*—In any province where the youth court is a superior court, a review under subsection (9) shall be made by the court of appeal of the province.

(12) *Extension of time to make application.*—A court to which an application is made under subsection (9) or (10) may at any time extend the time within which the application may be made.

(13) *Notice of application.*—A person who proposes to apply for a review under subsection (9) or (10) or for leave to apply for a review under subsection (10) shall give notice of his application for a review or for leave to apply for a review in such manner and within such period of time as may be directed by rules of court.

(14) *Form of transfer to ordinary court.*—An order made under subsection (1) may be in Form 6.

Time of application: subsection 16(1)

An application may be made at any time after an information has been laid and prior to adjudication. Subsection 20(3) of the J.D.A. allowed an application for transfer even after disposition.

Age of young person: subsection 16(1)

The young person must be alleged to have committed the offence after attaining the age of 14. Some jurisprudence under the J.D.A. took the relevant date for the determination of age to be the date of a transfer hearing; this jurisprudence is not applicable under the Y.O.A.

Types of offence: subsection 16(1)

Subsection 16(1) requires that a young person be alleged to have committed an indictable offence other than one referred to in s. 483 of the *Criminal Code*, after having attained the age of 14. The indictable offences referred to in s. 483 for which a young person cannot be transferred include: theft, obtaining by false pretenses, fraud and possession of stolen property where the subject matter of the offence is worth less then $200, and a number of other less serious offences. A young person cannot be transferred to adult court for a purely summary offence. In R. v. K.J.H. (1980), 5 Man. R. (2d) 14, 54 C.C.C. (2d) 238, [1980] 6 W.W.R. 644 (Q.B.) it was held that there could be a transfer application in regard to a hybrid offence, an offence for which the Crown has an election to proceed summarily or by indictment. This follows from the *Interpretation Act*, para. 27(1)(a), which deems hybrid offences to be indictable unless the Crown elects otherwise, and the decision in K.J.H. should probably be followed under the Y.O.A. (but see to the contrary, R. v. B. (1979), 51 C.C.C. (2d) 251 (B.C.S.C)).

Who may apply?: subsection 16(1)

An application for transfer may be brought by the Attorney General or his agent, but not by a private prosecutor. The application may also be brought by the young person or his counsel, who may, for example, be seeking such advantages of ordinary court as a preliminary inquiry or a jury trial. Subsection 16(1) reverses the effect of such decisions as R. v. Metz, [1977] 5 W.W.R. 374, 36 C.C.C. (2d) 22 (Man. C.A.) and makes clear that a judge may not initiate an application on his own.

"Opportunity to be heard": subsection 16(1)

Subsection 16(1) specifies that the transfer decision shall be made after affording the prosecutor, the young person and the parents of the young person "an opportunity to be heard". The Y.O.A. does not specify what kind of a hearing must be held, but decisions under the J.D.A. suggest that all of those mentioned have a right to be present, to call evidence, to cross-examine witnesses, to examine all of the documents which the court receives and to make submissions before a decision is made. In R. v. F.J.Y. (unreported decision) Ont. Prov. Ct. (Fam. Div.), November 30, 1979, Andrews C.J. Prov. Ct. stated that in regard to a J.D.A., s. 9 application:

> The transfer itself is not strictly of a judicial nature. It is more an administrative proceeding. ... In effect, the Court is not bound to observe the strict rules of trial procedure, but must at least observe the rules of natural justice. ... The Court may receive hearsay evidence at a hearing of this kind, but, of course cannot base its evidence solely upon it. ... The Court, of course must

never base its decision upon secret or undisclosed information or upon matters that may be solely in the personal knowledge of the judge.

See also *R. v. Arbuckle*, [1967] 3 C.C.C. 380, 59 W.W.R. 605, 1 C.R.N.S. 318 (B.C.C.A.); and *R. v. F.* (1974), 20 C.C.C. (2d) 11 (B.C.S.C.). It would seem that the characterization of the transfer process put forth by these decisions under the *J.D.A.*, is applicable to the Y.O.A. For example, s-s. 16(3) requires a pre-disposition report to be considered by a court at a transfer hearing. Such a report will invariably be filled with hearsay comments which would be inadmissible under a strict application of the rules of evidence.

Paragraph 11(3)(b) of the Y.O.A. provides that where a young person is not represented, the judge presiding at a transfer hearing must advise the young person of his right to be represented by counsel, and give him a reasonable opportunity to obtain counsel. Further, under s-ss. 11(4) and (5) if the young person wishes to obtain counsel but is unable for any reason to do so, the judge shall direct that representation be arranged under the auspices of provincial authorities. Given the very serious nature of a transfer application, a young person should generally be represented by counsel and not, for example, merely assisted by an adult under s-s. 11(7).

The transfer decision: subsection 16(1)

The transfer decision is one of the most important with which a youth court is faced. The court must be "of the opinion that in the interest of society and having regard to the needs of the young person", the young person should be proceeded with in ordinary court. The words of s-s. 16(1) of the Y.O.A. are not dissimilar to those found in s-s. 9(1) of the *J.D.A.*, but there is very clearly a major change in emphasis. The phrasing of s-s. 16(1) indicates that the "interest of society" is of primary importance, although the needs of the young person are also to be considered and balanced against the interest of society.

In considering a transfer application, the youth court must take into account all the factors listed in s-s. 16(2), and also consider and apply the general principles articulated in s. 3 of the Y.O.A. It is submitted that if the prosecutor seeks transfer, then the onus is upon the Crown to satisfy the court that transfer is appropriate, and this onus is a heavy one. It is clearly in the interest of society to be protected from criminal activity (para. 3(1)(b)), and this may often suggest that transfer to adult court is appropriate in the case of a serious offence, as longer custodial sentences can be imposed. On the other hand, both society and the young offender have an interest in rehabilitation so as to ensure that the young person commits no further offences. This objective is generally more likely to be achieved if the young person is not transferred, but rather kept in a system where staff, facilities and programs are specifically directed towards the young person's level of development and maturity and where he will be given special opportunities for rehabilitation (para. 3(1)(c)).

If the young person applies for transfer, usually for tactical reasons such as a preference for a jury trial, then it is submitted the onus should be upon him to satisfy the court that this is appropriate. In such circumstances, however, it is submitted that the onus may not be a high one, as the young person should have the right to be able to indicate a desire to waive the special protections afforded in youth court (see paras. 3(1)(e) and 16(2)(c)). The interest of society and needs of the young person for a trial in ordinary court may coincide. It is clear, however, that transfer applications are not simply a matter of consent. The young person does not have "an election", and the court has a duty to form an opinion that a transfer is appropriate.

Effect of transfer: subsection 16(1)

Where a transfer order is made in respect of a charge facing a young person, that charge is then proceeded with in "ordinary court" in accordance with the law ordinarily applicable to an adult charged with the offence. "Ordinary court" is defined in s-s. 2(1) of the Y.O.A. to mean that court "which would have jurisdiction in respect of an offence alleged" but for the Y.O.A. Depending on the offence, the matter could be dealt with by a magistrate, a judge alone or a judge and jury; in most instances the accused young person will have an election in ordinary court as to the method of trial. If a young person is transferred to ordinary court under s. 16 of the Y.O.A. the rules of procedure applicable to adults will apply. As s. 73 of the Y.O.A. repeals s. 441 of the *Criminal Code*, the proceedings will be open to the public; under certain circumstances defined in s. 442 of the *Code*, as amended by s. 74 of the Y.O.A., the public may be excluded in proceedings under the *Code*. A young person convicted in ordinary court faces sentence under the provisions of the *Code*, or other relevant statute, such as the *Narcotics Control Act*. The judge in ordinary court, sentencing a young person who has been transferred will presumably consider age as an important factor, but generally the sentencing principles applicable to adults will apply: see *R. v. Chamberlain* (1974), 22 C.C.C. (2d) 361 (Ont. C.A.). Thus a young person might face a sentence of life imprisonment in an adult facility after transfer, depending of course on the maximum sentence for the offence and the sentence actually imposed. Section 660.1 of the *Criminal Code*, as enacted by s. 75 of the Y.O.A., allows the adult and juvenile correctional authorities to place in a facility for young persons, a young person sentenced to an adult facility after transfer. A judge in ordinary court cannot directly sentence a young person to a facility for young persons, although he would not be precluded from making such a recommendation to correctional authorities.

Considerations by youth court: subsection 16(2)

Subsection 16(2) contains a number of factors which a youth court *must* take into account in considering an application under s-s. 16(1). Under s. 9 of the *J.D.A.*, courts have often considered all or a number of the criteria listed in s-s. 16(2), although not specifically required to do so. See, for example, *Re B. and M.* (1975), 33 C.R.N.S. 362 (Ont. Prov. Ct.); and *Re N.N.C.* (1978), 6 R.F.L. (2d) 254 (Alta. Juv. Ct.).

Seriousness and circumstances of alleged offence: paragraph 16(2)(a)

Under the Y.O.A. the youth court must consider the seriousness of the offence when deciding whether to transfer. Some decisions under the *J.D.A.* seem to suggest that in certain very serious cases like murder, transfer is obligatory. However, as noted in *R. v. Smith* (1975), 28 C.C.C. (2d) 368 (Man. C.A.), by O'Sullivan J.A. in dissent, Parliament has not statutorily required transfer for any particular offence; the seriousness of the offence is merely one factor the court is to consider. The jurisprudence under the *J.D.A.* suggests that in assessing the "seriousness . . . and circumstances" of the offence, the court may consider:

— the alleged offence itself, including maximum sentence for adults;

— the degree of violence, injury or damage to property;

— the effect of the alleged offence on the victim, and society in general;

— general or local crime problems; and

— the apparent attitude of the alleged offender, e.g. callousness.

The court apparently need *not* be satisfied, beyond a reasonable doubt or otherwise, that the offence actually occurred. Rather, it seems that the court is to consider evidence including hearsay evidence, about the alleged offence, and for the purposes of the transfer decision accept the allegations.

"Age, maturity, character . . . background . . . and record": paragraph 16(2)(b)

Paragraph 16(2)(b) makes clear that the youth court is to consider the individual young person, his age, maturity, character and background, and not simply his offence, when deciding a transfer application. Some of this information should be available through a pre-disposition report: see s-s. 16(3). The more amenable the young person seems to the program and facilities of the juvenile system, the greater the reluctance the youth court should be to transfer.

The youth court is required to consider the previous record of criminal convictions; the likelihood of transfers increases with the seriousness and length of the record. Note that if a sufficient period has elapsed since a previous conviction, part or all of the record may have been destroyed under s. 45 of the Y.O.A. and may not be used for any purpose, including transfer applications.

Adequacy of legislative provisions: paragraph 16(2)(c)

Paragraph 16(2)(c) requires a comparison of the adequacy of different legislative provisions to deal with the circumstances of the case, depending on whether transfer occurs. A major consideration in this regard will usually be the limitations placed on maximum duration of two or three years for dispositions made under s. 20 of the Y.O.A.; if it is felt a longer period in the correctional system is required, transfer is necessary. On the other hand, if a youth court judge wishes to ensure that a young person is placed in a juvenile facility, he must deal with the youth under the Y.O.A.

A young person may seek transfer to take advantage of certain provisions of the *Criminal Code*, such as those providing for jury trials.

Availability of treatment or correctional resources: paragraph 16(2)(d)

Paragraph 16(2)(d) requires the youth court judge to assess and compare the resources in the juvenile and adult systems, which would be available to the person upon a finding of guilt. This provision allows the court to recognize that a young person may have exhausted the resources available in the juvenile system. The judge should generally receive testimony or documentary evidence or hear representations about the facilities, particularly in the juvenile system. It is inappropriate for the judge to base his assessment on his own personal knowledge of the resources, without at least directing the parties to this issue and soliciting any evidence or representations they may wish to offer.

The young person and the Crown are both guaranteed the right to make representations and hence participate in the decision-making process. Clearly, counsel can make representations "on behalf of" the young person, but arguably others, such as a social worker, a relative or a parent, may also, with leave of the court, make representations on his behalf. Any of these persons might well be called as part of the defence's case, as well as by the prosecution. Parents are assured of an "opportunity to be heard" in their own right under s-s. 16(1).

Other factors: paragraph 16(2)(f)

Paragraph 16(2)(f) gives the court a broad discretion to consider "any other factors that the court considers relevant." One factor that courts considered under the *J.D.A.* is that a co-accused is an adult. A trial with an adult co-accused can only occur if the case is transferred: see for example, *R. v. Haig* (1970), 1 C.C.C. (2d) 299, [1971] 1 O.R. 75 (C.A.). In some cases under the *J.D.A.*, the courts considered that the defence of insanity might be raised. It was felt that s. 542 of the *Criminal Code* providing for confinement in "strict custody" of those acquitted by reason of insanity did not apply to juvenile proceedings, and hence such cases should be transferred. Under the Y.O.A., ss. 51 and 52, it is clear that the insanity provisions of the *Criminal Code* apply to young persons, and this is no longer a reason for transfer.

Pre-disposition reports: subsection 16(3)

Subsection 16(3) requires that a youth court have a pre-disposition report prepared, and that this report shall be considered by the court in deciding a transfer application. Defined in s-s. 2(1) of the Y.O.A., a pre-disposition report means "a report on the personal and family history and present environment of a young person made in accordance with section 14." Subsection 14(2) outlines the minimum contents of such a report. The scope of such a report is broad, and it may provide a court with valuable information. All of the provisions of s. 14 regarding preparation, disclosure and presentation of pre-disposition reports apply when they are used in transfer proceedings. Further, as provided by s. 15, a youth court judge who hears an application for transfer or examines a pre-disposition report, cannot thereafter conduct a trial in regard to that offence, subject to exceptions in s-s. 15(2) which allows a judge to continue to preside if the parties consent and the judge is satisfied he has not been predisposed by the report.

If appropriate, a youth court judge may also order a medical or psychological report under s. 13 before deciding whether to transfer a young person.

Dispensing with hearing: subsection 16(4)

The Y.O.A. provides an expeditious procedure for dealing with a transfer application by the Crown, where the young person is charged with an offence alleged to have been committed "while the young person was being proceeded against in ordinary court pursuant to an order previously made" under s-s. 16(1), or "serving a sentence as a result of proceedings in ordinary court" after transfer. The youth court may act on the written or oral application of the Crown and need not hold a hearing or consider a pre-disposition report. Subsection 16(4) probably reflects present practice, and facilitates the process of dealing with all charges against a young person in a single court.

There are some qualifications to this expeditious process:

— the subsequent offences must belong to the class of offences to which transfer proceedings apply (indictable and not referred to in s. 483 of the *Code*);

— the application must be made by the Crown; s-s. 16(4) of the Y.O.A. does not apply if the young person is seeking transfer;

— the provision is permissive; the youth court still has the option of holding a hearing or considering a predisposition report.

Reasons: subsection 16(5)

The youth court must give reasons either "where [it] makes an order or refuses to make an order under subsection (1)." These reasons are to form part of the record of the proceedings in the youth court; they need not be written, but if given orally, a record (mechanical recording or stenographer's notes) must be kept to comply with s. 40. The requirement of s-s. 16(5) emphasizes the importance of a formal judicial determination of the issue, and facilitates any review which might occur.

No further application: subsection 16(6)

Where a youth court refuses to grant a transfer application, there can be no further applications. Thus, an applicant for transfer cannot go from judge to judge or reapply to the same judge in an attempt to secure an order. Where the applicant is dissatisfied with the original result, the proper procedure is to apply for review under s-s. 16(9).

Effect of an order: subsections 16(7) and (8)

When a transfer order is made under s-s. 16(1), proceedings are discontinued under the Y.O.A. in youth court and the young person is dealt with thereafter in ordinary court. If the young person is acquitted in ordinary court, proceedings cannot be recommenced in youth court in regard to the charge dealt with in ordinary court. The ordinary court can only deal with the specific offence which is the subject of the transfer order. Other offences alleged to have been committed prior to or at the same time as the offence in respect of which the order is made, remain within the jurisdiction of the youth court, unless a separate transfer order is made. Offences which are alleged to have been committed by the young person, subsequent to a transfer order, must also be the subject of a separate transfer order, or dealt with in youth court. However, in regard to offences alleged to have been committed while a young person was already subject to a transfer order, or serving a sentence after trial in an ordinary court, s-s. 16(4) provides an expeditious process for transfer.

Applications may be made simultaneously in regard to separate offences (multiple charges or counts), and a single hearing held, though each application must formally result in a separate order.

Review of transfer order: subsections 16(9) to (13)

Subsections 16(9) to (13) provide a process for reviewing a youth court's transfer order or its refusal to make such an order. Subsection 16(9) refers to a decision being "reviewed". In R. v. West, [1973] 1 O.R. 211, 20 C.R.N.S. 15, 9 C.C.C. (2d) 369 (C.A.), Gale C.J.O. discussed the meaning of the term "reviewed" in s. 608.1 of the *Criminal Code*, which allows review of decisions regarding judicial interim release. He commented that (at C.C.C. p. 375):

> [T]he review should take the general form of an ordinary appeal and not a hearing *de novo* or one in which either side has the *right* to submit additional material to the Court of Appeal. However, while no such *right* exists, the Court, as in appeals, can grant leave in the usual way and upon the usual grounds to a party to produce new evidence.

These remarks would seem to accurately describe the review process contemplated by s-ss. 16(9) and (10) of the Y.O.A.

The young person and Crown both have a right to seek an initial review under s-s. 16(9); the review is from a youth court to a superior court. The superior court may "in its discretion, confirm or reverse the decision of the youth court." In R. v. Smith (1973), 13 C.C.C. (2d) 374, 6 N.B.R. (2d) 494 (C.A.), Hughes C.J.N.B. stated that, under s. 608.1 of the *Code*, the duty of a court reviewing a judicial interim release (at C.C.C. p. 377):

[W]ould appear to be to examine the record judicially and render the decision which we think "should have been" made by the Judge of first instance giving proper regard to his findings of fact and the inferences he has drawn.

Subsection 16(10) provides that the decision of a superior court reviewing a transfer decision under s. 16(9), may in turn be reviewed by the court of appeal. The review by the court of appeal is by leave only, and is not a matter of right.

"Superior court" and "court of appeal" are defined in s. 2 of the *Criminal Code* (see also s. 761). In most provinces the "superior court" is the Supreme Court. It seems likely that in most jurisdictions the youth court will be a provincial court; if the youth court should be the superior court, then s-s. 16(11) provides there is a right of review only from this court to the court of appeal. There is no further right of review or appeal beyond the court of appeal of the province in which the youth court sits.

Subsections 16(9) and (10) require an application for review or for leave to review to be made within 30 days of the decision appealed. In *R. v. Jean B.*, [1980] 1 S.C.R. 80, 48 C.C.C. (2d) 479n *sub nom. R. v. Boisvert*, it was held that an application was "made" when it was filed and served; there need not be an actual hearing within the time specified. *Jean B.* involved an interpretation of s. 37 of the *J.D.A.*, which governs juvenile delinquency appeals, and would probably govern the interpretation of s-ss. 16(9) and (10) of the Y.O.A.

Subsection 16(12) gives the reviewing court the jurisdiction to extend the time for making an application. Subsection 607(2) of the *Criminal Code* governs extension of time for making an appeal. The jurisprudence under that provision suggests that in deciding whether to grant an extension, the court will consider the length and the circumstances of the delay, any prejudice resulting, and the *bona fides* of the party seeking an extension.

Notice of application: subsection 16(13)

Subsection 16(13) provides that notice of the application for review or for leave to apply for review shall be given in such manner and within such period of time as may be directed by rules of court. This contemplates rules being formulated under s. 67 or 68 of the Y.O.A., such rules may be similar to those made under s. 438 of the *Code*.

Form of transfer order: subsection 16(14)

A transfer order made pursuant to s-s. 16(1) may be in Form 6 of schedule appended to Y.O.A.

SAMPLE FORM

FORM 6
THE YOUNG OFFENDERS ACT
IN THE YOUTH COURT FOR ONTARIO

ORDER OF TRANSFER TO ORDINARY COURT

Canada
Province of Ontario
County of Queens

Whereas David Smith of 25 First Avenue, Anytown, Ontario , being a young person within the meaning of the *Young Offenders Act*, and having attained the age of fourteen years, is alleged, in an information sworn on the 3rd day of June , 19 82 , to have committed the following offence:

robbery: to wit on the second day of June, 1982 did steal two hundred and fifty dollars from The Corner Milk Store, 2 West Street, Anytown, Ontario and at the same time thereat did use threats of violence contrary to section 303 of the *Criminal Code of Canada*;

And whereas that offence is an indictable offence other than one referred to in section 483 of the *Criminal Code*;

And whereas it would appear that, in the interests of society and having regard to the needs of David Smith , he should be proceeded with in ordinary court;

I, Thomas Brown , Judge of the Youth Court in and for the County of Queens , hereby order that David Smith be proceeded with before the court that would, except for the *Young Offenders Act*, have jurisdiction in respect of that offence.

Dated this 24th day of June , 19 82, at Anytown in the Province of Ontario.

"Thomas Brown"
. . . .
A Judge of the Youth Court

Restrictions on publication at transfer hearing: section 17

SECTION 17

17. (1) *Order restricting publication of information presented at transfer hearing.*—Where a youth court hears an application for a transfer to ordinary court under section 16, it shall

(a) where the young person is not represented by counsel or,

(b) on application made by or on behalf of the young person or the prosecutor, where the young person is represented by counsel,

make an order directing that any information respecting the offence presented at the hearing shall not be published in any newspaper or broadcast before such times as

(c) an order for a transfer is refused or set aside on review and the time for all reviews against the decision has expired or all proceedings in respect of any such review have been completed; or

(d) the trial is ended, if the case is transferred to ordinary court.

(2) *Offence.*—Every one who fails to comply with an order made pursuant to subsection (1) is guilty of an offence punishable on summary conviction.

(3) *Meaning of "newspaper".*—In this section, "newspaper" has the meaning set out in section 261 of the *Criminal Code*.

Publicity ban: subsection 17(1)

The publication ban provided for by s-s. 17(1) is intended to protect the young person from exposure to publicity, as do the provisions of ss. 38 and 39 of the Y.O.A. It is also intended to ensure that if a young person is transferred to adult court, he is ensured a fair trial. There may be highly prejudicial information revealed at a transfer hearing, including the circumstances of the alleged offence; it could be most unfair to have this publicly revealed before a trial in ordinary court, especially if there is to be a jury trial. The rationale behind s-s. 17(1) of the Y.O.A. is similar to that which provides for a publicity ban on evidence at a preliminary inquiry in ordinary court (*Criminal Code*, s. 467).

Subsection 17(1) requires that when a transfer application is made, the youth court judge *shall* make an order banning the publication of any information presented at a transfer hearing, in either of the following situations:

— where the young person is *not* represented by counsel, para. 17(1)(a); or

— where the young person is represented by counsel and an application is made by the young person or the prosecutor, para. 17(1)(b).

Subsection 17(1) does not give the youth court judge discretion; thus the only situation in which an order banning publicity will not be made is where the young person is represented by counsel and neither the young person nor prosecutor requests a ban.

The ban under s-s. 17(1) extends until:

— an order for transfer is refused, or the order to transfer is set aside on review, para. 17(1)(c); or

— if an order for transfer is made, until the trial in ordinary court is completed, para. 17(1)(d).

The ban in s-s. 17(1) is in addition to the restrictions on publication of information revealing the identity of young persons charged in proceedings under the Y.O.A., found in s. 38.

"Published or broadcast": subsections 17(1) and (3)

The ban covers information published in any "newspaper," as defined by s. 261 of the *Criminal Code*. This might conceivably preclude the reporting of a decision in a transfer hearing in some law reports, prior to the expiry of the order under paras. 17(1)(c) or (d), although one wonders whether a traditional law report would be held to be a "newspaper". "Broadcasting" is defined in the *Interpretation Act*, R.S.C. 1970, c. I-23, s. 28 to mean "any radio-communication [defined to include radio and television] in which the transmissions are intended for direct reception by the general public."

Offence: subsection 17(2)

Subsection 17(2) provides that the violation of a s-s. 17(1) order is an offence punishable upon summary conviction in ordinary court. If the identity of the young person is revealed it may also constitute an offence under s-s. 38(1).

Proceedings in ordinary court after transfer: sections 73 and 74

Section 73 of the Y.O.A. repeals s. 441 of the *Code*, and hence any proceedings in ordinary court after transfer are presumed to be open and subject to public reporting. Section 74 of the Y.O.A. amends s-s. 442(1) of the *Code*, but still permits all or any members of the public to be excluded from all or part of the proceedings in ordinary court if it is "in the interest of public morals, the maintenance of order or the proper administration of justice."

TRANSFER OF JURISDICTION
(Section 18)

Introduction

As a rule, a youth court judge only has jurisdiction to deal with offences committed within the province in which he sits. Section 18 of the Y.O.A. allows a young person alleged to have committed an offence in one province to enter a guilty plea and receive disposition in another province, provided the Attorney General of the province where the offence was committed consents. Section 18 is designed to allow a young person who commits an offence in one province to be dealt with by the youth court where he resides, and is generally equivalent to the provisions of s-s. 434(3) of the *Code* for adults. Section 18 is intended to allow a young person to be dealt with by a court close to his home, to encourage the involvement of parents, and to allow the benefits of parental supervision and community-based corrections to be utilized whenever possible. Section 18 will also permit outstanding charges against a young person from different jurisdictions to be resolved at one time.

The provisions of s. 18 of the Y.O.A. are in addition to those found in ss. 25 and 26 which provide for the transfer of a young person subject to a disposition under the Act from one province to another.

SECTION 18

18. (1) *Transfer of jurisdiction.*—Notwithstanding subsections 434(1) and (3) of the *Criminal Code*, where a young person is charged with an offence that is alleged to have been committed in one province, he may, if the Attorney General of the province where the offence is alleged to have been committed consents, appear before a youth court of any other province and,

(a) where the young person signifies his consent to plead guilty and pleads guilty to that offence, the court shall, if it is satisfied that the facts support the charge, find the young person guilty of the offence alleged in the information; and

(b) where the young person does not signify his consent to plead guilty and does not plead guilty, or where the court is not satisfied that the facts support the charge, the young person shall, if he was detained in custody prior to his appearance, be returned to custody and dealt with according to law.

(2) *Young person transferred to ordinary court in other province.*—Where a person is charged with an offence that is alleged to have been committed in a province in which he is a young person, that person may be proceeded against in accordance with subsection 434(3) of the *Criminal Code* before the ordinary court in another province in which he is an adult.

(3) *Adult transferred to youth court in other province.*—Where a person is charged with an offence that is alleged to have been committed in a province in which he is an adult, he may be proceeded with in accordance with subsection (1) before a youth court in another province in which he is a young person.

Transfer of jurisdiction: subsection 18(1)

Subsection 18(1) allows a young person charged with an offence alleged to have been committed in one province to appear before a youth court in another province, essentially for the purpose of entering a guilty plea and receiving a disposition. If a young person wishes to have an adjudication after a full trial, this must be held in the province where the offence was committed. (See Salhany, *Canadian Criminal Procedure*, 3rd ed. (1978), pp. 13-26 and 245-46 for a discussion of such matters as jurisdiction over offences committed in more than one province, venue (place of trial), general rules and special statutory provisions regarding jurisdiction.)

Subsection 18(1) should be used to allow a young person to face charges in the province of his residence, or to have outstanding charges from different provinces resolved at one time. A young person can only be dealt with by a youth court outside the province where he is alleged to have committed the offence if the Attorney General of the province where the offence is alleged to have been committed consents.

Section 18 may be utilized if a young person is initially arrested or summonsed to appear in a province outside the one in which the offence is alleged to have been committed. It may also be used if the initial appearance is in the province where the offence is alleged to have been committed, and subsequent appearances occur in another province. For s. 18 to be a basis for jurisdiction, the young person must appear in the youth court outside the province where the offence is alleged to have been committed, signify his consent to plead guilty and plead guilty. The court must then consider the facts of the case, as presented by the prosecutor, and be "satisfied that the facts support the charge." (See s. 19 of the Y.O.A. and the following discussion concerning the duty of a youth court on a guilty plea in regard to satisfying itself that the facts support the charge.) If the youth court is satisfied the facts support the charge, it shall find the young person guilty of the offence and make a disposition under s. 20. The young person will thereafter be dealt with in regard to that disposition by the youth court in the province that made the disposition.

If the young person does not signify his intention to plead guilty and does not plead guilty, or the court is not satisfied that the facts support the charge, para. 18(1)(b) requires the young person to be "dealt with according to law." This will require a youth court in the province where the offence is alleged to have been committed to deal with the charges, and if the young person was detained in custody prior to his appearance in court, will require his return to custody pending resolution of his case. Even in this case, if the young person is found guilty and a disposition imposed, the administration of the disposition may be transferred to another province under ss. 25 and 26 of the Y.O.A.

Transitional transfer provisions: subsections 18(2) and (3)

Subsections 18(2) and (3) of the Y.O.A. deal with situations which may arise prior to the establishment of a uniform national definition of "young person" on April 1, 1985 (see s. 2 of the Y.O.A.). Until that time, a 16 or 17 year old may be a "young person" in one province and an adult in another.

Subsection 18(2) provides that a person alleged to have committed an offence in a province in which he is a young person, may be dealt with in the ordinary (adult) court of another province in which he is an adult (usually the province of his residence); under these circumstances he is not to be dealt with in youth court in the second province. The transfer of jurisdiction in these circumstances will be in accordance with s-s. 434(3) of the *Code*, which is generally similar to s-s. 18(1) of the *Y.O.A.* Under s-s. 434(3) of the *Code*, the Attorney General responsible for the prosecution in the province where the offence is alleged to have been committed must consent to the transfer, and the accused must signify his consent to plead guilty and must plead guilty; however, the judge in ordinary court receiving the plea has no special obligation to satisfy himself that the facts support the charge.

Under s-s. 18(3), where a person is charged with an offence that is alleged to have been committed in a province in which he is an adult, he may be proceeded with in accordance with s-s. 18(1) before a youth court in another province in which he is a young person (usually the province of his residence). Subsection 434(3) of the *Code* has no application in these circumstances and the accused is not to be dealt with in ordinary court in the second province.

ADJUDICATION
(Section 19)

Introduction

Sections 12 and 19 of the Y.O.A. impose quite significant obligations on a youth court in regard to the acceptance of a plea and the rendering of an adjudication. Subsection 12(3) requires that before accepting a plea from a young person who is not represented, the court must explain to him that he may plead guilty or not guilty, and must satisfy itself that the young person understands the charge against him; if the court is not satisfied that the young person understands the charge, s-s. 12(4) requires it to enter a plea of not guilty and proceed with a trial. Section 19 requires that in all cases, regardless of whether or not the young person is represented by counsel, before accepting a guilty plea, the court must be "satisfied that the facts support the charge"; if the court is not satisfied, s-s. 19(2) requires the court to enter a plea of not guilty and proceed with a trial. Subsection 19(2) also provides for conducting a trial when a young person pleads not guilty.

In practice under the J.D.A., some juvenile court judges have been following the procedures outlined in ss. 12 and 19 of the Y.O.A. Under these sections a young person is guaranteed the protection which is only given to an adult at the discretion of a judge (see *Adgey v. The Queen*, [1975] 2 S.C.R. 426, 23 C.R.N.S. 298, 13 C.C.C. (2d) 177, 39 D.L.R. (3d) 553). The purpose of ss. 12 and 19 is not to discourage guilty pleas or to require unnecessary trials, but rather to ensure that a young person understands the charges he faces, and that if a conviction occurs, it is warranted in the circumstances. It is felt that the limited financial resources and the level of intellectual and emotional development of many young persons require these special protections.

SECTION 19

19. (1) *Where young person pleads guilty.*—Where a young person pleads guilty to an offence charged against him and the

youth court is satisfied that the facts support the charge, the court shall find the young person guilty of the offence.

(2) *Where young person pleads not guilty.*—Where a young person pleads not guilty to an offence charged against him, or where a young person pleads guilty but the youth court is not satisfied that the facts support the charge, the court shall proceed with the trial and shall, after considering the matter, find the young person guilty or not guilty or make an order dismissing the charge, as the case may be.

Where young person pleads guilty: subsections 19(1) and (2)

Subsection 19(1) provides that if a young person pleads guilty to an offence, the court has an obligation to conduct an inquiry to satisfy itself that the facts support the charge. This obligation exists regardless of whether the young person is represented by counsel. If the court is "satisfied that the facts support the charge", it shall find the young person guilty of the offence. Subsection 19(2) provides that if the court is not satisfied the facts support the charge, it shall proceed with the trial, receive evidence, consider the matter, and render an adjudication. In practice, if the judge is not satisfied that the facts support the charge, the prosecutor may choose to stay the proceedings (*Criminal Code*, s. 732.1) or may decide to call no evidence, in which case a dismissal will result; thus it is not necessary that there be a full trial.

Section 19 does not specify the nature of the inquiry which a youth court must conduct to "satisfy" itself that the facts support the charge. Citing *R. v. Anderson* (1912), 5 W.W.R. 1052, 22 C.C.C. 455, 16 D.L.R. 203, 7 Alta. L.R. 102 (C.A.), the *Encyclopedia of Words and Phrases: Legal Maxims (Canada)*, 3rd ed. (1979), Vol. 4, p. 121, defines "satisfy" to mean: "to free from uncertainty, doubt or anxiety, to set at rest the mind." This suggests a judge should have a high level of assurance that the facts support the charge; if the judge has real doubt or uncertainty about the matter, he should proceed under s-s. 19(2).

In *Adgey v. The Queen*, [1975] 2 S.C.R. 426, 23 C.R.N.S. 298, 13 C.C.C. (2d) 177, 39 D.L.R. (3d) 553, the majority of the Supreme Court of Canada rejected the view that a judge has an obligation to conduct an inquiry after a guilty plea has been entered; this continues to be the law applicable in adult proceedings. However, in proceedings under the Y.O.A., s. 19 does impose such an obligation, and the remarks of Laskin J. (as he then was), in dissent in *Adgey*, shed some light on the nature of the inquiry required under the Y.O.A. Laskin J. stated (S.C.R. at pp. 444-45):

> No doubt, a trial judge must have regard to the factual accuracy of a plea of guilty ... If those advanced by the Crown do not sustain the charge and conviction, then the guilty plea must be struck out ... I readily agree, moreover, that if the accused gives a version of the facts, after a narration by the Crown ... the trial judge would in effect be holding a trial after a plea of guilty if he was bound to assess the respective versions as to their credibility and weight. However, either the narration by the Crown or by the accused or by both may raise a question not only as to the factual accuracy of the plea but as well as to the propriety of the plea of guilty in terms of the accused's understanding and appreciation of it and its unequivocal character. ...
>
> The duty of the Court respecting an inquiry as to the "legality" (if I may make such a compendious reference) of the plea of guilty, must, it seems to me be complemented by a duty of the Crown to adduce facts which, taken to be true, support the charge and conviction. ... It would, in my view, be unsatisfactory to leave to the discretion of the Crown whether or not to adduce facts supportive of the charge and conviction. The trial judge could undoubtedly call for them, but the issue at that stage ought not to involve him in anything more than being satisfied that what is alleged, taking it to be true, completes the elements of a conviction of a plea of guilty ...

The remarks of Laskin J. in *Adgey* and the provisions of ss. 12 and 19 of the Y.O.A. suggest the following procedure upon receipt of a plea of guilty. The prosecutor should be asked to state the facts upon which the charge rests. The young person, or counsel if he has one, should be asked if he agrees with these facts, or wishes to add any facts, or provide additional facts or an alternative interpretation of the facts. The judge should then consider whether all of the facts alleged, if proven true, contain all of the elements of the offence necessary in law to sustain a conviction, or whether they reveal an obvious defence; if the judge is satisfied that all the elements are present and no obvious defence appears to exist, he should find the young person guilty. If there is any material discrepancy in the version of the facts presented by the Crown and that presented by the accused, the judge should proceed with the trial in accordance with s-s. 19(2). Such a discrepancy may in itself be reason for not being satisfied the facts support the charge, or may indicate a lack of understanding of the charge, in which case s-s. 12(4) requires the court to proceed with the trial.

If the judge orders that the case proceed to trial, it would usually be desirable to adjourn the case before proceeding to hear the evidence. The young person should have an opportunity to prepare for trial, and in particular, if not represented, to obtain counsel. Where a trial is required by the court under s-s. 19(2) because the court is not satisfied that the facts support the charge (s-s. 19(1)), or not satisfied that a young person understands the charge (s-s. 12(4)), the case should be conducted in the same manner as a trial resulting from a not guilty plea; there is the normal obligation on the prosecution to prove all elements of its case, with the young person having the right to make a full answer and defence.

Where young person pleads not guilty: subsection 19(2)

Where a young person enters a plea of not guilty, the court shall "proceed with the trial," and after "considering the matter," render an adjudication as required by s-s. 19(2). It is clear that the youth court must "proceed with the trial" in accordance with the general principles, practices and procedures which are applicable in adult court, except as they are modified by the Y.O.A. This procedure is established by the Declaration of Principle, and in particular para. 3(1)(e) guaranteeing the rights and freedoms of young persons. This is also made clear by ss. 51 and 52 of the Y.O.A., which provide that proceedings under the Y.O.A. are governed by the *Criminal Code*, though they are generally to be conducted as proceedings for summary conviction offences.

Thus, when a youth court proceeds with the trial, it must apply the principles and rules applicable in adult proceedings. Some examples are as follows:

— the burden of proof rests upon the prosecution, unless otherwise provided for by law; for example, in regard to the defence of insanity, s-s. 16(4) of the *Code* places the burden of proving insanity upon the young person;

— the standard of proof is the normal criminal standard of proof beyond a reasonable doubt, unless otherwise provided for by law, for example, when the defence of insanity is raised, it must only be established on the balance of probabilities;

— the laws of evidence are applicable as in adult proceedings, except as modified by the Y.O.A., ss. 56 to 63;

— the substantive features of the criminal law and *Criminal Code*, including all of the defences available in adult proceedings are applicable, such as insanity at the time of the offence (s. 16 of the *Code*), and the defence of *res judicata* (*Kienapple v. The Queen*, [1975] 1 S.C.R. 729, 44 D.L.R. (3d) 351, 15 C.C.C. (2d) 524, 26 C.R.N.S. 1, 1 N.R. 322);

— the provisions of the *Code* applicable to summary conviction offences, except as modified by the Y.O.A.; for example the issue of fitness to stand trial on account of insanity may be raised pursuant to the *Code*, s. 543, modified by s. 13 of the Y.O.A.;

— the only parties to the proceedings are the prosecutor and the young person, and each has a right to cross-examine witnesses called by the other, subject to s-s. 13(5) of the Y.O.A. dealing with cross-examination concerning a medical or psychological report;

— the right of the accused to make a full answer and defence, and also his privilege against self-incrimination.

For a further consideration of the procedures applicable in youth court, see discussion of s. 52 below.

DISPOSITIONS
(Sections 20 to 26)

Introduction

The *Young Offenders Act* takes a different approach to disposition from that taken in the *Juvenile Delinquents Act*. The *J.D.A.* focusses on the treatment and rehabilitation of the young person, relying heavily on a social welfare approach. Section 38 of the *J.D.A.* directs that "as far as practicable every juvenile delinquent shall be treated, not as a criminal, but as a misdirected and misguided child, and one needing aid, encouragement, help and assistance." Considerations of punishment and deterrence are not central to the *J.D.A.*, nor is the protection of the public.

The Y.O.A. changes this emphasis on treatment. One of the fundamental aims of the Y.O.A. is to recognize the special needs and circumstances of young persons which necessarily call for continued emphasis on treatment and rehabilitation. The Act, however, balances the young person's needs with the public's interest and places much more emphasis on public protection than the *J.D.A.*

The principles of responsibility, accountability and the protection of society are fundamental to the Y.O.A.'s philosophy on disposition. Paragraph 3(1)(a) states that young persons are not to be held as accountable as adults, but "young persons who commit offences should nonetheless bear responsibility for their contraventions." The new approach includes a right to "the least possible interference with freedom that is consistent with the protection of society, having regard to the needs of young persons and the interests of their families" (para. 3(1)(f)). The recognition in para. 3(1)(b) that society must "be afforded the necessary protection from illegal behaviour" ensures that the interest of society is considered.

Despite its adherence to these principles, the Y.O.A. recognizes the continued need of young persons for treatment and rehabilitation. Paragraph 3(1)(c) allows that: "... because of their state of dependency and level of development and maturity, [young persons] also have special needs and require guidance and assistance." The guarantee of a right to the least possible interference with freedom consistent with the protection of society in para. 3(1)(f) is meant to safeguard against overuse of custodial and other restrictive measures as well as treatment facilities and programs. This is an important right, especially in view of the wide range of dispositions available under the Y.O.A.

The Y.O.A. also recognizes the fact that parents are responsible for their children. Its provisions seek to acknowledge, support and maintain the relationship between parent and child as much as possible: para. 3(1)(h) states that "young persons should be removed from parental supervision either partly or entirely only when measures that provide for continuing parental supervision are inappropriate."

Along with a distinct shift in philosophy, the Y.O.A. introduces several changes from the provisions of the J.D.A. All dispositions under the Y.O.A. must be of fixed duration. This is not the case under the J.D.A. which permits indefinite committal to training school and other indeterminate dispositions, adjournments for indefinite periods, and the returning of juveniles to court for dispositional review at any time, up to the age of 21. Sections 28 to 32 of the Y.O.A. make clear that a process of judicial review is available from a youth court disposition. The Y.O.A. removes some of the broad judicial discretion in the area of disposition that exists under the J.D.A., while seeking to direct the exercise of judicial discretion in accordance with the various principles set out in s. 3 of the Y.O.A., the Declaration of Principle. The Y.O.A. also clarifies various issues which had arisen under the J.D.A.; for example, under the J.D.A. there was doubt whether a juvenile could receive an absolute discharge. Under the Y.O.A., the power to grant absolute discharges has been expressly conveyed to youth court judges.

SECTION 20

20. (1) *Dispositions that may be made.*—Where a youth court finds a young person guilty of an offence, it shall consider any pre-disposition report required by the court, any representations made by the parties to the proceedings or their counsel or agents and by the parents of the young person and any other relevant information before the court, and the court shall then make any

one of the following dispositions, or any number thereof that are not inconsistent with each other:

(a) by order direct that the young person be discharged absolutely, if the court considers it to be in the best interests of the young person and not contrary to the public interest;

(b) impose on the young person a fine not exceeding one thousand dollars to be paid at such time and on such terms as the court may fix;

(c) order the young person to pay to any other person at such time and on such terms as the court may fix an amount by way of compensation for loss of or damage to property, for loss of income or support or for special damages for personal injury arising from the commission of the offence where the value thereof is readily ascertainable, but no order shall be made for general damages;

(d) order the young person to make restitution to any other person of any property obtained by the young person as a result of the commission of the offence within such time as the court may fix, if the property is owned by the other person or was, at the time of the offence, in his lawful possession;

(e) if any property obtained as a result of the commission of the offence has been sold to an innocent purchaser, where restitution of the property to its owner or any other person has been made or ordered, order the young person to pay the purchaser, at such time and on such terms as the court may fix, an amount not exceeding the amount paid by the purchaser for the property;

(f) subject to section 21, order the young person to compensate any person in kind or by way of personal services at such time and on such terms as the court may fix for any loss, damage or injury suffered by that person in respect of which an order may be made under paragraph (c) or (e);

(g) subject to section 21, order the young person to perform a community service at such time and on such terms as the court may fix;

(h) make any order of prohibition, seizure or forfeiture that may be imposed under any Act of Parliament or any regulation made thereunder where an accused is found guilty or convicted of that offence;

(i) subject to section 22, by order direct that the young person be detained for treatment, subject to such conditions as the court considers appropriate, in a hospital or other place where treatment is available, where a report has been made in respect of the young person pursuant to subsection 13(1) that recommends that the young person undergo treatment for a condition referred in paragraph 13(1)(e);

(j) place the young person on probation in accordance with section 23 for a specified period not exceeding two years;

(k) subject to section 24, commit the young person to custody, to be served continuously or intermittently, for a specified period not exceeding

(i) two years from the date of committal, or

(ii) where the young person is found guilty of an offence for which the punishment provided by the *Criminal Code* or any other Act of Parliament is imprisonment for life, three years from the date of committal; and

(l) impose on the young person such other reasonable and ancillary conditions as it deems advisable and in the best interest of the young person and the public.

(2) *Coming into force of disposition.*—A disposition made under this section shall come into force on the date on which it is made or on such later date as the youth court specifies therein.

(3) *Duration of disposition.*—No disposition made under this section, except an order made under paragraph (1)(h) or (k), shall continue in force for more than two years and, where the youth court makes more than one disposition at the same time in respect of the same offence, the combined duration of the dispositions, except in respect of an order made under paragraph (1)(h) or (k), shall not exceed two years.

(4) *Combined duration of dispositions.*—Where more than one disposition is made under this section in respect of a young person with respect to different offences, the continuous combined duration of those dispositions shall not exceed three years.

(5) *Disposition continues when adult.*—A disposition made under this section shall continue in effect, in accordance with the terms thereof, after the young person against whom it is made becomes an adult.

(6) *Reasons for the disposition.*—Where a youth court makes a disposition under this section, it shall state its reasons therefor in the record of the case and shall

(a) provide or cause to be provided a copy of the disposition, and

(b) on request, provide or cause to be provided a transcript or copy of the reasons for the disposition to the young person in respect of whom the disposition was made, his counsel, his parents, the provincial director, where the provincial director has an interest in the disposition, the prosecutor and, in the case of a custodial disposition made under paragraph (1)(k), the review board, if any has been established or designated.

(7) *Limitation on punishment.*—No disposition shall be made in respect of a young person under this section that results in a punishment that is greater than the maximum punishment that would be applicable to an adult who has committed the same offence.

(8) *Application of Part XX of Criminal Code.*—Part XX of the *Criminal Code* does not apply in respect of proceedings under this Act except for sections 683, 685 and 686 and subsections 655(2) to (5) and 662.1(2), which provisions apply with such modifications as the circumstances require.

(9) *Section 722 of Criminal Code does not apply.*—Section 722 of the *Criminal Code* does not apply in respect of proceedings under this Act.

(10) *Forms.*—A disposition made under this section, other than a probation order, may be in Form 7.

(11) *Form of probation order.*—A probation order made under this section may be in Form 8 and the youth court shall specify in the order the period for which it is to remain in force.

SECTION 21

21. (1) *Where a fine or other payment is ordered.*—The youth court shall, in imposing a fine on a young person under paragraph 20(1)(b) or in making an order against the young person under paragraph 20(1)(c) or (e), have regard to the present and future means of the young person to pay.

(2) *Fine option program.*—A young person against whom a fine is imposed under paragraph 20(1)(b) may discharge the fine in whole or in part by earning credits for work performed in a program established for that purpose

(a) by the Lieutenant Governor in Council of the province in which the fine was imposed; or

(b) by the Lieutenant Governor in Council of the province in which the young person resides, where an appropriate agreement is in effect between the government of that province and the government of the province in which the fine was imposed.

(3) *Rates, crediting and other matters.*—A program referred to in subsection (2) shall determine the rate at which credits are earned and may provide for the manner of crediting any amounts earned against the fine and any other matters necessary for or incidental to carrying out the program.

(4) *Representations respecting orders under paras. 20(1)(c) to (f).*—In considering whether to make an order under paragraphs 20(1)(c) to (f), the youth court may consider any representations made by the person who would be compensated or to whom restitution or payment would be made.

(5) *Notice of orders under paras. 20(1)(c) to (f).*—Where the youth court makes an order under paragraphs 20(1)(c) to (f), it shall cause notice of the terms of the order to be given to the person who is to be compensated or to whom restitution or payment is to be made.

(6) *Consent of person to be compensated.*—No order may be made under paragraph 20(1)(f) unless the youth court has secured the consent of the person to be compensated.

(7) *Order for compensation or community service.*—No order may be made under paragraph 20(1)(f) or (g) unless the youth court

(a) is satisfied that the young person against whom the order is made is a suitable candidate for such an order; and

(b) is satisfied that the order does not interfere with the normal hours of work or education of the young person.

(8) *Duration of order for service.*—No order may be made under paragraph 20(1)(f) or (g) to perform personal or community services unless such services can be completed in two hundred and forty hours or less and within twelve months of the date of the order.

(9) *Agreement to performance of community service.*—No order may be made under paragraph 20(1)(g) unless the youth court is satisfied that the person or organization for whom the community service is to be performed has agreed to its performance.

SECTION 22

22. (1) *Consent for treatment order.*—No order may be made under paragraph 20(1)(i) unless the youth court has secured the

consent of the young person, the parents of the young person and the hospital or other place where the young person is to be detained for treatment.

(2) *Where consent of parent dispensed with.*—The youth court may dispense with the consent of a parent required under subsection (1) if it appears that the parent is not available or if the parent is not, in the opinion of the court, taking an active interest in the proceedings.

Dispositional hearing: subsection 20(1)

After adjudication and a finding of guilt, the youth court must make a disposition. The dispositions available are set out in s-s. 20(1). In arriving at a disposition, a judge must consider a pre-disposition report, before making a custodial order, and may order and consider a pre-disposition report before making any other disposition. A medical or psychological report may also be prepared pursuant to s. 13 of the Y.O.A. for use at disposition.

The youth court must consider any representations made by the parties, counsel for the parties or the young person's parents. Additionally, the youth court may consider any other relevant information before the court, for example, representations made by the victim. In making representations to the court, the parties have the right to call witnesses and to file documents. The general rule that evidence as to sentence need not be proved strictly according to the rules of evidence applies to disposition proceedings in youth court.

In *R. v. McGrath*, [1962] S.C.R. 739, 38 C.R. 115, 39 W.W.R. 304, 133 C.C.C. 57, the Supreme Court of Canada approved the following statement of accepted practice before imposing a sentence (from *Crankshaw's Criminal Code of Canada*, 7th ed., at p. 912):

"After conviction, accurate information should be given as to the general character and other material circumstances of the prisoner even though such information it not available in the form of evidence proper, and such information when given can rightly be taken into consideration by the judge in determining the quantum of punishment, unless it is challenged and contradicted by or on behalf of the prisoner, in which case the judge should either direct proper proof to be given or should ignore the information."

As the rules of evidence are relaxed during the disposition stage, there is a tendency for proceedings to become more informal than during the adjudication stage. It is essential to remember that the proceedings continue to be a judicial process, however, and as such the usual safeguards guaranteed to the accused continue to apply. As is the case before adjudication, the young person has a right to be represented during the dispositional stage of the hearing: see s. 11 of the Y.O.A. Any statements made about the young person should be made in his presence so that he (or his counsel) has the opportunity of contradicting such statements: see *R. v. Martin*, [1947] 2 D.L.R. 529, 3 C.R. 64, 19 M.P.R. 310, 87 C.C.C. 209 (N.B.C.A.); and *R. v. Benson and Stevenson* (1951), 100 C.C.C. 247, 13 C.R. 1, 3 W.W.R. 29 (B.C.C.A.).

The judge's role at disposition must continue to be one of impartial arbitor. The judge must weigh the interests of society, but must also ensure that the proceedings are conducted in a manner consistent with the needs and rights of the young person. The judge may participate in the proceedings to a certain extent, but even at disposition, the judge should ensure that he does not "descend into the arena." Improper intervention by the judge in the dispositional proceedings may be confusing or embarrassing to the parties or their counsel.

In *R. v. Donovan* (1947), 4 C.R. 212 at p. 219, 8 C.C.C. 86, 20 M.P.R. 44 (N.B.C.A.) Richards J.A. remarked that while there was not an absolute bar to judicial questioning at the time of disposition: "Such questioning . . . ought rarely to be done, but the door should not be closed entirely. Some discretion should be left to the trial Judge." To a similar effect, see *R. v. Edwards* (1907), 13 C.C.C. 202, 17 Man. R. 288 (C.A.). The Canadian Association of Provincial Court Judges, *Canadian Sentencing Handbook* (1982), provides the following caution in regard to a judge's role at sentencing (p. 9):

> In seeking information the judge must find a balance between the need for information and the demands of fairness and natural justice . . .

However, in *R. v. Morelli* (1977), 37 C.C.C. (2d) 392 at p. 395 (Ont. Prov. Ct.), August Prov.Ct.J. took a broader view:

> After a finding of guilt or conviction a Judge has the undoubted right to inquire into any matter on which he desires information

before sentence and to call such evidence that is necessary for this purpose without the consent of either party but, this information should be given in open Court . . .

If the judge begins to question the young person directly, for example, about his motivation for committing an offence, query whether this might under certain circumstances be construed as a violation of the right of the young person not to incriminate himself, as guaranteed by para. 11(c) of the *Charter of Rights*.

The dispositions available under s-s. 20(1) are available alone or in combination, provided they are not inconsistent with each other. All dispositions are subject to the provisions of s-ss. 20(3) and (4) which limit the duration of disposition.

Absolute discharge: paragraph 20(1)(a)

Paragraph 20(1)(a) of the *Young Offenders Act* provides that a young person may be granted an absolute discharge similar in effect to that which an adult might receive in ordinary court pursuant to s. 662.1 of the *Criminal Code*. Under the *Juvenile Delinquents* Act there was conflicting authority about the applicability of these provisions to juvenile proceedings: see *R. v. K.* (1980), 55 C.C.C. (2d) 324, [1980] 6 W.W.R. 355 *sub nom. R. v. Kloschinsky* (Alta. Q.B.) and *contra, R. v. Stimpson*, [1974] 3 W.W.R. 598, 26 C.R.N.S. 130, 17 C.C.C. (2d) 181 *sub nom. R. v. S.* (Man. Prov.Ct.). The enactment of para. 20(1)(a) of the Y.O.A. resolves this uncertainty. An absolute discharge may be ordered "if the court considers it to be in the best interests of the young person and not contrary to the public interest." Unlike the *Criminal Code*, the Y.O.A. does not provide for conditional discharge as a similar effect is achieved by ss. 36 and 45 of the Y.O.A., governing the effect of dispositions.

The conditions to be satisfied before a discharge is ordered are the same as those required by s. 662.1 of the *Criminal Code*. The interpretation of the phrase "best interests of the accused and not contrary to the public interest" was discussed in *R. v. Fallofield* (1973), 22 C.R.N.S. 342, 13 C.C.C. (2d) 450, [1973] 6 W.W.R. 472 (B.C.C.A.). The first condition, that a discharge be in the best interests of the accused was said (at C.R.N.S. p. 347) to:

... presuppose that the accused is a person of good character, without previous conviction, that it is not necessary to enter a conviction against him in order to deter him from future offences or to rehabilitate him, and that the entry of a conviction against him may have significant adverse repercussions.

The British Columbia Court of Appeal also explained that, while the public interest "must be given due weight, [it] does not preclude the judicious use of the discharge provisions" (at p. 347). For a similar statement of the criteria for granting a discharge, see R. v. Sanchez-Pino (1973), 11 C.C.C. (2d) 53, [1973] 2 O.R. 314, 22 C.R.N.S. 50 (C.A.). Discharges will be granted where it is felt that the court process has served its purpose through the trial stage alone and no further intervention by way of disposition is necessary or desirable. It is important to note that discharges are not to be applied routinely to any criminal offence: R. v. Derkson (1972), 20 C.R.N.S. 129, 9 C.C.C. (2d) 97 (B.C. Prov. Ct.). Evidence that an accused has received a previous discharge may be led at disposition to satisfy the judge that a further discharge would not be in the interest of the accused and would be contrary to the public interest: see R. v. Tan, [1975] 2 W.W.R. 747, 22 C.C.C (2d) 184 (B.C.C.A.).

Fine: paragraph 20(1)(b) and subsections 21(1) to (3)

Paragraph 20(1)(b) permits the imposition of a fine of up to $1,000, "to be paid at such time and on such terms as the court may fix." The limit under the J.D.A. is $25; the increased maximum under the Y.O.A. reflects inflation and the increased earning capabilities of some young persons, particularly 16 and 17 year olds. To prevent the imposition of an excessively large fine or an undue burden on the young person, the Act specifically provides in s-s. 21(1) that in imposing a fine the youth court shall "have regard to the present and future means of the young person to pay." Moreover, there is no provision for the young person to be taken into custody upon default of payment of a fine, unless so ordered by the youth court following a review of the disposition. Subsections 20(8) and (9) of the Y.O.A. stipulate that ss. 646 and 722 of the Criminal Code, providing imprisonment for failure to pay a fine, do not apply to a young person. Instead, upon default, a young person will be subject to the judicial review of disposition provisions of s. 33 of the Y.O.A.; at a review hearing a youth court might impose a custodial disposition for a failure to pay a fine, if there is wilful failure or refusal to pay the fine.

Subsection 21(2) allows a provincial government to establish a program under which a young person may perform some type of work rather than pay a fine. If a province establishes such a program, the young person has the option of participating or making monetary payment. A fine option program will help alleviate any financial distress which could result if a young person is obliged to raise a sum of money to pay a fine. Subsection 21(3) provides that the actual rate of crediting the work performed and any other matters necessary for or incidental to the program will be determined by the province.

Normally, a fine option program may be used by a young person if such a program is established in the province in which the fine was imposed. Paragraph 21(2)(b) also allows a young person to benefit from such a program if the youth resides in a province other than the one in which the fine was imposed. There must be a program in the province of the young person's residence and an agreement in effect between the government of the province in which the young person resides and the government of the province where the fine was imposed.

A fine option program may be established by the Lieutenant Governor in Council (provincial Cabinet) and does not require provincial legislation.

Compensation: paragraph 20(1)(c) and subsections 21(1), (4) and (5)

The youth court's dispositional alternatives include the power to make an order for compensation. Compensation orders are consistent with the Y.O.A.'s principles of responsibility and accountability. Their inclusion in the Act also reflects the growing concern in the criminal justice system for victims of crime. In R. v. Zelensky, [1978] 2 S.C.R. 940, [1978] 3 W.W.R. 693, 2 C.R. (3d) 107, 21 N.R. 372, 41 C.C.C. (2d) 97, 86 D.L.R. (3d) 179, the Supreme Court of Canada described compensation as a valid objective of sentencing, concluding that it was within the federal Parliament's jurisdiction over criminal law and procedure to enact legislation dealing with compensation.

Orders pursuant to para. 20(1)(c) may be made to cover a broad range of losses including compensation for the following: loss of or damage to property, for example, a broken window. Loss of income or support or "special damages" for personal injury arising from the commission of an offence, for example, medical expenses and medication for an elderly lady whose leg was broken during a robbery. Compensation orders are suitable in cases where the value of the loss is readily ascertainable. According to the Supreme Court in *Zelensky*: "[It is not] a function of the criminal court to force agreement to enable it to make an order for compensation" (at S.C.R. p. 961). Thus if the amount is in dispute or if the amount is not ascertainable, a compensation order should not be made under para. 20(1)(c).

A youth court may not make an order for "general damages", as this is an administratively difficult assessment better performed by the civil courts. Watson, Borins and Williams define general damages as items for which there is "no precise measure", including present, past and future pain and suffering and loss of enjoyment of life and future economic loss. Special damages "consist of the out-of-pocket expenses and other actual loss which the plaintiff [victim] has incurred in consequence of his injuries to the date his damages are assessed at trial. They include such items as medical and hospital expenses, ambulance fees and lost wages." (*Canadian Civil Procedure: Cases and Materials*, p. 6-53).

The youth court shall "have regard to the present and future means of the young person to pay" before making a compensation order. This provision is to prevent the imposition of an order that is too onerous for the young person. Note also that a young person without money may still compensate the victim by performing personal service pursuant to para. 20(1)(f). Subsection 21(4) provides that the youth court may consider representations made by the person who would be compensated under para. 20(1)(c) in deciding whether to make such an order. If the youth court decides to order compensation, s-s. 21(5) states that the youth court "shall cause notice of the terms of the order to be given to the person who is to be compensated."

Restitution: paragraph 20(1)(d) and subsections 21(4) and (5)

The Y.O.A. also provides for restitution orders. Restitution is the return of a specific piece of stolen property to the rightful owner or the person who was in lawful possession at the time the offence was committed. The Act provides for restitution "to any other person of any property obtained by the young person as a result of the commission of the offence." Restitution orders will likely be made in cases of theft or possession of stolen goods. If the property has been damaged during the commission of the offence, compensation may be ordered pursuant to para. 20(1)(c) in addition to restitution.

In considering whether to make a restitution order, the court may consider representations by the person to whom restitution would be made according to s-s. 21(4). Notice of the terms of a restitution order must be given under s-s. 21(5) to the person receiving restitution.

Compensation of innocent purchaser: paragraph 20(1)(e) and subsections 21(1), (4) and (5)

Sometimes property obtained as a result of the commission of an offence may be sold to an innocent purchaser. Generally, the common law provides that the true owner has a civil right to recover the stolen property, even after sale to an innocent purchaser. Although the right of the true owner under Quebec law differs somewhat from the situation in the common law provinces, in many situations the true owner in Quebec has the same right. If property is returned to its true owner after the commission of an offence by a young person, a youth court may order compensation pursuant to para. 20(1)(e) for any innocent purchaser who thereby suffers loss. The youth court may order the young person to pay the purchaser "an amount not exceeding the amount paid by the purchaser for the property."

The same provisions apply in the case of compensation for innocent purchasers as with other forms of compensation and restitution. The youth court must have regard to "the present and future means of the young person to pay," pursuant to s-s. 21(1). Representations by the innocent purchaser may be considered by a youth court judge under s-s. 21(4), and, if an order is made, the purchaser is to receive notice of its terms, in accordance with s-s. 21(5).

Personal services: paragraph 20(1)(f) and subsections 21(4) to (8)

An order may be made under para. 20(1)(f) for the young person to compensate "any person in kind or by way of personal services" for any losses suffered in respect of which an order for compensation may be made for a victim of crime or an innocent purchaser under para. 20(1)(c) or (e). An order under para. 20(1)(f) would be appropriate where the young person has little or no money and his earning capacity is low, for example, if he is attending school or if he is unemployed. In fact, s-s. 21(7) qualifies the availability of such an order for compensation by specifying that the order must not interfere with the normal hours of work or education of the young person. Subsection 21(7) also requires the youth court to satisfy itself that the young person is a suitable candidate for an order under para. 20(1)(f). As an order for compensation by way of personal services will require a degree of personal involvement, it would be preferable for the young person to display some willingness to perform personal services, although his consent to such a disposition is not required. An example of an order under para. 20(1)(f) might require a young person who vandalised a house to do some gardening work for the home owner. To ensure that one who has suffered loss is not unwillingly forced into contact with the young offender, s-s. 21(6) adds an important condition: no order may be made under para. 20(1)(f) "unless the youth court has secured the consent of the person to be compensated." As with other forms of compensation and restitution, the person to be compensated may make representations to the youth court pursuant to s-s. 21(4) when the court is considering an order under para. 20(1)(f). If an order is made, s-s. 21(5) requires that notice of its terms are to be given to the person who is to be compensated. Personal service orders must be completed within 12 months of the date of the order and a maximum of 240 hours of work may be assigned; s-s. 32(9) allows a judicial extension of a further 12 months to complete the order.

Community service order: paragraph 20(1)(g) and subsections 21(7) to (9)

An order may be made pursuant to para. 20(1)(g) requiring the young person to perform community service. Community service orders are appropriate where there is no private victim or the victim does not wish to be directly compensated. As stated in a 1979 *Report on the State of Community Service Orders in the Provincial Court (Family Division), Province of Ontario*, the purpose is "to sensitize an offender to the aftermath of an event by emphasizing the relationship between an offence and the ethical responsibilty imposed by society to make reparation." Community service orders have been used for other offences such as public mischief, breaking and entering, arson and wilful damage, all of which involve damage to property. They might also be appropriate for other offences such as causing a disturbance. Examples of such orders would include volunteer work for a community group, visits to a senior citizens' home or perhaps cleaning up a park area.

Paragraph 21(7)(a) provides that the youth court must be satisfied that the young person is "a suitable candidate" for a community service order. The determination of criteria will be up to the youth court but, in view of the direct personal involvement and the degree of cooperation required, a certain amount of willingness on the part of the young person would be preferable. There may, however, be situations where the court will deem it appropriate to compel a young person to perform such a disposition, despite his lack of consent or willingness. Subsection 21(9) recognizes that the cooperation of the beneficiary of the services is essential; it stipulates that no community service order may be made unless the person or organization for whom the community service is to be performed has agreed to its performance. The youth court must also ensure that the order does not interfere with the normal hours of work or education of the young person, according to para. 21(7)(b). Community service orders must be completed within 12 months of the date of the order and a maximum of 240 hours of work may be assigned pursuant to s-s. 21(8). Subsection 32(9) allows a judicial extension of a further 12 months to complete the order.

Prohibition: paragraph 20(1)(h)

Under para. 20(1)(h) the youth court may "make any order of prohibition, seizure or forfeiture that may be imposed under any Act of Parliament or any regulation made thereunder where an accused is found guilty or convicted of that offence." There are a number of sections of the Criminal Code and other federal enactments that provide for orders of prohibition, seizure or forfeiture: for example, an order of prohibition respecting firearms may be made under ss. 98 and 101 of the Code; seizure of obscene matter is provided for under s. 160 of the Code; and an order for forfeiture of a controlled drug may be made under s-s. 37(8) or s. 45 of the Food and Drugs Act. Where the circumstances allow for it, any order under one of these sections applying to adults may be made in the case of a young person.

In some circumstances, a similar order might also be made under para. 20(1)(l) which empowers the youth court to "impose on the young person such other reasonable and ancillary conditions as it deems advisable."

Detention for treatment: paragraph 20(1)(i) and section 22

An additional option is available to the court where a report prepared by a "qualified person" recommends that the young person undergo treatment for a condition referred to in para. 13(1)(e), namely, "a physical or mental illness or disorder, a psychological disorder, an emotional disturbance, a learning disability or mental retardation." The youth court may direct that the young person be detained for treatment in a hospital or other place where treatment is available. This disposition may form part of or be in lieu of any other disposition. Paragraph 20(1)(i) is subject to s. 22, which requires the consent of the young person, the parents of the young person and the hospital or other place of treatment. Subsection 22(2) permits the youth court to dispense with the consent of the parent, if the parent is not available or if the parent is not taking an active interest in the proceedings. No provision is made for dispensing with the consent of the young person; in appropriate circumstances it may be possible to require civil commitment of a young person in a treatment facility under provincial mental health legislation, without the consent of the young person or his parents.

The power of the court to make a disposition requiring the young person to undergo treatment is distinct from the issues of fitness for trial and insanity. The question whether an accused is fit to stand trial arises at any time before adjudication. Section 543 of the *Criminal Code* applies to proceedings under the Y.O.A. by virtue of s-s. 13(8). If the accused is incapable of conducting his defence on account of insanity, he will be kept in custody in a mental health facility for an indeterminate period "at the pleasure of the lieutenant governor," until he is well. Similarly, by virtue of s. 51 and s-s. 52(2) of the Y.O.A., young persons who desire to enter a plea of not guilty by reason of insanity are dealt with under the *Code* as well. If acquitted by reason of insanity, the young person is also committed to custody in a mental hospital for an indeterminate period. In the case of a young person who is the subject of a treatment order under para. 20(1)(i), however, an adjudication has taken place and the young person has been found guilty of an offence; clearly the young person was fit to stand trial and insanity at the time of the offence was not in issue. Furthermore, the treatment order is for a determinate period. Moreover, the review procedures under ss. 28 to 32 of the Y.O.A. continue to apply.

Probation: paragraph 20(1)(j)

See discussion below under s. 23.

Custody: paragraph 20(1)(k)

See discussion below under s. 24.

Other reasonable conditions: paragraph 20(1)(l)

The final item in the list of dispositions provides that the youth court may "impose on the young person such other reasonable and ancillary conditions as it deems advisable and in the best interest of the young person and the public." This is a flexible provision that will allow for a variety of novel dispositions. The wording suggests that a para. 20(1)(l) disposition cannot stand on its own and should be made in combination with any of the other dispositions listed in s. 20. See comments of Laskin C.J.C. concerning para. 20(1)(g) of the *J.D.A.* in *Attorney General for Ontario and Viking Houses v. Regional Municipality of Peel*, [1979] 2 S.C.R. 1134, 104 D.L.R. (3d) 1 at p. 12, 29 N.R. 244, 49 C.C.C. (2d) 103. This case suggests that an order under para. 20(1)(l) of the Y.O.A. would probably be made in combination with a probation order, although not restricted thereto.

A similar provision in para. 20(1)(g) of the *J.D.A.* was used to make an order prohibiting the juvenile from driving for four months in *Re Strahl*, [1968] 2 C.C.C. 34, 2 C.R.N.S. 178, 60 W.W.R. 765 *sub nom. R. v. Strahl* (Man. Q.B.). In that case the judge referred to s. 38 of the *J.D.A.*, providing "that the care and custody and discipline of a juvenile delinquent shall approximate as nearly as may be that which should be given by his parents ..." to justify the suspension of driving privileges. Since the philosophy of the Y.O.A. differs significantly from that of the J.D.A., an order suspending driving privileges under the Y.O.A. would only be appropriate in more limited circumstances; for example, an order suspending driving privileges may be considered where a young person used a vehicle in the course of committing an offence.

Another use of para. 20(1)(g) of the J.D.A. was to include a condition that a juvenile on probation attend a wilderness camp, see R. v. Dapic, [1977] 5 W.W.R. 447, 36 C.C.C. (2d) 461, 40 C.R.N.S. 156 (B.C.S.C.). It would seem that such an order could also be made under the Y.O.A.: see, however, comments below concerning para. 23(2)(f) which suggest that para. 20(1)(l) cannot be used to place a young person in custody.

Disposition coming into force: subsection 20(2)

A disposition made under s. 20 comes into force "on the date on which it is made or on such later date as the youth court specifies." The power to postpone the starting date of a disposition gives the court some flexibility, for example to allow the young person an opportunity to finish a term at school before the commencement of a custodial disposition. Unless a delay in instituting the disposition is specifically ordered, however, the disposition takes effect immediately. Note that s-s. 23(7) specifies that a probation order must take effect immediately, unless the probation order follows a period of custody. Thus the court may not postpone the commencement of probation under s-s. 20(2).

Duration of disposition: subsections 20(3) and (4)

All dispositions under the Y.O.A. are to be for a fixed length of time. This represents a significant change from the J.D.A. which allowed indeterminate dispositions. Subsections 20(3) and (4) fix a maximum duration for all dispositions under s. 20. As a general rule, s-s. 20(3) limits the duration of most dispositions under s. 20 to two years. Exceptions apply with respect to an order of prohibition, seizure or forfeiture under para. 20(1)(h) (the length of which is limited by the legislation providing for the order) and an order committing the young person to custody under para. 20(1)(k) (the length of which can extend to a maximum of three years for offences carrying a life sentence in the case of an adult). In almost all instances, it is believed that a period of control for up to two years in length is sufficient. The same limitation applies "where the youth court makes more than one disposition at the same time in respect of the same offence." Again, the total length of dispositions imposed cannot exceed two years.

Subsection 20(4) sets out another exception to the "two-year rule." It establishes a three-year maximum on the combined length of continuous dispositions imposed on the young person in respect to different offences. It is clear that the three-year limitation applies when a young person receives dispositions in regard to two or more offences committed at different times at the same dispositional hearing.

There is arguably some ambiguity about how s-s. 20(4) should be interpreted when a young person is receiving a disposition for one offence, and is already subject to a disposition previously made under the Y.O.A. The words of s-s. 20(4) appear to speak from the time of the making of the last disposition. Thus, a youth court judge making a disposition in regard to a young person already subject to a Y.O.A. disposition, cannot make an order that will result in the young person being subject to a "continuous combined duration" of more than three years from the time the judge makes that disposition. For example, suppose a young person commits an offence, receives a custodial disposition of two years, and while in custody commits a further offence for which a disposition hearing is held one year and 11 months after the original disposition was made. The maximum disposition which can be imposed under the Y.O.A. (assuming subpara. 20(1)(k)(ii) applies), is a three-year custodial disposition to run *concurrently* with the unexpired portion of the original disposition; that is, the youth court can add a maximum of two years and 11 months to the original disposition so that the "continuous combined dispositions" from the time of final disposition, do not exceed three years. This interpretation of s-s. 20(4) renders it generally consistent with subpara. 20(1)(k)(ii).

If a disposition made in regard to one offence has expired at the time of the dispositional hearing for a second offence, then s-s. 20(4) ceases to apply in respect of the first offence; of course s-s. 20(3) applies to any dispositions made at the second hearing.

The basis for the three-year maximum on dispositions under the Y.O.A., found in subpara. 20(1)(k)(ii), is that any benefit a young person can receive from involvement with the juvenile correction system should occur within that period. Any need for an extension beyond the three-year period would suggest that the young person has "outgrown" the juvenile system, and would be unlikely to benefit from further exposure to the dispositions provided in the Y.O.A.; transfer to adult court under s. 16 should be considered in such circumstances.

Disposition continues when adult: subsection 20(5)

Subsection 20(5) is self-explanatory: "[a] disposition . . . shall continue in effect . . . after the young person against whom it has been made becomes an adult." This section should be read in conjunction with s-s. 24(14) which provides that after a young person serving a custodial disposition has reached the age of 18, the youth court may direct that he serves his disposition or the remaining portion of the disposition in a provincial correctional facility for adults. Even when the young person is transferred to an adult facility pursuant to s-s. 24(14), the youth court retains jurisdiction over him for purposes of dispositional review.

Reasons for the disposition: subsection 20(6)

By virtue of s-s. 20(6), the youth court is under an obligation to state its reasons for making a disposition in the record of the case. It must provide or cause to be provided a copy of the disposition to the young person, his counsel, his parents, the provincial director where the provincial director has an interest in the disposition, and the prosecutor. In the case of a custodial disposition, the review board, if one has been established, must also receive a copy of the disposition. A disposition may be in Form 7, except a probation order, which may be in Form 8. See sample forms at end of discussion of s. 20.

Upon request, any of the persons listed above may receive a transcript or copy of the reasons for disposition. Although a fee could be set under s. 67 or 68, query whether the words "shall provide" suggest an obligation to provide a copy of the reasons without charge. This subsection recognizes the importance which the Y.O.A. places on the young person and his parents knowing the exact reasons for any disposition.

The provisions of s-s. 20(6) do not require that a judge render his decision in writing. Procedures for recording the judge's oral reasons must, however, be in operation so that written reasons can be made available on request.

Limitation on punishment: subsection 20(7)

Another provision of the Y.O.A. which contrasts with the J.D.A. is the limitation on punishment found in s-s. 20(7), which provides that no "punishment that is greater than the maximum punishment that would be applicable to an adult who has committed the same offence" may be imposed. The *Criminal Code* and other legislation set out a number of offences for which there are maximum punishments. Noteworthy in this context are the maximum penalties applicable under the *Criminal Code*, s. 722 for summary conviction offences; these are a fine of $500, imprisonment for six months or both. For a "hybrid offence" (one which is indictable or summary at the election of the Crown), the offence is treated as indictable unless the Crown makes a contrary election, and hence the maximum applicable to sentences for summary conviction offences does not apply: see the *Interpretation Act*, para. 27(1)(a).

Criminal Code provisions inapplicable: subsections 20(8) and (9)

Subsection 20(8) makes the provisions of Part XX of the *Criminal Code* inapplicable in respect of Y.O.A. proceedings, with several exceptions. Part XX of the *Code* deals with "Punishments, Fines, Forfeitures, Costs and Restitution of Property." Because the Y.O.A. institutes its own set of procedures with respect to these matters, the *Code* provisions are made inapplicable. By express inclusion the provisions of s. 683 (pardon), s. 685 (remission) and s. 686 (royal prerogative of mercy) continue to apply. Subsections 655(2) to (5) dealing with restitution of property before the court where there is no conviction, also apply under the Y.O.A., as does s-s. 662.1(2), specifying the period for which an appearance notice, promise to appear, summons, undertaking or recognizance is in effect.

Subsection 20(9) provides that s. 722 of the *Code* does not apply to proceedings under the Y.O.A. Section 722, which governs punishment for summary conviction offences, provides in s-s. (1) that the maximum punishment, unless otherwise stipulated, cannot exceed $500 or six months' imprisonment or both;

s-ss. 722(2) to (11) provide generally for fines and default in payment thereof. As the Y.O.A. contains its own range of dispositions for all offences as well as provisions for default, it is unnecessary to make use of s. 722 for these purposes. However, as s-s. 20(7) stipulates that no disposition for a young person shall result in a punishment greater than the maximum punishment applicable to an adult who commits the same offence, it is submitted that where the legislative provision creating the summary conviction offence does not specify a penalty, the general limitations on sanctions in s-s. 722(1) would govern. This interpretation does not involve a direct application of s-s. 722(1); rather, it is arrived at by referring to the legislative provisions which create specific summary conviction offences, which in turn, where no maximum is specified, incorporate s-s. 722(1). This interpretation accords with the clear legislative intent of s-s. 20(7) of the *Young Offenders Act*, namely, not to expose young persons to more serious sanctions than adults. (See L. Wilson, *Juvenile Courts in Canada* (Toronto: Carswell, 1982), p. 200.) Section 15 of the *Charter of Rights*, guaranteeing equal benefit of the law without discrimination based on age (to come into effect April 17, 1985), would seem to require such an interpretation.

Probation: section 23

"Probation is a form of disposition under which an offender who has been found to have committed an offence may be released by the court, subject to the supervision of a probation officer and to certain conditions imposed by the court" (*Juvenile Delinquency in Canada: The Report of the Department of Justice Committee on Juvenile Delinquency* (1965), at p. 173). Probation is used very frequently for both young offenders and adults. It is desirable because it allows the young person to receive supervision and treatment, if necessary, while being subject to minimal restrictions on his freedom. Although the definition above envisions a probation officer's supervision as part of a probation order, a young person may be placed on probation without having to report to a probation officer. In such cases, usually involving less serious crimes, supervision by parents or another responsible person is adequate.

Probation has been frequently used under the J.D.A. through committal to the care or custody of a probation officer, placement with supervision or visitation by a probation officer or by virtue of the power to impose "such further and other conditions as may be deemed advisable." Because the *J.D.A.* does not specify acceptable conditions of probation as does s. 663 of the *Criminal Code* and does not set out procedures to be followed on breach, an issue has arisen as to what this procedure properly should be. The Y.O.A. clarifies issues such as these. The Y.O.A. provisions are exhaustive and apply to young persons in lieu of the *Criminal Code* provisions dealing with probation. Thus, the *Code* offence of "breach of probation" does not apply to young persons who are in breach of their probation orders. Under the Y.O.A. a young person in breach of the terms of his probation may be dealt with only by way of review pursuant to s. 33.

Paragraph 20(1)(j) and Section 23

20. (1) Where a youth court finds a young person guilty of an offence ... the court shall then make any one of the following dispositions,

. . .

(j) place the young person on probation in accordance with section 23 for a specified period not exceeding two years;

23. (1) *Conditions that must appear in probation orders.*—The following conditions shall be included in a probation order made under paragraph 20(1)(j):

(a) that the young person bound by the probation order shall keep the peace and be of good behaviour;

(b) that the young person appear before the youth court when required by the court to do so; and

(c) that the young person notify the provincial director or the youth worker assigned to his case of any change of address or any change in his place of employment, education or training.

(2) *Conditions that may appear in probation orders.*—A probation order made under paragraph 20(1)(j) may include such of the following conditions as the youth court considers appropriate in the circumstances of the case:

(a) that the young person bound by the probation order report to and be under the supervision of the provincial director or a person designated by him or by the youth court;

(b) that the young person remain within the territorial jurisdiction of one or more courts named in the order;

(c) that the young person make reasonable efforts to obtain and maintain suitable employment;

(d) that the young person attend school or such other place of learning, training or recreation as is appropriate, if the court is satisfied that a suitable program is available for the young person at such place;

(e) that the young person reside with a parent, or such other adult as the court considers appropriate, who is willing to provide for the care and maintenance of the young person;

(f) that the young person reside in such place as the provincial director or his delegate may specify;

(g) that the young person comply with such other reasonable conditions set out in the order as the court considers desirable, including conditions for securing the good conduct of the young person and for preventing the commission by the young person of other offences.

(3) *Communication of probation order to young person and parent.*—Where the youth court makes a probation order under paragraph 20(1)(j), it shall

(a) cause the order to be read by or to the young person bound by the probation order;

(b) explain or cause to be explained to the young person the purpose and effect of the order and ascertain that the young person understands it; and

(c) cause a copy of the order to be given to the young person and to a parent of the young person, if the parent is in attendance at the proceedings against the young person.

(4) *Copy of probation order to parent.*—Where the youth court makes a probation order under paragraph 20(1)(j), it may cause a copy of the report to be given to a parent of the young person not in attendance at the proceedings against the young person if the parent is, in the opinion of the court, taking an active interest in the proceedings.

(5) *Endorsement of order by young person.*—After a probation order has been read by or to a young person and explained to him pursuant to subsection (3), the young person shall endorse the order acknowledging that he has received a copy of the order and acknowledging the fact that it has been explained to him.

(6) *Validity of probation order.*—The failure of a young person to endorse a probation order pursuant to subsection (5) does not affect the validity of the order.

(7) *Commencement of probation order.*—A probation order made under paragraph 20(1)(j) comes into force

(a) on the date on which the order is made; or

(b) where the young person in respect of whom the order is made is committed to continuous custody, on the expiration of the period of custody.

(8) *Notice to appear.*—A young person may be given notice to appear before the youth court pursuant to paragraph (1)(b) orally or in writing, and where the notice is in writing it may be in Form 9.

(9) *Warrant to arrest young person.*—If a young person to whom a notice is given in writing to appear before the youth court pursuant to paragraph (1)(b) does not appear at the time and place named in the notice and it is proved that a copy of the notice was served on him, a youth court may issue a warrant to compel the appearance of the young person.

Mandatory conditions: subsection 23(1)

Subsection 23(1) sets out three conditions that must appear in a probation order. They are straightforward and need little explanation. The first condition states that the young person "shall keep the peace and be of good behaviour." Secondly, the young person must "appear before the youth court when required by the court." This provision allows the youth court judge to make contact with the young person to discuss informally the terms of the probation order and the young person's compliance with it. It does not allow the youth court to change the probation order; rather it is an option available to reinforce the court's order, if necessary, without invoking the review mechanisms. A formal review of the probation order for reasons other than failure to comply must be carried out under s. 32. Section 33 deals with review of probation orders where the young person has wilfully failed or refused to comply with the order. The final mandatory condition is that the young person "notify the provincial director or the youth worker assigned to his case of any change of address or any change in his place of employment, education or training."

Conditions that may appear in a probation order: subsection 23(2)

In addition to the mandatory conditions listed in s-s. 23(1), the youth court may impose one or more of the conditions in s-s. 23(2), as long as the conditions are not inconsistent with each other. The optional conditions should allow the court to issue a probation order which will meet the particular needs of the young person.

The first in the list of conditions set out in s-s. 23(2) requires reporting to a supervisor who could be the provincial director or "a person designated by him or by the youth court." It is expected that the designated individual would, in most instances, be a youth court worker (probation officer), although the court could appoint any other person that it sees fit. Another condition is an order pursuant to para. 23(2)(b) that the young person "remain within the territorial jurisdiction of one or more courts named in the order." This is a commonly imposed term of probation used to ensure that the young person receives the benefit of supervision ordered for him.

The youth court may order that the young person "make reasonable efforts to obtain and maintain suitable employment" pursuant to para. 23(2)(c). If the young person is not working an order might be made under para. 23(2)(d) requiring the young person to attend school or "such other place of learning, training or recreation as is appropriate." Such an order would be in addition to any provincial education attendance laws and would be appropriate only "if the court is satisfied that a suitable program is available for the young person."

Paragraph 23(2)(e) empowers the court to make an order "that the young person reside with a parent, or such other adult as the court considers appropriate, who is willing to provide for the care and maintenance of the young person." This condition is clearly phrased so that an order may be made for the young person to reside with a natural person only, not a corporation: this corresponds with the approach of the Supreme Court of Canada to orders under the *J.D.A*: *A.-G. Ont. and Viking Houses v. Regional Municipality of Peel*, [1979] 2 S.C.R. 1134, 104 D.L.R. (3d) 1, 49 C.C.C. (2d) 103, 29 N.R. 244. Under para. 23(2)(e) of the Y.O.A., financial responsibility for providing care for the young person is clearly assumed by the adult with whom the young person is ordered to reside and hence there are no cost implications for provincial or municipal governments.

Paragraph 23(2)(e) apparently allows for a residential placement even in the face of a contrary subsisting custody order of a higher court. The cases of *R. v. C.F.*; *R. v. F.G.* (1977), 34 C.C.C.

(2d) 333 (Ont. Prov. Ct.) held that an order under the J.D.A. that placed the juveniles in the custody of their fathers superseded prior custody orders of the Supreme Court of Ontario, entrusting the youths to the custody of their respective mothers. The custody order of another court, whether made under federal or provincial legislation, would last "until the issue is raised again in another Court having jurisdiction to hear the matter" (p. 336). While such a disposition under the Y.O.A. may suspend the effect of an existing custody order, it does not affect the validity of the custody order or its continued effect following the expiry of the disposition under the Y.O.A.

Another condition of probation which may be imposed is set out in para. 23(2)(f), providing for an order "that the young person reside in such place as the provincial director or his delegate may specify." This provision allows the placement of a young person in a facility operated by provincial child welfare authorities, a private agency, or by an individual. The provision would seem broad enough to allow the provincial director to specify that the young person reside at a wilderness camp or at some residential educational facility.

Although the words of para. 23(2)(f) appear very broad, it would not seem reasonable to interpret them as giving the provincial director an unfettered discretion for this provision applies only to residential placements and cannot be used to order detention or custody. Specific provisions of the Y.O.A. restrict the placement of young persons in various facilities, and para. 23(2)(f) should not be used to circumvent these provisions. For example, para. 20(1)(i) and s. 22 restrict detention in a hospital or other treatment facility. Paragraph 20(1)(k) and s. 24 contain a number of provisions ensuring that a young person is placed in custody only under restricted circumstances, with clear requirements for judicial control over the commitment process. Subsection 24(10) provides that a young person committed to custody under para. 20(1)(k) will be held separate and apart from any adult charged with or convicted of an offence. It would be both illogical and inappropriate to interpret para. 23(2)(f) as giving the provincial director authority to place a young person in a hospital or other treatment facility, in a place of custody as defined in s. 24 of the Y.O.A., or in an adult correctional facility. The provincial director's discretion under para. 23(2)(f) is, by necessary implication, limited by other provisions in the Act.

Normally before a para. 23(2)(f) condition is included in a probation order, one would expect that the provincial director or his delegate would present a plan at a dispositional hearing concerning the place of residence. If this plan is not followed by the authorities having care of the young person, there would be grounds for a dispositional review under s. 32.

The province will assume the costs of the placement when an order is made under para. 23(2)(f).

Another possible condition of probation is "that the young person comply with such other reasonable conditions set out in the order as the court considers desirable ...". Such conditions may be included "for securing the good conduct of the young person and preventing the commission by the young person of other offences." Examples include a curfew, writing an essay about an appropriate topic, a requirement that the young person obtain counselling, a non-association order, and an order prohibiting a young person from driving a car (see Re Strahl, [1968] 2 C.C.C. 34, 2 C.R.N.S. 178, 60 W.W.R. 765, sub nom. R. v. Strahl (Man. Q.B.)). It should be emphasized that the condition must be reasonable, and may serve the purpose of securing the good conduct of the young person and may aid in preventing the commission of other offences.

Communication of terms of the probation order: subsections 23(3) to (6)

Subsection 23(3) requires the youth court to ensure that the terms of any probation order are communicated to the young person. The court shall cause the probation order to be read by or to the young person (para. 23(3)(a)). The court further shall explain or cause to be explained the purpose and effect of the probation order, and the judge has an obligation to ascertain that the young person understands the order (para. 23(3)(b)). The words of s-s. 23(3) do not demand that the order be read or explained to the young person by the judge in the courtroom. A youth court worker can acquaint the young person with the terms of the probation order outside the courtroom, though the judge must ascertain that the young person understands the effect of the order. A copy of the probation order must be given to the young person, and to a parent, if in attendance at the proceedings (para. 23(3)(c)).

A parent not in attendance at youth court proceedings may none the less receive a copy of the probation order pursuant to s-s. 23(4) if the parent "is, in the opinion of the court, taking an active interest in the proceedings." Sending a copy to the parent through the mail would be adequate. Although no guidelines have been set out to assist a judge in determining whether a parent is "taking an active interest in the proceedings," it would seem desirable for the judge to err on the side of causing notice to be given. If the parents are likely to be involved in supervising the probation order or if they will be helpful in ensuring that the young person observe certain conditions of the order, for example, if the young person is living at home and he has a curfew imposed upon him, it would seem essential to inform the parents of the terms of the probation.

The Y.O.A. does not specify the consequences of a failure to communicate the terms of the probation order to the young person, but a failure to do so might be brought up at a subsequent review under s. 33; clearly the young person may not be guilty of wilful breach under s. 33 if he did not understand exactly what conditions were imposed on him earlier. Common practice under the J.D.A. has been to require that the young person be informed of the consequences of breach of probation at the dispositional hearing: see *Racicot v. The Queen* (1978), 2 Canadian Journal of Family Law 195 (Ont. H.C.) and *Re Juvenile J. (No. 2)* (1978), 2 Canadian Journal of Family Law 196 (Ont. Prov. Ct.). The Y.O.A. clarifies the nature of the obligation to communicate the terms of probation and the consequences of breach.

Subsection 23(5) requires the young person to acknowledge the explanation of the probation order and his receipt of a copy by "endorsing" the order. An endorsement would most likely be the young person's signature, or in rare circumstances, for example if he was illiterate, his mark. This requirement is to ensure that the young person understands the significance of the probation order. According to s-s. 23(6), however, failure to sign the order does not affect its validity; thus the young person cannot thwart the process by refusing to endorse the order.

Commencement of probation order: subsection 23(7)

A probation order comes into effect on the date on which the order is made, except where the young person is committed to continuous custody; in the latter case the probation order comes into force on the expiration of the period of custody. Subsection 23(7) specifically modifies the provisions of s-s. 20(2) which generally permit a youth court judge to order that a disposition take effect at a later date.

Appearance before youth court: subsections 23(8) and (9)

Paragraph 23(1)(b) provides that the youth court can require the appearance of the young person at any time. Subsection 23(8) makes provision for notifying the young person to appear. Notice may be given orally or in writing; if in writing, notice may be given in Form 9: see sample Form 9 at end of discussion of s. 23. If the young person does not appear as required after receiving notice, the youth court is empowered to compel the attendance of the young person by warrant pursuant to s-s. 23(9). Note, however, that the purpose of requiring an appearance is to maintain contact with the young person on an informal level, not to review the disposition formally. Formal reviews are to be carried out in accordance with ss. 32 and 33, and, unless there has been a wilful breach of probation within s. 33, the youth court cannot impose a more onerous disposition after review. The informal procedure under para. 23(1)(b) will usually be set in motion by a youth court worker who has reason to think it would be beneficial to bring the young person before the youth court, for example, if the court worker has been having difficulties with the young person. The worker can contact the clerk of the youth court or a youth court judge and request that notice be given pursuant to s-s. 23(8) requiring a young person to appear, and if necessary, have a warrant issued pursuant to s-s. 23(9).

Form of probation order: subsection 20(11)

Subsection 20(11) provides that a probation order may be in Form 8. If probation is combined with another disposition then both dispositions may be in Form 8.

SAMPLE FORM

FORM 8
THE YOUNG OFFENDERS ACT
IN THE YOUTH COURT FOR ONTARIO

PROBATION ORDER

Canada
Province of Ontario
County of Queens

Whereas on the 28th day of June 19 82 , in the Youth Court at 100 Main Street, Anytown, Ontario , David Smith of 25 First Avenue, Anytown, Ontario a young person within the meaning of the *Young Offenders Act* was tried and found guilty of the following offence:

robbery: to wit on the second day of June, 1982, David Smith did steal two hundred and fifty dollars from The Corner Milk Store, 2 West Street, Anytown, Ontario, and at the same time thereat did use threats of violence contrary to section 303 of the *Criminal Code of Canada.*

And be it remembered that on 8th day of July 19 82 , I Thomas Brown Judge of the Youth Court in and for the County of Queens ordered David Smith to perform the following community service:

For a period of twenty months from the date of this order and during the period of probation herein described, David Smith shall perfom two hours per week of service at the Anytown Community Centre under the direction of Mr. George O'Hara, Director of Youth Activities, such service to be in the assistance of Mr. O'Hara in the organization and maintenance of a junior swimming program for handicapped children.

And in addition thereto placed David Smith on probation on the conditions hereinafter prescribed;

Now therefore David Smith , in this order called the young person, shall, for the period of twenty months from the date of this order comply with the following conditions:

1. that the young person shall keep the peace and be of good behaviour;

2. that the young person appear before the Youth Court when required by the court to do so;

3. that the young person notify the provincial director or the youth worker assigned to his case of any change of address or any change in his place of employment, education or training;

4. that the young person attend Sir John A. MacDonald High School in Anytown, Ontario and comply with the requirements of the academic program as directed by Mr. Timothy Jones, Vice-Principal; and

5. that the young person report to the youth worker assigned to his case, on the first Monday of every month for the period of the probation.

Dated this 8th day of July 19 82 at Anytown in the Province of Ontario

"Thomas Brown"
....
A Judge of the Youth Court

I, David Smith , being the young person referred to in this probation order hereby acknowledge that I have read the order, that the order has been explained to me and that I have received a copy of the order.

"David Smith"
....

SAMPLE FORM

FORM 9
THE YOUNG OFFENDERS ACT
IN THE YOUTH COURT FOR ONTARIO

NOTICE TO APPEAR BEFORE YOUTH COURT
PURSUANT TO PROBATION ORDER

Canada
Province of Ontario
County of Queens

To David Smith of 25 First Avenue, Anytown, Ontario ,
a young person within the meaning of the *Young Offenders Act*:

Whereas by order dated the 8th day of July 19 82 you were
placed on probation for a period of twenty months commencing on the date of the order;

And whereas pursuant to the conditions of the probation order
you are bound to appear before the Youth Court when required
by the court to do so;

This is therefore to require you to appear before the Youth
Judge sitting at 100 Main Street, Anytown, Ontario on Fri-
day the 22nd day of October 19 82 at 2:00 o'clock, in
the after noon to be dealt with in accordance with the *Young
Offenders Act*;

And further this is to notify you that if you do not attend at the
time and place stated herein a warrant may be issued for your
arrest.

Dated this 13th day of October 19 82 at Anytown in
the Province of Ontario.

"Thomas Brown"
. . . .
A Judge of the Youth Court

Custodial dispositions: section 24

A custodial disposition is the most serious disposition that can be ordered by a youth court. Although there are different forms of custodial dispositions, all forms of custody impose continuous supervision and restrict the young person's access to the community.

The principles set out in paras. 3(1)(f) and (h) of the Y.O.A. declare that a young person has "a right to the least possible interference with freedom that is consistent with the protection of society" and prescribe removal from parental supervision "only when measures that provide for continuing parental supervision are inappropriate." These principles indicate that custody is to be used as a last resort, only when the young person has committed a serious crime or when he presents a serious threat to the community.

The Y.O.A. establishes two types of custody, open and secure. At no time is a secure custodial disposition to be ordered unless committal is necessary for the protection of the public. The Act forbids the use of secure custodial facilities except for serious offences; further restrictions apply in the case of young persons under the age of 14. Other safeguards apply to any order committing a young person into custody; for example, the youth court must consider a pre-disposition report before making a custodial disposition. The young person is given an absolute right of appeal in regard to disposition, in contrast with the provisions of the J.D.A., requiring special leave to appeal.

Paragraph 20(1)(k) and Section 24

20. (1) Where a youth court finds a young person guilty of an offence ... the court shall make any one of the following dispositions ...

(k) subject to section 24, commit the young person to custody, to be served continuously or intermittently, for a specified period not exceeding

(i) two years from the date of committal, or

(ii) where the young person is found guilty of an offence for which the punishment provided by the *Criminal Code* or any other Act of Parliament is imprisonment for life, three years from the date of committal ...

24. (1) *Definitions.*—In this section,

"open custody" means custody in

(a) a community residential centre, group home, child care institution, or forest or wilderness camp, or

(b) any other like place or facility

designated by the Lieutenant Governor in Council of a province or his delegate as a place of open custody for the purposes of this Act, and includes a place or facility within a class of such places or facilities so designated;

"secure custody" means custody in a place or facility designated by the Lieutenant Governor in Council of a province for the secure containment or restraint of young persons, and includes a place or facility within a class of such places or facilities so designated.

(2) *Order of committal to specify type of custody.*—Where the youth court commits a young person to custody under paragraph 20(1)(k), it shall specify in the order of committal whether custody is to be open custody or secure custody.

(3) *Conditions for secure custody.*—Subject to subsection (4), no young person who is found guilty of an offence shall be committed to secure custody unless the young person was, at the time the offence was committed, fourteen years of age or more and unless

(a) the offence is one for which an adult would be liable to imprisonment for five years or more;

(b) the offence is an offence under section 132 (prison breach) or subsection 133(1) (escape or being at large without excuse) of the *Criminal Code* or an attempt to commit such offence; or

(c) the offence is an indictable offence and the young person was

(i) within twelve months prior to the commission of the offence found guilty of an offence for which an adult would be liable to imprisonment for five years or more, or adjudged to have committed a delinquency under the *Juvenile Delinquents Act* in respect of such offence, or

(ii) at any time prior to the commission of the offence committed to secure custody with respect to a previous offence, or committed to custody in a place or facility for the secure containment or restraint of a child, within the meaning of the *Juvenile Delinquents Act*, with respect to a delinquency under that Act.

(4) *Idem.*—A young person who is found guilty of an offence and who was, at the time the offence was committed, under the age of fourteen years may be committed to secure custody if

(a) the offence is one for which an adult would be liable to life imprisonment;

(b) the offence is one for which an adult would be liable to imprisonment for five years or more and the young person was at any time prior to the commission of the offence found guilty of an offence for which an adult would be liable to imprisonment for five years or more or adjudged to have committed a delinquency under the *Juvenile Delinquents* Act in respect of such offence; or

(c) the young person is found guilty of an offence under section 132 (prison breach) or subsection 133(1) (escape or being at large without excuse) of the *Criminal Code* or an attempt to commit such offence.

(5) *Idem.*—The youth court shall not commit a young person to secure custody unless the court considers a committal to secure custody to be necessary for the protection of society having regard to the seriousness of the offence and the circumstances in which it was committed and having regard to the needs and circumstances of the young person.

(6) *Place of custody.*—A young person who is committed to custody shall be placed in open custody or secure custody, as specified in the order of committal, at such place or facility as the provincial director or his delegate may specify and may, during the period of custody be transferred by the provincial director or his delegate from one place or facility of open custody to another or from one place or facility of secure custody to another.

(7) *Transfer from secure custody to open custody.*—The provincial director or his delegate may, with the written authorization of the youth court, transfer a young person from a place or facility of secure custody to a place or facility of open custody.

(8) *Transfer from open custody to secure custody.*—Subject to subsection (9), no young person who is committed to open custody may be transferred to a place or facility of secure custody except in accordance with section 33.

(9) *Idem.*—The provincial director or his delegate may transfer a young person from a place or facility of open custody to a place or facility of secure custody for a period not exceeding fifteen days if the young person escapes or attempts to escape lawful custody or is, in the opinion of the director or his delegate, guilty of serious misconduct.

(10) *Young person to be held separate from adults.*—Subject to this section, a young person who is committed to custody under paragraph 20(1)(k) shall be held separate and apart from any adult who is charged with or convicted of an offence against any law of Canada or a province.

(11) *Pre-disposition report.*—Before making an order of committal to custody under paragraph 20(1)(k), the youth court shall consider a pre-disposition report.

(12) *Committal to custody deemed continuous.*—A young person who is committed to custody under paragraph 20(1)(k) shall be deemed to be committed to continuous custody unless the youth court specifies otherwise.

(13) *Availability of place of intermittent custody.*—Before making an order of committal to intermittent custody under paragraph 20(1)(k), the youth court shall require the prosecutor to make available to the court for its consideration a report of the provincial director or his delegate as to the availability of a place of custody in which an order of intermittent custody can be enforced and, where the report discloses that no such place of custody is available, the court shall not make such an order.

(14) *Transfer to adult facility.*—Where a young person is committed to custody under paragraph 20(1)(k), the youth court may, on application of the provincial director or his delegate made at any time after the young person attains the age of eighteen years, after affording the young person an opportunity to be heard, authorize the provincial director or his delegate to direct that the young person serve his disposition or the remaining portion thereof in a provincial correctional facility for adults, if the court considers it to be in the best interests of the young person or in the public interest, but in any such event the provisions of this Act shall continue to apply in respect of that person.

(15) *Where disposition and sentence concurrent.*—Where a young person is committed to custody under paragraph 20(1)(k) and is concurrently under sentence of imprisonment imposed in ordinary court, that person may serve his disposition and sentence, or any portions thereof, in a provincial correctional facility for adults or in a place of custody for young persons.

(16) *Warrant of committal.*—Where a young person is committed to custody under paragraph 20(1)(k), the youth court shall issue or cause to be issued a warrant of committal, which may be in Form 10.

Definitions: subsection 24(1)

There are two types of custody available under the Y.O.A.: "open" and "secure". Each juvenile facility will be designated by the province as being "open" and "secure". Examples of "open custody" listed in para. 24(1)(a) include a community residential centre, a group home, a child care institution and a forest or wilderness camp. Open facilities do not devote resources to prevent the young person from leaving. On the other hand, secure facilities are designed to restrain or contain the young person. The definition of "secure custody" is a place or facility "for the secure containment or restraint of young persons." Physical security is not the only consideration, however, as a place with a high staff to young person ratio might be classified as secure without physical control over the young person; the requisite control could be achieved through close supervision.

It is important to distinguish between the two levels of custody so that the right to the least possible interference with freedom is maintained. If the provincial authorities were to place a young person whose disposition specified "open custody" in "secure custody", the young person could initiate a review or seek a remedy by way of prerogative writ. The designation of open or secure facilities is the responsiblity of the Lieutenant Governor in Council (Cabinet) of a province.

Judicial specification of level of custody: subsections 24(2) to (5)

Subsection 24(2) provides that the youth court must specify to which level of custody, open or secure, it is committing a young person. Under s-s. 24(6) the provincial director or his delegate may decide upon the precise facility within the level of custody. It is felt that the judiciary rather than the provincial social service or correctional authorities should bear the responsibility for determining the extent to which a young person will be deprived of his liberty. It is also believed that determination of the level of custody in open court will help to maintain and increase the confidence of young persons and the public in the juvenile justice system. The provision allowing provincial authorities to assign the young person to any facility within the designated level gives the provinces flexibility to plan and implement effective programs and enables them to use their resources most effectively.

There are a number of objective and subjective criteria which must be satisfied before a court makes an order for committal to secure custody. The two objective elements are age and seriousness of the offence. The criteria for the committal of offenders 14 years or older are set out in s-s. 24(3). A young person 14 or over must be convicted of an offence for which an adult would be liable to imprisonment for five years or more, or must be convicted of a violation or an attempted violation of the *Criminal Code*, s. 132 (prison breach) or s-s. 133(1) (escape or being at large without excuse). In addition, a young person, 14 or over, may be committed to secure custody under para. 24(3)(c) if a disposition is being made in regard to any indictable offence, and (i) in the previous 12 months he was convicted of an offence for which an adult would be liable to imprisonment for five years or more, or (ii) at any previous time he was committed to a secure facility.

Subsection 24(4) governs the committal to secure custody of young persons between the ages of 12 and 14 at the time of the offence; it provides for committal only in the most serious circumstances. The young person must have been convicted of an offence for which an adult would be liable to life imprisonment, or convicted of a violation or attempted violation of the *Criminal Code*, s. 132 (prison breach) or s-s. 133(1) (escape or being at large without excuse). A young person between 12 and 14 may also be committed to secure custody under para. 24(4)(b) if a disposition is being made in regard to an offence for which an adult would be liable to imprisonment for five years or more and the young person has previously been convicted of such an offence.

Subsections 24(3) and (4) expressly provide for the consideration of previous adjudications in respect of offences committed when the *Juvenile Delinquents Act* was in force.

Even when a young person has been found guilty of committing an offence for which he may receive a secure custodial disposition under s-s. 24(3) or (4), the Act prescribes a subjective test which must be satisfied before the order is made. Subsection 24(5) provides that secure custody must be "necessary for the protection of society having regard to the seriousness of the offence and the circumstances in which it was committed and having regard to the needs and circumstances of the young person." This permits consideration by the youth court of the circumstances surrounding the offence, the necessity for physical restraint of the young person, the facilities and programs for treatment or rehabilitation of the youth and other factors. Although this provision allows a subjective evaluation that includes the needs of the young person, secure custody must be necessary for the protection of the public.

Place of custody: subsections 24(6) to (9)

Once the designation of "open" or "secure" custody has been made by the youth court, the responsibility for placement of the young person in a particular custodial facility falls to the provincial director or his delegate. Under s-s. 24(6) the provincial director has complete freedom to place the young person and to transfer him from one facility to another, as long as the young person remains within the designated level of custody. The provincial director, however, is restricted in changing the level of custody imposed by the judge because it is felt that a judicial disposition should not be unilaterally altered by provincial social service or correctional authorities.

Transfers from secure custody to open custody may be made by the provincial director or his delegate with the "written authorization of the youth court" pursuant to s-s. 24(7). Although the judge's approval is necessary there is no need for a hearing because the move is from a more restrictive to a less restrictive facility. If the youth court judge refuses to grant his written approval for such a move, the provincial director may seek a hearing by the youth court to review a disposition under s. 28.

Transfers from open custody to secure custody may not be made without going through the s. 33 procedures for review. This ensures that the young person is not committed to more restrictive secure custody without a hearing. Moreover, a s. 33 review can only occur if there has been an escape or attempt to escape custody (open or secure), or there has been a wilful failure or refusal to comply with a disposition. Query whether under certain limited circumstances, a refusal by a young person to participate in the program of a custodial facility might be considered so substantial as to constitute a wilful failure to comply with a disposition.

Subsection 24(9) provides that as an exceptional measure the provincial director or his delegate may transfer a young person from open to secure custody without court authorization "if the young person escapes or attempts to escape lawful custody" or if the young person is "in the opinion of the director or his delegate, guilty of serious misconduct." A transfer under s-s. 24(9) may only be "for a period not exceeding fifteen days." If the young person is kept in secure custody in excess of 15 days or without just cause, the young person could institute a civil suit or seek relief in the form of a prerogative writ or both. In addition there might well be administrative consequences for the provincial director or his delegate.

No definition of "serious misconduct" has been set out in the Act to aid in the interpretation of s-s. 24(9). The intention is clearly to provide the power to deal with young persons in exceptional circumstances. The word "serious" should be stressed. Conduct that might be described as "serious" could involve an unusual threat to the safety of the young person or others living or working in the open facility with the young person. In exceptional circumstances, the persistent breach of the rules of the facility, if sufficiently important to the operation of the facility, might merit the description "serious misconduct."

Custody separate from adults: subsections 24(10), (14) and (15)

Subsection 24(10) states that, subject to s. 24, a young person committed to custody "shall be held separate and apart from any adult who is charged with or convicted of an offence against any law of Canada or a province."

Subsection 24(14) permits the transfer of a young person to a provincial correctional facility for adults when the young person has reached the age of 18 years. Application must be made to the youth court and the young person must be afforded an opportunity to be heard; as the transfer represents a substantial alteration to the original disposition, judicial review is justified. The young person has the right to counsel, and the rules of natural justice apply. The rules of evidence might be relaxed, however, as is usual at a post-adjudication hearing. An order under s-s. 24(14) is appropriate "if the court considers it to be in the best interests of the young person or in the public interest." These tests are alternatives, if a transfer were necessary in the public interest an order might be made even if it was not in the best interests of the young person to be so transferred. It should be noted that this transfer provision is not intended to reflect general practice. It is an option to be resorted to in appropriate cases.

A transfer under s-s. 24(14) does not have the same effect as a s. 16 transfer to adult court. Subsection 24(14) explicitly provides that "the provisions of this Act shall continue to apply"; the young person is placed in an adult facility, but the judicial review provisions of the Y.O.A. continue to apply.

In the rare situations where a young person is committed to custody under para. 20(1)(k) of the Y.O.A. and the young person is concurrently under sentence of imprisonment in ordinary court, s-s. 24(15) provides that the young person may serve his disposition and sentence in either an adult facility or a place of custody for young persons. The correctional authorities are to decide where the young person will be confined.

Pre-disposition report: subsection 24(11)

A pre-disposition report prepared pursuant to s. 14 is mandatory before an order of committal to custody is made, whether the custody is open or secure. The report is considered necessary in determining the appropriateness of a custodial disposition and should be designed to give a variety of relevant information to the youth court, for example, by pointing out personality characteristics, describing the family and education background, etc.

Intermittent custody: subsections 24(12) and (13)

Young persons are ordinarily deemed by s-s. 24(12) to be committed to continuous custody, unless otherwise specified.

If a place is available, an order of committal to intermittent custody may be made by the youth court. Subsection 24(13) provides that before making an order of committal to intermittent custody, the court shall require the prosecutor to make available to the court a report of the provincial director or his delegate on "the availability of a place of custody in which an order of intermittent custody can be enforced." If no place is available, an order for intermittent custody may not be made. The provisions of the *Criminal Code* dealing with intermittent sentences for adult offenders do not apply by virtue of s-s. 20(8), which makes Part XX of the *Code* inapplicable to young persons.

Form for order of disposition: subsection 20(10)

Subsection 20(10) provides that a disposition made under s. 20, other than a probation order, may be in Form 7. Form 7, included in the Schedule following the Act, sets out precedents for all of the dispositions in s. 20, such as absolute discharge, imposition of fine, a compensation order and so on. A sample of Form 7 for a committal to custody follows on next page.

Warrant of committal: subsection 24(16)

Subsection 24(16) specifies that a warrant of committal to custody may be in Form 10. A sample of Form 10 follows on page 216.

SAMPLE FORM

FORM 7
THE YOUNG OFFENDERS ACT
IN THE YOUTH COURT FOR ONTARIO

ORDER OF DISPOSITION

Canada
Province of Ontario
County of Queens

Whereas on the 26th   day of August 19 82 , in the Youth
Court at   100 Main Street, Anytown, Ontario, Mary Powell
of 452 Blair Road, Anytown, Ontario a young person within
the meaning of the *Young Offenders Act* was on her own admission
found guilty of having committed the following offence:

theft: to wit Mary Powell on the 13th day of July, 1982
at Anytown, Ontario did steal a Sony television and
recorder, Serial Nos. 48774 B and 2236 CF respectively, the property of the County of Queens Board of
Education, of a value of $1345 dollars, contrary to
Section 294(a) of the *Criminal Code of Canada.*

Be it remembered that on the 15th day of September 19 82,
I Thomas Brown Judge of the Youth Court in and for the
County of Queens committed Mary Powell to secure
custody in County of Queens Youth Centre or such place of
secure custody as the provincial director or his delegate may
specify for a period of nine months commencing on the 16th
day of September 19 82 .

Dated this 15th day of September 19 82 at Anytown in the Province of Ontario.

"Thomas Brown"
. . . .
A Judge of the Youth Court

Note: Destruction of Records
Section 45 provides for the destruction of records where a young
person who is found guilty of an offence has not been charged
with or found guilty of a further offence for a period of five years
after all dispositions are completed in the case of an indictable
offence or two years in the case of a summary conviction offence.

SAMPLE FORM

FORM 10
THE YOUNG OFFENDERS ACT
IN THE YOUTH COURT FOR ONTARIO

WARRANT OF COMMITTAL TO CUSTODY

Canada
Province of Ontario
County of Queens

To the peace officers in the County of Queens and to the person in charge of the place of custody specified herein:

Whereas Mary Powell of 425 Blair Road, Anytown, Ontario , a young person within the meaning of the *Young Offenders Act*, was on the 26th day of August 19 82 , found guilty of the following offence:

> theft: to wit Mary Powell on the 13th day of July, 1982 at Anytown, Ontario did steal a Sony television and recorder, Serial Nos. 48774 B and 2236 CF respectively, the property of the County of Queens Board of Education, of a value of $1345 dollars, contrary to Section 294(a) of the *Criminal Code* of Canada;

And whereas Mary Powell was committed in custody in the County of Queens Youth Centre or such other place of secure custody as the provincial director or his delegate may specify for a period of nine months to be served continuously commencing on the 16th day of September 19 82.

This is therefore to command you to take Mary Powell and safely convey her to such place of custody and to deliver her to the person in charge thereof, together with the following precept:

This is to command you, the person in charge of the said place of custody, to receive Mary Powell into your custody and to keep her there safely in accordance with the order committing her to custody, and for so doing this is a sufficient warrant.

Dated this 15th day of September 19 82 at Anytown in the Province of Ontario.

"Thomas Brown"
. . . .
A Judge of the Youth Court

Transfer of disposition: section 25

SECTION 25

25. (1) *Transfer of disposition.*—Where a non-custodial disposition has been made in respect of a young person and the young person or a parent with whom he resides is or becomes a resident of a territorial division outside the jurisdiction of the youth court that made the disposition, whether in the same or in another province, a youth court judge in the territorial division in which the disposition was made may, on the application of the Attorney General or his agent or on the application of the young person or his parent with the consent of the Attorney General or his agent, transfer the disposition and such portion of the record of the case as is appropriate to a youth court in the other territorial division, and all subsequent proceedings relating to the case shall thereafter be carried out and enforced by that court.

(2) *No transfer outside province before appeal completed.*—No disposition may be transferred from one province to another under this section until the time for an appeal against the disposition or the finding on which the disposition was based has expired or until all proceedings in respect of any such appeal have been completed.

(3) *Transfer to a province where person is adult.*—Where an application is made under subsection (1) to transfer the disposition of a young person to a province in which the young person is an adult, a youth court judge may, with the consent of the Attorney General, transfer the disposition and the record of the case to the youth court in the province to which the transfer is sought, and the youth court to which the case is transferred shall have full jurisdiction in respect of the disposition as if that court had made the disposition, and the person shall be further dealt with in accordance with this Act.

Transfer of disposition: section 25

Section 25 recognizes the increased mobility of Canadian families and young persons by providing for a judicial transfer of a non-custodial disposition from one youth court jurisdiction to another, where the young person is a resident of a different jurisdiction or where the young person, his parent or family move to a new jurisdiction. The transfer may occur within a province or between provinces. Subsection 25(1) provides that the Attorney General or his agent in the province where the original disposition was made must consent to the transfer. The consent of the Attorney General in the receiving province, however, is not required; this obviates the possibility of a virtual veto of such a transfer which would perhaps prevent the young person from taking up residence with his parents.

It should be noted that s. 25 eliminates jurisdictional problems with respect to non-custodial dispositions only. Section 26 provides for interprovincial agreements to allow a young person placed on probation or committed to custody in one province to be dealt with in another province. Section 25 should be distinguished from s. 18 which permits the transfer to another province of a pending charge against a young person, prior to adjudication, if the young person signifies his intention to enter a guilty plea. Under s. 18 the youth court in the province to which the charge is transferred accepts the plea, makes an adjudication, and makes a disposition; the consent of the original province's Attorney General or his agent is also necessary under s. 18.

The most frequent use of s. 25 transfers will probably concern probation orders. Administrative coordination between the provinces will be necessary for the transfer process to function smoothly. Subsection 25(1) provides that all subsequent proceedings relating to the case, such as judicial review of disposition under ss. 32 and 33, shall thereafter be carried out and enforced by the court to which the case is transferred. The original court has no further role to play.

Subsection 25(1) also specifies that "such portion of the record ... as is appropriate to a youth court in the other territorial division" may be transferred. See comments on s. 40 discussing what constitutes the "record" of a youth court.

It would not appear that a hearing is necessary under s. 25, although a youth court that is inclined to refuse an application under the section might choose to afford the young person an opportunity to be heard. Owing to the recognition the Y.O.A. gives to the parent-child relationship and the obligations of parents towards their children, it would seem that a court should normally grant an application under s. 25 which is based upon a parental move.

Subsection 25(2) provides that no disposition may be transferred under s. 25 until the time for an appeal has lapsed, or, if an appeal has been made, until all appeal proceedings have been completed.

Subsection 25(3) has been included to deal with the difference in maximum ages that may exist on a province-by-province basis until April 1, 1985, when a uniform maximum age will apply across Canada. If a young person applies pursuant to s-s. 25(1) to move to another jurisdiction where he is an adult, the youth court judge may transfer the disposition and the record to the youth court of the receiving province. If such a transfer if made, the youth court in the receiving province has full jurisdiction and the original disposition continues as if the youth court in the receiving province had made it. Moreover, s-s. 25(3) states that "the person shall be further dealt with in accordance with this Act". This provision permits the continuation of a disposition and allows for review under the Y.O.A.

Interprovincial agreements governing disposition transfer: section 26

SECTION 26

26. (1) *Interprovincial arrangements for probation or custody.*— Where an appropriate agreement has been made between two provinces, young persons who have been placed on probation or committed to custody in one province under section 20 may be dealt with under the probation order or held in custody in the other province.

(2) *Youth court retains jurisdiction.*—Subject to subsection (3), where a young person is dealt with under a probation order or held in custody pursuant to this section in a province other than that in which the disposition was made, the youth court of the province in which the disposition was made shall, for all purposes of this Act, retain exclusive jurisdiction over the young person as if the young person were dealt with or held within that province, and any warrant or process issued in respect of the young person may be executed or served in any place in Canada outside the province where the disposition was made as if it were executed or served in that province.

(3) *Waiver of jurisdiction.*—Where a young person is dealt with under a probation order or held in custody pursuant to this

section in a province other than that in which the disposition
was made, the youth court of the province in which the disposition was made may, with the consent of the Attorney General of
that province and the young person, waive its jurisdiction, for
the purpose of any proceeding under this Act, to the youth court
of the province in which the young person is dealt with or held,
in which case the youth court in the province in which the
young person is so dealt with or held shall have full jurisdiction
in respect of the disposition as if that court had made the
disposition.

Interprovincial agreements: section 26

Subsection 26(1) allows any two provinces to make an agreement so that a young person who is placed on probation or
committed to custody in one province may be dealt with in
another province. A transfer under s. 26 does not require judicial
consent or a court order, though under s-s. 26(3) a waiver of
court jurisdiction may be sought after a young person has been
transferred pursuant to a s. 26 agreement. A s. 26 transfer cannot
be effected solely on the application of the young person, and his
consent is not required.

Agreements under s. 26 will be useful in two situations. First,
where the young person or his family moves, provincial authorities can make arrangements for transfer of a disposition without
the need for judicial involvement. If the young person is on
probation, a transfer pursuant to s. 26 may be administratively
easier to effect than a judicial transfer under s. 25. If the young
person is in custody and his family moves to another province,
the correctional authorities may want the youth moved so as to
be close to his family, but to remain in custody — this can only
be accomplished under s. 26.

The second situation where an order under s. 26 will be available is to allow one province to use custodial or other facilities in
another province, and particularly, to take advantage of special
programs in one province that are not readily available elsewhere.
For example, small provinces such as Prince Edward Island can
send young persons to custodial facilities in Nova Scotia if facilities are lacking in P.E.I. In some areas of the country, the nearest
specialized institutions are not necessarily to be found within
provincial boundaries; for example, communities in Northwest-

ern Ontario may look to Manitoba for specialized facilities rather than to Southern Ontario.

Pursuant to s-s. 26(2), in the event of a transfer under s-s. 26(1), the youth court of the province that made the original order retains exclusive jurisdiction over the young person, notwithstanding the fact that the young person is serving his disposition out of the province. To enforce this out of province jurisdiction, s-s. 26(2) provides that any warrant or process of the youth court of the province where the original order was made may be executed or served outside the province, and has effect throughout Canada.

Notwithstanding s-s. 26(2), the youth court of the original province may waive its jurisdiction to the youth court of the other province pursuant to s-s. 26(3). To do this the consent of both the Attorney General of the original province and of the young person is required. Note here that the Attorney General alone has the authority to consent, unlike the situation in s-s. 25(1) where either the Attorney General or his agent may consent. If the original youth court waives jurisdiction, the receiving youth court has "full jurisdiction in respect of the disposition as if that court had made the disposition."

The original youth court has no obligation to hold a hearing before deciding to waive jurisdiction under s-s. 26(3). If the Attorney General and the young person both consent the youth court might well be reluctant to intervene and to refuse to allow a waiver; nevertheless the court may feel that it has an independent duty, and may choose to hold a hearing to consider the situation, though such action should not ordinarily be necessary.

APPEALS
(Section 27)

Introduction

Section 27 of the *Young Offenders Act* provides for an appeal procedure very different from that of the *Juvenile Delinquents Act*. Section 37 of the *J.D.A.* permits appeals only with special leave to be granted if the appellate judge considers that it is "essential in the public interest or for the due administration of justice that such leave be granted." If leave is granted, an appeal under the *J.D.A.* follows the provisions of the *Criminal Code* relating to appeals from conviction on indictment, applied *mutatis mutandis*.

The Y.O.A. provides for appeals as of right. The *Criminal Code* procedure applies to Y.O.A. appeals; however, unlike the *J.D.A.*, the Y.O.A. maintains the distinction between appeals from summary conviction and indictable offences. The provisions of s. 27 of the Y.O.A. recognize that young persons affected by the criminal law should have the same appeal rights as adults.

SECTION 27

27. (1) *Appeals.*—An appeal lies under this Act from a finding of guilt, an order dismissing an information or a disposition made under section 20,

(a) in the case of an indictable offence or an offence that the Attorney General or his agent elects to proceed with as an indictable offence, in the same manner as if the finding of guilt were a conviction, the order dismissing the information were a verdict of acquittal or the disposition were a sentence, in a prosecution by indictment in ordinary court; and

(b) in the case of an offence punishable on summary conviction or an offence that the Attorney General or his agent elects to proceed with as an offence punishable on summary conviction, in the same manner as if the finding of guilt were a conviction, the order dismissing the information were an order dismissing the information or the disposition were a sentence, in proceedings by way of summary conviction in ordinary court.

(2) *Deemed election.*—For the purposes of appeals under this Act, where no election is made in respect of an offence that may be prosecuted by indictment or proceeded with by way of summary conviction, the Attorney General or his agent shall be deemed to have elected to proceed with the offence as an offence punishable on summary conviction.

(3) *Where the youth court is a superior court.*—In any province where the youth court is a superior court, an appeal under paragraph (1)(b) shall be made to the court of appeal of the province.

(4) *Where the youth court is a county or district court.*—In any province where the youth court is a county or district court, an appeal under paragraph (1)(b) shall be made to the superior court of the province.

(5) *Appeal to the Supreme Court of Canada.*—No appeal lies pursuant to paragraph (1)(a) from a judgment of the court of appeal in respect of a finding of guilt or an order dismissing an information to the Supreme Court of Canada unless leave to appeal is granted by the Supreme Court of Canada within twenty-one days after the judgment of the court of appeal is pronounced or within such extended time as the Supreme Court of Canada or a judge thereof may, for special reasons, allow.

(6) *No appeal from disposition on review.*—No appeal lies from a disposition under sections 28 to 32.

Appeals: subsections 27(1), (3), (4), (5) and (6)

Appeal lies as of right from a finding of guilt, an order dismissing an information, or a disposition. Subsection 27(6) of the Y.O.A. provides that there is no appeal from a review of disposition under ss. 28 to 32; because no disposition can be made more onerous under these sections, the substantive rights of the young offender are not affected. There is an appeal from a dispositional review under s. 33, since an additional penalty may be ordered pursuant to that section: see s-s. 33(10).

Subsection 52(2) of the Y.O.A. preserves the summary and indictable character of offences under the Act and different appeal procedures for summary and indictable offences are provided for by s-s. 27(1). Paragraph 27(1)(a) provides that an adjudication or disposition for an indictable offence prosecuted in youth court is the same as if the offence were prosecuted by indictment in ordinary court; thus appeals are governed by the *Criminal Code*, Part XVIII, "Appeals — Indictable Offences."

Under s. 603 of the *Code*, an appeal lies to the provincial court of appeal; appeals may be based on questions of law alone or with leave of the court of appeal on mixed questions of law and fact. In addition, the court of appeal has a discretion to grant leave where other sufficient grounds exist. Leave is required for an appeal regarding disposition alone (para. 603(1)(b) of *Code*). There may be an appeal where the accused is found unfit to stand trial or not guilty by reason of insanity (s-s. 603(2) of *Code*).

Paragraph 27(1)(b) provides that an adjudication or disposition for a summary conviction offence prosecuted in youth court is the same as if the offence were prosecuted summarily in ordinary court; thus the provisions of ss. 747 to 771 of the *Code* govern these appeals. Under these sections of the *Code*, there is some variation between jurisdictions as to which court the appeal lies; in jurisdictions where the youth court is a provincial court, appeals lie to the "appeal court" (as defined in s. 747 of the *Code*), with limited rights of appeal to the court of appeal under s. 771. Subsections 27(3) and (4) of the Y.O.A. specify that in regard to a summary conviction matter, in any province where the youth court is a superior court, an appeal lies to the court of appeal (s-s. 27(3)), and where the youth court is a county or district court, an appeal is made to the superior court of the province (s-s. 27(4)). The provisions of the *Code* in regard to summary matters provide some flexibility as to whether the appeal is on the record, on the basis of a stated case, or even by trial *de novo* (see s. 755 and ss. 761 to 770 of the *Code*).

In addition to the relevant provisions of the *Code*, the appeal procedure will be governed by any applicable provincial criminal appeal rules enacted pursuant to s. 438 of the *Criminal Code*. On appeal procedure generally, see Salhany, *Canadian Criminal Procedure*, 3rd ed. (1978), Chapter 9. The criminal appeal rules for all the provinces are set out in D. Watt, *Criminal Law Precedents*, Vol. 2 (Toronto: Carswell, 1978).

Subsection 27(5) of the Y.O.A. limits recourse to the Supreme Court of Canada. An appeal to the highest court from a judgment of the court of appeal lies only in regard to an adjudication for an indictable offence and not for a disposition, disposition review or adjudication for a summary conviction offence. Further, an appeal to the Supreme Court of Canada requires leave of that

Court; leave must be granted within 21 days, unless the Court grants an extension for "special reasons".

The right of appeal in the Y.O.A. is statutory and extends only to the specific matters set out in the Act. A number of decisions cannot be appealed, for example, an order of exclusion from the court under s. 39, or a decision under para. 40(2)(e) regarding disclosure of records. Some sections of the Y.O.A. create specific appeal or review procedures for certain decisions, for example s-ss. 16(9) to (13), which govern review of a transfer decision by a higher court. There may also be a possibility of judicial review of some decisions of youth courts through the use of prerogative writs, even in the absence of express statutory provision in the Y.O.A.

Deemed election: subsection 27(2)

Where no election is made in respect of a "hybrid offence" (an offence which can be proceeded with on indictment or summarily), s-s. 27(2) deems that the prosecutor has elected to proceed with the offence as an offence punishable on summary conviction. This accords with jurisprudence on this matter dealing with adult offenders. Although para. 27(1)(a) of the *Interpretation Act* deems an offence to be an indictable offence until the Crown elects otherwise, if no election is endorsed on the record and the trial proceeds, the offence will be deemed a summary conviction offence. (See Salhany, *Canadian Criminal Procedure*, 3rd ed. (1978), pp. 231-32 and cases cited there.) As a consequence of this rule, the Crown should consider exercising its right to elect at the first opportunity; in any event the Crown must elect before the accused enters his plea. See D. A. MacDougall, "The Crown Election" (1979), 5 C.R. (3d) 315.

REVIEW OF DISPOSITIONS
(Sections 28 to 34)

Introduction

The disposition review provisions of the Y.O.A. are set out in sections 28 to 34. The function of a review is to ascertain whether a disposition is still appropriate after some time has elapsed or circumstances have changed or to provide for proper enforcement in cases of wilful failure to comply with a disposition. This accords with the principles of the Y.O.A. that dispositions are to be geared to needs which may change (para. 3(1)(c)), and that young persons are guaranteed the right to the least possible interference with their freedom that is consistent with the protection of society (para. 3(1)(f)).

Sections 28 to 34 form a procedural code; review is available to the young person under one of these sections. Review of custodial dispositions is available pursuant to ss. 28 and 29. Under s. 28, there is an automatic review by a youth court after one year. Upon request, review may take place after six months from the date of the disposition or earlier, with leave of the court, where the young person has made progress with the disposition, there has been a change in circumstances or where the young person can otherwise satisfy the youth court that grounds for review exist.

Section 29 provides a procedure that allows the provincial director to make a recommendation for release of the young person from custody. If the provincial director's recommendation is acceptable to the court, it is not necessary to conduct a hearing or to make a court appearance.

Under s. 30, review of custodial dispositions may be carried out by provincial review boards. These boards are empowered to take over the s. 28 and 29 functions of a youth court, other than the release of a young person from custody to probation, which must be effected by the court. Any decision of a review board is made reviewable by a youth court under s. 31.

Review of non-custodial dispositions is governed by s. 32. The youth court may confirm or vary non-custodial dispositions on review; as well the court is empowered to terminate the disposition outright, unlike the situation under ss. 28 and 29. Provincial review boards have no jurisdiction to review non-custodial dispositions.

Review under ss. 28 to 32 may not result in a more onerous disposition. Section 33 is the only provision for review allowing for the imposition of a more severe disposition. Review under s. 33 can occur only where there has been a wilful failure or refusal to comply with the disposition or the young person has escaped or attempted to escape from custody, and any such allegation must be proved beyond a reasonable doubt.

The provisions for review of disposition under the Y.O.A. contrast with the provisions of the *Juvenile Delinquents Act*, which are less structured and broader. According to s-s. 20(3) of the J.D.A., once adjudged delinquent, a juvenile can be brought back before the Juvenile Court at any time before he is 21; the Court may then make any disposition listed in s-s. 20(1). The review provisions of the J.D.A. are potentially subject to abuse. For example, there is no duty on the Court to carry out a full hearing regarding allegations of wilful breach of a disposition. Moreover, at the time of review under the J.D.A., a delinquent may be subject to transfer to adult court pursuant to s. 9.

The Y.O.A. sets out a number of procedures that must be followed upon review, thus ensuring that the young person has a fair hearing. Provision is made for such matters as notice, and progress reports are required to provide the court with adequate information about the young person. At every stage of review proceedings, the young person has the right to counsel. The possibility of transfer to ordinary court at the time of review does not exist under the Y.O.A.

It should be noted that a disposition review under ss. 28, 29, 31 to 33 need *not* be conducted by the youth court judge who made the initial disposition. See discussion following s. 64, substitution of judges.

Youth court hearing to review custody

SECTION 28

28. (1) *Automatic review of disposition involving custody.—* **Where a young person is committed to custody pursuant to a**

disposition made in respect of an offence for a period exceeding one year, the provincial director of the province in which the young person is held in custody shall cause the young person to be brought before the youth court forthwith at the end of one year from the date of the most recent disposition made in respect of the offence, and the youth court shall review the disposition.

(2) *Idem.*—Where a young person is committed to custody pursuant to dispositions made in respect of more than one offence for a total period exceeding one year, the provincial director of the province in which the young person is held in custody shall cause the young person to be brought before the youth court forthwith at the end of one year from the date of the earliest disposition made, and the youth court shall review the dispositions.

(3) *Optional review of disposition involving custody.*—Where a young person is committed to custody pursuant to a disposition made in respect of an offence, the provincial director may, on his own initiative, and shall, on the request of the young person, his parent or the Attorney General or his agent, on any of the grounds set out in subsection (4), cause the young person to be brought before the youth court at any time after six months from the date of the most recent disposition made in respect of the offence or, with leave of a youth court judge, at any earlier time, and, where the youth court is satisfied that there are grounds for the review under subsection (4), the court shall review the disposition.

(4) *Grounds for review under subsection (3).*—A disposition made in respect of a young person may be reviewed under subsection (3)

(a) on the ground that the young person has made sufficient progress to justify a change in disposition;

(b) on the ground that the circumstances that led to the committal to custody have changed materially;

(c) on the ground that new services or programs are available that were not available at the time of the disposition; or

(d) on such other grounds as the youth court considers appropriate.

(5) *No review where appeal pending.*—No review of a disposition in respect of which an appeal has been taken shall be made under this section until all proceedings in respect of any such appeal have been completed.

(6) *Youth court may order appearance of young person for review.*—Where a provincial director is required under subsections (1) to (3) to cause a young person to be brought before the youth court and fails to do so, the youth court may, on application made by the young person, his parent or the Attorney General or his agent, or on its own motion, order the provincial director to cause the young person to be brought before the youth court.

(7) *Progress report.*—The youth court shall, before reviewing under this section a disposition made in respect of a young person, require the provincial director to cause to be prepared, and to submit to the youth court, a progress report on the performance of the young person since the disposition took effect.

(8) *Additional information in progress report.*—A person preparing a progress report in respect of a young person may include in the report such information relating to the personal and family history and present environment of the young person as he considers advisable.

(9) *Written or oral report.*—A progress report shall be in writing unless it cannot reasonably be committed to writing, in which case it may, with leave of the youth court, be submitted orally in court.

(10) *Provisions of subsections 14(4) to (10) to apply.*—The provisions of subsections 14(4) to (10) apply, with such modifications as the circumstances require, in respect of progress reports.

(11) *Notice of review from provincial director.*—Where a disposition made in respect of a young person is to be reviewed under subsection (1) or (2), the provincial director shall cause such notice as may be directed by rules of court applicable to the youth court or, in the absence of such direction, at least five clear days notice of the review to be given in writing to the young person, his parents and the Attorney General or his agent.

(12) *Notice of review from person requesting it.*—Where a review of a disposition made in respect of a young person is requested under subsection (3), the person requesting the review shall cause such notice as may be directed by rules of court applicable to the youth court or, in the absence of such direction, at least five clear days notice of the review to be given in writing to the young person, his parents and the Attorney General or his agent.

(13) *Statement of right to counsel.*—Any notice given to a parent under subsection (11) or (12) shall include a statement that

the young person whose disposition is to be reviewed has the right to be represented by counsel.

(14) *Service and form of notice.*—A notice under subsection (11) or (12) may be served personally or may be sent by registered mail and, in the case of a notice to a young person, may be in Form 11 and, in any other case, may be in Form 12.

(15) *Notice may be waived.*—Any of the persons entitled to notice under subsection (11) or (12) may waive the right to such notice.

(16) *Where notice not given.*—Where notice under subsection (11) or (12) is not given in accordance with this section, the youth court may

(a) adjourn the proceedings and order that the notice be given in such manner and to such persons as it directs; or

(b) dispense with the notice where, in the opinion of the court, having regard to the circumstances, notice may be dispensed with.

(17) *Decision of the youth court after review.*—Where a youth court reviews under this section a disposition made in respect of a young person, it may, after affording the young person, his parents, the Attorney General or his agent and the provincial director or his agent an opportunity to be heard, having regard to the needs of the young person and the interests of society,

(a) confirm the disposition;

(b) where the young person is in secure custody, by order direct that the young person be placed in open custody; or

(c) release the young person from custody and place him on probation in accordance with section 23 for a period not exceeding the remainder of the period for which he was committed to custody.

(18) Form of disposition.—A disposition made under subsection (17) may be in Form 13.

Automatic review of custodial dispositions: subsections 28(1) and (2)

Section 28 provides for a review hearing by a youth court where a young person has been committed to custody. Review is mandatory at the end of one year from disposition, where the young person has been committed to custody for a period of more than one year.

Under s-s. 28(1), a duty is placed on the provincial director to cause a young person committed to custody for more than one year to be brought before a youth court at the end of one year. This automatic review is included in the Act to ensure that the disposition remains relevant to the needs of the young person and also to make the most effective use of resources.

If a young person is committed to custody as a result of dispositions for more than one offence, s-s. 28(2) provides for mandatory review at "the end of one year from the date of the earliest disposition made." Subsection 28(2) applies if all of the dispositions are made at one hearing and applies to all consecutive or concurrent custodial dispositions, exceeding a total period of one year. It also applies if there is an initial custodial disposition, and one or more subsequent custodial dispositions are made while the first one is still in effect, so that the total of the custodial dispositions exceeds one year.

Optional review: subsections 28(3) and (4)

Subsection 28(3) provides for a review of custodial dispositions earlier than the one-year period specified in s-ss. 28(1) and (2). There is a right to apply for a review before a youth court at any time after six months from the date of the most recent disposition or dispositional review in respect of the offence. The review may be initiated by the provincial director on his own motion. Alternatively, the young person, his parent, or the Attorney General or his agent, may request that the provincial director cause the young person to be brought before the youth court; the provincial director must comply with such a request. Grounds for a disposition review under s-s. 28(3) are set out in s-s. 28(4), and are as follows: the young person has made sufficient progress to justify a change in disposition; circumstances that led to the committal to custody have changed materially; new services are available; or "on such other grounds as the youth court considers appropriate." If any of these grounds are established, the youth court must review the disposition.

It is also possible for the provincial director, the young person, his parent, or the Attorney General or his agent, to seek youth court review of a custodial disposition at an earlier time, before the expiration of six months from the most recent disposition or last review. Leave of a youth court judge is required before such a review occurs; the youth court judge must be satisfied that there are grounds for review under s-s. 28(4). Leave for a review hearing may be granted after giving the parties an opportunity to make summary representations, or presumably may be dealt with on the basis of written submissions.

No review where appeal pending: subsection 28(5)

Subsection 28(5) makes clear that appeal proceedings must be completed before a review of disposition can take place under s-ss. 28(1) to (3).

Failure of provincial director to cause appearance of young person: subsection 28(6)

Subsection 28(6) provides a remedy if the provincial director fails to cause a young person to be brought before the youth court, as required by s-ss. 28(1) to (3). In such an instance, the young person, his parent, or the Attorney General or his agent may apply to a youth court for an order requiring the provincial director to bring the young person before the court; as well, the youth court may make such an order on its own motion. Breach of a youth court order made pursuant to s-s. 28(6) would constitute contempt of court and would be punishable as such under s. 47 of the Y.O.A.

Progress reports: subsections 28(7) to (10)

Subsection 28(7) requires that prior to a review hearing under s. 28 a progress report shall be prepared and submitted to the youth court on the performance of the young person since the disposition took effect. The provincial director is officially responsible to cause the report to be prepared; the youth court worker will usually be charged with its preparation. The object of the report is to provide the court with adequate information about the young person to facilitate the review procedure. Subsection 28(8) permits the author to include "such information relating to the personal and family history and present environment of the young person as he considers advisable." There is flexibility regarding the contents of the report according to this formula.

Subsection 28(9) requires a progress report to be in writing, "unless it cannot reasonably be committed to writing"; with leave of the court in such circumstances a progress report may be submitted orally in court. If a lack of time or resources necessitates oral submission of a progress report, the parties should, where possible, be informed of its contents before presentation of the report so that they will be put on notice and can respond to it. A judge may consider an adjournment in preference to allowing an oral report if a party objects to its submission as it is more difficult for a party to prepare to challenge an oral report than a written one.

Subsection 28(10) provides that the procedural provisions of s-ss. 14(4) to (10), dealing with pre-disposition reports, are adopted in regard to progress reports "with such modifications as the circumstances require." By adopting the provisions of s-s. 14(4), a progress report is specifically made part of the youth court record. Provision is made for distribution of the report to the young person, a parent in attendance at court, the young person's counsel and the prosecutor (para. 14(5)(a)). If a parent is not in attendance but is taking an active interest in the proceedings, the youth court may cause a copy of the report to be given to the parent (para. 14(5)(b)). The opportunity to cross-examine the person who made the report is given to the young person, his counsel or an adult who is assisting the young person pursuant to s-s. 11(7), and the prosecutor (s-s. 14(6)).

Further dissemination of the progress report is permitted by the adoption of s-ss. 14(8) and (9). The first provision allows copies or transcripts of the report to be furnished to "any court that is dealing with matters relating to the young person" and to "any youth worker to whom the young person's case has been assigned"; as well, the court may furnish the report, or a part thereof, to any person who in the opinion of the court has a valid interest in the proceedings. Subsection 14(9) operates so as to permit the provincial director to make the progress report available to a person supervising or having custody of the young person, or to a person who is directly assisting in the care or treatment of the young person.

The application of s-s. 14(10) generally forbids the use in evidence of any statement made by a young person in the course of preparation of a progress report in any civil or criminal proceedings, except for the purposes of a proceeding under s. 16 (transfer), s. 20 (disposition) or ss. 28 to 32 (disposition review).

For a more complete discussion on s-ss. 14(4) to (19), see the discussion under s. 14 "Pre-disposition report."

Notice of review: subsections 28(11) to (16)

The Y.O.A. contains detailed provisions to ensure that adequate notice of review proceedings is given to the young person, his parents and the Attorney General or his agent. The legislation uses the word "parents," and presumably includes all parents of the young person. If there are difficulties in locating or notifying all parents, s-s. 28(16) provides for substituted service or dispensing with notice. Subsection 28(11) specifies that "such notice as may be directed by rules of court applicable to the youth court" must be given. If notice is not dealt with by rules of court enacted pursuant to ss. 67 or 68 of the Y.O.A., a minimum of five clear days' notice of review must be given in writing to each of the persons mentioned in s-s. 28(11).

Subsection 28(11) imposes responsibility upon the provincial director to see that notice is given of a review commenced pursuant to s-s. 28(1) or (2). An equivalent responsibility is placed on "the person requesting the review" by s-s. 28(12), where review is initiated before one year under s-s. 28(3). Subsection 28(13) provides that notice to parents must include a statement advising the parents that the young person has the right to be represented by counsel. Subsection 11(9) requires the same statement on any notice of review of disposition given to the young person.

Notice under s-s. 28(11) or (12) may be sent by registered mail or served personally according to s-s. 28(14). Subsection 62(1) of the Y.O.A. provides that service "may be proved by oral evidence given under oath by, or by the affidavit or statutory declaration of, the person claiming to have personally served it or sent it by mail." A notice to a young person may be in Form 11. Notice to any other person may be in Form 12: see samples at the end of discussion of s. 28.

Any person entitled to notice under s-s. 28(11) or (12) may waive his right to notice pursuant to s-s. 28(15). In the event that notice is not given in accordance with s. 28, the youth court may, pursuant to s-s. 28(16), make an order dispensing with service of notice or it may adjourn the proceedings to allow time for notice to be served in accordance with the direction of the court. The provisions for substitutional service and the dispensing of notice are similar to the provisions in s. 9 governing notice to parents: see the discussion of s-s. 9(10).

Decision of the youth court: subsections 28(17) and (18)

Before making a new disposition or confirming the old disposition, the youth court must afford the young person, his parents, the Attorney General or his agent and the provincial director or his agent an opportunity to be heard pursuant to s-s. 28(17). This provision ensures that the rules of natural justice apply to reviews, with all parties having the right to call witnesses and cross-examine the witnesses called by other parties. Even though the right to a hearing is guaranteed, the strict rules of evidence do not apply to dispositional hearings. See comments above on the conduct of a disposition hearing under s. 20.

No disposition imposed on review under s. 28 may be more onerous than the original disposition. The youth court is limited to three options on review: it may confirm the disposition; it may change the level of custody from secure to open; and it may release the young person from custody and place him on probation for a period not exceeding the remainder of the period for which he was committed to custody. Note also that there is no provision for outright release from custody, without a period of probation. A further review under s. 32 would be necessary to secure the termination of probation.

In deciding whether to release a young person from custody, or to reduce the level of custody, the youth court must have regard to "the needs of the young person and the interests of society." The court should consider the Declaration of Principles, set out in s. 3, and will doubtless refer to the factors mentioned in s-s. 28(4). The court will thus consider whether the young person has made sufficient progress to justify a change in disposition, whether the circumstances that led to the commission of the offence have materially changed, and whether new services or programs that were not available at the time of disposition are now available. The court may consider any other factors it considers appropriate. In assessing these factors, the court must consider the interest of society and the needs of the young person.

Subsection 28(18) permits the use of Form 13 for a disposition made under s-s. 28(17). See sample forms on the following pages.

SAMPLE FORM

FORM 11
THE YOUNG OFFENDERS ACT
IN THE YOUTH COURT FOR ONTARIO

NOTICE TO YOUNG PERSON OF REVIEW
OF DISPOSITION

Canada
Province of Ontario
County of Queens

To: Mary Powell of 425 Blair Road, Anytown, Ontario ,
a young person within the meaning of the *Young Offenders Act,*

Whereas on the 26th day of August 19 82 , you were
found guilty of the following offence:

theft: to wit Mary Powell on the 13th day of July, 1982
at Anytown, Ontario did steal a Sony television and
recorder, Serial Nos. 48774 B and 2236 CF respectively, the property of the County of Queens Board of
Education, of a value of $1345, contrary to Section
294(a) of the *Criminal Code of Canada;*

And whereas by order of disposition dated the 15th day of
September 19 82, it was ordered;

that Mary Powell be committed to secure custody in
the County of Queens Youth Centre for a period of
sixteen months commencing on the 16th day of September, 1982.

And whereas a review of the disposition is required pursuant to
subsection 28(1) of the *Young Offenders Act:*

This is therefore to notify you that the review will be heard
before the Youth Court at 100 Main Street, Anytown, Ontario on Monday the 19th day of September 19 83 , at
10:00 o'clock in the fore noon;

And this is to notify you that you have the right to be represented by counsel.

Dated this 8th day of September 19 83 at Anytown
in the Province of Ontario.

"James Flynn"
....
A Judge of the Youth Court

SAMPLE FORM

FORM 12
THE YOUNG OFFENDERS ACT
IN THE YOUTH COURT FOR ONTARIO

NOTICE OF REVIEW OF DISPOSITION

Canada
Province of Ontario
County of Queens

To John Smith of 25 First Ave., Anytown, Ontario being a parent of, a person under a legal duty to provide for or a person who has in law or in fact the custody or control of David Smith of 25 First Ave., Anytown, Ontario :

Whereas on the 28th day of June 19 82 , David Smith was found guilty of the following offence:

robbery: to wit on the second day of June, 1982, David Smith did steal two hundred and fifty dollars from The Corner Milk Store, 2 West Street, Anytown, Ontario, and at the same time thereat did use threats of violence contrary to section 303 of the *Criminal Code of Canada*;

And whereas by probation order dated the 8th day of July 19 82 , it was ordered:

1. that David Smith be placed on probation commencing on the date of that order for a period of twenty months and subject to the conditions therein prescribed; and

2. that David Smith perform, at the Anytown Community Centre, two hours per week of community service for a period of twenty months as described in the order.

And whereas an application has been made by John Smith for a review of the disposition;

This is therefore to notify you that the review will be heard before the Youth Court on Tuesday the 16th day of January 19 83 , at 10:00 o'clock in the fore noon:

And this is to notify you that David Smith has the right to be represented by counsel.

And this is to notify you that you or any other person who is a parent of, a person under a legal duty to provide for or a person who has in law or in fact the custody and control of David Smith may appear at the hearing and will be given an opportunity to be heard.

Dated this 8th day of January 19 83 , at Anytown in the Province of Ontario.

"Thomas Brown"
....
A Judge of the Youth Court

SAMPLE FORM

FORM 13
THE YOUNG OFFENDERS ACT
IN THE YOUTH COURT FOR ONTARIO

DISPOSITION ON REVIEW

Canada
Province of Ontario
County of Queens

Whereas on the 26th day of August 19 82 , you were found guilty of the following offence:

theft: to wit Mary Powell on the 13th day of July, 1982 at Anytown, Ontario did steal a Sony television and recorder, Serial Nos. 48774 B and 2236 CF respectively, the property of the County of Queens Board of Education, of a value of $1345, contrary to Section 294(a) of the *Criminal Code of Canada.*

And whereas by order of disposition dated the 15th day of September 19 82 , it was ordered

that Mary Powell be committed to secure custody in Anytown Group Home for a period of sixteen months commencing on the 16th day of September, 1982:

And whereas a review of the disposition has been heard by the Youth Court

Be it remembered that on the 29th day of March 19 83 , I, James Flynn , Judge of the Youth Court, following the review ordered:

Mary Powell be committed to open custody in the County of Queens Youth Centre for the remainder of the period prescribed in the order of disposition dated the 15th day of September, 1982.

Dated this 29th day of March 19 83 , at Anytown in the Province of Ontario.

"James Flynn"
. . . .
A Judge of the Youth Court

Release from custody on recommendation of provincial director: section 29

SECTION 29

29. (1) *Recommendation of provincial director for probation.*— Where a young person is held in continuous custody pursuant to a disposition, the provincial director may, if he is satisfied that the needs of the young person and the interests of society would be better served if the young person were released from custody and placed on probation, cause notice in writing to be given to the young person, his parents and the Attorney General or his agent that he recommends that the young person be released from custody and placed on probation and give a copy of the notice to the youth court, and the provincial director shall include in the notice the reasons for his recommendation and the conditions that he would recommend be attached to a probation order.

(2) *Application to court for review of recommendation.*—A youth court shall, where notice of a review of a disposition made in respect of a young person is given under subsection (1), on the application of the young person, his parents or the Attorney General or his agent made within ten days after service of the notice, forthwith review the disposition.

(3) *Subsections 28(5), (7) to (10) and (12) to (18) apply.*— Subsections 28(5), (7) to (10) and (12) to (18) apply with such modifications as the circumstances require, in respect of reviews made under this section and any notice required under subsection 28(12) shall be given to the provincial director.

(4) *Where the court does not review the disposition.*—A youth court that receives a notice under subsection (1) recommending that a young person be released from custody and placed on probation shall, if no application for a review is made under subsection (2),

(a) release the young person and place him on probation in accordance with section 23, in which case the court shall include in the probation order such conditions referred to in that section as it considers advisable having regard to the recommendations of the provincial director; or

(b) where the court deems it advisable, make no direction under this subsection unless the provincial director requests a review under this section.

(5) *Where the provincial director requests a review.*—Where the provincial director requests a review under paragraph (4)(b),

(a) the provincial director shall cause such notice as may be directed by rules of court applicable to the youth court or, in the absence of such direction, at least five clear days notice of the review to be given in writing to the young person, his parents and the Attorney General or his agent; and

(b) the youth court shall forthwith, after the notice required under paragraph (a) is given, review the disposition.

(6) *Form of notice.*—A notice given under subsection (1) may be in Form 14.

Recommendation of provincial director for probation: subsections 29(1), (2), (4) and (5)

Section 29 provides that the provincial director may initiate a young person's release from custody to probation by making a recommendation for release to the youth court. The provincial director may thus play a major part in bringing about early release. The granting of the power to the provincial director to initiate early release without going so far as to permit him to alter unilaterally a custodial disposition is consistent with the complementary roles of the judiciary and juvenile correctional services, and recognizes that ultimate control over dispositions rests with the judiciary.

Detailed procedures are set out in s. 29 to ensure that the rights and interests of a young person, his parents and society are safeguarded. Notice of the provincial director's recommendation must be given to the young person, his parents, and the Attorney General or his agent, and where applicable, to the review board pursuant to s-s. 30(3). A copy of the notice must be given to the youth court. Subsection 29(1) specifies that the reasons for the provincial director's recommendation must be included in the notice, as must the conditions that the provincial director recommends for the young person's probation order.

Within ten days of the receipt of the provincial director's notice recommending release of the young person from custody on probation pursuant to s-s. 29(1), the young person, his parents, or the Attorney General or his agent, may apply to the youth court for a review hearing to consider the matter.

If no application is made for a review hearing, the youth court has two options under s-s. 29(4). The youth court may follow a provincial director's recommendation and release the young person from custody, placing him on probation on such terms as it considers advisable having regard to the recommendations of the provincial director; however, the court is not bound by the conditions of probation suggested by the provincial director. Alternatively, the youth court, where it deems it advisable, may make no direction unless the provincial director requests a review. Thus if the judge is of the opinion that a hearing is necessary, he may decline to make any order. The provincial director then has the option of requesting a review or abandoning or postponing his recommendation to release. Should the provincial director request a review under para. 29(4)(b), para. 29(5)(a) provides that notice must be given to the young person, his parents, and the Attorney General or his agent. Subsection 30(3) provides that where applicable, notice be given to a review board. Notice must be in accordance with the rules of court made pursuant to s. 67 or 68; if no rules of court apply, a minimum of five clear days' notice must be given. After the notice required by para. 29(5)(a) is given, the youth court shall forthwith hold a review hearing.

Procedure on review: subsections 29(3) and (6)

A youth court hearing is required in order to consider a provincial director's recommendation to release a young person from custody on probation if a review is sought by the young person, his parents or the Crown under s-s. 29(2). Alternatively, a hearing must be held where a judge refuses to accept the recommendation and the provincial director requests a review under para. 29(4)(b). The conduct of such a review hearing is governed by s-s. 29(3), which adopts many of the provisions of s. 28, making review hearings under the two sections quite similar.

One such provision, adopted in s-s. 29(3), is found in s-s. 28(5), providing that no review can take place in respect of a disposition that is being appealed until all appeal proceedings have been completed.

A progress report on the young person's performance since the disposition took effect must be prepared and submitted to the court; the provisions of s-ss. 28(7) to (10) apply to such reports. Information in the report may relate to the young person's personal history, his family history and his present environment. The report is to be in writing, with leave of the court, an oral report may be submitted. The report is part of the youth court record. The young person, a parent in attendance, his counsel and the prosecutor must receive copies of a written report prior to the hearing, and a parent with an active interest may receive a copy (s-s. 14(5)). Cross-examination of the author of the report is specifically provided for.

Copies of the progress report shall be supplied on request to other courts dealing with the young person and to a youth court worker assigned to the young person's case. Copies may be supplied on request to any person who, in the opinion of the court, has a valid interest in the proceedings — for example, a person supervising the young person or directly assisting in his care or treatment. Any statement made by the young person in the preparation of a progress report may not be used in civil or criminal proceedings, except under s. 16 (transfer), s. 20 (disposition) or ss. 28 to 32 (disposition review).

The person requesting review must comply with the notice requirements set out in s-ss. 28(12) to (16), with such modifications as the circumstances require; as well, the person requesting review shall give notice to the provincial director pursuant to s-s. 29(3). Such notice as the rules of court require, or at least five clear days' notice if no rules have been made, is mandatory. Any notice given to a parent or young person must include a statement of the young person's right to counsel; notice may be served personally or sent by registered mail. The right to notice may be waived. Where notice has not been given, in accordance with s-s. 28(16), the youth court may order an adjournment so notice may be given as directed, or the court may dispense with notice altogether. Notice to a young person may be in Form 11. Notice to a parent, the Attorney General or his agent or the provincial director may be in Form 12. See sample forms at the end of comments.

Subsection 29(3) also incorporates the provisions of s-s. 28(17), which ensure the young person, his parents, the Attorney General or his agent, and the provincial director or his agent, have an opportunity to be heard. As well, the effect of s-s. 28(17) is that no disposition imposed on review may be more onerous than the disposition under review. After a review under s. 29, the youth court may change the level of custody from secure to open custody, release the young person and place him on probation or confirm the disposition. In deciding on the appropriate course of action, the youth court shall have regard to "the needs of the young person and the interests of society"; the court should also consider the factors set out in s-s. 28(4).

A disposition under s. 29 may be in Form 13: see p. 239. A notice under s-s. 29(1) may be in Form 14: see sample below.

As the procedure for a s. 29 hearing largely adopts the procedure for the conduct of a s. 28 hearing, reference should be made to the discussion following that section.

SAMPLE FORM

FORM 14
THE YOUNG OFFENDERS ACT
IN THE YOUTH COURT FOR ONTARIO

NOTICE BY PROVINCIAL DIRECTOR OF INTENTION TO RELEASE YOUNG PERSON FROM CUSTODY

Canada
Province of Ontario
County of Queens

To: Mary Powell of 452 Blair Road, Anytown, Ontario , a young person within the meaning of the *Young Offenders Act*:

Whereas on the 26th day of August 19 82 , you were found guilty of the following offence:

theft: to wit Mary Powell on the 13th day of July, 1982 at Anytown, Ontario did steal a Sony television and recorder, Serial Nos. 48774 B and 2236 CF respectively, the property of the County of Queens Board of Education, of a value of $1345, contrary to Section 294(a) of the *Criminal Code of Canada*;

And whereas by order of disposition dated the 15th day of September 19 82 , it was ordered

that Mary Powell be committed to secure custody in County of Queens Youth Centre for a period of sixteen months commencing on the 16th day of September, 1982:

And whereas it appears that the needs of Mary Powell and the interests of society would be best served if Mary Powell were released from custody and placed on probation for the remainder of the disposition;

This is therefore to notify you that I recommend that Mary Powell be released from custody and placed on probation by the Youth Court;

And this is also to notify you that unless you or any other party entitled to apply to the Youth Court or the Review Board established or designated for the purposes of section 30 of the *Young Offenders Act*, if any, for a review of the disposition so applies within a period of ten days from the date of service of this notice Mary Powell will in accordance with subsection 29(4) of the *Young Offenders Act* be placed on probation by the Youth Court at the expiry of that period:

And this is also to notify you that I recommend that Mary Powell be placed on probation for the following reasons:

1. The progress report indicates that Mary Powell has participated in drug abuse programs during her period in custody and has responded well to them;

2. Mary Powell has re-established a relationship with her mother, Mrs. Helen Powell, and intends to return to her mother's home. Mrs. Powell, for her part, feels that Mary would now be better off with her;

3. Mary Powell has indicated a desire to continue her education at Great Lakes Community College;

4. Mary Powell has during her stay in custody improved her attitude and is now prepared to get on with her life without drugs;

5. The youth worker from the County of Queens Youth Centre feels that nothing is to be gained by Mary Powell's continued committal to custody.

And this is to notify you that I recommend the following conditions to Mary Powell's probation order:

1. that Mary Powell live at her mother's residence at 452 Blair Road, Anytown, Ontario; and

2. that Mary Powell attend the drug abuse program conducted at the Regional Drug Research Centre, Anytown, Ontario.

Dated this 8th day of February 19 83 , at Anytown in the Province of Ontario.

"J. Paul Henry"

. . . .

Provincial Director

Review boards: sections 30 and 31

Sections 30 and 31 allow individual provinces to establish review boards to carry out the "duties and functions of a youth court" under ss. 28 and 29 in regard to review of a custodial disposition. A review board does not have the authority to release a young person from custody and place him on probation, although it can recommend to a youth court that the young person be released from custody and placed on probation. If the young person, his parents, the provincial director or the Crown do not object to the recommendation, a youth court must follow the recommendation of a review board to release the young person and place him on probation, though the youth court may decide to impose any conditions of probation it considers advisable, having regard to the recommendations of the review board.

The review board's jurisdiction is limited to review of custodial dispositions. Alteration of non-custodial dispositions is entirely in the hands of the youth court under ss. 32 and 33. The review board's "duties and functions" include the holding of a hearing at which the young person, his parents, the Crown and the provincial director have an opportunity to be heard. Section 11 of the Y.O.A. assures the young person of the right to representation at a review board hearing. There are provisions in s. 30 ensuring that those involved receive adequate notice of the proceedings. There must be a progress report prepared for the review board hearing, and the parties must have an opportunity to cross-examine the maker of the report.

Where there is no application made to the youth court for a review hearing, the review board's recommendation goes into effect without a court hearing. If, however, an application for review is made by the young person, his parents, the Crown or the provincial director, the youth court must conduct a hearing pursuant to s. 31 to consider the recommendation. The Y.O.A. does not specify the exact nature of the review to be conducted by the youth court; however, it is evident that s-s. 31(2) requires a full hearing rather than simply a review on the record of the board's proceedings. Subsection 31(2) incorporates the provisions for notice, requires the submission of a progress report and affords those involved an opportunity to be heard as set out in s-ss. 28(7) to (10) and (12) to (18). Section 11 guarantees the young person's right to counsel at such a youth court hearing.

The effect of ss. 30 and 31 is to allow provinces to set up review boards to consider whether a custodial disposition should be continued. The members of the boards need not have legal training, and may bring other special expertise to the issue. The proceedings need not follow strict procedural and evidentiary rules which govern trials in youth court. Although proceedings before a review board may be relatively informal compared to those in a youth court, a board must comply with certain procedural standards. The Y.O.A. specifies many of the procedures to be followed, for example in regard to affording those involved, notice and an opportunity to be heard, and providing the young person with a right to counsel. Further, it is submitted that as a review board is required under s-s. 30(1) to "carry out the duties and functions of a youth court" under ss. 28 and 29, it is a tribunal carrying out an essentially judicial function. Hence, in addition to the statutory requirements, the review board is to follow the rules of natural justice and might be well advised to follow similar procedural standards as would normally be expected in a dispositional hearing conducted by a youth court.

In any event, the Y.O.A. ensures a degree of judicial control over the review board process, and guarantees a right to review by a youth court if any of the parties involved are dissatisfied with the recommendations of a review board.

SECTION 30

30. (1) *Review board.*—Where a review board is established or designated by a province for the purpose of this section, that board shall, subject to this section, carry out in that province the duties and functions of a youth court under sections 28 and 29 other than releasing a young person from custody and placing him on probation.

(2) *Other duties of review board.*—Subject to this Act, a review board may carry out any duties or functions that are assigned to it by the province that established or designated it.

(3) *Notice under section 29.*—Where a review board is established or designated by a province for the purposes of this section, the provincial director shall at the same time as any notice is given under subsection 29(1) cause a copy of the notice to be given to the review board.

(4) *Notice of decision of review board.*—A review board shall cause notice of any decision made by it in respect of a young

person pursuant to section 28 or 29 to be given forthwith in writing to the young person, his parents, the Attorney General or his agent and the provincial director, and a copy of the notice to be given to the youth court.

(5) *Decision of review to take effect where no review.*—Subject to subsection (6), any decision of a review board under this section shall take effect ten days after the decision is made unless an application for review is made under section 31.

(6) *Decision respecting release from custody and probation.*— Where a review board decides that a young person should be released from custody and placed on probation, it shall so recommend to the youth court and, if no application for a review of the decision is made under section 31, the youth court shall forthwith on the expiration of the ten day period referred to in subsection (5) release the young person from custody and place him on probation in accordance with section 23, and shall include in the probation order such conditions referred to in that section as the court considers advisable having regard to the recommendations of the review board.

(7) *Form of notice of decision of review board.*—A notice of a decision of the review board under this section may be in Form 15.

SECTION 31

31. (1) *Review by youth court.*—Where the review board reviews a disposition under section 30, the youth court shall, on the application of the young person in respect of whom the review was made, his parents, the Attorney General or his agent or the provincial director, made within ten days after the decision of the review board is made, forthwith review the decision.

(2) *Subsections 28(5), (7) to (10) and (12) to (18) apply.*— Subsections 28(5), (7) to (10) and (12) to (18) apply, with such modifications as the circumstances require, in respect of reviews made under this section and any notice required under subsection 28(12) shall be given to the provincial director.

Composition and duties of review boards: subsections 30(1) and (2)

Section 30 of the Y.O.A. permits a province to set up a "review board" to carry out the responsibilities of a youth court in regard to review of custodial dispositions of young persons. If a province chooses to have a review board, it must determine its composition, either establishing a completely new tribunal, or designating an existing body as a "review board". Subsection 30(1) provides that the board shall, "subject to this section, carry out ... the duties and functions of a youth court under sections 28 and 29 other than releasing a young person from custody and placing him on probation."

A review board may hold a review hearing under s. 28 (automatic and optional review) and confirm the original custodial disposition or direct that where a young person has been in secure custody be instead placed in open custody (paras. 28(17)(a) and (b)). The board cannot directly order the release of a young person from custody and place him on probation as a youth court may do under para. 28(17)(c). The review board may only make a recommendation to this effect to the youth court which is bound to follow the recommendation for release, unless a request for review is made. In implementing a recommendation for release, the court may impose such conditions of probation as it considers advisable, having regard to the recommendations of the board (s-s. 30(6)).

Where a province has established a review board, it would also have jurisdiction under s. 29. In exercising this jurisdiction, the board would have to assess a provincial director's recommendation for release, and would, upon receipt of an application, conduct a review hearing pursuant to s-s. 29(2). The board cannot, however, order the release of a young person and place him on probation; the release must be effected by the youth court pursuant to s-s. 30(6).

Subsection 30(2) provides that "[s]ubject to this Act, a review board may carry out any duties or functions that are assigned to it by the province ...". Thus, in addition to the board's review jurisdiction, a province may assign other duties falling within the jurisdiction of provincial authorities.

The duties of a review board include ensuring that a progress report is prepared and is considered by the board, and that all those entitled are given a copy and an opportunity to cross-examine the person who prepared the report (s-ss. 28(7) to (10)). The board must also ensure that the notice provisions of s-ss. 28(11) to (16) are complied with.

Section 11 of the Y.O.A. applies to review board hearings, thus a young person must be advised of his right to obtain counsel and must be given a reasonable opportunity to obtain counsel.

Furthermore, if a young person wishes to obtain counsel but is unable to do so, either on his own or after reference to a legal aid or assistance program, the board must make a direction for the appointment of counsel.

A review board has a "duty to act fairly" and it seems clear that a review board has a duty to comply with the rules of natural justice: see *Re Abel and Advisory Review Board* (1980), 31 O.R. (2d) 520, 119 D.L.R. (3d) 101 (C.A.). Thus, a young person should have a right in proceedings before a review board to challenge evidence, cross-examine witnesses and call his own evidence. Any legislation, whether federal or provincial, which governs review boards is subject to the *Charter of Rights*, in particular s. 7 of the *Charter* which provides: "Everyone has the right . . . to liberty and security of person and the right not to be deprived thereof except in accordance with the principles of fundamental justice."

Notice: subsection 30(3)

To ensure that any review board which is set up is kept informed about development in regard to young persons in custody, s-s. 30(3) requires the provincial director to cause a copy of any notice given under s-s. 29(1) to be given to the review board. Subsection 29(1) requires that the provincial director give notice to various persons of his recommendations that a young person be released from custody and placed on probation. If no request is made under s-s. 29(2) for a review hearing, the young person must be released pursuant to the recommendation of the provincial director, although the terms of probation may be varied by the youth court.

Notice of decision of review board: subsection 30(4)

Subsection 30(4) provides that notice of any decision made by the review board under s. 28 or 29 must be given "forthwith in writing to the young person, his parents, the Attorney General or his agent and the provincial director." The youth court is also to receive a copy of the notice.

Effect of decision of review board: subsections 30(5) and (6)

The recommendation of the review board goes into effect ten days after the decision is made, according to s-s. 30(5), unless an application for a review hearing by a youth court is made under s. 31. Thus, for example, if the board recommends release from secure custody into open custody, the order will take effect ten days after the board's decision unless review is sought under s. 31. Subsection 30(6) provides an exception to the s-s. 30(5) procedure where the decision of the review board is to recommend the young person's release from custody to probation. In such a case s-s. 30(6) provides that the youth court must follow the board's recommendation and release the young person unless an application for a review hearing concerning the board's decision is made within ten days. In making the probation order, however, the court may impose such conditions as it "considers advisable having regard to the recommendations of the review board." If a request for review is made, the provisions of s. 31 apply. Notice of a decision of a review board may be in Form 15.

SAMPLE FORM

FORM 15
THE YOUNG OFFENDERS ACT
IN THE YOUTH COURT FOR ATHABASKA

NOTICE OF DECISION BY REVIEW BOARD

Canada
Province of Athabaska
County of Kings

To: Jacques Labonte of 1880 Rue Regent Street, Centreville, Athabaska , being a young person within the meaning of the *Young Offenders Act*:

Whereas on the 30th day of September 19 82 , you were found guilty of the following offence:

Indecent Assault: to wit Jacques Labonte on the 6th day of August, 1982, at Centreville, in the Province of Athabaska, did indecently assault Anne Bennett, a female person, contrary to Section 149 of the *Criminal Code of Canada*:

And whereas on the 13th day of October 19 82 , it was ordered that Jacques Labonte be committed to custody for a period of eighteen months commencing on the 13th day of October 19 82 .

And whereas on the   17th   day of   October   19 83   , the Review Board ordered:

that the disposition contained in the order dated the 13th day of October 1982 be confirmed.

This is therefore to notify you that, unless you or any other party entitled thereto, applies to the Youth Court for a review of the decision within ten days after the date of the decision the order of the Review Board will take effect on the expiration of the ten days or, where   Jacques Labonte   is to be placed on probation, on the endorsement by the Youth Court of the Review Board's decision.

Dated this   17th   day of   October   19 83 , at   Centreville in the Province of Athabaska.

"Bradley St. Clair"
. . . .
Chairman
Province of Athabaska
Disposition Review Board

Review by youth court: subsections 31(1) and (2)

If any of those involved in the process are dissatisfied with the review board's decision, review may be requested pursuant to s-s. 31(1). The persons who may request a review are the young person, his parents, the Attorney General or his agent, or the provincial director. The provisions adopted by s-s. 31(2) include the requirements of s-ss. 28(7) to (10) concerning a progress report, including provision for cross-examination of the person who prepared it. It would seem that a progress report prepared and submitted to the review board may be used again for the youth court's review hearing. Subsection 31(2) also adopts the provisions of s-ss. 28(12) to (16) governing notice of the youth court's review hearing, and in addition, provides that notice be given to the provincial director. Section 11 ensures the rights of the young person in regard to counsel, including the right to have counsel appointed by direction of the court under s-s. 11(4). See discussion above concerning s-ss. 28(5), (7) to (10) and (12) to (18) concerning conduct of youth court hearings.

The Y.O.A. does not specify the nature of "the review" of a review board's decision which a youth court is to undertake pursuant to s. 31; it would seem, however, that it is not simply a review of the transcript of the review board's proceedings which is contemplated. Subsection 31(2) adopts s-s. 28(17) which imposes on a youth court a duty to render a decision only after affording the young person, his parents, the Attorney General or his agent, and the provincial director or his agent "an opportunity to be heard". Subsection 28(17) gives the youth court a broad discretion to render a decision "having regard to the needs of the young person and the interests of society." The general scheme of the Y.O.A. contemplates that review boards should conduct intermediary hearings, and that their decisions concerning release be final unless a review thereof is required by any of the parties. All of this suggests that in conducting a review under s. 31, a youth court may refer to the proceedings before a review board and its decision, but should be able to make a fresh decision. Further, those involved should be free to again adduce evidence already heard by the review board. For example, s-s. 31(2), adopting s-s. 28(10), which in turn adopts s-s. 14(6), assures the young person and any adult assisting him and the prosecutor a right to cross-examine the makers of the progress report at a youth court hearing reviewing a board decision.

In seeking a review by the youth court of the review board's decision pursuant to s. 31, a party involved might wish to have access to documents used by the review board. It can be argued that since the review board is carrying out the "duties and functions" of a youth court, its records, by necessary implication, are governed by s. 40 of the Y.O.A. As these boards, for the purposes of reviewing a custodial disposition, are given analogous powers to those of a youth court and will be making similar decisions, a liberal and remedial approach, consistent with the spirit of the Y.O.A., would suggest that this view should prevail. Hence, those involved would have a right of access to any documents used by the board. The jurisprudential concept of "procedural fairness" also lends support to this conclusion.

In the absence of explicit legislative provision, however, it may be argued that these are not technically youth court records and that therefore s. 40 does not apply. If this argument is accepted, it follows that s. 43 will govern review board records and will ensure that such records are not improperly disclosed and are eventually destroyed. Section 43 does not guarantee the young person, his counsel or his parents access to the records. However, if there is a review by a youth court of the review board's decision, the young person would have access under s. 40 to any documents sent by the review board for consideration by the youth court. This would include documents which a review board might initially have withheld from the young person (subject to para. 13(6)(b) allowing withholding of medical and psychological reports from a young person). If s. 43 does apply, existing jurisprudence suggests that in the absence of valid legislation to the contrary, the review board must act fairly and at least counsel for a young person should have access to all documents on which the board relies in making its decision; see *Re Abel and Advisory Review Board* (1980), 31 O.R.(2d) 520, 119 D.L.R. (3d) 101 (C.A.).

Review of non-custodial dispositions: section 32

Review of dispositions which do not involve custody are made pursuant to s. 32, and may only be conducted by a youth court. There is a right to a review six months after a disposition is made, and earlier with leave of the court. A progress report may be ordered by the court, although it is not mandatory. The youth court must conduct a hearing at which the provisions of s. 11 regarding representation for the young person apply, including the obligation of the court to direct that counsel be appointed if the young person wishes to obtain counsel but is unable to do so, either on his own or through a legal aid or assistance program.

As a general rule, except with the consent of the young persons, a disposition "more onerous" than the remaining portion of the original disposition cannot be imposed on the young person as a result of a review under s. 32. A more onerous disposition may only be imposed under s. 33, where it has been proven beyond a reasonable doubt that there has been "wilful failure or refusal to comply" with a disposition.

The purpose of a s. 32 review is to ensure that a disposition remains relevant and to allow a disposition to be altered so that a young person can take advantage of new programs or opportunities.

SECTION 32

32. (1) *Review of dispositions not involving custody.*—**Where a youth court has made a disposition in respect of a young person but has not committed him to custody, the youth court shall, on**

the application of the young person, his parent, the Attorney General or his agent or the provincial director, made at any time after six months from the date of the disposition or, with leave of a youth court judge, at any earlier time, review the disposition if the court is satisfied that there are grounds for review under subsection (2).

(2) *Grounds for review.*—A review of a disposition may be made under this section

(a) on the ground that the circumstances that led to the disposition have changed materially;

(b) on the ground that the young person in respect of whom the review is to be made is unable to comply with or is experiencing serious difficulty in complying with the terms of the disposition;

(c) on the ground that the terms of the disposition are adversly affecting the opportunities available to the young person to obtain services, education or employment; or

(d) on such other grounds as the youth court considers appropriate.

(3) *Progress report.*—The youth court may, before reviewing under this section a disposition made in respect of a young person, require the provincial director to cause to be prepared, and to submit to the youth court, a progress report on the performance of the young person since the disposition took effect.

(4) *Subsections 28(8) to (10) apply.*—Subsections 28(8) to (10) apply, with such modifications as the circumstances require, in respect of any progress report required under subsection (3).

(5) *Subsections 28(5) and (12) to (16) apply.*—Subsections 28(5) and (12) to (16) apply, with such modifications as the circumstances require, in respect of reviews made under this section and any notice required under subsection 28(12) shall be given to the provincial director.

(6) *Compelling appearance of young person.*—The youth court may, by summons or warrant, compel a young person in respect of whom a review is to be made under this section to appear before the youth court for the purposes of the review.

(7) *Decision of the youth court after review.*—Where a youth court reviews under this section a disposition made in respect of a young person, it may, after affording the young person, his parents, the Attorney General or his agent and the provincial director or his agent an opportunity to be heard,

(a) confirm the disposition;

(b) terminate the disposition and discharge the young person from any further obligation of the disposition; or

(c) vary the disposition or make such new disposition listed in section 20, other than a committal to custody, for such period of time, not exceeding the remainder of the period of the earlier disposition, as the court deems appropriate in the circumstances of the case.

(8) *New disposition not to be more onerous.*—Subject to subsection (9), where a disposition made in respect of a young person is reviewed under this section, no disposition made under subsection (7) shall, without the consent of the young person, be more onerous than the remaining portion of the disposition reviewed.

(9) *Exception.*—A youth court may under this section extend the time within which an order to perform personal or community service is to be complied with by a young person where the court is satisfied that the young person requires more time to comply with the order, but in no case shall the extension be for a period of time that expires more than twelve months after the date of the disposition reviewed would expire.

(10) *Form of disposition.*—A disposition made under subsection (7) may be in Form 13.

(11) *Form of summons or warrant.*—A summons referred to in subsection (6) may be in Form 16 and a warrant referred to in that subsection may be in Form 17.

Review of non-custodial dispositions: subsections 32(1) and (2)

Review of non-custodial dispositions is dealt with under s. 32 of the Y.O.A. and is a matter for the youth court only. A review board has no jurisdiction to hear such a review. Review may be sought under s. 32 by the young person, his parents, the Attorney General or his agent, or the provincial director. Review is available as of right after six months from the date of the disposition, or earlier with leave of a judge if he is satisfied that there are grounds for review. The grounds for a review pursuant to s. 32 are as follows: a material change in circumstances, an inability or serious difficulty in complying with the disposition, adverse effects of the disposition on the opportunities available to the young person to obtain services, education or employment, or "such other grounds as the youth court considers appropriate."

It is clear from these grounds that a disposition should be altered if it imposes excessive hardship on the young person. The Y.O.A.'s provisions for review ensure that dispositions continue to be relevant; they also afford the young person an opportunity to have the disposition altered so that advantage may be taken of new programs.

Progress reports: subsections 32(3) to (5)

A progress report may be required during review of a non-custodial disposition. Unlike the situation regarding review of custodial dispositions, progress reports are not mandatory, and they should only be required where such a report would be helpful in reviewing the disposition. Subsection 32(4) adopts the provisions of s-ss. 28(8) to (10), with such modifications as the circumstances require, establishing the procedure to be followed with respect to progress reports. A number of detailed provisions are summarized briefly below. A more complete commentary can be found in the comments on s. 28.

The progress report "on the performance of the young person since the disposition took effect" may also include personal information and material on the young person's family history and his present environment. As a general rule, the report is to be in writing; with leave of the court, however, an oral report may be submitted. Oral reports are likely to be appropriate when the parties indicate that the contents of the report do not appear contentious. The report is a part of the youth court record. The young person, a parent (if in attendance at the proceedings), his counsel and the prosecutor must receive copies of the report. The court may cause a copy of the report to be given to a parent not in attendance if the parent, in the court's opinion, is taking an active interest in the proceedings. Cross-examination of the author of the report is specifically provided for. Copies of the progress report shall, on request, be supplied to other courts dealing with the young person and to the youth worker assigned to the young person's case. Copies may be supplied to any person who, in the opinion of the court, has a valid interest in the proceedings; for example, a person supervising the young person or directly assisting in his care or treatment may have access to progress reports. Any statement made by the young person in the preparation of a progress report may not be used in civil or criminal proceedings except under s. 16 (transfer), s. 20 (disposition) or ss. 28 to 33 (disposition review) of the Y.O.A.

Subsection 32(5) adopts the provisions of s-s. 28(5), which stipulate that no review of a disposition that is being appealed is permitted "until all proceedings in respect of any such appeal have been completed." As well, s-s. 32(5) adopts s-ss. 28(12) to (16), provisions respecting notice. Where review is requested by the young person, his parents or the Attorney General or his agent, the person requesting the review must comply with these notice requirements. Subsection 32(5) specifically makes provision for notice to the provincial director in accordance with the requirements of s-s. 28(12). Such notice must be in accordance with the rules of court, if no rules of court have been made, there must be at least five clear days' notice. Notice to the young person and to a parent must include a statement of the young person's right to counsel (s-ss. 11(9) and 28(13)); notice may be served personally or sent by registered mail. The right to notice may be waived. Where notice has not been given as required by the Y.O.A., the youth court may order an adjournment so that notice may be given as directed, or the court may dispense with notice altogether. Notice to a young person may be in Form 11. Notice to a parent, the Attorney General or his agent, the provincial director or any other person may be in Form 12.

Compelling appearance of young person: subsection 32(6)

As it is in most instances desirable for the young person to be present at a review hearing, the youth court has the power to compel the young person's appearance by summons or warrant if the young person fails to attend voluntarily after receiving notice of a review hearing. If the young person is arrested pursuant to a warrant, the release provisions of s. 453.1 of the *Criminal Code* would apply, allowing the officer in charge of the station where the young person was taken to release him where the warrant is endorsed pursuant to s-s. 455.3(6). If the young person was to be detained in custody pending the review hearing, such detention should be in accordance with the provisions of ss. 7 and 8 of the Y.O.A., requiring a judicial decision to detain, usually made by a youth court judge, and requiring detention separate from adults, except under unusual circumstances.

Although the young person has a right to have an opportunity to be heard before a review decision is made, a youth court may review his disposition without the young person being present. If there is a likelihood that the youth court is planning to terminate the disposition, it may be unnecessary to compel his attendance under s-s. 32(6). Indeed, if the young person is making satisfactory progress, it may not be felt necessary to compel his attendance. In such cases, a youth court worker may convey the views of the young person to the court.

Decision of the youth court: subsections 32(7) to (9)

Subsection 32(7) requires the youth court to afford the young person, his parents, the Attorney General or his agent, and the provincial director or his agent, an opportunity to be heard. Subsection 32(7) provides the youth court with three options: to confirm, terminate or vary the disposition. In deciding whether to confirm, terminate or vary the original disposition, the youth court should consider the grounds for review set out in s-s. 32(2): material change in circumstances, inability or serious difficulty in complying with disposition, adverse effect of disposition on opportunities to obtain services, education or employment, or other "appropriate" grounds. If the court terminates the disposition, it will discharge the young person from any further obligation respecting the disposition. There is no requirement that the young person be placed on probation following review as there is in the case of release from custody under s. 28 or 29. In varying the disposition, the youth court may impose any disposition listed in s. 20, except committal to custody. A new disposition under s-s. 32(7) may not exceed "the remainder of the period of the earlier disposition."

An important limitation is placed on the power to vary the disposition by s-s. 32(8), which forbids the imposition of a "disposition more onerous than the remaining portion of the disposition reviewed," unless the young person gives his consent or unless s-s. 32(9) applies. This means that the new disposition cannot be more onerous than the remaining unfulfilled obligations imposed by the initial disposition, unless agreed to by the young person. Generally the only means of imposing a more severe disposition is review pursuant to s. 33, where there has been a wilful failure or refusal to comply with a disposition or an escape or attempted escape. The young person cannot be subjected to a harsher disposition at any review under the Y.O.A without such a finding.

The variety of dispositions in s. 20 may cause difficulty in determining when a disposition is "more onerous." It is easy to see that a term of probation of nine months duration is more onerous than one six months long, but it is not obvious how to evaluate one disposition, for example, a community service order, in comparison with another, such as a fine. To avoid this very problem, s-s. 32(8) makes provision for the young person to consent to a more onerous disposition. Thus, where the court is in any doubt as to whether a variation of the original disposition might be "more onerous", it should secure the consent of the young person.

There is one exception to the rule laid down by s-s. 32(8): s-s. 32(9) provides for an extension of the time in which the young person has to perform personal or community services. No extension may last more than 12 months after the date on which the disposition was originally scheduled to expire. Subsection 32(9) permits an extension of time only; it does not permit the imposition of a greater amount of time to be spent performing community or personal services.

Forms: subsections 32(10) and (11)

A disposition under s-s. 32(7) may be in Form 13 (see p. 239 for sample). A summons referred to in s-s. 32(6) may be in Form 16 and a warrant referred to in s-s. 32(6) may be in Form 17. See sample forms below.

SAMPLE FORM

FORM 16
THE YOUNG OFFENDERS ACT
IN THE YOUTH COURT FOR ONTARIO

SUMMONS FOR APPEARANCE ON REVIEW

Canada
Province of Ontario
County of   Queens

To: David Smith of 25 First Avenue, Anytown, Ontario , being a young person within the meaning of the *Young Offenders Act*:

Whereas on the 28th day of June 19 82 , you were found guilty of the following offence:

robbery: to wit on the second day of June, 1982, David Smith did steal two hundred and fifty dollars from The Corner Milk Store, 2 West Street, Anytown, Ontario, and at the same time thereat did use threats of violence contrary to section 303 of the *Criminal Code of Canada*;

And whereas by probation order dated the 8th day of July 19 82 , it was ordered:

1. that David Smith be placed on probation commencing on the date of that order for a period of twenty months and subject to the conditions therein prescribed; and

2. that David Smith perform, at the Anytown Community Centre, two hours per week of community service as described in the order.

And whereas it has been made to appear to me by information supplied by Janet Carter, the youth worker assigned to your case , that you should be brought back before the Youth Court for a review of the disposition because the informant says she has reasonable and probable grounds to believe and does believe:

1. that David Smith has failed to report to Janet Carter, the youth worker assigned to his case on the first Monday of October 1982, and November 1982 as required by condition prescribed in the probation order dated 8 July 1982; and

2. that David Smith has failed to attend Sir John A. MacDonald High School during the months of October and November of 1982, as required by condition prescribed in the probation order dated 8 July 1982; and

3. that David Smith has failed to perform the community service as ordered by the Youth Court in the order dated 8 July, 1982.

This is therefore to command you to appear before the Youth Court at 100 Main Street, Anytown, Ontario on Tuesday the 16th day of December 19 82 , at 10:00 o'clock in the fore noon, for the purpose of this review and to be dealt with according to the *Young Offenders Act*.

You have the right to be represented by counsel on your appearance.

Dated this 1st day of December 19 82 , at Anytown in the Province of Ontario.

"Thomas Brown"
....
A Judge of the Youth Court

SAMPLE FORM

FORM 17
THE YOUNG OFFENDERS ACT
IN THE YOUTH COURT FOR ONTARIO

WARRANT TO COMPEL APPEARANCE ON REVIEW

Canada
Province of Ontario
County of Queens

To the peace officers in the County of Queens .

Whereas on the 28th day of June 19 82 , David Smith of, 25 First Avenue, Anytown, Ontario , a young person within meaning of the *Young Offenders Act*, was found guilty of the following offence:

robbery: to wit on the second day of June, 1982, David Smith did steal two hundred and fifty dollars from The Corner Milk Store, 2 West Street, Anytown, Ontario, and at the same time thereat did use threats of violence contrary to section 303 of the *Criminal Code of Canada*;

And whereas by probation order dated the 8th day of July 19 82 , it was ordered:

1. that David Smith be placed on probation commencing on the date of that order for a period of twenty months and subject to the conditions therein prescribed; and

2. that David Smith perform, at the Anytown Community Centre, two hours per week of community service as described in the order.

And whereas it has been made to appear to me by information supplied by Janet Carter, the youth worker assigned to his case , that he should be brought back before the Youth Court for a review of the disposition because the informant says she has reasonable and probable grounds to believe and does believe;

1. that David Smith has failed to report to Janet Carter, the youth worker assigned to his case on the first Monday of October 1982, and November 1982 as required by condition prescribed in the probation order dated 8 July 1982; and

2. that David Smith has failed to attend Sir John A. MacDonald High School during the months of October and November of 1982, as required by condition prescribed in the probation order dated 8 July 1982; and

3. that David Smith has failed to perform the community service as ordered by the Youth Court in the order dated 8 July, 1982;

4. that David Smith failed to appear at the Youth Court at 100 Main Street, Anytown, Ontario, on Tuesday the 16th day of December, 1982, as required by the Summons for Appearance on Review (Form 16) dated 1st day of December, 1982.

This is therefore to command you forthwith to arrest David Smith and bring him before the Youth Court at   100 Main Street, Anytown, Ontario for the purpose of this review and to be dealt with according to the *Young Offenders Act*.

And you are also required, on arresting David Smith to inform him that he has the right to be represented by counsel on his appearance.

Dated this 16th day of December 19 82 , at Anytown in the Province of Ontario.

"Thomas Brown"

. . . .

A Judge of the Youth Court

Review of disposition for failure to comply: section 33

Section 33 allows for a youth court review where there has been a wilful failure or refusal to comply with a disposition, or where a young person committed to custody has escaped or attempted to escape. Section 33 governs both custodial and noncustodial dispositions; it is the principal review provision of the Y.O.A. allowing for the imposition of a more onerous disposition as a result of a breach. As the young person may be penalized as a result of a s. 33 review, certain protections are afforded him. The court must be satisfied beyond a reasonable doubt of the wilful failure or refusal to comply with the disposition, or of the escape or attempted escape from custody. A progress report must be prepared for the consideration of the court, and there is a right of appeal. The young person is also assured of his s. 11 right to counsel, including the right to have the court make a direction for the appointment of counsel under s-s. 11(4), if the young person is unable to obtain counsel.

SECTION 33

33. (1) *Review of disposition where failure to comply.*—Where a youth court has made a disposition in respect of a young person and the Attorney General or his agent or the provincial director or his delegate lays an information alleging that the informant, on reasonable and probable grounds, believes that the young person has

(a) wilfully failed or refused to comply with the disposition or any term of condition thereof, or

(b) in the case of a committal to custody under paragraph 20(1)(k), escaped or attempted to escape custody,

the youth court shall, on application of the informant made at any time before the expiration of the disposition or within six months thereafter, by summons or warrant, require the young person to appear before the court and shall review the disposition.

(2) *Subsections 28(7) to (10) apply.*—Subsections 28(7) to (10) apply, with such modifications as the circumstances require, in respect of reviews made under this section.

(3) *Notice of review from the provincial director.*—Where the provincial director or his delegate applies for a review of a disposition under subsection (1), he shall cause such notice as may be directed by rules of court applicable to the youth court or, in the absence of such direction, at least five clear days notice of the review to be given in writing to the parents of the young person in respect of whom the disposition was made and to the Attorney General or his agent.

(4) *Notice of review from the Attorney General or his agent.*— Where the Attorney General or his agent applies for a review of a disposition under subsection (1), the Attorney General or his

agent shall cause such notice as may be directed by rules of court applicable to the youth court or, in the absence of such direction, at least five clear days notice of the review to be given in writing to the parents of the young person in respect of whom the disposition was made and to the provincial director or his delegate.

(5) *Subsections 28(13) to (16) apply.*—Subsections 28(13) to (16) apply, with such modifications as the circumstances require, in respect of notices given under subsection (3) or (4).

(6) *Decision of the youth court after review.*—Where the youth court reviews under this section a disposition made in respect of a young person, it may, subject to subsection (8), after affording the young person, his parents, the Attorney General or his agent and the provincial director or his agent an opportunity to be heard, and if it is satisfied beyond a reasonable doubt that the young person has

(a) wilfully failed or refused to comply with the disposition or any term or condition thereof, or

(b) in the case of a committal to custody under paragraph 20(1)(k), escaped or attempted to escape custody,

vary the disposition or make any new disposition listed in section 20 that the court considers appropriate.

(7) *Limitation on custody.*—No disposition shall be made under this section committing a young person to custody

(a) for a period in excess of six months, where the disposition under review was not a committal to custody or was a committal to custody that has expired; or

(b) for a period that expires more than six months after the disposition under review was to expire, where the disposition under review was a committal to custody that has not expired.

(8) *Postponement of performance of previous dispositions.*—Notwithstanding any other provision of this Act, where a young person is committed to custody under this section, the youth court may order that the performance of any other disposition made in respect of the young person be postponed until the expiration of the period of custody.

(9) *Prosecution under section 132 or 133 of Criminal Code.*—Where a disposition is reviewed under this section on the ground set out in paragraph (1)(b), the young person may not be prosecuted under section 132 or 133 of the *Criminal Code* for the same act and, where a young person is prosecuted under either of those sections, no review may be made by the youth court under this section by reason of the same act.

(10) *Appeals.*—An appeal from a disposition of the youth court under this section lies as if the order were a disposition made under section 20 in respect of an offence punishable on summary conviction.

(11) *Form of disposition.*—A disposition made under subsection (6) may be in Form 13.

(12) *Form of summons or warrant.*—A summons referred to in subsection (1) may be in Form 16 and a warrant referred to in that subsection may be in Form 17.

(13) *Form of information.*—An information referred to in subsection (1) may be in Form 18.

Review of disposition where failure to comply: subsection 33(1)

Review under s. 33 can result in the imposition of a new disposition that is more onerous than the original disposition. This is the principal provision of the Y.O.A. which permits the imposition of a more severe disposition where there has been a breach (see also s-ss. 32(8) and (9)). Section 33 applies to all dispositions, custodial and non-custodial alike.

A young person is subject to review if an informant lays an information that he has reasonable and probable grounds for believing that the young person has "wilfully failed or refused to comply with the disposition or any term or condition" or that the young person has "escaped or attempted to escape custody." The informant must be one of the following: the Attorney General or his agent, or the provincial director or his delegate. Upon receiving an information under s. 33, the youth court must require the young person to appear before the court for review of the disposition. An information may be in Form 18 (see sample at end of discussion of this section).

The youth court can require the young person to attend by having a summons issued to him, commanding the young person to appear in youth court at a specified time. Subsection 455.5(2) of the *Code* requires the summons to be personally served on the young person, or if he cannot conveniently be found, it may be left for him at his last or usual place of residence with a person who appears to be at least 16 years of age. A summons may be in Form 16.

A warrant for the arrest of the young person may be issued if he refuses to comply with the summons. The judge may initially issue a warrant instead of a summons if he is satisfied on "reasonable and probable grounds ... that it is necessary in the public interest" (*Criminal Code*, s. 455.3(4)), for example to ensure his attendance. If a young person is arrested pursuant to a warrant issued under s. 33 of the Y.O.A., the provisions of s. 453.1 of the *Code*, governing release by the officer in charge of the police station where the young person is brought, are applicable provided the warrant has been endorsed in accordance with s-s. 455.3(6) of the *Code*. If it is necessary to detain the young person in custody pending a review, such detention must be in accordance with the provisions of ss. 7 and 8 of the Y.O.A., requiring detention separate from adults, except under unusual circumstances. A warrant issued under s-s. 33(1) may be in Form 17. Any summons or warrant issued pursuant to s-s. 33(1) must comply with s-s. 11(9) and include a statement that the young person has a right to be represented by counsel.

If the young person is already in custody prior to a s. 33 review, an order may be made pursuant to s. 460 of the *Code* by the youth court judge, ordering his custodians to bring the young person before the court for the review.

An application for a s. 33 review may be made at any time before the expiration of the disposition, or within six months thereafter.

Progress report: subsection 33(2)

Subsection 33(2) adopts the provisions of s-ss. 28(7) to (10) with regard to progress reports. A progress report must be prepared and submitted to the youth court before a decision is made on a s. 33 review. Except with leave of the court, the report must be in writing. Generally the young person, his counsel, the prosecutor, and a parent attending the proceedings will receive a copy of the report. The parties generally have a right to cross-examine the maker of the report. Statements made by a young person "in the course of the preparation" of a progress report are not admissible "in evidence against him in any civil or criminal proceedings except in proceedings under section 16 or 20 or sections 28 to 32": see s-s. 14(10), adopted through s-s. 28(10). The purpose of s-s. 14(10) is to promote the confidence of the

young person and ensure his cooperation in the process of preparing the progress report. The statements made by the young
person are not to be "admissible in evidence against him." It is
submitted that in the context of s. 33, this means a statement
made by the young person *cannot* be used to prove that the young
person wilfully failed or refused to comply with a disposition, or
escaped or attempted to escape custody. It is, however, submitted that if a court is satisfied that such a breach occurred, then
the court can use the statements of the young person for the
purpose of deciding on an appropriate course of action, as s-s.
33(6) allows the court to make "any *new* disposition listed in
section 20 that the court considers appropriate." It is submitted
that such statements would then be admissible in accordance
with s. 20, not s. 33. If such use could not be made of the
statements of the young person, it would effectively reduce the
value of any interview with the young person for the purpose of
preparing a progress report for the s. 33 hearing, and would be
taking an unnecessarily broad view of the meaning of the phrase
"admissible in evidence against him."

Notice: subsections 33(2) and (4) to (6)

Pursuant to s-ss. 33(3) and (4), notice of a review hearing must
be given in accordance with the rules of court, if the rules of
court do not specify any notice requirements, a minimum of five
clear days' notice must be given in writing. Notice must go to the
young person's parents, the Attorney General or his agent, and
the provincial director; it would seem that notice should be given
to all parents within the Act's definition of "parent," unless
further direction is given by the court (see s-s. 28(16)). If the
provincial director brings the application for review, he is responsible under s-s. 33(3) to see that notice is given to the parents and the Attorney General or his agent. Conversely, if the
application is brought by the Attorney General, it is his responsibility to ensure that notice is given pursuant to s-s. 33(4) to the
young person's parents and the provincial director or his
delegate.

Subsections 28(13) to (16) are also made applicable to review
under s. 33 by s-s. 33(5). Notice to parents must include a
statement of the young person's right to counsel and may be
served personally or sent by registered mail. The right to notice
may be waived. Where notice has not been given in accordance

with the Act, the youth court may order an adjournment so that notice may be given as directed, or the court may dispense with notice altogether (s-s. 28(16)). Notice to a parent, the Attorney General or his agent, the provincial director or his delegate, or any other person may be in Form 12. See discussion of s-ss. 28(13) to (16) for further comments.

The young person will receive notice of the proceedings pursuant to a summons or warrant issued under s-s. 33(1).

Decision of the youth court: subsections 33(6) to (8)

When a youth court conducts a review under s. 33, it has an obligation to afford the young person, his parents, the Attorney General or his agent, and the provincial director or his agent, "an opportunity to be heard" (s-s. 33(6)). The court has a duty under s. 11 to advise the young person of his right to obtain counsel, give the young person a reasonable opportunity to obtain counsel, and, if the young person wishes to obtain counsel but is unable to do so, either on his own or through a legal aid or assistance program, must direct that counsel be appointed to represent the young person under s-s. 11(4).

Subsection 33(6) requires that before varying a disposition or making a new one under s. 20, the court must be satisfied "beyond a reasonable doubt" that the young person has wilfully failed or refused to comply with the disposition of any term or condition thereof, or if committed to custody has escaped or attempted to escape custody. The Y.O.A. does not specify what type of hearing must be conducted under s-s. 33(6). It is submitted, however, that in general the rules of evidence and procedure which are applicable at trial should govern the proceedings. This view follows from a consideration of the consequences of the proceedings, from the fact that a s. 33 review may take place instead of charges under the *Criminal Code* (s. 132 or 133) or that a s. 33 review may occur in the place of charges under various provisions of Part XX of the *Code*. In addition, the nature of the standard of proof specified in s-s. 33(6) is "proof beyond a reasonable doubt," the criminal standard of proof. Thus the onus should be on the prosecution to prove its case; the prosecution may be conducted by the Attorney General or his agent, or the provincial director or his agent. It is submitted that the young person should not be compelled to give evidence against himself at this stage of the proceeding, although he should, of course, have the right to testify and call witnesses. Witnesses should give evidence under oath and should be subject to cross-examination. Evidence should be taken in accordance with the rules of evidence applicable for trials.

A s. 33 review must be based on a wilful failure or refusal to comply with a disposition or an escape or attempted escape from custody. A failure or refusal to comply with a disposition could arise out of a refusal to pay a fine, or a breach of the terms of probation. It may be argued that if a young person is placed in open custody, and wilfully refuses to follow the rules governing the facility in which he is placed, this may constitute a violation of para. 33(6)(a). A breach of the terms of a temporary release granted under s. 35 of the Y.O.A., for example, by failing to return to custody when required, would probably constitute a violation of para. 33(6)(a), rather than para. 33(6)(b), as it would not constitute an "escape."

If the court is satisfied beyond a reasonable doubt that one of the conditions of para. 33(6)(a) or (b) has occurred, it may "vary the disposition or make any new disposition in section 20 that the court considers appropriate", the court may also decide to confirm the original disposition. It is submitted that at this stage of a s. 33 review, the youth court can modify its procedure and generally adopt the procedure applicable at a disposition hearing under s. 20. Thus, at this stage it is appropriate for the court to give the parents an opportunity to be heard, and the court may receive the progress report (see s-s. 33(2) comments above concerning progress reports).

If the court is not satisfied beyond a reasonable doubt that the young person has violated para. 33(6)(a) or (b), the information must be dismissed. The young person will continue with the original disposition, though the judge may make some informal remarks to the young person, just as he could do if the young person were required to appear under para. 23(1)(b). If the court is satisfied a violation has occurred, it has a broad discretion to vary the original disposition. A custodial disposition made under s-s. 33(6) is limited to a maximum of six months under s-s. 33(7), whether the disposition is a new committal to custody or in addition to an original committal. Subsection 33(8) allows the court to commit a young person to custody under s. 33 and postpone the performance of any other disposition, such as a period of probation, until the expiration of the period of custody.

In reviewing a disposition under s. 33, a court might conceivably order a less onerous disposition. For example, a court might be satisfied beyond a reasonable doubt that a young person committed a minor breach of a term of probation, but on balance is of the view that the period of probation should be reduced or terminated — the court has discretion to do this under s. 33.

Prevention of double jeopardy: subsection 33(9)

Prison breach and escape from lawful custody are punishable under ss. 132 and 133 of the *Criminal Code*. Subsection 33(9) makes clear that the Crown must elect whether to prosecute a young person under the *Code* or to proceed with review under s. 33: the young person may not be subject to both provisions because that amounts to double jeopardy. A prosecution under s. 132 or 133 of the *Code* could be initiated either by the Crown or by a private prosecutor; for example, the provincial director could start proceedings under the *Code* provisions, if he so desired, if no charges were laid by the Crown.

A young person who fails to comply with a non-custodial disposition can only be dealt with under the Y.O.A., by means of s. 32 and where the default is wilful, by s. 33. Subsection 20(8) of the Y.O.A. provides that Part XX of the *Criminal Code*, which governs punishments, fines, probation and other sentences in regard to adult offenders, does not apply to proceedings under the Y.O.A. Hence, a failure to pay a fine, a breach of probation and other failures to comply with non-custodial dispositions made under the Y.O.A., can only be dealt with under that Act.

Appeals: subsection 33(10)

Subsection 33(10) permits an appeal from a disposition made under s. 33 as if it were a disposition under s. 20 for an offence punishable on summary conviction. A general right to appeal from a finding of guilt, an order dismissing an information, or a disposition made under s. 20, is provided for in s. 27 of the Y.O.A. An appeal from a disposition made pursuant to s. 33 is provided for specifically in s-s. 33(10). By way of contrast, no right of appeal is given with respect to dispositions made pursuant to ss. 28 to 32 (see s-s. 27(6)), as only s. 33 allows a disposition more onerous than the original disposition.

It is also submitted that the young person may rely on s. 27 to appeal the finding that he has wilfully failed or refused to comply with a disposition, or escaped or attempted to escape custody, and the prosecutor may appeal a dismissal of the information. The terms "finding of guilt" and "order dismissing the informa-tion" in s-s. 27(1), seem to apply to this type of finding. Further-more, it should be noted that the exclusion contained in s-s. 27(6) relates only to the reviews under ss. 28 to 32, thereby clearly implying that s. 27 applies to a review under s. 33.

In view of the maximum disposition and s-ss. 33(10) and 27(2), it is suggested that any appeal of the finding of the court be treated as an appeal from a conviction of a summary convic-tion offence.

Forms: subsections 33(11) to (13)

A disposition made in accordance with s-s. 33(6) may be in Form 13 (see p. 239). A summons may be in Form 16 (see p. 260). A warrant may be in Form 17 (see p. 262). An information may be in Form 18 (see the sample Form 18 on the following page).

SAMPLE FORM

FORM 18
THE YOUNG OFFENDERS ACT
IN THE YOUTH COURT FOR ONTARIO

INFORMATION

Canada
Province of Ontario
County of Queens

This is the information of Janet Carter , of The Department of Youth Services , being a delegate of the provincial director, hereinafter called the informant:

The informant says that she has reasonable and probable grounds to believe and does believe that David Smith of, 25 First Avenue, Anytown, Ontario , a young person within meaning of the *Young Offenders Act*, wilfully failed to or refused to comply with a disposition of the Youth Court ordered on the 8th day of July 19 82 , or with a term or condition thereof, as follows:

1. that David Smith has failed to report to Janet Carter, the youth worker assigned to his case on the first Monday of October 1982, and November 1982 as required by condition prescribed in the probation order dated 8 July 1982; and

2. that David Smith has failed to attend Sir John A. MacDonald High School during the months of October and November of 1982, as required by condition prescribed in the probation order dated 8 July 1982; and

3. that David Smith has failed to perform the community service as ordered by the Youth Court in the order dated 8 July, 1982.

Sworn before me this 15th)	"Janet Carter"
day of December 19 82)	
at Anytown in the)	. . . .
Province of Ontario.)	Informant

"Susan A. Barber"
. . . .
A Justice of the Peace in and for
the County of Queens

Disposition on review: section 34

SECTION 34

34. *Sections 20 to 26 apply to dispositions on review.*—Subject to sections 28 to 33, subsections 20(2) to (8) and sections 21 to 26 apply, with such modifications as the circumstances require, in respect of dispositions made under sections 28 to 33.

Section 34 provides that the dispositions imposed as a result of a review under ss. 28 to 33 are subject to the same limitations and conditions that apply to original dispositions as a result of s-ss. 20(2) to (8) and ss. 21 to 26. For example, where a young person is released from custody pursuant to s. 29 and placed on probation, the mandatory terms set out in s-s. 23(1) apply to the probation order, as well as any other terms the judge chooses to impose under s-s. 23(2). The new disposition may not exceed the maximum duration of disposition prescribed by s-s. 20(3). See the earlier discussion of ss. 20 to 26.

TEMPORARY RELEASE FROM CUSTODY
(Section 35)

Introduction

Legislation governing adults in correctional facilities allows for temporary release programs: see s. 26 of the *Penitentiary Act*, R.S.C. 1970, c. P-6, permitting temporary absence, and the similar provisions enacted in s. 36 of the *Prisons and Reformatories Act*, R.S.C. 1970, c. P-21. Day parole is permitted under the *Parole Act*, R.S.C. 1970, c. P-2. Provincial legislation in most provinces allows adults confined in provincial correctional institutions to enjoy the same privileges. The Y.O.A. contains equivalent provisions for the temporary release of young persons for limited periods of time. The young person may be released for up to 15 days for medical, compassionate or humanitarian reasons, or for the purpose of rehabilitation or re-integration into the community. Release for a specified number of hours on a daily basis is also provided for so that the young person may work, attend school, or participate in a training program.

The specific provisions for temporary release in the Y.O.A. are new to the juvenile corrections system, the J.D.A. gave the authority to determine the terms of the young person's committal to the provinces. In many places, some form of temporary release has in fact been used by provincial authorities. By virtue of s. 35, temporary release for young offenders has now received legislative sanction.

Temporary release is a non-judicial process. The person responsible for the program is the provincial director; the circumstances in which release is available are set out in s. 35. Unless policy directives are issued to define in greater detail when temporary release is available, each case will be considered and assessed on it own merits. Additional policy restrictions could include a minimum time spent in custody before eligibility for release and limits on the number of temporary leaves per person.

SECTION 35

35. (1) *Temporary absence or day release.*—The provincial director of a province or his delegate may, subject to any terms or

conditions that he considers desirable, authorize a young person committed to custody in the province pursuant to a disposition made under this Act

(a) to be temporarily released for a period not exceeding fifteen days where, in his opinion, it is necessary or desirable that the young person be absent, with or without escort, for medical, compassionate or humanitarian reasons or for the purpose of rehabilitating the young person or re-integrating him into the community; or

(b) to be released from custody on such days and during such hours as he specifies in order that the young person may

(i) attend school or any other educational or training institution,

(ii) obtain or continue employment or perform domestic or duties required by the young person's family, or

(iii) participate in a program specified by him that, in his opinion, will enable the young person to better carry out his employment or improve his education or training.

(2) *Limitation.*—A young person who is released from custody pursuant to subsection (1) shall be released only for such periods of time as are necessary to attain the purpose for which the young person is released.

(3) *Revocation of authorization for release.*—The provincial director of a province or his delegate may, at any time, revoke an authorization made under subsection (1).

(4) *Arrest and return to custody.*—Where the provincial director or his delegate revokes an authorization for a young person to be released from custody under subsection (3) or where a young person fails to comply with any term or condition of his release from custody under this section, the young person may be arrested without warrant and returned to custody.

(5) *Prohibition.*—A young person who has been committed to custody under this Act shall not be released from custody before the expiration of the period of his custody except in accordance with subsection (1) unless the release is ordered under sections 28 to 33 or otherwise according to law by a court of competent jurisdiction.

Temporary absence and day release: subsections 35(1) to (3)

The provincial director or his delegate is authorized by s-s. 35(1) to release a young person from custody for a temporary absence or day release. There is no right to temporary absence; it is an administrative matter, and there is no recourse to the courts if it is not granted. Temporary release includes a release of up to 15 days, without the young person returning to custody at night. Day release may be for such part of a day as the circumstances require.

Under para. 35(1)(a), a young person may be released temporarily for up to 15 days, where, in the provincial director's opinion, it is necessary or desirable to release the young person "for medical, compassionate or humanitarian reasons or for the purpose of rehabilitating the young person or re-integrating him into the community." Release under para. 35(1)(a) would be appropriate for attendance at a funeral, or where the young person needs medical treatment, or to prepare the young person for the end of his custodial term. Temporary release may be with or without an escort.

Day release, governed by para. 35(1)(b), allows for release of a young person "on such days and during such hours" as the provincial director specifies. Such day release may be for the purpose of allowing the young person to attend "school or any other educational or training institution." It may also be to allow a young person to "obtain or continue employment" or to "perform domestic or other duties required by the young person's family"; this last category might include caring for young siblings, or a child or an elderly relative, or working on a family farm. Day release may also be granted to allow a young person to participate in a program to improve the employment, education or training prospects of the young person. There is no legislative provision for providing an escort for a young person on day release. Although theoretically an escort might be provided, it is felt that a young person who requires an escort is not ready for day release.

Subsection 35(1) allows the imposition of any "terms or conditions" considered desirable in regard to temporary absence or day release. For example, the young person could be restricted as to his method of travel, required not to associate with certain persons outside the custodial facility and prohibited from consuming drugs or alcohol. In regard to temporary absence, a young person might be required to report to a local police station.

Subsection 35(1) applies to all young persons serving a custodial disposition under the Y.O.A., whether the young person is detained in custody in open or secure facilities for young persons, or whether an order has been made under s-s. 24(14) of the Y.O.A. to place the young person in a provincial correctional facility for adults. Subsection 24(14) expressly provides that a young person so transferred remains subject to the Y.O.A.; hence the temporary release provisions of the Y.O.A. would apply.

Subsection 35(2) provides that the young person is to be at liberty only "for such periods of time as are necessary to attain the purpose for which the young person is released." Although there are no restrictions on the granting of multiple continuous temporary absence permits, there is no reason to believe that the authorities would abuse these provisions. If permanent release of the young person was desired, the provincial director may use s. 29 of the Y.O.A. to recommend the release of the young person from custody and his placement on probation. The review provisions of s. 28 are also available to the provincial director, as well as to the young person, his parents and the Attorney General.

With the exception of these provisions for temporary release, young persons are not to be released from custody under the Y.O.A. unless released pursuant to the review provisions of ss. 28 to 33 or "otherwise according to law by a court of competent jurisdiction."

Revocation of temporary absence or day release: subsections 35(3) and (4)

According to s-s. 35(3) an authorization made under s-s. 35(1) may be revoked at any time. If the authorization for temporary release is revoked, or if the young person fails to comply with any term or condition of his release, s-s. 35(4) provides that the young person may be arrested without warrant and returned to custody.

A young person absent from custody without authorization may be subject to prosecution under s. 133 of the *Criminal Code* for being at large without lawful excuse. It should first be noted that the young person must have knowledge of the revocation of his temporary release pursuant to s-s. 35(3) before a charge under para. 133(1)(b) of the *Code* will stand. Moreover, cases such as *R. v. Seymour* (1980), 52 C.C.C. (2d) 305 (Ont. C.A.) should be noted. There, an adult released temporarily from a provincial correctional institution was prosecuted under para. 133(1)(b) of the *Code*. In this case, Seymour had been drinking in violation of one of the conditions of his temporary release. Despite the provisions of the provincial enactment authorizing temporary releases, Seymour was not convicted; the judge held that it was only a wilful breach of a condition which shows an intention by the inmate to withdraw himself from the control (in the sense of custody) of the correctional authorities that renders him unlawfully at large without lawful excuse.

EFFECT OF TERMINATION
OF DISPOSITION
(Section 36)

Introduction

In the Declaration of Principle, the Y.O.A. recognizes that young persons "should not in all instances be held accountable in the same manner or suffer the same consequences for their behaviour as adults." Various provisions in the Act provide for more lenient treatment of young offenders than adults and offer young persons some special protections. It is hoped that these provisions will minimize the negative impact on young persons of their involvement in the juvenile justice system. One such provision is s. 36 of the Y.O.A.; it provides that for many purposes, a young person shall be deemed not to have been convicted upon completion of his disposition.

Section 36 is designed to give the young person an incentive to complete his disposition and to thus promote the rehabilitation of the young offender. In light of the young person's age, it is felt that after completion of his diposition, he should not have his previous mistakes held against him; this is particularly important in regard to employment opportunities, as otherwise the young person may be denied the benefit of job experience.

Section 36 is not a complete prohibition on the subsequent use of a conviction under the Y.O.A. For example, even after the completion of a disposition, a previous conviction may be used in subsequent transfer applications, disposition and sentencing hearings, and bail applications. Section 45 of the Y.O.A. provides a much broader prohibition against use of a previous conviction under the Y.O.A. Section 45 requires the destruction of the young person's record following a certain period of time after completion of the disposition, provided the young person has not subsequently been convicted of another offence. Section 36 is available in the interim between completion of disposition and the time when destruction is required under s. 45. Once the provisions of s. 45 become applicable, s-s. 45(5) provides that for all purposes, a young person shall be deemed not to have committed the offence and the fact of previous conviction cannot be used for any purpose. The requirements for destruction under s. 45 are intentionally more onerous, and thus will serve as a long-term incentive for the rehabilitation of the young offender.

SECTION 36

36. (1) *Effect of absolute discharge or termination of dispositions.*—Subject to section 12 of the *Canada Evidence Act,* where a young person is found guilty of an offence, and

(a) a youth court directs under paragraph 20(1)(a) that the young person be discharged absolutely, or

(b) all the dispositions made under this Act in respect of the offence have ceased to have effect,

the young person shall be deemed not to have been found guilty or convicted of the offence except that,

(c) the young person may plead *autrefois convict* in respect of any subsequent charge relating to the offence;

(d) a youth court may consider the finding of guilt in considering an application for a transfer to ordinary court under section 16;

(e) any court or justice may consider the finding of guilt in considering an application for judicial interim release or in considering what dispositions to make or sentence to impose for any offence; and

(f) the National Parole Board or any provincial parole board may consider the finding of guilt in considering an application for parole.

(2) *Disqualifications removed.*—For greater certainty and without restricting the generality of subsection (1), an absolute discharge under paragraph 20(1)(a) or the termination of all dispositions in respect of an offence for which a young person is found guilty removes any disqualification in respect of the offence to which the young person is subject pursuant to any Act of Parliament by reason of a conviction.

(3) *Applications for employment.*—No application form for or relating to

(a) employment in any department, as defined in section 2 of the *Financial Administration Act,*

(b) employment by any Crown corporation as defined in Part VIII of the *Financial Administration Act,*

(c) enrolment in the Canadian Forces, or

(d) employment on or in connection with the operation of any work, undertaking or business that is within the legislative authority of the Parliament of Canada,

shall contain any question that by its terms requires the applicant to disclose that he has been charged with or found guilty of an offence in respect of which he has, under this Act, been discharged or has completed all the dispositions.

(4) *Punishment.*—Any person who uses or authorizes the use of an application form in contravention of subsection (3) is guilty of an offence punishable on summary conviction.

(5) *Finding of guilt not a previous conviction.*—A finding of guilt under this Act is not a previous conviction for the purposes of any offence under any Act of Parliament for which a greater punishment is prescribed by reason of previous convictions.

Effect of discharge or termination of disposition: subsections 36(1) and (2)

Where the youth court gives an absolute discharge or imposes a disposition and it has been completed, the young person is deemed by s-s. 36(1) "not to have been found guilty or convicted of the offence." The effect of this provision is limited by the exceptions included in s-s. 36(1).

The first exception set out in s-s. 36(1) applies to preserve the effect of s. 12 of the *Canada Evidence Act*, which provides that if a person testifies at his own trial or at the trial of another person, he may be questioned regarding previous convictions under the Y.O.A. This provision is in accordance with the decision of the Supreme Court of Canada in *Morris v. The Queen*, [1979] 1 S.C.R. 405, 6 C.R. (3d) 36, 43 C.C.C. (2d) 129, 91 D.L.R. (3d) 161, 23 N.R. 109 which held that the cross-examination of a witness on his record as a juvenile was admissible in evidence under s. 12 of the *Canada Evidence Act* for the purpose of establishing or attacking credibility. It should be noted, however, that when the s. 45 provisions for destruction of the young person's record come into effect, he is deemed not to have committed the offence. If questioned about his record during court proceedings pursuant to s. 12 of the *Canada Evidence Act*, he may properly deny a conviction under the Y.O.A., once the record is required to be destroyed under s. 45.

Subsection 36(1) provides for the use of a conviction under the Y.O.A. in judicial and other proceedings. Paragraph 36(1)(c) allows the young person to enter a special plea of *autrefois convict* based on the conviction for an offence for which he has completed the disposition or received an absolute discharge. This special plea prevents the young person from being twice convicted of the same offence (see s. 535 of the *Criminal Code*). In view of the *Canadian Charter of Rights and Freedoms*, para. 11(h), providing that if a person has been found guilty of an offence and punished, he shall not be tried for it again, it also seems that a young person could use the conviction as the basis of the common law defence of *res judicata* ("the issue has been decided"), which technically is somewhat broader than *autrefois convict* (see *Kienapple v. The Queen*, [1975] 1 S.C.R. 729, 15 C.C.C. (2d) 524, 26 C.R.N.S. 1, 1 N.R. 322, 44 D.L.R. (3d) 351).

Paragraph 36(1)(d) provides that in considering an application to transfer the young person to ordinary court under s. 16 of the Y.O.A., the deeming provision is of no effect; the youth court may consider the previous conviction. Under para. 36(1)(e), the finding of guilt may also be considered during a court's consideration of an application for judicial interim release (whether a young person or adult), before the imposition of disposition under the Y.O.A., or before the imposition of sentence in ordinary court. See, however, s-s. 36(5) of the Y.O.A. which provides that a finding of guilt is not to be treated as a previous conviction for the purpose of any offence for which a greater punishment is automatically prescribed by reason of a previous conviction. Under para. 36(1)(f), the National Parole Board or any provincial parole board may consider the finding of guilt in considering an application for parole, which may be made after the young person becomes an adult. To facilitate subsequent use of a record, a court pursuant to paras. 40(3)(f) and (g), and a parole board pursuant to para. 40(3)(d), are given access to the young person's record on request.

Subsection 36(2) of the Y.O.A. confirms that the effect of s-s. 36(1) is to ensure that even after an absolute discharge or the completion of all dispositions, a young person is not to suffer "any disqualification in respect of the offence to which the young person is subject pursuant to any Act of Parliament by reason of a conviction." An example of a disqualification to which a young person would be subject if this provision was not included in the Y.O.A. is found in s-s. 682(3) of the *Criminal Code*, which disqualifies persons convicted of certain offences from contracting with the Crown.

Employment applications: subsections 36(3) and (4)

Subsection 36(3) of the Y.O.A. protects young persons by prohibiting specified employers from asking certain questions on job applications that relate to past involvement in proceedings under the Y.O.A. This should ensure that a person's opportunities for finding employment are not hindered by previous involvement in the juvenile justice system. Subsection 36(3) provides that the application forms concerning specified employment shall not contain "any question that by its terms requires the applicant to disclose that he has been charged with or found guilty of an offence" under the Y.O.A., in respect of which he has received an absolute discharge or completed all dispositions. The prohibition of s-s. 36(3) governs applications concerning employment in any federal department or any federal Crown corporation, or for "employment on or in connection with the operation of any work, undertaking or business that is within the legislative authority of the Parliament of Canada"; this last category extends to railways, banks and all other enterprises within federal jurisdiction. The prohibition of s-s. 36(3) also applies to application forms for enrolment in the Canadian Forces.

The federal government lacks the legislative authority to forbid the disclosure of a conviction under the Y.O.A. on application forms for employment in enterprises outside the federal jurisdiction. Provincial governments and enterprises within the provincial jurisdiction may continue to ask such questions, unless the provinces enact similar provisions.

The penalty for requiring disclosure contrary to s. 36 is set out in s-s. 36(4), using or authorizing the use of an application form in contravention of s-s. 36(3) is a summary conviction offence. Punishment for summary conviction offences is provided for in the *Criminal Code*, and is currently six months in jail, a $500 fine or both.

Finding of guilt not a previous conviction: subsection 36(5)

Further legislative recognition of the principle that a young person's mistakes should not be held against him indefinitely can be found in s-s. 36(5), which provides that a young person's conviction for an offence under the Y.O.A. is not a "previous conviction" for the purposes of any offence under any Act of Parliament. For certain offences, the enacting legislation specifies that a heavier penalty must be imposed for a second, or subsequent, convictions. For example, para. 234(1)(b) of the *Criminal Code* provides that a person convicted of a second offence of impaired driving is subject to a mandatory minimum of 14 days' imprisonment, while subsequent impaired driving offences are punishable by a minimum of at least three months' imprisonment. Subsection 36(5) is an example of a situation where the young person is not held as strictly accountable as an adult; in effect the young person may be given a second chance.

Paragraph 36(1)(e) specifically allows a court to make use of a previous conviction under the Y.O.A. for the purpose of imposing a disposition in youth court or a sentence in ordinary (adult court). The effect of s-s. 36(5) is only to free a court from the mandatory requirement of imposing a more severe sanction if there has been a previous conviction. Once a record of conviction is required to be destroyed in accordance with s. 45, however, it cannot be used for any purpose.

YOUTH WORKERS
(Section 37)

Introduction

The Y.O.A. creates a new classification of personnel within the juvenile justice system, "the youth worker". These workers will perform many of the functions carried out by juvenile probation officers under ss. 30 and 31 of the *J.D.A.*

SECTION 37

37. *Duties of youth worker*.—The duties and functions of a youth worker in respect of a young person whose case has been assigned to him by the provincial director or his delegate include

(a) where the young person is bound by a probation order that requires him to be under supervision, supervising the young person in complying with the conditions of the probation order or in carrying out any other disposition made together with it;

(b) where the young person is found guilty of any offence, giving such assistance to him as he considers appropriate up to the time the young person is discharged or the disposition of his case terminates;

(c) attending court when he considers it advisable or when required by the youth court to be present;

(d) preparing, at the request of the provincial director or his delegate, a pre-disposition report or a progress report; and

(e) performing such other duties and functions as the provincial director requires.

Youth workers: section 37

According to the definition in s-s. 2(1) of the Y.O.A., youth workers are "to perform, either generally or in a specific case . . . any of the duties or functions of a youth worker under this Act." A certain class of persons may be designated by the province as youth workers. This designation may be made by an Act of the provincial legislature or by the Lieutenant Governor in Council (provincial Cabinet) or his delegate. Persons not so designated or appointed may also qualify as a "youth worker", if they are carrying out any of the duties or functions of a youth worker, as the definition is a functional one.

Section 37 of the Y.O.A. outlines four specific tasks that may be performed by a youth worker: supervising the young person in complying with the conditions of the probation order or in carrying out any other disposition made in conjunction with the probation order; assisting the young person until his disposition has been completed; attending court proceedings "when he considers it advisable or when required by the youth court to be present"; and preparing pre-disposition and progress reports. Section 37 also authorizes a youth worker to perform "such other duties and functions as the provincial director requires."

Youth workers are provincial employees, the exact nature of their duties may depend upon provincial directives. Various officers may act in the capacity of youth workers regardless of the title of their positions; for example, probation officers or child welfare workers may assume the responsibilities of a youth worker. Especially in remote areas, the practice of dividing a worker's time between other duties such as supervising adult probationers or doing child welfare work, and young offenders work, may continue to be commonplace. It is not essential that a youth worker be employed full time in assisting young offenders.

PROTECTION OF PRIVACY
OF YOUNG PERSONS
(Sections 38 and 39)

Introduction

Sections 38 and 39 of the Y.O.A. are designed to protect the young person's privacy during youth court proceedings by forbidding publication of information serving to identify the young person and by allowing exclusion of the public from the court in certain circumstances. The court's concern goes beyond privacy, however, as an exclusionary order may be made in order to protect the young person from harm, or in the interests of public morals, the maintenance of order, or the proper administration of justice.

The approach to the issue of privacy adopted in the Y.O.A. differs significantly from that taken in the *Juvenile Delinquents Act*, particularly as that Act was interpreted in recent judicial pronouncements. Subsection 12(1) of the *J.D.A.* provides that trials shall take place "without publicity". In *C.B. v. The Queen* (1981), 62 C.C.C. (2d) 107, 24 R.F.L. (2d) 225, 127 D.L.R. (3d) 482, [1981] 6 W.W.R. 701 (S.C.C.), the Supreme Court of Canada overturned a number of lower court decisions and held that s-s. 12(1) of the *J.D.A.* means that trials are to be held *in camera*. As a result, reporters and other members of the public may not attend trials involving *J.D.A.* prosecutions. The *J.D.A.* does not give a judge any discretion to allow members of the public to attend. Further s-s. 12(3) of the *J.D.A.* prohibits the publication of any report revealing the identity of any child charged with a delinquency, except with special leave of the court.

The Y.O.A. reverses the effect of the Supreme Court's decision in *C.B. v. The Queen*. The general rule under the Y.O.A. is that like adult proceedings, youth court proceedings are to be open to the public. Young persons are to be seen to be responsible for their acts, and in this respect these provisions are consistent with para. 3(1)(a) of the Act. The shift from *in camera* proceedings to open court is considered both necessary and desirable for a number of reasons, notably: to help maintain public confidence in the juvenile justice system, to safeguard the rights of young persons by conducting proceedings openly, and to foster community awareness and involvement in juvenile corrections and justice. However, in recognition of the special status of young persons, under specified circumstances, the youth court judge has a discretion to exclude the public from the proceedings.

Specific provisions have been included in the Y.O.A. to maintain the special status of young persons and to ensure that their needs are not jeopardized by proceedings in open court. These provisions recognize that young people should not in all instances be treated exactly as adults. Such is the aim of s. 38, which forbids the publication of any report of an offence or of proceedings involving a young person that names or contains information serving to identify the young person charged with the offence. This section provides similar protection for any young person or child involved in the proceedings, either as a victim or a witness.

SECTION 38

38. (1) *Identity not to be published.*—No person shall publish by any means any report

(a) of an offence committed or alleged to have been committed by a young person, unless an order has been made under section 16 with respect thereto, or

(b) of a hearing, adjudication, disposition or appeal concerning a young person who committed or is alleged to have committed an offence

in which the name of the young person, a child or a young person aggrieved by the offence or a child or a young person who appeared as a witness in connection with the offence, or in which any information serving to identify such young person or child, is disclosed.

(2) *Contravention.*—Every one who contravenes subsection (1)

(a) is guilty of an indictable offence and is liable to imprisonment for not more than two years; or

(b) is guilty of an offence punishable on summary conviction.

(3) *Magistrate has absolute jurisdiction on indictment.*—Where an accused is charged with an offence under paragraph (2)(a), a

magistrate has absolute jurisdiction to try the case and his jurisdiction does not depend on the consent of the accused.

No publication of identity: subsection 38(1)

Subsection 38(1) provides that no person shall publish any
report of an offence committed by a young person, which names
or in any way identifies the young person charged, or a child
(under 12 years of age) or young person "aggrieved by the offence", or a child or young person appearing as a witness. The
prohibition covers reports of both the actual offence and any
hearing, adjudication, disposition or appeal under the Y.O.A.
The effect of s-s. 38(1) terminates in regard to the young person
charged with the offence once an order has been made transferring the young person to ordinary (adult) court under s. 16 of the
Y.O.A. Although s-s. 38(1) ceases to have effect if a transfer
order is made, an order banning publication of information presented at the transfer hearing pursuant to s. 17, will continue in
effect until the trial in adult court has ended (see s. 17 and
following discussion).

The rationale behind preventing publicity is based on a recognition that a young person involved in the criminal justice system
may be stigmatized or "labelled" if his involvement becomes
known to his peers or the community at large. An American case
involving an 11-year-old boy charged with committing second
degree murder provides some evidence that publicity associated
with the proceedings can cause serious psychological harm. The
boy's picture appeared once in the newspaper and television
footage showed him leaving the courthouse; as well, his name was
published frequently in news reports until the date of a court
order restraining publication. The conclusion of the study was
that "publicity placed additional stress on [the youth] during a
difficult period of adjustment in the community, and it interfered
with his adjustment at various points when he was otherwise
proceeding adequately." See D. C. Howard, J. T. Grisso and R.
Neems, "Publicity and Juvenile Court Proceedings" (1977), 11
Clearinghouse Review 203.

"A young person aggrieved": subsection 38(1)

Subsection 38(1) refers to a "child or young person aggrieved." This clearly includes a victim, but may be broader: see

subpara. 39(1)(a)(iii) referring to a "young person who is aggrieved by or the victim of the offence." A young person aggrieved by an offence might, for example, include the child of a rape victim.

"Publish": subsection 38(1)

The use of the word "publish" in s-s. 38(1) creates some uncertainty, as it normally has two different meanings. The word "publish" may mean either (see *Random House Dictionary*, 1969, p. 1162):

> to issue or cause to be issued, in copies made by printing or other processes for sale or distribution to the public, as a book, periodical, map, piece of music, engraving or the like.
>
> or
>
> to make publicly or generally known

The first definition limits "publish" to the printed word: the second is broader and would take in any medium through which information is disseminated. As this section creates an offence, it must be construed narrowly. Moreover, s. 38 contrasts with the wording of s. 17 of the Y.O.A., which states that "information ... shall not be published in any newspaper or broadcast ...". The use of both "publish" and "broadcast" in s. 17 might suggest that the term "publish", as used in the Y.O.A., should be given a narrow meaning. However, direct comparison of s. 17 of the Y.O.A. and s. 38 might not be appropriate as in s. 38 "publish" is modified by the expansive phrase, "by any means".

The term "publish" is also used in s. 263 of the *Criminal Code*. However, since libel is restricted to printed matter, the definition of publishing in s. 263 and the case law on the issue do not resolve the problem that has been identified in s. 38.

In *Re A.-G. Man. and Radio OB Ltd.* (1976), 70 D.L.R. (3d) 311, 31 C.C.C. (2d) 1, [1976] 4 W.W.R. 147 (Man. Q.B.), Solomon J. held that in regard to a radio broadcast concerning a juvenile charged with murder, the radio announcer "breached s-ss. 12(1) of the [*Juvenile Delinquents*] Act by publishing, during his radio programme, information which could easily identify the juvenile" (at p. 316 D.L.R.), the issue of the meaning of "publish" was not directly addressed by Solomon J. but the court clearly intended it to have a very broad meaning. In *Smith v. Daily*

Mail Publishing, 99 S. Ct. 2667, 443 U.S. 97 (1979), the United States Supreme Court considered legislation dealing with publication of identifying information at juvenile trials, and specifically distinguished electronic media from newspapers. The implications of *Smith* are considered further below, suffice it to note that if "publish" in s. 38 of the Y.O.A. is given a narrow meaning so as to restrict the print medium only, the section may be subject to challenge under the *Canadian Charter of Rights and Freedoms*.

On balance, the broader definition of "publish" is more logical and preferable. The addition of the words "by any means" to s-s. 38(1) is meant to confirm that the broader meaning was intended. Further, and more importantly, the purpose of s. 38, including its intended protection of young persons and children, would be entirely undermined if "publish" was confined to the print media.

Procedure: subsections 38(2) and (3)

Subsection 38(2) provides that offences created by s-s. 38(1) are hybrid: the Crown has an election, and may choose to prosecute by way of summary conviction or indictment. Subsection 38(3) provides that all charges under s-ss. 38(1) are within the absolute jurisdiction of a magistrate in adult court, thus eliminating any choice for the accused regarding manner of trial. This simplifies and expedites the procedures for this type of prosecution.

Contempt of court

The offence created by s-s. 38(2) for contravening the publication restrictions found in ss. 17 and 38 of the Y.O.A. is supplementary to the more general provisions of the law of contempt. Reports in the media may also constitute criminal contempt if they are "calculated to prejudice mankind against the accused before the case is heard": see *Re A.-G. Man. and Radio OB Ltd.*, [1976] 4 W.W.R. 147, 70 D.L.R. (3d) 311, 31 C.C.C. (2d) 1 (Man. Q.B.).

A Charter of Rights challenge to section 38?

It is possible that the validity of s. 38 of the Y.O.A. may be challenged as an infringement of "freedom of the press and other media communication", as guaranteed by para. 2(b) of the *Canadian Charter of Rights and Freedoms*.

In one American case, such a challenge was successful, although its applicability to Canada is debatable. In *Smith v. Daily Mail Publishing*, 99 S. Ct. 2667, 443 U.S. 97 (1979) the United States Supreme Court held unconstitutional state legislation making it an offence if the name of any child involved in a juvenile court proceeding was "published in any newspaper without a written order of the court"; the legislation violated the First Amendment of the American Constitution, guaranteeing freedom of the press. Chief Justice Burger, delivering the opinion of the Court, recognized that the state had an interest in protecting the anonymity of the juvenile offender "because publication of the name may encourage further antisocial conduct and also may cause the juvenile to lose future employment or suffer other consequences" (at p. 104 U.S.), but he concluded that the state interest could not justify the imposition of criminal sanctions. Justice Rehnquist, in a concurring opinion, held that the state's interests in preserving the anonymity of juvenile offenders was of the "highest order", and "far outweighs any minimal interference with freedom of the press that a ban on publication of the youths' names entails" (at p. 107 U.S.). Although Justice Rehnquist ruled the statute unconstitutional, as it restricted only newspapers and not the electronic media, he concluded that "a generally effective ban on publication that applied to all forms of mass communication, electronic and print media alike, would be constitutional" (at p. 111 U.S.).

The approach of Canadian courts to the *Charter* is still in its intitial stages of development, but it would seem that the approach of Justice Rehnquist, with its balancing of interests, will be adopted in view of s. 1 of the *Charter*, which explicitly recognizes that the freedoms of the *Charter* are subject "to such reasonable limits prescribed by law as can be demonstrably justified in a free and democratic society." This would suggest that s. 38 of the Y.O.A. could not be successfully challenged under the *Charter*, provided the words "publish by any means" are given a broad interpretation.

In *R. v. J.(R.)*, [1982] W.D.F.L. 791, 7 W.C.B. 507 (Ont. Prov. Ct.), it was held that s-s. 12(1) of the *J.D.A.*, with its requirement that hearings occur *in camera*, was unconstitutional for violating the *Charter* and that a reporter could be present during a juvenile trial. However, Genest Prov. J. expressly held that the provisions of s-ss. 12(3) and (4) prohibiting the publication of information identifying the juvenile was reasonable and justified and hence permissible under s. 1 of the *Charter*. A limitation on the freedom of the press guaranteed by s. 2 of the *Charter* is justified in the interest of protecting youths from the harmful effects of public identification in the media.

See S. D. Cohen, "Reconciling Media Access with Confidentiality for the Individual in Juvenile Court" (1980), 20 Santa Clara Law Review 405; and *Re F. P. Publications (Western) Limited and The Queen* (1979), 2 Man. R. (2d) 1, 108 D.L.R. (3d) 153, 51 C.C.C. (2d) 110, [1980] 1 W.W.R. 504 (C.A.). See also the discussion under s. 39 of the Y.O.A. concerning challenges to that section based on para. 11(d) of the *Charter* guaranteeing a "fair and public hearing".

Exclusion from hearing: section 39

SECTION 39

39. (1) *Exclusion from hearing.*—**Subject to subsection (2), where a court or justice before whom proceedings are carried out under this Act is of the opinion**

(a) that any evidence or information presented to the court or justice would be seriously injurious or seriously prejudicial to

(i) the young person who is being dealt with in the proceedings,

(ii) a child or young person who is a witness in the proceedings,

(iii) a child or young person who is aggrieved by or the victim of the offence charged in the proceedings, or

(b) that it would be in the interest of public morals, the maintenance of order or the proper administration of justice to exclude any or all members of the public from the court room,

the court or justice may exclude any person from all or part of the proceedings if the court or justice deems that person's presence to be unnecessary to the conduct of the proceedings.

(2) *Exception.*—**A court or justice may not, pursuant to subsection (1), exclude from proceedings under this Act**

(a) the prosecutor;

(b) the young person who is being dealt with in the proceedings, his parent, his counsel or any adult assisting him pursuant to subsection 11(7);

(c) the provincial director or his agent; or

(d) the youth worker to whom the young person's case has been assigned.

(3) *Exclusion after adjudication or during review.*—The youth court, after it has found a young person guilty of an offence, or the youth court or the review board, during a review of a disposition under sections 28 to 33, may, in its discretion, exclude from the court or from a hearing of the review board, as the case may be, any person other than

(a) the young person or his counsel,

(b) the provincial director or his agent,

(c) the youth worker to whom the young person's case has been assigned, and

(d) the Attorney General or his agent,

when any information is being presented to the court or the review board the knowledge of which might, in the opinion of the court or review board, be seriously injurious or seriously prejudicial to the young person.

Exclusion from youth court hearing: subsection 39(1)

The youth court judge may exclude any person from the courtroom, with the exception of a limited number of participants specifically mentioned in s-s. 39(2), or in the case of a dispositional hearing or review, those mentioned in s-s. 39(3). Subsection 39(1) establishes two sets of criteria for exclusion. The youth court judge is empowered to order exclusion to protect a young person or child from serious prejudice or harm; as well, a judge may make an order for exclusion in the interests of public morals, the maintenance of order, or the proper administration of justice. A person may only be excluded if his presence is "unnecessary to the conduct of the proceedings."

The first set of criteria in para. 39(1)(a) allows exclusion if any evidence or information presented to the court or justice would be "seriously injurious" or "seriously prejudicial" to a young person or child in any of three categories: the young person charged with the offence, a child or young person appearing as a witness, and a child or young person "aggrieved by or the victim of the offence." For a discussion of the word "aggrieved" see comments under s-s. 38(1).

The test to be satisfied in s-s. 39(1) is a stringent one — harm must be "seriously injurious" or "seriously prejudicial." Two types of harmful communications are covered by these words. The situation where a young person is harmed by hearing information which is shocking, distasteful or delicate is covered by the word "injurious." The conveying of information to someone other than the young person so that the young person is indirectly harmed is included in "prejudicial." The fact that injury or prejudice may result, is not sufficient to justify an exclusionary order; the use of the word "would" suggests that the likelihood of harm must be reasonably probable or certain. Further, the harm must be a serious harm before any person may be excluded pursuant to s-s. 39(1).

The second set of criteria for exclusion is broadly worded in para. 39(1)(b); exclusion is permitted in the interest of "public morals, the maintenance of order or the proper administration of justice." Since s-s. 39(1) uses the same words as s. 442 of the *Criminal Code*, the jurisprudence which has developed in relation to s. 442 may be relevant. Exclusion of the public on the basis of the "proper administration of justice" is not justified solely because of the embarrassment of witnesses: *R. v. Quesnel and Quesnel* (1979), 51 C.C.C. (2d) 270 (Ont. C.A.). The discretion to exclude the public must be exercised cautiously and only as circumstances demand: *R. v. Warawuk* (1978), 42 C.C.C. (2d) 121, [1978] 5 W.W.R. 389, 10 A.R. 541 (C.A.).

The power to exclude under s-s. 39(1) exists in addition to the usual rules regarding the exclusion of witnesses. The trial judge has a discretion to make an order excluding all or any of the witnesses for the Crown or the defence (except the accused). However, even where a witness has intentionally disregarded the court's exclusion order, a witness cannot be prevented from testifying although refusal to leave the courtroom may affect the weight given to the witness's testimony: *R. v. Wilson* (1973), 6 N.S.R. (2d) 395, 25 C.R.N.S. 47, 14 C.C.C. (2d) 258 (C.A.); leave to appeal to S.C.C. refused 14 C.C.C. (2d) 258n (S.C.C.).

Persons who may not be excluded: subsection 39(2)

Subsections 39(2) and (3) provide that certain persons may not be excluded from proceedings under the Y.O.A., these two subsections should be considered together. Subsection 39(2) provides that the persons specified may not be excluded from the proceedings, prior to disposition; those mentioned in s-s. 39(2) have an unfettered right to be present at a pre-trial detention hearing, transfer proceedings and until the judge renders an ajudication at trial. Subsection 39(3) provides that the specified persons may not be excluded from a disposition hearing or a disposition review. The list in s-s. 39(3) is somewhat narrower than that in s-s. 39(2); there are some persons who have the right to be present until adjudication is completed, under s-s. 39(2), but who may be excluded thereafter as they are not mentioned in s-s. 39(3).

Those who may not be excluded prior to disposition because they are mentioned in s-s. 39(2) are: the prosecutor, the young person, his parent, his counsel or an adult assisting the young person pursuant to s-s. 11(7), the provincial director or his agent, and the youth worker assigned to the young person's case. The prosecutor includes a "private prosecutor", as defined in the *Criminal Code*.

Exclusion at disposition or review: subsection 39(3)

Subsection 39(3) permits exclusion during review or after adjudication if there is information being presented, "the knowledge of which might . . . be seriously injurious or seriously prejudicial to the young person." Certain individuals may not be excluded: the young person; his counsel; the provincial director or his agent; the young person's youth worker; and the Attorney General or his agent. Note that this list is shorter than that in s-s. 39(2). Following adjudication, a private prosecutor, the young person's parents and an adult assisting the young person under s-s. 11(7) may be excluded. The provisions of s-s. 39(3) reflect a concern that the wide range of information, including reports containing personal information, presented at a dispositional hearing or review not be broadly disseminated. For example, a young person who has had an abortion without the parents knowing might be seriously prejudiced if her parents were to learn of the abortion. Similarly, an adult relative assisting the young person under s-s. 11(7) might learn something, knowledge of which could be injurious to the young person. Subsection 39(3) requires the court or review board to be of the opinion that "the knowledge ... *might* ... be *seriously* injurious or *seriously* prejudicial to the young person." This suggests that the potential injury must be substantial, and not slight, but that there need not be certainty that the injury will occur; the risk of injury is sufficient. Subsection 39(3) may be contrasted with s-s. 39(1); the latter requires the court to be of the opinion that the information "*would* be *seriously* injurious or *seriously* prejudicial", and imports a much greater degree of certainty that injury will occur.

Presence of young person: subsections 39(2) and (3)

The combined effect of s-ss. 39(2) and (3) is to recognize the young person's right to be present throughout the proceedings. Although the general rule is that attendance is required, para. 577(2)(b) of the *Criminal Code* states that the court may "permit the accused to be out of court during the whole or any part of his trial on such conditions as the court considers proper." This provision of the *Code* is applicable to youth court proceedings pursuant to s-s. 52(3) of the Y.O.A. Moreover, it contemplates the court acceding or responding to a request from the young person to be absent; the court should not respond to requests from third parties such as the prosecutor or a parent, unless the latter makes the request on behalf of the young person. If the young person is not represented, however, it would seem that the judge should not exercise his discretion to allow the young person to be out of court except in very limited circumstances. If the young person is represented, a request to be absent from the court can only be made with the young person's approval or authority. See *R. v. Page*, [1969] 1 C.C.C. 90, 64 W.W.R. 637 (B.C.C.A.) where a conviction in an adult proceeding was quashed because counsel for the accused waived his client's right to be present without the client's express authorization, there was no need to demonstrate prejudice nor was it necessary for the accused to object at trial.

See also para. 577(2)(c) of the *Code* allowing a judge to order exclusion of a young person during the trial of the issue of whether he is unfit to stand trial by reason of insanity, if the judge is satisfied that the presence of the young person might have an "adverse effect" on his "mental health". Consider also the discussion of s-ss. 13(5) and (6) of the Y.O.A. above, where it was suggested these provisions of the Y.O.A. might be interpreted so as to allow exclusion of a young person during cross-examination of the author of a medical or psychological report, if the presence of the young person "would be likely to be detrimental to the young person or would be likely to result in bodily harm to, or be detrimental to the mental condition of, a third party."

A Charter of Rights challenge to section 39?

Section 39 of the Y.O.A., which gives a youth court discretion to exclude members of the public from proceedings may be challenged as violating rights guaranteed in the *Charter of Rights*. Paragraph 2(b) of the *Charter* guarantees freedom of "expression, including freedom of the press and other media of communication," while para. 11(d) of the *Charter* provides that "any person charged with an offence has the right . . . to be presumed innocent until proven guilty . . . in a fair and *public* hearing." Thus, s. 39 may be challenged either by a young person claiming his right to a "public hearing" is being violated, or by a person excluded from the hearing. It is submitted that s. 39 should withstand constitutional challenge.

There are a few recent Canadian cases decided under the *Charter* which are directly relevant and some American decisions which are, as well, of considerable assistance.

In *Reference re Constitutional Validity of Section 12 of The Juvenile Delinquents Act* (1982), 38 O.R. (2d) 748, 70 C.C.C. (2d) 257, 29 R.F.L. (2d) 1 (H.C.); affd 3 C.C.C. (2d) 515, 41 O.R. (2d) 113 *sub nom. Re Southam Inc. and The Queen (No. 1)* (C.A.), a declaration was made that s-s. 12(1) of the *J.D.A.* which provides for an absolute prohibition on public attendance at juvenile trials, was unconstitutional as a violation of "freedom of expression including freedom of the press and other media" as guaranteed by s. 2 of the *Charter of Rights*. The court focussed on the fact that s-s. 12(1) of the *J.D.A.* gave the court no discretion, and stated that while there are circumstances in which an exclusion of the public is justifiable, there is a presumption that the public should be present: see *MacIntyre v. A.-G. N.S.* (1982), 40 N.R. 181, 65 C.C.C. (2d) 129, 26 C.R. (3d) 193, 132 D.L.R. (3d) 385, 49 N.S.R. (2d) 609 (S.C.C.). In *obiter dicta*, Smith J. (at p.

754 O.R.) specifically compared the constitutional validity of provisions of the *J.D.A.* and the *Y.O.A.*:

> That the courts possess an inherent jurisdiction to forbid access in certain narrow instances, is beyond dispute. The question is whether, since the enactment of the Charter, a legislature or Parliament may pre-empt an entire field by enacting legislation that provides *in camera* hearings for certain classes of cases regardless of circumstances. ... It is of significance that the new legislation to be shortly proclaimed [the Y.O.A.] lifts the present broad legislative restriction on public proceedings and confers a discretion on the court. The new provisions will be consonant with the *Canadian Charter of Rights and Freedoms* which is designed to remove all potential for abuse and arbitrariness. The basic rights in the Charter are those of all citizens regardless of age.
>
> The courts may be called upon to develop the parameters for the exercise of discretion where children are involved whether that discretion is exercised pursuant to the common law to present statutory provisions such as those found in the *Criminal Code* or to the new *Young Offenders Act* ... when it shortly comes into force. But the state has not satisfied me that a blanket denial of a public hearing without any cause being shown other than general social purposes can be justified. And when dealing with a legislative violation of a fundamental freedom ... the burden of persuasion rests with the legislators.

It is submitted that the comments of Smith J. in regard to the validity of s. 39 of the Y.O.A. are correct. The accused young person and the public both have a presumptive constitutional right to attend a hearing under the Y.O.A. However, these rights may be restricted if it is necessary to do so to protect a child or young person from the trauma or harm of a public hearing, or to protect the public interest in the administration of justice or the public morals. See *Globe Newspaper Company v. Superior Court for the County of Norfolk*, 102 S.Ct. 2613 (1982) where the United States Supreme Court suggested that there is a compelling state interest which would justify legislation restricting public access to trials where the victim of a sexual offence is a minor, provided the legislation allows a court to determine on a case-by-case basis whether the state's legitimate concern for the minor victim's well-being necessitates closure. See also *R. v. J.(R.)*, [1982] W.D.F.L. 791, 7 W.C.B. 507 (Ont. Prov. Ct.) and *Richmond Newspapers v. Virginia*, 448 U.S. 555, 100 S.Ct. 2814 (1980).

MAINTENANCE AND USE OF RECORDS
(Sections 40 to 46)

Introduction

The *Young Offenders Act* establishes a procedure for the compiling and maintaining of records concerning a young person dealt with under the Act, including those of the youth court, police, government departments and agencies, and private individuals and agencies; the Act also governs fingerprints and photographs of young persons. The Y.O.A. protects the privacy of young persons by ensuring that access to these records is limited, and also offers the young person an incentive to avoid further criminal activity by providing for the automatic destruction of records, if the young person has no further convictions for a specified period.

The *Juvenile Delinquents Act* is silent about records. Under the J.D.A., record keeping practice has varied across the country, and conflicting jurisprudence has developed around such issues as obtaining fingerprints from children. The desire for standardized practice and for clearer legislative direction regarding access to the young person's record has led to the enactment of the detailed provisions in ss. 40 to 46 of the Y.O.A.

Concern has been expressed about the constitutionality of these new provisions. It has been suggested that ss. 40 to 46 are *ultra vires* the federal government, since records could be classified as coming within the provincial power of the "administration of justice" under s-s. 92(14) of the *Constitution Act, 1867*. However, a sounder approach is to regard these provisions as *intra vires* the jurisdiction of the federal government as "criminal law and procedure" under s-s. 91(27) of the *Constitution Act, 1867*. See A.-G. B.C. v. Smith, [1967] S.C.R. 702, 2 C.R.N.S. 277, [1969] 1 C.C.C. 244, 61 W.W.R. 236, 65 D.L.R. (2d) 82 and R. v. Hauser et al., [1979] 1 S.C.R. 984, 98 D.L.R. (3d) 193, 8 C.R. (3d) 89, [1979] 5 W.W.R. 1, 26 N.R. 541, 46 C.C.C. (2d) 481.

Youth court records: section 40

SECTION 40

40. (1) *Clerk of youth court to keep records.*—The clerk of every youth court shall keep, separate from records of cases in ordinary court, a complete record of every case arising under this Act that comes before the youth court.

(2) *Records to be made available to specified persons and bodies.*—A record of a case kept pursuant to subsection (1) shall, during the course of proceedings in the case and during the term of any disposition made in the case, be made available for inspection on request to

(a) counsel for or a parent of the young person to whom it relates;

(b) the prosecutor;

(c) any judge who hears the case on appeal;

(d) any member of a department or agency of a government in Canada that is engaged in the supervision or care of the young person or in the administration of a disposition relating to the young person; and

(e) any other person who is deemed by a youth court judge to have a valid interest in the proceedings against the young person or in the work of the youth court, to the extent directed by the judge.

(3) *Idem.*—A record of a case kept pursuant to subsection (1) shall, on request, be made available for inspection at any time before or after proceedings in the case are completed to

(a) the young person to whom it relates, subject to subsection (4);

(b) counsel acting on behalf of the young person;

(c) the Attorney General of the province in which the youth court hearing the case has jurisdiction or any person authorized in writing by the Attorney General for the purposes of this section;

(d) the National Parole Board or any provincial parole board, for the purpose of considering an application for parole made by the young person after he has become an adult;

(e) any peace officer, for the purpose of investigating any offence that the young person is, on reasonable and probable grounds, suspected of having committed;

(f) any court that is dealing with the young person pursuant to provincial child welfare or youth protection legislation;

(g) any court or justice, for the purpose of sentencing the young person after he becomes an adult, if the young person is found guilty of an offence under an Act of Parliament or the legislature of a province or a regulation made thereunder;

(h) any provincial detention or correctional centre or any penitentiary in which the young person is held in custody after he becomes an adult or is transferred to ordinary court under section 16;

(i) the provincial director, if the young person is being dealt with pursuant to provincial child welfare or youth protection legislation that authorizes the provincial director to obtain the information in the record;

(j) any person, for the purpose of determining whether to grant security clearances required by the Government of Canada or the government of a province for the purposes of employment or the performance of services;

(k) any person who is deemed by a youth court judge to have a valid interest in the record, for research or statistical purposes, if the judge is satisfied that the disclosure is desirable in the public interest; and

(l) any other person who is deemed, or any person within a class of persons that is deemed, by a youth court judge to have a valid interest in the record, if the judge is satisfied that the disclosure is desirable in the interest of the proper administration of justice.

(4) *Non-disclosure of reports to young person.*—Where a youth court has withheld the whole or a part of a report from a young person, his parents or a private prosecutor, pursuant to subsection 13(6) or 14(7), the record or part thereof shall not be made available for inspection under this section to the young person, his parents or the private prosecutor, as the case may be.

(5) *Disclosure of information in records and copies of records.*— Any person to whom a record is required to be made available for inspection on request under this section may be given any information contained in the record and may be given a copy of any part of the record.

(6) [*Record of copies*].—The youth court shall keep a record of all copies given under subsection (5) and the persons to whom they are given.

(7) *Introduction into evidence.*—Nothing in paragraph (3)(f) or (g) authorizes the introduction into evidence of any part of a record that would not otherwise be admissible in evidence.

(8) *Disclosure for research or statistical purposes.*—Where a record is made available for inspection to any person under paragraph (3)(k), that person may subsequently disclose any information contained in the record, but may not disclose the information in any form that could reasonably be expected to identify the young person to whom it relates.

Youth court records: subsection 40(1)

Subsection 40(1) states that the clerk of every youth court shall keep a "complete record of every case" before the youth court. The section is mandatory — a record must be kept of every case that comes before the youth court, and these records must be kept separate from those kept for ordinary court (adult court). Youth court records are distinct from police records (ss. 41 and 42) and government and private records (s. 43).

Definition of "record": section 40

The Y.O.A. does not specify what constitutes a "complete record." Subsection 552(2) of the *Criminal Code* requires the ordinary court to "keep a record of every arraignment and of proceedings subsequent to arraignment"; the wording of the Y.O.A. is broader.

For the purposes of the Y.O.A. the "complete record" should include such items as the information, a written notation concerning each time the case was before the court and indicating the plea, adjudication, and disposition, if any. Certain provisions of the Y.O.A. specify that some documents are part of the "record": s-s. 13(9), a medical or psychological report, s-s. 14(4), a pre-disposition report, and subpara. 44(5)(a)(i), fingerprints and photographs received into evidence. Subsection 16(5) provides that the reasons for a youth court's decision on a s. 16 transfer application should form part of the record. Similarly under s-s. 20(6) reasons for disposition form part of the record. Oral reasons for a transfer or disposition decision, or an oral pre-disposition report given under s. 14(3), must be "recorded," but need not be transcribed; it is sufficient to keep a mechanical or stenographic recording. It would also seem that other documents, court forms and exhibits would constitute part of the "complete record" required by the Y.O.A.

There must be a stenographic or mechanical recording of the evidence of witnesses testifying in proceedings under the Y.O.A. This is a result of the incorporation of the summary conviction procedures of the *Criminal Code* in s. 52 of the Y.O.A.: see s-s. 736(3) and s. 468 of the *Code*. Though there must be a stenographic or mechanical recording, neither the *Code* nor Y.O.A. require the entire recording to be transcribed; transcription may be requested by a party in conjunction with an appeal.

It may be argued that since the Y.O.A. does not specifically refer to such stenographic or mechanical recordings, they are not within the "complete record" of s. 40. If this argument is accepted, then while it is necessary to have recordings of youth court proceedings, they need not be destroyed, as s. 45 of the Y.O.A. does not apply. Notwithstanding the above argument, however, it is submitted that a stenographic or mechanical recording does form part of the "complete record" of s. 40, and hence is subject to the limited access and destruction provisions of ss. 40 and 45. This approach is based on a policy of ensuring that a young person is adequately protected and access to the recordings of the proceedings is limited, and in due course the record is destroyed as required by s. 45. Accordingly, youth court clerks and youth court reporters will have to ensure that appropriate measures are taken in regard to the storage and destruction of mechanical and stenographic recordings of the proceedings.

The content of the "complete record" may perhaps be further defined under s. 67 of the Y.O.A., which empowers the Governor in Council to make regulations generally for carrying out the purposes and provisions of the Act. In addition, this section permits the Governor in Council to make regulations establishing uniform rules of court for youth courts across Canada, including rules regulating the practice and procedure to be followed by youth courts. Such regulations would be applicable uniformly across Canada.

Similarly, but on a provincial level, s. 68 allows judges of the youth court to make rules to regulate the duties of the officers of the youth court in the province and any other matter considered expedient to attain the ends of justice and carrying into effect the provisions of the Act. Thus, judges in each province may have the power to define the content of the record, where it has not specifically been dealt with in the Y.O.A. or by federal regulation.

Rules and regulations under s. 67 or 68 are not to be inconsistent with the Y.O.A., and could specify the manner in which records are to be kept. If judicial interpretation should result in a narrow view being taken of the meaning of a "complete record," rules or regulations could elaborate on record keeping requirements, but they could not cut down on the scope of the Act.

Appeal court records

The records of an ordinary court hearing an appeal or review of a decision of a youth court are not directly governed by s. 40 of the Y.O.A. Paragraphs 40(2)(a) and (b) allow the parties to have access to the youth court record which permits preparation of an appeal, and para. 40(2)(c) specifically allows the appellate court to have access to the youth court record. Any portions of the youth court record which come into the records of an appellate court are not to be disclosed, by virtue of s-s. 46(2), and s. 45 further requires the destruction of copies of those portions of the youth court record acquired by the appellate court. Thus, some parts of the appellate records may technically be exempt from the Y.O.A., but some portions will be subject to the access and destruction provisions of the Act. Those responsible for record keeping in the appellate courts will have to handle their records in such a manner as to comply with the provisions of the *Young Offenders Act*.

Review board records

Under s. 30 of the Y.O.A. provincial governments may decide to establish review boards to carry out the "duties and functions of a youth court" in regard to review of custodial dispositions. It is submitted that as such boards are carrying out the "duties and functions" of a youth court, by necessary implication the records of such boards are to be treated as youth court records and are governed by s. 40. However, in the absence of explicit legislative provision, it could be argued that it is more appropriate to consider that these are not technically youth court records and are not governed by s. 40. If this argument is accepted, then review board records would be governed by s. 43 of the Y.O.A. See also the discussion under ss. 31 and 43.

Disclosure: subsections 40(2) and (3)

Section 40 sets out detailed rules relating to disclosure of records. Subsection 40(2) is the more limited provision, since it deals only with requests for disclosure "during the course of proceedings and during the term of any disposition." Essentially s-s. 40(2) is directed to those persons directly involved in the proceedings. Subsection 40(3), a broader provision than s-s. 40(2), states that disclosure may be made "at any time before or after proceedings in the case are completed." The wording of s-s. 40(3) is broad enough to include a request for disclosure made during the proceedings. Thus, a young person has a right of access to his court record at any time under s-s. 40(3).

Disclosure to whom: paragraphs 40(2)(a) to (d)

Subsection 40(2) provides a list of persons who may obtain access to the court record "during the course of the proceedings" and who pursuant to s-s. 40(5) may obtain copies of any part of the record. Counsel for the young person or a parent has this right under para. 40(2)(a). Paragraph 40(2)(b) gives this right to the prosecutor; the definition of prosecutor found in s. 2 of the *Criminal Code* includes a private prosecutor. Paragraph 40(2)(c) allows access to the court record by any judge who hears the case on appeal.

Paragraph 40(2)(d) permits access to a member of "a department or agency of a government" supervising or caring for the young person or administering a disposition relating to the young person and clearly directs the release of records to youth court workers and training school administrators. This raises the issue whether Children's Aid Societies in Ontario, Nova Scotia and Manitoba come within para. 40(2)(d) as an "agency of a government." While these agencies are government funded and are subject to a large degree of control, both through their budgets and through government regulation, they are distinct legal entities with community based boards of directors. In any event, if a Children's Aid Society is not an "agency of a government," it could apply for access to court records pursuant to paras. 40(2)(e) and (3)(l).

Disclosure, who decides: paragraphs 40(2)(a) to (d)

Disclosure under paras. 40(2)(a) to (d) is an administrative matter within the clerk's powers. As long as the clerk is satisfied as to the identity of the person seeking disclosure, it must be made to a person qualified under these paragraphs.

Disclosure to "any other person" having a "valid interest": paragraph 40(2)(e)

Paragraph 40(2)(e) extends disclosure to "any other person ... deemed by a youth court judge to have a valid interest in the proceedings ... or in the work of the youth court." This provision contrasts with the immediately preceding paragraphs because a determination by a youth court judge is required. The Y.O.A. does not require a judge to hold any kind of a hearing before rendering a decision; the Act will be satisfied by an informal process. It is left to the discretion of each judge to determine an appropriate procedure, subject to any rules or regulations which may be promulgated. The judge, in his discretion, will determine whether the young person or any other persons should be given notice of any application, and whether anyone will be permitted to make representations. For example, if an individual wants access to the record of a particular young person, but the validity of his interest is borderline, it might be appropriate to give the young person notice of this before making a decision. On the other hand, if a newspaper reporter doing a background story on the youth court wishes to examine all the records of the youth court for a particular month, a judge may decide to allow this without giving notice to any the young people involved; of course the reporter would be subject to s. 38 concerning disclosure of the identity of young persons. If the circumstances require, a judge might consider appointment of an *amicus curiae* to represent the interests of a class of young persons, rather than giving each notice. Disclosure under para. 40(2)(e) may be limited to the extent directed by the judge, such that only relevant and necessary portions of the record will be disclosed.

The requirement that a person have a "valid interest" appears to narrow the class of people who will have access to the young person's record during the course of proceedings, although the Act does not define this term. The section includes a person with "an interest in the proceedings" or "in the work of the court."

Examples of persons who may have an interest in the proceedings are the victim, close relatives of the victim, and possibly the child's doctor.

Disclosure under subsection 40(3)

Subsection 40(3) gives a specified list of persons a right to access to court records, and to obtain copies under s-s. 40(5), at any time before, after and during a proceeding.

Paragraph 40(3)(a) gives the young person a right to access, thus ensuring that the young person is able to use the records in preparation for and during any legal proceedings. Counsel for the young person is included in para. 40(3)(b), but only to the extent that he is acting "on behalf of the young person." "Counsel" is defined in s. 2 of the *Criminal Code* as a "barrister or solicitor". This definition does not, therefore, seem to extend to articling students or clerks, nor does it include other agents or representatives of the young person. Unlike para. 40(2)(a), which allows for disclosure of records to a parent, or counsel for a young person, para. 40(3)(b) does not include reference to parents. The parents' right to disclosure is more limited than the young person's, as no specific right to access records is given to them after the completion of disposition; parents may seek access under para. 40(3)(l).

Some of the provisions of s-s. 40(3) limit the circumstances under which access can be obtained. For example, the National Parole Board has a right of access, in the case of an application for parole made by the young person after he has become an adult (para. 40(3)(d)). Similarly, any institution in which the young person is held in custody after he becomes an adult may request disclosure (para. 40(3)(h)). Access is also granted under para. 40(3)(j) for the purpose of determining whether to grant security clearances required by the provincial or federal government.

Under para. 40(3)(c), the provincial Attorney General or any person authorized in writing by him has a right to access to the record, without the need to specify a reason.

Disclosure to police investigator: paragraph 40(3)(e)

Paragraph 40(3)(e) provides for access to an investigating peace officer with "reasonable and probable grounds" for suspecting the young person of having committed an offence. The person who determines whether reasonable and probable grounds exist has not been specified. It seems that the youth court clerk is given this responsibility; note that paras. 40(3)(k) and (l) specify that certain questions of access must be determined by the judge. As with paras. 40(2)(a) to (d), it seems that paras. 40(3)(a) to (j) are to be administered by the clerk of the youth court.

Disclosure for other proceedings: paragraphs 40(3)(f), (g) and (i)

Disclosure of the youth court record is also available to any court for the purpose of sentencing the young person after he has become an adult (para. 40(3)(g)). The purpose of this provision is to make available to the sentencing judge information revealing a pattern of crime before, and continuing into, adulthood. Any court dealing with the young person under provincial child welfare or youth protection legislation also has a right to disclosure (para. 40(3)(f)). As well, where such legislation authorizes the provincial director to obtain the information in the record, if the provincial director is dealing with the young person under such legislation, he may have access to the record (para. 40(3)(i)). Note, however, that s-s. 40(7) clearly states that neither para. 40(3)(f) nor (g) renders admissible evidence that would otherwise not be admissible according to the rules of evidence in the court proceedings. A previous youth court record cannot be used for any purpose after the time prescribed by s. 45 of the Y.O.A. requiring destruction of the records has elapsed: see s-s. 45(5). See also paras. 36(1)(c) to (f) concerning use of a record of conviction in subsequent proceedings.

Disclosure to researchers or persons having a "valid interest": paragraphs 40(3)(k) and (l)

Any person "deemed by a youth court judge to have a valid interest in the record, for research or statistical purposes" may have access to youth court records pursuant to para. 40(3)(k), provided the disclosure is in the "public interest". Paragraph 40(3)(l) extends disclosure to any other person deemed by a youth court judge to have a valid interest in the record, provided disclosure "is desirable in the interest of the proper administration of justice."

Anyone seeking disclosure under para. 40(3)(k) or (l) must satisfy a youth court judge that he has a "valid interest." This term is also used in para. 40(2)(e). What constitutes a "valid interest"? Clearly in these situations a valid interest must be consistent with either the public interest (para. 40(3)(k)) or the interest of the proper administration of justice (para. 40(3)(l)).

An example of a "person" wanting disclosure under para. 40(3)(l) might be one operating an alternative measures (diversion) program under s. 4. The disclosure of youth court records might be required to enable the program operators to ascertain whether destruction of their own records is required under s-s. 45(2).

In assessing an application for access under para. 40(3)(k) the judge should consider the nature of the research being conducted. The objectives of the researcher and his qualifications (high school student vs. post-graduate university work) are to be assessed. Note that s-s. 40(8) permits a researcher obtaining information under para. 40(3)(k) to disclose this information, but not in "any form that could reasonably be expected to identify the young person to whom it relates." The researcher is also exempted under s-s. 45(3) from the destruction of records provisions of the Y.O.A.; this saves the researcher from the difficulties associated with destruction and allows long-term studies to be conducted, subject to s-s. 40(8).

Subsection 46(2) generally prohibits the disclosure of information by those who have access to records.

The Y.O.A. does not require a judge to hold a formal hearing before rendering a decision under para. 40(3)(k) or (l). An informal procedure will satisfy the Act: see discussion on para. 40(2)(e).

In deciding an application under s-ss. 40(2) or (3), the judge should consider the fundamental principles articulated in s. 3 of the Y.O.A. Paragraph 3(1)(e) provides that the young person has rights and freedoms in his own right. Indiscriminate disclosure of the young person's record without a determination of the presence of a sufficient degree of public interest may violate the young person's right to privacy.

Limitation on disclosure: subsection 40(4)

Subsections 13(6) and 14(7) provide that medical, psychological or pre-dispositional reports may, under specified circumstances, be withheld from a young person, his parents or a private prosecutor. Where this has been done, even though these reports constitute part of the youth court record, they shall not be available for inspection under s-ss. 40(2) and (3) to a person from whom they have been withheld under s-ss. 13(6) and 14(7). This will require some special precautions on the part of youth court clerks, some form of "red flagging" of these records will be necessary. Others who have obtained copies of these documents will have to exercise similar care.

Copies of records: subsections 40(5) and (6)

A person who has access to court records under s-s. 40(2) or (3) may be given a copy of any part of the record under s-s. 40(5). Presumably under s. 67 or 68 regulations or rules may be prescribed to set fees for providing copies. Under s-s. 40(6) the youth court must keep a record of all copies given out along with a list of the persons to whom copies are given. Such records facilitate the operation of the destruction provisions in s. 45. Note that apparently no record need be kept of persons who merely inspect the files and who might in the course of inspection make handwritten notes of the information in the file.

Police records: sections 41 and 42

The importance of the records of various local, provincial and national police forces to the enforcement and administration of justice is recognized by the Y.O.A. Section 41 deals with what is commonly referred to as a "criminal record," while s. 42 is somewhat broader and includes police records relating directly to the investigation of alleged offences. Note that s. 44 deals with fingerprints and photographs which could form an integral part of actual investigative police records. Records of ancillary police services and associated police agencies, such as forensic laboratories, fall under s. 43 dealing with government records.

Central repository records: section 41

SECTION 41

41. (1) *Records in central repository.*—**A record of any offence of which a young person has been found guilty under this Act may be kept in such central repository as the Commissioner of**

the Royal Canadian Mounted Police may, from time to time, designate for the purpose of keeping criminal history files or records on offenders or keeping records for the identification of offenders.

(2) *Police force to provide record.*—Where a young person is found guilty of an offence under this Act, the police force responsible for the investigation of the offence shall provide a record of the offence for inclusion in any central repository designated pursuant to subsection (1).

(3) *Subsections 40(2) to (8) apply.*—Subsections 40(2) to (8) apply, with such modifications as the circumstances require, in respect of records kept pursuant to subsection (1).

"Record": section 41

"Record" and "criminal history files" are not defined in the Act, although the record in s. 41 is clearly different from the youth court records in s. 40. The "record" which may be kept pursuant to s. 41 could include such factual information about the young person, the offence, and the disposition as the following:

— young person	— identifying information including:
	• name, address, school, etc.
	• date and place of birth
	• physical description
	• parents' names and addresses
	• finger print section (F.P.S.) number
— offences	— nature of offence
	— Act and section number
	— date of conviction
— disposition	— jurisdiction and court
	— nature of disposition
	— date of completion

Subsection 41(1) uses the terms "criminal history files", "records on offenders" and "records for the identification of offenders"; these terms would appear to be roughly synonymous. The use of these synonyms ensures that terminology employed by different law enforcement agencies is included. Further, the words seem susceptible to broad interpretation, and the records can be expanded to include additional information which may be considered relevant.

Subparagraph 44(5)(a)(ii) requires that where a young person accused of committing an indictable offence is found guilty of that offence, the original or a copy of any fingerprints and print of any photograph of the young person shall be kept as part of the s. 41 record in the central repository.

Records of offence: section 41

Records maintained under s. 41 relate only to offences of which a young person has been found guilty. "Offence" is limited by the definition in s-s. 2(1) to the Y.O.A. to "an offence created by an Act of Parliament or by any legislation, rule, order, by-law or ordinance made thereunder other than an ordinance of the Yukon Territory or the Northwest Territories."

It appears that the wording of s. 41 does not allow the central repository to retain fingerprints which are sent for a fingerprint search prior to conviction. After a search and a reply to the submitting force has been made, the prints will have to be returned or destroyed, as there is no authority for their retention in these circumstances (see para. 44(5)(a)).

"Central repository": subsection 41(1)

The Commissioner of the Royal Canadian Mounted Police is given authority to designate a facility for the purpose of storage and retrieval of these records. No doubt this repository will be patterned on the existing adult storage facility and will likely be located at the R.C.M.P. headquarters in Ottawa. Such a centralized repository incorporates the following advantages:

— it will promote effective investigation of crime and identification of criminals in the interests of public protection and the effective administration of justice;

— it will ensure access to information in a young person's record for those persons so entitled (see s-s. 41(3)); and

— it will enable a young person to obtain, at any time, a complete summary of his record and allow him to verify that destruction has in fact occurred (see s-s. 41(3) and s. 45).

Record provided to central repository: subsection 41(2)

Subsection 41(2), in conjunction with s-s. 41(1), contemplates a scheme whereby the investigating police department, upon conviction of the young person, shall furnish the designated central repository with the information which constitutes the "record of the offence." Prior to the conviction of a young person, a record will exist and will be available only at the police department responsible for, or participating in, the investigation of the offence, as provided for under s. 42.

Since the investigating department must provide the information subsequent to a conviction, the Act ensures that the information available in the central repository will be complete. Where more than one department has been involved in the investigation, the department which was responsible for the carriage of the prosecution must comply with providing the record.

Access to the central repository: subsection 41(3)

Subsection 41(3) adopts s-ss. 40(2) to (8), with such changes as the circumstances require, in respect of the records kept in the central repository. Thus, certain persons have a right to disclosure, some have a right under specified circumstances, and others may make an application to youth court to have access to the records. There is to be no disclosure of records other than in the circumstances specified in s-ss. 40(2) and (3) (see s-s. 46(2)). Under para. 40(3)(c), the young person has a right of access to his record at any time and, pursuant to s-s. 40(5), may have a copy of his record; this will allow the young person to ensure that his record has been destroyed as required by s. 45.

For paras. 40(2)(a) to (d) and 40(3)(a) to (j), the keeper of the central repository is to satisfy himself as to identity and eligibility of the person seeking access. If access is sought under para. 40(2)(e) or 40(3)(k) or (l), the issue must be decided by a youth court judge. The Y.O.A. does not require that any person be given notice of such an application or that a formal hearing be held. Before allowing access to the records of the central repository under s. 41 pursuant to para. 40(2)(e) or 40(3)(k) or (l), a judge might consider giving notice to the Commissioner of the Royal Canadian Mounted Police. See also discussion of para. 40(2)(e).

The record kept pursuant to s. 41 might be referred to as the young person's "criminal record". Subject to s-ss. 36(1) and 45(5) it may be used in subsequent proceedings in youth court and adult court: see also para. 40(3)(g). It may also be used in a child welfare or youth protection hearing: see para. 40(3)(f). Admissibility of the record in subsequent court proceedings is subject to the rules of evidence, see s-s. 40(7). In practice such records are introduced by certified copy and identification of the accused person is made by testimony of a police officer or by fingerprint evidence.

Police records: section 42

SECTION 42

42. (1) *Police records.*—A record of any offence alleged to have been committed by a young person may be kept by any police force responsible for, or participating in, the investigation of the offence.

(2) *Records available to members of police force.*—A record kept pursuant to subsection (1) may be made available for inspection at any time to any member of the police force keeping the record.

(3) *Records may be made available to specified persons.*—A record kept pursuant to subsection (1) may, in the discretion of the police force keeping the record, be made available for inspection to any person or body referred to in subsection 40(2) or (3) for the purposes and in the circumstances set out in those subsections.

(4) *Subsections 40(4) to (8) apply.*—Subsections 40(4) to (8) apply, with such modifications as the circumstances require, in respect of records kept pursuant to subsection (1).

(5) *Police records may be made available to peace officers.*—A record kept pursuant to subsection (1) may be made available for inspection at any time to a peace officer if access to the record is necessary in the investigation of any offence that a person is suspected of committing or in respect of which a person has been arrested or charged, whether as a young person or as an adult.

"Record of any offence alleged": subsection 42(1)

It should be noted that "record" as used in this section is broader than "record" in s. 41. Since the record in s. 42 is not dependent upon conviction, but relates to the investigation of the offence, the scope of information which can be included is not as restricted as in s. 41. The record in s. 42 apparently refers to all of the documentation compiled by the police force in the investigation of an offence and would include general investigation reports, complaints, occurrence reports, as well as any forensic laboratory reports. This record may also contain personal information about the young person suspected of being involved. Section 42 does not require a police force to maintain a record but it does govern the maintenance of, access to, and destruction of any documents and other material which form part of the "record of any alleged offence."

As the term "record" is not defined, it is not clear whether it can be so broadly interpreted as to include the notes and notebook used by a policeman in the investigation of an offence alleged to have been committed by a young person. The statute refers to records kept by a "police force," rather than those of a peace or police officer, which suggests the individual officer's notes are not included. Further, as an officer's personal notes are of a more private nature than an official file at a police station, and as such are not available to the public, one might argue that the potential for prejudice to young persons from the existence of such notes is relatively minimal. On the other hand, any notes made by a police officer would be made in the course of his official duties and arguably are a part of the records of the "police force." One of the main objectives of the record provisions in the Act is the protection of young persons from unauthorised release of information and this suggests that a police officer's notes should be included in the s. 42 record. It would seem anomalous to allow an individual police officer to keep a personal record of the offence when all other records are required to be destroyed. If it is accepted that an officer's notes are included, he will have to comply with the provisions of s. 45 regarding destruction of records. For example, if the notes were taken in connection with an offence where the accused is a young person, the officer would have to destroy the relevant portion of his notes where the youth is acquitted or where the charge has been withdrawn or stayed; other provisions of s. 45 may require destruction at a later date even if the young person is convicted.

It would not seem that physical evidence would constitute part of a police "record" but tape recordings, videotapes or photographs would be considered part of this record. Fingerprints and photographs of the young person are part of the s. 42 record, but are also subject to the additional constraints of s. 44.

Section 42 has no application until it is "alleged" that an offence has been committed by a young person. An information does *not* have to be laid for a young person to be "alleged" to have committed an offence; it is sufficient if the young person is a suspect in a case. A young person who is merely a witness or is otherwise named in the record (although not as a suspect), is not entitled to access pursuant to s-s. 42(3); nor, for example, is there a requirement for the destruction of a police record concerning an offence committed by an adult and naming a young person as a witness.

Participating police force: subsection 42(1)

The nature of criminal investigation often necessitates a number of police forces being involved in a single investigation. Where more than one force is participating in the investigation of an offence alleged to be committed by a young person, each force may keep a record, and each is subject to the Act.

It would appear from para. 44(5)(b) that fingerprints and photographs can be kept only by "the police force responsible for the investigation leading to the laying of the information against the young person," and a police force merely "participating in" the investigation of an alleged offence would be precluded from keeping fingerprints or photographs.

Police access to police records: subsections 42(2) and (5)

Pursuant to s-s. 42(2), the files maintained by the police force are accessible to members of the same force, subject only to any internal policy which is within the discretion of the force to implement. This is contrasted with what appears to be a higher test for access for members of another force under s-s. 42(5).

Subsection 42(5) provides for access to police officers from forces other than the force keeping the record. This subsection does not appear to impose as high a test for access as is the case with police officer's access to court records (see para. 40(3)(e)), although the use of the word "necessary" suggests that the information sought from the record must have a measure of importance related to the investigation. It is for the record keeper of the force to determine the issue of necessity, with any uncertainty being resolved by the chief of the force.

Subsection 42(5) allows access in situations where charges are not yet laid; mere suspicion is enough to justify the request for access.

Discretionary access to police records: subsections 42(3) and (4)

Subsection 42(3) allows a person or body referred to in s-s. 40(2) or (3) to seek access to the police record, but it is in the discretion of the police force keeping the record to refuse access. This means that the young person does not have a right of access to the police record although such a right exists with respect to the record of conviction maintained under s. 41. Subsection 42(3) is generally consistent with the protection of personal information provisions of the *Canadian Human Rights Act*, S.C. 1976-77, c. 33, subpara. 53(b)(iii) whereby police investigative files are exempt from the general access provisions of that legislation (see also *Access to Information Act Bill*, S.C. 1980-81-82-83, c. 111).

The effect of s-s. 42(3) of the Y.O.A. is to place the integrity of the investigation of an offence ahead of the right to access of a s. 42 record. More specifically police may be concerned about the disclosure of information concerning the following:

(i) police investigative methods;

(ii) witness names and information identifying witnesses;

(iii) an investigation of co-accused or suspects who were not charged.

Thus, although a person has satisfied a youth court judge that he should have access to police records under para. 40(2)(e) or 40(3)(k) or (l), access to these records may still be denied by the police. This subsection also may operate to deny access to the courts as provided for under paras. 40(3)(f) and (g).

Subsection 42(4) is similar to s-s. 41(3) and makes these subsections of s. 40 dealing with the process of disclosure and provision of copies applicable to police records. The right to receive a copy pursuant to s-s. 40(5) is also within the discretion of the police force, and it would seem that a copy of the record may be denied although a force may choose to make the record available for inspection.

The police have an absolute discretion as to whether to allow access to their records to statutorily authorised persons. Given the sensitive nature of material in police files, the concern about the release of information about investigative methods and a fear that information in the records might ultimately be revealed to the individuals named, it was felt necessary to give the police control over their records.

Apparently, the only constraint upon the police right to refuse access to their records is a requirement of good faith.

Police files and records have generally not been subject to subpoena in court proceedings on the basis of Crown privilege: see however, *Smerchanski v. Lewis* (1980), 31 O.R. (2d) 705, 117 D.L.R. (3d) 716, 18 C.P.C. 29 (C.A.) which limits the scope of the doctrine. Any right to subpoena police files for various proceedings exists in addition to those rights of disclosure created by the Y.O.A.

Government and private records: section 43

Section 43 deals with a range of records kept by government agencies and departments and by private individuals and organizations, in connection with a young person being dealt with under the Y.O.A. Any records within s. 43 are subject to the provisions of the Act limiting access and requiring disclosure and destruction.

SECTION 43

43. (1) *Government records.*—**A department or agency of any government in Canada may keep records containing information obtained by the department or agency**

(a) for the purpose of an investigation of an offence alleged to have been committed by a young person;

(b) for use in proceedings against a young person under this Act;

(c) for the purpose of administering a disposition;

(d) for the purpose of considering whether, instead of commencing or continuing judicial proceedings under this Act

against a young person, to use alternative measures to deal with the young person; or

(e) as a result of the use of alternative measures to deal with a young person.

(2) *Private records.*—Any person or organization may keep records containing information obtained by the person or organization

(a) as a result of the use of alternative measures to deal with a young person alleged to have committed an offence; or

(b) for the purpose of administering or participating in the administration of a disposition.

(3) *Record may be made available to specified persons and bodies.*—Any record kept pursuant to subsection (1) or (2) may, in the discretion of the department, agency, person or organization keeping the record, be made available for inspection to any person or body referred to in subsections 40(2) or (3) for the purposes and in the circumstances set out in those subsections.

(4) *Subsections 40(4) to (8) apply.*—Subsections 40(4) to (8) apply, with such modifications as the circumstances require, in respect of records kept pursuant to subsections (1) and (2).

Government records: subsection 43(1)

Subsection 43(1) covers records of any government agency or department at any level — federal, provincial or municipal — other than those governed by ss. 40 to 42 and 44. Subsection 43(1) permits the government department or agency to keep records for the following specified purposes:

(a) investigation of an offence,

(b) use in proceedings against a young person,

(c) purposes of administering a disposition,

(d) consideration of use of alternative measures, under s. 4 or

(e) dealing with a young person by alternative measures.

Any records within this definition are subject to the access and destruction provisions of Y.O.A. Subsection 43(1) authorizes the keeping of records by the provincial director, Crown attorneys, probation officers, training schools and other treatment or custody facilities. Medical and psychiatric facilities directly operated by provincial health departments would also seem to fall within the scope of this provision. Naturally records of government departments or agencies which do not relate to matters specified in s-s. 43(1) are not within the Act. For example, if a young person who is convicted under the Y.O.A. is a ward of a Department of Social Services, the records of the Department concerning the ward do not generally become subject to the access, disclosure and destruction provisions of the Y.O.A. These records, however, would be subject to the Y.O.A. provisions to the extent that they were obtained for use in proceedings under the Act, or for the purposes of administering a disposition.

"Department or agency": subsection 43(1)

The term "department or agency of any government in Canada" is not defined in the Y.O.A., and its exact scope is not clear (see the discussion of Children's Aid Societies under paras. 40(2)(a) to (d), above). The definition is important, for the types of records encompassed by s-s. 43(1) are much broader than those of s-s. 43(2); any records within the provisions of the Y.O.A. are subject to the disclosure and destruction provisions of the Act. Accordingly, in each case where an agency or department purports to have authority to maintain records concerning a young person, its status as a government agency or department must be determined. If it is not a government agency or department, its authority for maintaining such records must be found in s-s. 43(2).

Records of persons or organizations: subsection 43(2)

The records of persons or organizations containing information obtained as a result of the use of alternative measures, or for the purpose of administering or participating in the administration of a disposition are subject to the provisions of the Y.O.A.

The Y.O.A. does not, however, govern other records of private persons or organizations. Thus records of a community agency which counselled a young person prior to the commission of an offence are not subject to the Act, but if the agency becomes involved in supervising a disposition of the young person, those portions of the young person's file obtained as a result of supervising the disposition are subject to the Act. Similarly, the records of a store's security service used in the prosecution of a young person are *not* governed by the Y.O.A., though the police files on the same case are governed by s. 41.

Discretionary disclosures: subsections 43(3) and (4)

Subsection 43(3), like its counterpart s-s. 42(3), gives discretion to the record keeper in deciding whether to give disclosure to the persons designated in s-ss. 40(2) and (3) to the record in question. Presumably the record keeper has a discretion to allow disclosure of part of a record, while retaining the right to withhold other parts. Pursuant to s-s. 46(2), disclosure of information and access to records is only to be given to those specified in s-ss. 40(2) and (3). Application can be made to a youth court under paras. 40(2)(e) and 40(3)(k) and (l) for permission to have disclosure of the records, but the record keeper retains final discretion to refuse disclosure, even after court approval.

It was not felt necessary to give a right to dislosure of records governed by s. 43, even though these include such records as those used for alternative measures and by review boards, as:

— every young person is given access to court records (s. 40) and criminal records (s. 41), and this is thought sufficient to allow a young person to conduct court proceedings and enforce rights under the Act,

— much of the information contained in records governed by s. 43 is obtainable pursuant to other provisions in the Act,

— in regard to records of individuals, agencies and organizations involved in alternative measures, it was felt that these records are limited in scope and usefulness, and further, the young person only participates in alternative measures voluntarily,

— the agencies, organizations and individuals referred to in s. 43 are not usually considered part of the judicial system, and it was felt inappropriate to impose the costs and inconveniences mandatory disclosure might involve.

Naturally, any person mentioned in s-s. 40(2) or (3) might use other legislation to obtain disclosure. The provinces may enact legislation, or in some situations Part IV of the *Canadian Human Rights Act*, S.C. 1976-77, c. 33 might apply (see also *Access to Information Act*, S.C. 1980-81-82-83, c. 111).

Review board records

There may be potential difficulties in regard to access to documents and records used by the review boards, which individual provinces may choose to establish to deal with review of custodial dispositions under s. 30 of the Y.O.A. It can be argued that since the review boards are carrying out "the duties and functions" of a youth court, it is the necessary implication of the legislation that the review board's records are governed by s. 40. As these boards, for the purposes of reviewing a custodial disposition, are given analogous powers to those of a youth court and will be making similar decisions, a liberal and remedial approach, consistent with the spirit of the Y.O.A., would suggest that this view should prevail. Hence those involved would have a right of access to any document used by the board. The jurisprudential concept of "procedural fairness" also lends support to this conclusion.

In the absence of explicit legislative provision, however, it may be argued that these are not technically youth court records and therefore that s. 40 does not apply. If this argument is accepted, it follows that s. 43 will govern review board records and ensure that such records are not improperly disclosed and are eventually destroyed. Section 43, however, does not guarantee the young person, his counsel or his parents access to the records. However, if there is a review by a youth court of the review board's decision, under s. 40 the young person must have access to any documents sent by the review board for consideration by the youth court. This would include documents which a review board might initially have withheld from the young person (subject to para. 13(6)(b) allowing withholding of medical and psychological reports from a young person). If s. 43 applies, existing jurisprudence suggests that in the absence of valid legislation to the contrary, the review board must act fairly and at least counsel for a young person should have access to all documents on which the board relies in making its decision: see Re Abel and Advisory Review Board (1980), 31 O.R. (2d) 520, 56 C.C.C. (2d) 153, 119 D.L.R. (3d) 101 (C.A.).

A young person, his parents, the Attorney General or his agent or the provincial director have a right to review by the court of a review board decision (s. 31).

Fingerprints and photographs: section 44

Under the *Juvenile Delinquents Act* there have been conflicting judicial pronouncements concerning the fingerprinting and photographing of youths in connection with police investigations, and practices have varied considerably across the country. Section 44 of the Y.O.A. clarifies the law, giving police the same legislative authority to take fingerprints and photographs of young persons in cases where adults can be subjected to such a procedure with special protections to ensure that access will be strictly controlled. Fingerprints and photographs of young persons can only be taken with legislative authority, and not on the basis of consent. As well as the general destruction provisions of s. 45, there are specific and more stringent requirements in s-s. 44(4) regarding fingerprints and photographs. Although fingerprinting and photographing are an integral part of police investigative work, it is important to note that they are regarded as particularly sensitive and are accorded different treatment from that given other police records under ss. 41 and 42.

SECTION 44

44. (1) *Identification of Criminals Act applies.*—**Subject to this section, the** *Identification of Criminals Act* **applies in respect of young persons.**

(2) *Limitation.*—**No fingerprints or photograph of a young person who is accused of committing an offence shall be taken except in the circumstances in which an adult may, under the** *Identification of Criminals Act,* **be subjected to the measurements, processes and operations referred to in that Act.**

(3) *Subsections 40(2) to (8) apply.*—**Subsections 40(2) to (8) apply, with such modifications as the circumstances require, in respect of fingerprints or photographs taken pursuant to this section.**

(4) *Destruction of fingerprints and photographs.*—**Any fingerprints or photograph of a young person taken pursuant to this Act, and all copies, prints or negatives thereof, shall be destroyed forthwith**

(a) where the young person is acquitted, on the expiration of the time allowed for the taking of an appeal or, where an appeal is taken, when all proceedings in respect of the appeal have been completed; or

(b) where a young person is not charged with an offence or where the charge against the young person is dismissed for any reason other than an acquittal, withdrawn or stayed and no proceedings are taken against him for a period of three months, on the expiration of the three months.

(5) *Records kept where a young person is found guilty.*—Where a young person accused of committing an indictable offence is found guilty of the offence, the original or a copy of any finger-prints and a print of any photograph of the young person taken by or on behalf of a peace officer

(a) shall be kept

(i) as part of the youth court record of the young person where the fingerprints or a print of the photograph has been received in evidence by the youth court in any pro-ceeding relating to the offence, and

(ii) as part of any record of the offence kept in the reposi-tory referred to in subsection 41(1); and

(b) may be kept by the police force responsible for the inves-tigation leading to the laying of the information against the young person.

Legislative authority: subsections 44(1) and (2)

Subsection 44(1) authorizes police officers to fingerprint and photograph young persons in the same way as adults, pursuant to the provisions of the *Identification of Criminals Act*, R.S.C. 1970, c. I-1. That Act authorizes these procedures when a person is charged with or convicted of an indictable offence, or has been apprehended under the *Extradiction Act*, R.S.C. 1970, c. E-21 or the *Fugitive Offenders Act*, R.S.C. 1970, c. F-32.

Subsection 44(2) provides that fingerprints and photographs can *only* be taken pursuant to the provisions of the *Identification of Criminals Act*. Unlike with adults, the police cannot fingerprint or photograph a young person solely on the basis of his consent, there must be legislative authority. It might be argued that if fingerprints or photographs are taken in violation of s-s. 44(2) of the Y.O.A., they should be excluded from evidence at sub-sequent proceedings pursuant to the *Canadian Charter of Rights and Freedoms*, as violating rights under para. 11(d) and "bringing the administration of justice into disrepute" (s-s. 24(2) of the *Charter*).

Access to fingerprints and photographs: subsection 44(3)

Subsection 44(3) provides that s-ss. 40(2) to (8) governing access to records apply to fingerprints and photographs taken by the police. Thus, for example, under para. 40(3)(e) any peace officer having reasonable and probable grounds for suspecting that a young person has committed *any* offence, may have access to any fingerprints or photographs already taken of the young person, unless they have been destroyed pursuant to the provisions of the Y.O.A. Similarly, under para. 40(3)(a) the young person has a right to access. Notice that unlike in regard to police records (s. 42) and government and private records (s. 43), the keeper of fingerprints or photographs must disclose them to an authorized person.

It would seem unlikely that circumstances would justify a judicial disclosure of fingerprints or photographs under para. 40(2)(e), or 40(3)(k) or (l). Sufficient information should be available in the youth court records (s. 40) and police records (s. 41) for most researchers and other persons having a "valid interest" in the young person or the proceedings of the youth court.

Unauthorized disclosure is an offence under s-s. 46(2).

Destruction of fingerprints and photographs: subsection 44(4)

Subsection 44(4) requires the destruction of fingerprints and photographs when a young person is not convicted. Paragraph 44(4)(a) requires destruction upon acquittal. Paragraph 44(4)(b) deals with situations where the young person is not charged or proceedings are stayed or withdrawn, or there is a dismissal for any reason other than an acquittal (for example, quashing an information for a technical defect) and no new proceedings are taken for three months; in these situations fingerprints or negatives must be destroyed three months from the cessation of proceedings. Paragraph 44(4)(b) is subject to the *Extradition Act* and *Fugitive Offenders Act* which do not require that a charge be laid before fingerprints or photographs are taken.

When fingerprints or photographs have been taken and the young person is convicted, they may be stored pursuant to s-s. 44(5) and must be destroyed pursuant to s. 45.

Although s-s. 44(4) does not specifically deal with included offences, it would seem clear that where a young person is convicted of an included indictable offence, the fingerprints and photograph could be retained as per s-s. 44(5). Where a young person is originally charged with an indictable offence and his fingerprints or photograph are taken pursuant to s-s. 44(1) but is only convicted of an included summary conviction offence, his fingerprints and photograph would have to be destroyed.

Subsection 44(4) requires the destruction of all originals, as well as copies, prints and negatives.

Storage of fingerprints and photographs: subsection 44(5)

Subsection 44(5) provides for the storage of fingerprints and photographs in the following manner where a young person is found guilty of an indictable offence:

— where the prints/photos were used in court they shall form part of the court record and be stored accordingly under s. 40 (subpara. 44(5)(a)(i));
— they shall form part of any record kept in the central repository under s. 41 (subpara. 44(5)(a)(ii); and
— they may be kept by the police force responsible for the investigation (para. 44(5)(b)).

It is noteworthy that para. 44(5)(a) is mandatory whereas para. 44(5)(b) is permissive.

Although s-s. 42(1) provides for participating police forces to maintain a record, para. 44(5)(b) makes it clear that it is only the police force which was "responsible for the investigation leading to the laying of an information" which may retain fingerprints and photographs in their record. In a joint investigation, more than one force might have this responsibility, in which case both would qualify under para. 44(5)(b).

It also seems that the central repository must destroy or return to the submitting police force, fingerprints and photographs of young persons that are submitted prior to conviction for the purposes of criminal record checks. There is no authority in ss. 41 to 44 for the central repository to retain fingerprints and photographs until the young person has been convicted, and s. 46 makes it clear in these circumstances that they may not be kept.

Destruction of records: section 45

The philosophy of accountability and responsibility articulated in the Declaration of Principle found in s. 3 of the Y.O.A.

does not extend to the point that young persons are treated exactly as adults. The record destruction provisions of the Y.O.A. recognize that a young person should not be subject to consequences as severe as those imposed on an adult.

Section 45 gives a young person convicted of an offence an incentive to refrain from further involvement in illegal activity by providing for automatic destruction of records after a certain period of time if the young person has no further convictions. It is recognized that a young person should be given a second chance to begin life with a "clean record". Similar policy concerns are reflected in s. 36, which provides that for many purposes a young person will be deemed not to have been convicted of an offence under the Y.O.A. once any disposition made under the Act has ceased to have effect.

SECTION 45

45. (1) *Destruction of records.*—Where a young person is charged with an offence and

(a) is acquitted, or

(b) the charge is dismissed for any reason other than acquittal, withdrawn or stayed and no proceedings are taken against him for a period of three months,

all records kept pursuant to sections 40 to 43 and records taken pursuant to section 44 that relate to the young person in respect of the alleged offence and all copies, prints or negatives of such records shall be destroyed.

(2) *Idem.*—Where a young person

(a) has not been charged with or found guilty of an offence under this or any other Act of Parliament or any regulation made thereunder, whether as a young person or an adult,

(i) for a period of two years after all dispositions made in respect of the young person have been completed, where the young person has at any time been found guilty of an offence punishable on summary conviction but has never been convicted of an indictable offence, or

(ii) for a period of five years after all dispositions made in respect of the young person have been completed, where the young person has at any time been convicted of one or more indictable offences, or

(b) has, after becoming an adult, been granted a pardon under the *Criminal Records Act,* all records kept pursuant to sections 40 to 43 and records taken pursuant to section 44 that relate to the young person and all copies, prints or negatives of such records shall be destroyed.

(3) *Copy given for research or statistical purposes.*—Subsections (1) and (2) do not apply in respect of any copy of a record or part thereof that is given to any person pursuant to paragraph 40(3)(k), but does apply in respect of copies of fingerprints or photographs given pursuant to that paragraph.

(4) *Destruction on acquittal, etc.*—Any record that is not destroyed under this section because the young person to whom it relates was charged with an offence during a period referred to in that subsection shall be destroyed forthwith

(a) where the young person is acquitted, on the expiration of the time allowed for the taking of an appeal or, where an appeal is taken, when all proceedings in respect of the appeal have been completed;

(b) where no proceedings are taken against him for a period of six months, on the expiration of the six months; or

(c) where the charge against the young person is dismissed for any reason other than acquittal, withdrawn or stayed and no proceedings are taken against him for a period of six months, on the expiration of the six months.

(5) *Young person deemed not to have committed offence.*—A young person shall be deemed not to have committed any offence in respect of which records are required to be destroyed under subsection (1), (2) or (4).

(6) *Records not to be used.*—No record or copy, print or negative thereof that is required under this section to be destroyed may be used for any purpose.

(7) *Request for destruction.*—Any person who has under his control or in his possession any record that is required under this section to be destroyed and who refuses or fails, on a request made by or on behalf of the young person to whom the record relates, to destroy the record commits an offence.

(8) *Application to delinquency.*—This section applies, with such modifications as the circumstances require, in respect of records relating to the offence of delinquency under the *Juvenile Delinquents Act* as it read immediately prior to the coming into force of this Act.

Destruction if no conviction: subsection 45(1)

All records kept in connection with an alleged offence by a young person must be destroyed if he is acquitted of the charge, para. 45(1)(a). Records included would be youth court records (s. 40), police records (s. 42), and government and private records (s. 43); central repository records only arise after conviction (s. 41) and destruction of fingerprints and photographs is governed by s-s. 44(4) where the young person is acquitted. There is no specification of how soon after acquittal the records must be destroyed; presumably this must be done after the expiration of the time allowed for taking an appeal or, where an appeal is taken, when all proceedings in respect of the appeal have been completed.

Paragraph 45(1)(b) has similar provisions dealing with situations where a charge is withdrawn or stayed, and proceedings are not brought for three months. This paragraph also applies where a charge is dismissed for reasons other than acquittal, for example if there has been a dismissal because of the non-appearance of the prosecutor (*Criminal Code*, s. 734) or an information is quashed for a technical defect.

There is no express provision in s-s. 45(1) for the destruction of the record of an investigating police force which suspects a young person of having committed an offence, but has not laid any charges. Further, there is no express provision in the Act for the destruction of police records with respect to a young person suspected of an offence where no charge is laid *if* there is no conviction for a subsequent offence. This would suggest a force may keep its investigating records active indefinitely (contrast para. 44(4)(b) which specifies that fingerprints or photographs are to be destroyed if no charges are brought within three months). While one might reach this conclusion, it should be noted that it would be inconsistent with the effect of para. 45(2)(a).

Where a young person is suspected of committing an offence but not charged, subsequently is convicted of another offence, and then satisfies the requirements of para. 45(2)(a) for a "clean period", "*all* records kept pursuant to sections 40 to 43" shall be destroyed. In this instance, it would seem that "all records" includes records of an investigating force which has previously suspected a young person of an offence and not laid any charges.

The records of an agency administering a program of alternative measures in regard to a young person alleged to have committed an offence, but not formally charged (no information laid), are governed by the same legislative provisions as govern police investigating files regarding offences for which no charges are laid. While s-s. 45(1) does not require destruction, s-s. 45(2) will require destruction if there has been a conviction in regard to a subsequent charge and the required "clean period". This leads to the anomalous result that the records of a young person who has only been involved in alternative measures could be kept indefinitely whereas the records of a youth who has performed alternative measures, is convicted of a subsequent offence, and then satisfies the requirements for destruction will be destroyed. Notwithstanding this apparent gap in the legislation, it is suggested that, as a matter of practice, records from alternative measures involvement be destroyed if the young person has no further convictions, after two years if the original offence was summary, and after five years if the original offence was indictable.

Destruction after finding of guilt: subsections 45(2) and (4)

If a young person has been convicted under the *Young Offenders Act*, s-s. 45(2) provides that if there are no further charges for a specified time, then all records kept under ss. 40 to 44 are to be destroyed. The time specified is two years after the completion of the disposition of an offence if the original offence was summary, and five years after the completion of the disposition if the offence was indictable. Destruction will also be required if, after becoming an adult, the young person secures a pardon under the *Criminal Records Act*, R.S.C. 1970 (1st Supp.), c. 12.

If there are further charges before a record is destroyed under s-s. 45(2), but no conviction results, then s-s. 45(4) requires the ultimate destruction of the records. The destruction is suspended until the charges are dismissed, or there has been a reasonable period (six months) for their resolution.

If a young person is convicted of another offence before the period specified in s-s. 45(2) has expired, the records need not be destroyed; however, if there is a subsequent period free of further convictions, all records are to be destroyed. For example, if a 13-year-old boy is convicted of a summary conviction offence in January, 1990 and given six months' probation, then as a

14-year-old of an indictable offence in January, 1991 and given 12 months' probation and then has no further charges, in January, 1997, all of the records relating to both offences are to be destroyed — January, 1997 is five years after the completion of the last disposition.

Method of destruction: sections 44 and 45

The Act does not provide a specific mechanism for destruction. The word "destroy" suggests there is an onus on the record keeper to see that records are shredded, burned or otherwise mutilated so that they are no longer in a readable form. In the case of computer tapes, the recordings must be erased. Merely throwing records out as waste paper may not meet the requirements of the Act. There are frequent media reports of supposedly confidential government files which were to have been destroyed, but were only thrown out and ultimately discovered in a public place due to some unfortunate event like the rupture of a garbage bag.

At least initially, agencies and individuals with records, or copies of records, may have some difficulty in complying with the destruction provisions of the Y.O.A. It is in part because of anticipated difficulties that s-s. 45(7) limits criminal liability for failure to comply with the destruction of records requirements of the Act.

Copies: subsection 45(3)

As a rule, if a record is to be destroyed under s. 45, all copies of the record are to be destroyed. The requirement to keep a list of those who have received copies of records pursuant to s-s. 40(6), facilitates keeping track of those who have copies. An exception to this rule exists under s-s. 45(3) for researchers who obtain copies of records under para. 40(3)(k); this will facilitate long-term research and preserve potentially valuable research data. Even researchers must destroy copies of fingerprints and photographs, as these only serve identification purposes.

Effect of destruction: subsections 45(5) and (6)

Whenever records are required to be destroyed under s. 45, as a result of s-s. 45(5) a young person is deemed not to have committed any offence, even if the record is not in fact destroyed. Similarly, under s-s. 45(6) no record and no copy, print or negative thereof which is required by s. 45 to be destroyed, may be used for any purpose; in particular, they may not be used in subsequent proceedings. Subsections 45(5) and (6) protect the young person if there should be a failure to destroy records or copies.

Sanctions for failure to destroy: subsection 45(7)

Subsection 45(7) makes it an offence for any person who has under his control or in his possession, any record that is required under s. 45 to be destroyed, but *only* if that person has refused or failed to destroy the records *after* a request to do so, by or on behalf of the young person to whom the record relates. The penalty provision is found in s-s. 46(4).

The offence created by s-s. 45(7) is limited to situations of a specific request, as it is recognized that some agencies and individuals may have some difficulty in totally complying with all of the destruction provisions, particularly in the first few years of implementation of the Y.O.A. It is expected that in due course adequate methods and procedures will be developed to facilitate compliance with the Act.

Records, and copies of records, may be kept by the youth court, different police forces, a range of government departments and agencies, and private organizations and individuals. The destruction requirements of the Y.O.A. are further complicated by the fact that a person in possession of records may have some difficulty in ascertaining whether the young person in question has been charged with or convicted of further offences, and hence knowing when destruction is required under s-s. 45(2) or (4) as the case may be. Record keepers may choose to minimize these difficulties by destroying records within the periods specified by s-s. 45(2), unless they definitely have knowledge of subsequent convictions. Alternatively, a record keeper may seek access to the records of criminal history contained in the central repository pursuant to s. 41; such a record keeper would clearly seem to be a person having a "valid interest" under para. 40(3)(1).

Except in the case of a refusal or failure to comply with a request for destruction (s-s. 45(7)), there is no direct sanction in the Y.O.A. for a failure to destroy records as required by the Act.

However, if a record keeper fails to comply, it might be possible in some circumstances for a third party to obtain a prerogative writ of *"mandamus"* compelling compliance. Further, there might be circumstances in which a record keeper who fails to comply with the Act might be liable for damages, including the possibility of punitive damages if the failure is a result of a wilful refusal to attempt to comply. There might also be political or administrative pressures brought to bear on those who make no effort to comply. It also may be possible that charges could be brought under s. 115 of the *Criminal Code* for disobeying a statute.

Juvenile Delinquents Act records: subsection 45(8)

Subsection 45(8) provides that the provisions of s. 45 regarding destruction apply to records relating to the offence of delinquency under the *Juvenile Delinquents Act*, "with such modifications as the circumstances require." The intention is to make the new procedures apply to all existing records pertaining to delinquents. As the *J.D.A.* has been in force for over 70 years, it is recognized that it may not be realistic to destroy all records amassed under that Act. It is clear, however, that any records which should be destroyed, but are not, cannot be used for any purposes, and in particular, are not to be used in any court proceedings, s-s. 45(6). Further, if a young person or any person acting upon his behalf requests that specific records be destroyed, it will be an offence under s-s. 45(7) to refuse. In general, one would expect record keepers to make reasonable good faith efforts to comply with the Y.O.A.

Offence: section 46

Section 46 creates offences for failure to comply with the provisions of the Y.O.A. prohibiting disclosure, and in some circumstances provides for the punishment of those who fail to destroy records as required. The aim of creating offences is to encourage respect for and discourage abuse of the law.

SECTION 46

46. (1) *Prohibition against possession of records.*—No person shall knowingly have in his possession any record kept pursuant to sections 40 to 43 or any record taken pursuant to section 44, or any copy, print or negative of any such record, except as authorized or as required by those sections.

(2) *Prohibition against disclosure.*—Subject to subsection (3), no person shall knowingly

(a) make available for inspection to any person any record referred to in subsection (1), or any copy, print or negative of any such record,

(b) give any person any information contained in any such record, or

(c) give any person a copy of any part of any such record

except as authorized or required by sections 40 to 44.

(3) *Exception for employees.*—Subsection (1) does not apply, in respect of records referred to in that subsection, to any person employed in keeping or maintaining such records, and any person so employed is not restricted from doing anything prohibited under subsection (2) with respect to any other person so employed.

(4) *Offence.*—Any person who fails to comply with this section or commits an offence under subsection 45(7)

(a) is guilty of an indictable offence and liable to imprisonment for two years; or

(b) is guilty of an offence punishable on summary conviction.

(5) *Absolute jurisdiction of magistrate.*—The jurisdiction of a magistrate to try an accused is absolute and does not depend on the consent of the accused where the accused is charged with an offence under paragraph (4)(a).

Possessing records: subsection 46(1)

Subsection 46(1) forbids any person from knowingly having in his possession any "record," within the definitions of ss. 40 to 44, or any copies of any such records, except as authorized or required by the Act. It is an essential element of the offence that a person have knowledge of the existence of the records, but ignorance of the provisions of the Y.O.A. is no defence: see *Criminal Code*, s. 19. "Person" is defined in the *Interpretation Act*, R.S.C. 1970, c. I-23, s. 28 to include a corporation.

Disclosure of records: subsection 46(2)

Subsection 46(2) creates an offence for any person to knowingly make available a record, or a copy of a record, or any information contained in a record, except as authorized by the

Act. As with s-s. 46(1) knowledge is an essential element of the offence, and person includes a corporation.

It would seem that the disclosure must in some way be related to the compilation or maintenance of the record. Thus it would be an offence for a court clerk to reveal to an insurance adjuster that a young person had been convicted of impaired driving, as the clerk would be giving information contained in a record, the court record, which he had a duty to maintain. On the other hand, the young person himself could inform the adjuster of this fact with impunity.

Protection for employees: subsection 46(3)

Subsection 46(3) has two clauses dealing with two distinct situations, and providing that persons in those situations are not violating the provisions of the Y.O.A.

The first clause of s-s. 46(3) modifies the effect of s-s. 46(1), so that any person "employed in keeping or maintaining" records is exempt from s-s. 46(1). A very broad interpretation of this provision would suggest that any person who is an employee, and who in the course of his employment keeps records as defined by ss. 40 to 44, is exempt from the provisions of s-s. 46(1), whether or not the employer is authorized to have such records. A narrower, and more reasonable interpretation is that any employee of a person authorized to keep records, may in the course of his employment keep these records. It would seem unreasonable for a person to raise as a defence to a criminal charge the mere fact that it was his employer who directed him to do the act.

The second clause of s-s. 46(3) authorizes one person employed in keeping records to release those records to another person employed in keeping records. Clearly, this provision at least authorizes the transfer of records and exchange of information from one person employed in keeping records for a particular employer to another employee of the same employer. But no limitation has been placed on disclosure from one person to another person "so employed", and it would seem that one person employed in record keeping could disclose records to another person employed in record keeping by a different employer, provided both employers were authorized to keep the type of records in question.

Procedure: subsections 46(4) and (5)

Subsection 46(4) provides that the offences created by s-s. 45(7) and s. 46 are hybrid, and therefore the Crown must elect to proceed by summary conviction or by indictment.

Subsection 46(5) states that these offences are within the absolute jurisdiction of a magistrate, thus eliminating any choice for the accused regarding the manner of trial. This simplifies and expedites the procedure for this type of prosecution.

CONTEMPT OF COURT
(Section 47)

Introduction

Broadly defined, criminal contempt of court is conduct which obstructs or tends to obstruct the due administration of justice, or which tends to undermine the authority and discipline of the court. Criminal contempt also consists of behaviour which prejudices the ability of the court to conduct a fair trial. Examples of criminal contempt include the misconduct of fighting in court, interference with officers of the court, refusal by a witness to be sworn or to answer questions once sworn, the imputation of false motives to the court and the publication of information relating to proceedings before the court which would prejudice the outcome of the trial.

Criminal contempt may be committed "in the face" of the court, in which case it is usually dealt with summarily by the presiding judge. It may also be committed "constructively", that is "other than in the face of the court." Contempt in the face of the court is distinguished from constructive contempt on the basis that all the circumstances of the former are within the personal knowledge of the court. The refusal of a witness to be sworn and disruptive behaviour in the courtroom are examples of such contempt. Constructive contempt occurs when the facts of the alleged contempt are not within the direct knowledge of the court and where it is necessary for there to be testimony of witnesses or affidavit evidence to prove the occurrence of the contempt.

Constructive contempt is usually dealt with in proceedings commenced by an information or indictment. Contempt in the face of the court is normally proceeded against summarily, since the presiding judge can do so without unnecessarily having to call witnesses of issues of fact. By dealing with constructive contempt by information or indictment, the judge can avoid placing himself in the position of accuser, witness and adjudicator. However, constructive contempt may also be dealt with summarily if an emergency exists in which the dignity and authority of the court must be vindicated immediately. For a discussion of the distinction between contempt "in the face of the court" and constructive contempt, see *McKeown v. The Queen*, [1971] S.C.R. 446, 16 D.L.R. (3d) 390, 2 C.C.C. (2d) 1.

Subsection 5(5) of the Y.O.A. makes the youth court a "court of record". Consequently, it has the inherent power to punish for contempt committed in the face of the court. Moreover, s-s. 47(1) of the Y.O.A. considerably expands the traditional contempt jurisdiction of an inferior court of record by statutorily granting the youth court the same jurisdiction and power to deal with contempt as a superior court of criminal jurisdiction. A superior court has the inherent power, apart from statute, to punish contemptuous acts committed constructively against itself or another court.

The present juvenile court, in addition to any inherent power it may have to deal with contempt by virtue of the *J.D.A.*, s-s. 36(1) has the power to control order while it is sitting. The juvenile court does not have the jurisdiction to deal with constructive contempt against itself, nor can it punish a juvenile for contempt against another court, unless charges are laid pursuant to the *J.D.A.* The Y.O.A., s. 47, gives a considerably greater jurisdiction and authority to the youth court in dealing with contempt committed by young persons.

SECTION 47

47. (1) *Contempt against youth court.*—**Every youth court has the same power, jurisdiction and authority to deal with and impose punishment for contempt against the court as may be exercised by the superior court of criminal jurisdiction of the province in which the court is situated.**

(2) *Exclusive jurisdiction of youth court.*—**The youth court has exclusive jurisdiction in respect of every contempt of court committed by a young person against the youth court whether or not committed in the face of the court and every contempt of court committed by a young person against any other court otherwise than in the face of that court.**

(3) *Concurrent jurisdiction of youth court.*—**The youth court has jurisdiction in respect of every contempt of court committed by a young person against any other court in the face of that court and every contempt of court committed by an adult**

against the youth court in the face of the youth court, but nothing in this subsection affects the power, jurisdiction or authority of any other court to deal with or impose punishment for contempt of court.

(4) *Dispositions.*—Where a youth court or any other court finds a young person guilty of contempt of court, it may make any one of the dispositions set out in section 20, or any number thereof that are not inconsistent with each other, but no other disposition or sentence.

(5) *Section 636 of Criminal Code applies in respect of adults.*— Section 636 of the *Criminal Code* applies in respect of proceedings under this section in youth court against adults, with such modifications as the circumstances require.

(6) *Appeals.*—A finding of guilt under this section for contempt of court or a disposition or sentence made in respect thereof may be appealed as if the finding were a conviction or the disposition or sentence were a sentence in a prosecution by indictment in ordinary court.

Contempt jurisdiction of youth court: subsections 47(1) and (2)

Subsection 47(1) of the Y.O.A. provides that every youth court has the same power, jurisdiction and authority to deal with criminal contempt against the court as may be exercised by a superior court of criminal jurisdiction. As a result of s-s. 47(1), the youth court will have the statutory jurisdiction to deal with all contempts committed by young persons or adults against the youth court.

Concurrent contempt jurisdiction of the youth court: subsections 47(2) and (3)

Subsection 47(2) grants the youth court exclusive jurisdiction over all criminal contempts of court committed by a young person, other than those committed in the face of another court. The exclusive jurisdiction granted by s-s. 47(2) to deal with constructive contempts committed by young persons against other courts accords with the grant of superior court jurisdiction over contempt provided by s-s. 47(1). Subsection 47(3) further provides that the youth court will have jurisdiction in respect of every contempt of court committed by a young person against any other court. This jurisdiction of the youth court over young persons who commit contempt in the face of other courts will be concurrent with the jurisdiction of the other courts to deal with the contempt since s-s. 47(3) of the Y.O.A. provides that nothing in s-s. 47(3) affects the jurisdiction or power of any other ordinary court to deal with or impose punishment for contempt. Thus jurisdiction over adults who commit constructive contempt against the youth court will be shared between the youth court and the superior court of criminal jurisdiction. One should note the decision of R. v. Marsden (1977), 40 C.R.N.S. 11, 37 C.C.C. (2d) 107 (Que. S.C.) wherein it was held that a superior court has no jurisdiction over contempts committed in the face of an inferior court.

Disposition of young persons: subsection 47(4)

Where any court finds a young person guilty of criminal contempt of court, s-s. 47(4) of the Y.O.A. restricts the sanction to any one or more of the dispositions found in s. 20 of the Y.O.A. No other form of disposition or sentence is allowed; if more than one disposition under s. 20 is made they must be consistent with each other.

Application of section 636 of the Criminal Code: subsection 47(5)

Subsection 47(5) of the Y.O.A. only applies to adults. It specifically makes s. 636 of the Criminal Code applicable against adults in proceedings taken in youth court but allows for modifications as the circumstances require. Section 636 of the Criminal Code provides that any person who is required by law to attend or remain in attendance for the purpose of giving evidence, and without lawful excuse fails to attend or remain in attendance, is guilty of contempt of court; it provides that such a person may be proceeded against summarily and limits the punishment to a fine of $100 or imprisonment for 90 days or both. Moreover, a person found guilty pursuant to s. 636 of the Criminal Code may be ordered to pay the costs that are incident to the service of process or to the detention. Section 636 of the Code is exhaustive; that is, no other punishment may be imposed: Re Helik, [1939] 3 D.L.R. 56, 72 C.C.C. 76, [1939] 2 W.W.R. 123, 47 Man. R. 179 (K.B.).

Appeals: subsection 47(6)

Subsection 47(6) provides that for the purpose of an appeal, a finding of guilt, disposition or sentence for contempt of court under s. 47 of the Y.O.A. will be treated as a conviction or sentence respectively, of an indictable offence in ordinary court. Therefore, pursuant to the provisions of the *Criminal Code*, Part XVII, appeals will be to the "court of appeal" of the province in which the contempt was committed.

FORFEITURE OF RECOGNIZANCES
(Sections 48 and 49)

Introduction

Sections 51 and 52 of the Y.O.A. provide for the application of the *Criminal Code* where it is not inconsistent with the Y.O.A. Therefore, recognizances may be entered into by young persons pursuant to the provisions of ss. 453, 453.1, 457, and 745 of the *Code*. Sections 453.1 and 453 apply to an accused arrested with or without warrant, and if the conditions of each section are met, provide for his release from detention by the officer in charge of the police station; the accused may be required to enter into a recognizance to secure his release. Section 457 of the *Code* provides for the release of an accused by a justice if the accused was not released by the officer in charge; an accused person may be required to enter into a recognizance under s. 457. Generally these provisions of the *Code* are applicable to a young person after arrest, although s. 8 of the Y.O.A. stipulates that a justice will only deal with the judicial interim release of a young person if a youth court judge is not reasonably available. Section 745 of the *Code* provides that a recognizance may be required from a person to ensure that he keeps the peace and is of good behaviour. In some circumstances, these provisions of the *Code* may require a deposit (cash or other valuable security) or surety (guarantor) of the recognizance.

The object of a recognizance is to secure the performance of some act by a person. Thus, where a youth court requires an assurance that a young person will appear in court at a specified time, it may, as a condition of his release, require him to enter a recognizance, with or without deposit or sureties. Where sureties are required, the sureties also enter the recognizance as an added guarantee that the acts will be performed. For example, in a recognizance under s. 457, the surety's prime obligation is to ensure the appearance of the accused at the proper time and place. Theoretically, when bail is granted on the basis of a recognizance with sureties, the effect is not to set the accused free, but to transfer his custody from the officers of the law to the custody of the sureties. Bail, therefore, frees the accused from imprisonment prior to trial by having his sureties undertake that the accused will fulfill any conditions incident to his release and will appear at the time required.

A recognizance is a voluntary acknowledgement of an existing debt owing to the Crown, by which the principal (accused) and his sureties admit their respective liability to pay the Crown a certain sum of money, unless the principal (accused) fulfills certain conditions. Where the conditions are fulfilled and, for example, the accused appears in court as required, the recognizances are discharged; however, if the accused fails to appear at the time specified, the recognizances become subject to forfeiture. A hearing is held which allows the principal (accused) and the sureties an opportunity to show cause why the sum should not be forfeited. When a youth court judge orders forfeiture, the principal and his sureties become judgment debtors of the Crown, each in the amount the judge orders him to pay.

In addition to forfeiture proceedings, a young person could face criminal charges for breach of his recognizance. A young person who enters a recognizance to fulfill conditions and to appear for trial as a precondition of his release on bail may be charged under s. 133 of the *Code* if a breach of his recognizance occurs. Similarly, s. 746 of the *Criminal Code* provides that breach of a recognizance entered to keep the peace pursuant to s. 745 of the *Criminal Code* is an offence punishable on summary conviction.

SECTION 48

48. *Applications for forfeiture of recognizances.*—Applications for the forfeiture of recognizances of young persons shall be made to the youth court.

Jurisdiction of youth court: section 48

If a young person breaches a recognizance issued under ss. 453, 453.1 or 457 of the *Code* by failing to appear as required, or by breaching the peace or violating other conditions of a recognizance given pursuant to s. 745 of the *Code*, the young person and any of his sureties may be subject to forfeiture. Section 48 of the Y.O.A. provides that applications for forfeiture of recognizances given by young persons must be made to the youth court; both the young person and any sureties are subject to forfeiture in the youth court. Applications for forfeiture are usually submitted by the Crown. Part XXII of the *Criminal Code*, governing the "Effect and Enforcement of Recognizances," generally applies to proceedings under the Y.O.A., except as expressly modified by s. 48 or 49.

When a young person breaches his recognizance, a "certificate of default" pursuant to s. 704 of the *Code* is endorsed on the back of the recognizance by the presiding youth court judge or justice. The endorsement in Form 29 of the *Code* sets out the nature of the default, the reason for the default, if known, and whether the ends of justice have been defeated or delayed by the default. It also gives the names and addresses of the principal and any sureties of the recognizance. The certificate is evidence of the default to which it relates.

SECTION 49

49. (1) *Proceedings in case of default.*—**Where a recognizance binding a young person has been endorsed with a certificate pursuant to subsection 704(1) of the *Criminal Code*, a youth court judge shall,**

(a) on the request of the Attorney General or his agent, fix a time and place for the hearing of an application for the forfeiture of the recognizance; and

(b) after fixing a time and place for the hearing, cause to be sent by registered mail, not less than ten days before the time so fixed, to each principal and surety named in the recognizance, directed to him at his latest known address, a notice requiring him to appear at the time and place fixed by the judge to show cause why the recognizance should not be forfeited.

(2) *Order for forfeiture of recognizance.*—**Where subsection (1) is complied with, the youth court judge may, after giving the parties an opportunity to be heard, in his discretion grant or refuse the application and make any order with respect to the forfeiture of the recognizance that he considers proper.**

(3) *Judgment debtors of the Crown.*—**Where, pursuant to subsection (2), a youth court judge orders forfeiture of a recognizance, the principal and his sureties become judgment debtors of the Crown, each in the amount that the judge orders him to pay.**

(4) *Order may be filed.*—**An order made under subsection (2) may be filed with the clerk of the superior court or, in the**

province of Quebec, the prothonotary and, where an order is filed, the clerk or the prothonotary shall issue a writ of *fieri facias* in Form 30 set out in the *Criminal Code* and deliver it to the sheriff of each of the territorial divisions in which any of the principal and his sureties resides, carries on business or has property.

(5) *Where a deposit has been made.*—Where a deposit has been made by a person against whom an order for forfeiture of a recognizance has been made, no writ of *fieri facias* shall issue, but the amount of the deposit shall be transferred by the person who has custody of it to the person who is entitled by law to receive it.

(6) *Subsections 704(2) and (4) of Criminal Code do not apply.*—Subsections 704(2) and (4) of the *Criminal Code* do not apply in respect of proceedings under this Act.

(7) *Sections 706 and 707 of the Criminal Code apply.*—Sections 706 and 707 of the *Criminal Code* apply in respect of writs of *fieri facias* issued pursuant to this section as if they were issued pursuant to section 705 of the *Criminal Code*.

Proceedings in case of default: section 49

Paragraph 49(1)(a) of the Y.O.A. provides that when a recognizance binding on a young person has been endorsed with a certificate of default pursuant to s-s. 704(1) of the *Code*, the Attorney General or his agent may request that a youth court judge fix a time and place for a hearing of the application for forfeiture of the recognizance. When requested the judge must fix a time and a place for a hearing and send a notice to the principal (young person) and every surety named in the recognizance. The notice, as provided in para. 49(1)(b), must be directed to the principal and sureties at their latest known addresses and must inform them that they are to appear at that time and place to show cause why the recognizance should not be forfeited. The notice must be sent by registered mail, not less than ten days before the date for the hearing. Subsection 49(2) of the Y.O.A. clearly implies that a failure to comply with the notice requirements of s-s. 49(1) will result in a lack of jurisdiction over the application (see *R. v. Policha; Ex parte Pawlivsky*, [1970] 5 C.C.C. 172, 11 C.R.N.S. 199 *sub nom. Re Pawlivsky*, 73 W.W.R. 74 *sub nom. Pawlivsky v. The Queen* (Sask. Q.B.)).

Pursuant to s-s. 49(2) of the Y.O.A., the youth court judge hearing the forfeiture application, after giving the parties an opportunity to be heard, may either grant or refuse the application for forfeiture. The youth court judge may make any order with respect to the forfeiture of the recognizance as he considers proper. Though there will usually be a forfeiture if the conditions of the recognizance are not satisfied, this is not always the case. See R. v. Lauder, [1963] 2 C.C.C. 142 at p. 147, 39 C.R. 380, 41 W.W.R. 505 (Alta. Dist. Ct.) where the court stated there should not be a forfeiture in regard to a recognizance given to assure appearance in court if the accused has satisfied the court that "he had good and sufficient excuse for not appearing [at the time stipulated]", for example, due to accident or illness.

Subsection 49(3) of the Y.O.A. provides that where a recognizance is ordered forfeited, the principal and his sureties become judgment debtors of the Crown, each in the amount that the judge orders him to pay.

Where an order is made under s-s. 49(2) of the Y.O.A., it may be filed with the clerk of the superior court of the province, or in the province of Quebec, with the prothonotary. The clerk or the prothonotary shall issue a writ of *fieri facias* in Form 30, set out in the *Criminal Code*. (A writ of *fieri facias*, or "fi fa" — Latin meaning "to cause to be made" — instructs the sheriff to cause a sum of money to be produced by seizing property.) The writ of *fieri facias* is to be delivered to the sheriff of each territorial division in which property is owned by the principal or surety. The sheriff must then seize and sell sufficient property, both real and personal, of the principal and sureties to satisfy the order of forfeiture.

Subsection 49(5) of the Y.O.A. provides that no writ of *fieri facias* shall issue if a deposit of money or other valuable property was made when the recognizance was entered into and the deposit is sufficient to cover the forfeiture. Instead, the deposit is to be transferred to the person "entitled by law to receive it" (usually the provincial government, see *Code*, s. 651).

Subsection 49(7) of the Y.O.A. provides that ss. 706 and 707 of the *Criminal Code* apply in respect of writs of *fieri facias* issued pursuant to s. 49 of the Y.O.A., as if they were issued pursuant to s. 705 of the *Code*. Subsection 706(1) of the *Code* provides that such a writ of *fieri facias* may be executed by the sheriff to whom it is delivered and the property seized dealt with in the same manner as a writ of *fieri facias* issued out of a superior court. Subsection 706(2) of the *Code* entitles the Crown to the costs of execution in accordance with the tariff of the superior court of the appropriate province. Section 707 of the *Code* provides a procedure for the committal to custody or discharge of the sureties if their property is insufficient to cover the amount forfeited. In accordance with s. 707, and after appropriate notice, a time and place will be fixed for the sureties to show cause why they should not be committed if the forfeiture is not satisfied.

Subsection 49(6) provides that s-ss. 704(2) and (4) of the *Criminal Code* do not apply in respect of proceedings under the Y.O.A. The provisions of s-ss. 704(2) and (4) of the *Code* are adequately provided for in s-ss. 49(4) and (5) of the Y.O.A. respectively.

Liability of sureties: section 49

Subsection 698(1) of the *Criminal Code* applies to bind the sureties to a bail recognizance until the accused is either discharged or sentenced. Section 697 of the *Code* provides that the sureties continue to be bound to assure the appearance of the accused as required, regardless of trial adjournments or changes in the place of the trial. Section 699 of the *Code* provides that sureties are not discharged in their duty on the basis of the accused being re-arrested on the same or additional charges. A surety who wishes to discharge his obligation prior to the disposition of the young person can do so by virtue of ss. 701 and 702 of the *Code* in conjunction with ss. 49 and 51 of the Y.O.A., by bringing the young person and delivering him into the custody of the court. Similarly, s. 700 of the *Code* provides for the surety to apply to the youth court to relieve him of his obligation to ensure that a young person attends court; in this case a warrant for the arrest of the young person is issued, and upon the young person being placed in detention, the surety is discharged.

A surety's prime obligation under a bail recognizance is to ensure the appearance of the accused, and in the case of a peace bond under s. 745 of the *Criminal Code* is to ensure the good behaviour of the accused; the surety's recognizance is to effect these duties. The granting of bail on a recognizance with a surety is technically to change the custody of the accused from the officers of the law to the surety. Thus, if the accused fails to appear at the time required or he breaches a condition of the recognizance, the surety may be subject to forfeiture. The surety is responsible for the production of the young person or his good behaviour, as the case may be, and if the conditions are violated, the courts do not look favourably upon relieving the surety from forfeiture.

Subsection 49(2) of the Y.O.A. provides that the youth court judge has the discretion, after hearing the parties, to grant or refuse the forfeiture of the recognizance and to make any order in respect to the recognizance that he considers proper. If the surety "connived at the disappearance of the accused man, or aided it or abetted it, it would be proper to forfeit the whole of the sum. If he or she was wanting in due diligence to secure his appearance, it might be proper to forfeit the whole or a substantial part of it depending on the degree of fault. If he or she was guilty of no want of diligence and used every effort to secure the appearance . . . it might be proper to remit it entirely." See R. v. Southampton Justices, Ex parte Green, [1975] 2 All E.R. 1073, at pp. 1077-78 (C.A.); also R. v. Andrews (1975), 34 C.R.N.S. 344, 9 Nfld. & P.E.I.R. 168 (Nfld. S.C.).

Subsection 11(9) of the Y.O.A. provides that when a young person enters into a recognizance before an officer in charge (pursuant to s. 453 or 453.1 of the Code), a statement must be included in the recognizance that the young person has the right to be represented by counsel. Subsection 698(4) of the Code provides that the provisions of s. 697 and s-ss. 698(1), (2) and (3), which outline a surety's obligations, should also be endorsed on any recognizance.

Young persons as sureties

A young person cannot act as a surety for the recognizance of another person.

When a person undertakes to act as a surety for the recogniz-ance of another, the surety contracts to forfeit the sum specified if the principal fails to satisfy the terms of the recognizance (fails to appear or breaches the peace). An infant (a minor, in Canada a person under 18) cannot validly sign a recognizance as a surety since the contract, not being for the benefit of the infant, is void. See R. v. Leduc, [1972] 1 O.R. 458, 5 C.C.C. (2d) 422 (Dist. Ct.); R. v. Shrupka, [1977] 5 W.W.R. 233 (Man. Prov. Ct.).

INTERFERENCE WITH DISPOSITIONS
(Section 50)

Introduction

The purpose of s. 50 of the Y.O.A. is to ensure, through the use of criminal law and penal sanctions, that dispositions made pursuant to s. 20 of the Act are not interfered with by unauthorized persons.

SECTION 50

50. (1) *Inducing a young person, etc.*—Every one who

(a) induces or assists a young person to leave unlawfully a place of custody or other place in which the young person has been placed pursuant to a disposition,

(b) unlawfully removes a young person from a place referred to in paragraph (a),

(c) knowingly harbours or conceals a young person who has unlawfully left a place referred to in paragraph (a),

(d) wilfully induces or assists a young person to breach or disobey a term or condition of a disposition, or

(e) wilfully prevents or interferes with the performance by a young person of a term or condition of a disposition

is guilty of an indictable offence and is liable to imprisonment for two years or is guilty of an offence punishable on summary conviction.

(2) *Absolute jurisdiction of magistrate.*—The jurisdiction of a magistrate to try an adult accused of an indictable offence under this section is absolute and does not depend on the consent of the accused.

Interference with dispositions: section 50

Section 50 of the Y.O.A. creates a number of offences for the purpose of ensuring that no one interferes with a disposition imposed by a youth court under s. 20. Thus, if a young person wilfully breaches a term of his own disposition, he may be charged under s. 33 of the Y.O.A., or if appropriate, under s. 132

or 133 of the *Criminal Code* (prison breach or escape and being unlawfully at large without excuse). Any other person (adult or young person) who induces or assists in the breach may, if appropriate, be charged under s. 50 of the Y.O.A.

Presently s. 34 of the *J.D.A.* makes it a summary conviction offence to induce or attempt to induce a child to leave, or remove or attempt to remove a child from an institution where the child had been placed pursuant to the *J.D.A.* It is also an offence under that section to knowingly harbour or conceal a child who had escaped lawful custody. Section 34 of the *J.D.A.* provides that contravention can result in a fine not exceeding $100 or imprisonment not exceeding one year, or both. In comparison s. 50 of the Y.O.A. provides that if the Crown elects to proceed by indictment, the maximum sentence is two years' imprisonment; if the Crown elects to proceed summarily, the maximum sentence is a fine of $500, or six months' imprisonment or both.

Paragraphs 50(1)(a), (b) and (c) deal with interference with dispositions under which a young person has been committed to custody or placed in a residence pursuant to a disposition. Examples of places other than custody include a residential placement by the court or provincial director as a condition of probation under para. 23(2)(e) or (f).

Offences analogous to those under paras. 50(1)(a), (b) and (c) are contained in ss. 134 and 135 of the *Criminal Code* (permitting or assisting escape; and rescue or permitting escape). In appropriate cases, reference may be made to the jurisprudence under corresponding sections of the *Code*. For example, a prisoner is said to have escaped custody contrary to para. 133(1)(a) of the *Code* when he "without permission ... departed from the ... limits of his custody and it matters not if he remained on the prison property": *R. v. Piper*, [1965] 3 C.C.C. 135, 51 D.L.R. (2d) 534 at p. 537 (Man. C.A.). Thus it may be argued that para. 50(1)(a) or (b) of the Y.O.A. is violated even if the young person has not left the property on which he is in custody. In appropriate cases, it may be possible to charge those who assist a young person in escaping custody either under the *Code* or s. 50 of the Y.O.A., subject to the rules preventing "double jeopardy".

Section 50 of the Y.O.A. is a broader penal provision than the comparable sections of the *Criminal Code* pertaining to interference with adults in custody. For example, para. 50(1)(a) makes it an offence to "induce" a young person to unlawfully leave custody; this is broader than the *Code* notions of permitting, assisting or facilitating escape. Paragraph 50(1)(c) makes it an offence to "harbour or conceal" a young person who has unlawfuly left custody; this is also broader than the provisions of the *Code*, and may well require parents to report to the authorities the presence of their child in their home if he has unlawfully left custody. (See s. 250 of the *Code*, abduction of child under 14, which uses similar concepts of enticing and harbouring.)

Paragraphs 50(1)(d) and (e) of the Y.O.A. deal with interference with conditions of disposition not relating to custody or placement of a young person. There are no analogous provisions of the *Code* relating to interference with probation or other noncustodial adult sentences. These paragraphs also demonstrate the concern of the Y.O.A. with protecting young persons who are subject to dispositions from improper interference; the Act recognizes that young persons are more immature than adults, and perhaps more easily led astray.

As s. 50 of the Y.O.A. creates a number of criminal offences, no person can be convicted of violating s. 50 unless it is proven beyond a reasonable doubt that he had the requisite mental intention to commit the offence (the so-called *mens rea* — guilty mind). Paragraphs 50(1)(c), (d) and (e) set out the specific statutory mental requirements to be proved against the accused in order for a conviction; the accused must have been acting "knowingly" for para. 50(1)(c) and "wilfully" for paras. 50(1)(d) and (e). Paragraph 50(1)(a) will at least require evidence from which it can be inferred beyond a reasonable doubt that the accused not only committed the prohibited act (assisting escape), but that the accused additionally had the requisite *mens rea*. It seems clear that knowledge of the disposition, to the extent that the young person was in custody, must be proved for a conviction under para. 50(1)(a). Similarly para. 50(1)(b) creates an offence requiring *mens rea*. Mistake of fact will therefore operate as a defence to a charge under s. 50; in appropriate circumstances mistake of law might also be a defence, though never ignorance of the law.

Section 50 creates a hybrid offence, one for which the Crown may elect to proceed summarily or by indictment. Subsection 50(2) provides that if the Crown elects to proceed by indictment, the offence is within the absolute jurisidiction of a magistrate, thus eliminating any choice for the accused regarding the manner of trial. This simplifies and expedites the procedure for this type of prosecution.

An adult violating s. 50 of the Y.O.A. will be prosecuted only in ordinary (adult) court. A young person interfering in the disposition of another young person and thereby violating s. 50 of the Y.O.A. will, of course, be subject to prosecution in youth court, unless the case is transferred to ordinary court under s. 16.

APPLICATION OF THE CRIMINAL CODE
(Section 51)

SECTION 51

51. *Application of Criminal Code.*—**Except to the extent that they are inconsistent with or excluded by this Act, all the provisions of the *Criminal Code* apply, with such modifications as the circumstances require, in respect of offences alleged to have been committed by young persons.**

Application of the Criminal Code

By virtue of s. 51, all provisions of the *Criminal Code* apply to the Y.O.A., except to the extent that they are "inconsistent with or excluded by" the Y.O.A. While the Y.O.A. is a fairly comprehensive statute, it is by no means an exhaustive code of substantive or procedural law, and accordingly it adopts the provisions of the *Criminal Code* to fill the gaps. Section 51 not only allows for the application of the substantive and procedural provisions of the *Code*, but also, by virtue of s. 7 of the *Code*, allows for the application of all of the common law not modified by legislation.

Thus, the following are all applicable in respect of offences alleged to have been committed by young persons:

— all of the substantive offences created by the *Code*, except those excluded by the Y.O.A. (see e.g. s-s. 20(8) of the Y.O.A. rendering inapplicable various offences arising out of a breach of sentence, such as breach of probation, s. 666 of the *Code*);

— any defences available at common law (see s-s. 7(3) of the *Code*) or under the *Code* (some of which are available only to young persons — see e.g. s. 147 of the *Code* providing that certain types of sexual offences cannot be committed by a male under 14; though note the repeal of ss. 12 and 13 of the *Code*, governing incapacity on account of age, by s. 72 of the Y.O.A.);

— the evidentiary law applicable to prosecutions under the *Code*, subject to such modifications as are found in ss. 56 to 63 of the Y.O.A.;

— statutory and common law rules governing burden and onus of proof (e.g. s-s. 16(4) of *Code*, regarding presumption of sanity).

Section 51 of the Y.O.A. does not provide for the strict application of provisions of the *Code* in all cases, but rather allows for modifications in accordance with the circumstances and in accordance with the provisions of the Y.O.A. The provisions of the *Code* must be applied within the overall scheme of the Y.O.A. and are subject to its specific provisions.

The application of the *Criminal Code* to proceedings under the Y.O.A. is further amplified by provisions of the Y.O.A. dealing with jurisdiction and procedure. Sections 5 and 6 of the Y.O.A. give youth court judges the jurisdiction and powers of magistrates under the *Code*, and allow justices to deal with certain matters in regard to proceedings under the Act. Sections 52 to 55 of the Y.O.A. provide a procedural framework for the operation of the youth court, generally adopting the procedures established in the *Code* for summary offences, though retaining the distinction between summary and indictable offences.

The application of the provisions of the *Criminal Code* to proceedings under the Y.O.A. thus requires a knowledge and understanding of both pieces of legislation.

In regard to some matters, the *Criminal Code* is applied without modification. For example, if a young person raises the defence of insanity to a charge under the Y.O.A., the provisions of the *Code* dealing wih insanity (ss. 16, 542, 545 and 547) apply to young persons. The Y.O.A. makes no mention of insanity as a defence, and the combined effect of ss. 5, 51 and 52 of the Y.O.A. is to render the provisions of the *Code* applicable (note that in regard to insanity at the time of trial, s. 13 of the Y.O.A. modifies some of the *Code* procedures).

In regard to certain matters, the provisions of the *Code* have been somewhat modified to accommodate concerns or problems which are unique to the juvenile justice system. For example, a young person is arraigned and enters a plea as an adult would. However, there are special provisions which ensure that a young person understands the significance of his plea, and which require a youth court judge to satisfy himself that the facts support a guilty plea (ss. 11, 12 and 19 of the Y.O.A.). Another example of the modification of *Code* provisions by the Y.O.A. is in regard to pre-trial detention; in general, the substantive features of the *Code*'s pre-trial detention sections apply, but there are special protections in the Y.O.A. to ensure that young persons are usually detained separately from adults and dealt with by youth court judges (ss. 7 and 8 of the Y.O.A.).

There are certain matters for which the provisions of the Y.O.A. completely replace the *Criminal Code*. For example, in regard to disposition, the scheme created by the Y.O.A. excludes the operation of the sentencing provisions of the *Code* (ss. 20 to 26, 28 to 34 of the Y.O.A.).

PROCEDURE
(Sections 52 to 55)

Introduction

Sections 52 to 55 of the Y.O.A. govern certain procedural matters in regard to proceedings under the Act. Section 52 is by far the most important, providing a general procedural framework for proceedings under the Act. As a general rule, the summary conviction procedures of the *Criminal Code* are to apply to proceedings under the Y.O.A., for both summary conviction and indictable offences (s-s. 52(1)). However, offences are to retain their distinct character as summary or indictable (s-s. 52(2)), and this distinction is significant for such matters as disposition and appeals. Other provisions of ss. 52 to 55 deal with a range of procedural issues such as ensuring the attendance of the young person at trial, limitation periods, issuing subpoenas and the effect of warrants.

SECTION 52

52. (1) *Part XXIV and summary conviction trial provisions of Criminal Code to apply.*—**Subject to this section and except to the extent that they are inconsistent with this Act,**

(a) the provisions of Part XXIV of the *Criminal Code*, and

(b) any other provisions of the *Criminal Code* that apply in respect of summary conviction offences and relate to trial proceedings

apply to proceedings under this Act

(c) in respect of a summary conviction offence, and

(d) in respect of an indictable offence as if it were defined in the enactment creating it as a summary conviction offence.

(2) *Indictable offences.*—**For greater certainty and notwithstanding subsection (1) or any other provision of this Act, an indictable offence committed by a young person is, for the purposes of this or any other Act, an indictable offence.**

(3) *Attendance of young person.*—**Section 577 of the *Criminal Code* applies in respect of proceedings under this Act, whether the proceedings relate to an indictable offence or an offence punishable on summary conviction.**

(4) *Limitation period.*—In proceedings under this Act, subsection 721(2) of the *Criminal Code* does not apply in respect of an indictable offence.

(5) *Costs.*—Section 744 of the *Criminal Code* does not apply in respect of proceedings under this Act.

Summary conviction procedures to apply: subsection 52(1)

The *Criminal Code* divides offences into two categories, summary and indictable, with some offences being "hybrid", either summary or indictable at the election of the Crown. Summary conviction offences are generally less serious offences, with lower maximum penalties. The procedures governing proceedings for summary conviction offences are largely found in Part XXIV of the *Code*, ss. 720 to 772; these procedures are generally simpler and more expeditious than those which apply to indictable offences.

Subsection 52(1) of the Y.O.A. provides that in regard to proceedings under the Y.O.A., the procedure which will be followed will be that which governs summary conviction offences, regardless of whether the enactment creating the offence specifies that the offence is summary, indictable or hybrid. The applicable procedure is thus found in Part XXIV of the *Code* and other parts of the *Code* applicable to summary conviction offences, except to the extent that these provisions are modified by the specific provisions of the Y.O.A. As will be discussed below, the distinction between summary conviction and indictable offences is retained by s-s. 52(2) of the Y.O.A., and is most important for certain purposes, such as appeals and maximum dispositions, but generally the procedure for both types of offences is summary.

Thus, proceedings under the Y.O.A. will include the following:

— commencement of proceedings by information (a sworn written statement laid before a justice), ss. 723 and 724 of the *Code*;

— compelling attendance of the accused young person by means of summons or warrant, s. 728 of the *Code* adopts Parts XIV and XV of the *Code*;

— right of accused to object to form of information and right of prosecutor to amend, ss. 729 to 732 of the *Code*;

— arraignment of accused, s. 736 of the *Code* (see also ss. 11, 12 and 19 of the Y.O.A., imposing special duties on youth court);

— right of accused to make full answer and defence, s. 737 of the *Code*; and

— adjudication, ss. 739 to 743 of the *Code* (see also s. 19 of the Y.O.A.)

A proceeding under the Y.O.A. will never include an indictment, a preliminary trial or a jury trial, as these are features of proceedings by indictment.

For a fuller description of the procedure applicable to summary conviction proceedings, see Salhany, *Canadian Criminal Procedure*, 3rd ed. (1978), Chapter 7, "Summary Conviction Proceedings".

It is important to recognize the significance of the fact that s-s. 52(1) of the Y.O.A. adopts the summary conviction procedures "except to the extent that they are inconsistent with this Act." In effect, proceedings under the Y.O.A. combine procedures applicable in summary conviction proceedings faced by adults with certain unique provisions introduced by the Y.O.A. Some of the *unique features* of proceedings in youth court include:

— limited jurisdiction of a justice ss. 6 and 8;

— detention generally separate from adults, s. 7;

— notice to parents and order for attendance of parents, ss. 9 and 10;

— rights in regard to counsel, s. 11;

— duty of court in regard to arraignment and receiving plea, ss. 12 and 19;

— medical and psychological reports, s. 13;

— pre-disposition reports, s. 14;

— disposition provisions, ss. 20 to 26;

— disposition review, ss. 28 to 34;

— restrictions on publicity, s. 38;

— provision for exclusion of public, s. 39;

— provisions governing youth court records, ss. 40, 45 and 46; and

— provisions modifying laws of evidence, ss. 56 to 63.

There are also certain provisions of the Y.O.A. which modify the procedures applicable in summary conviction proceedings; these provisions of the Y.O.A. include those found in ss. 52 to 55 (specifically governing procedure) and other provisions such as those governing:

— appeals, s. 27;

— contempt, s. 47;

— substitution of judges, s. 64; and

— clerks, s. 65.

Thus, proceedings in youth court are not an exact replica of summary conviction proceedings in adult court; nor are they totally unique. Reliance must be placed on both the *Criminal Code* and the Y.O.A. to determine the correct procedure for youth court proceedings.

Indictable offences: subsection 52(2)

Subsection 52(2) of the Y.O.A. provides that notwithstanding the fact that s-s. 52(1) adopts the procedures applicable to summary conviction offences for offences which are defined in the enacting legislation to be indictable, for the purpose of the Y.O.A. or any other Act, the offence is an indictable offence. Thus, for all purposes other than procedure at trial, an indictable offence retains its character and nature. Classification of an offence as indictable is significant for:

— arrest and pre-trial detention, ss. 7 and 8;

— transfer to adult court, s. 16;

— consequences of defence of insanity (see discussion of s. 13);

— maximum duration of disposition, see s-s.20(7);

— appeal procedures, s. 27;

— requirements for destruction of records, s. 45; and

— limitation periods, s-s. 52(4).

Thus, in regard to "hybrid" offences, for which the prosecutor has an election to proceed by summary conviction or by indictment, the election retains significance with respect to the character of the offence. The *Interpretation* Act, R.S.C. 1970, c. I-23, para. 27(1)(a) provides that as a general rule a hybrid offence is deemed to be indictable unless an election is made by the prosecutor to treat the offence as summary. The Y.O.A. in s-s. 27(2), however, provides that for the purposes of an appeal, where no election is made in respect of a hybrid offence, it is deemed to be summary.

Attendance of young person: subsection 52(3)

Section 577 of the *Code* generally requires the presence in court of an accused person in regard to indictable offences, but not for summary offences. Subsection 52(3) of the Y.O.A. provides that s. 577 of the *Code* applies in respect to *all* offences dealt with under the Y.O.A., thus generally requiring the presence of a young person at court, regardless of whether the offence is summary or indictable. This ensures the attendance of young persons who may not always appreciate the significance of a court proceeding; thus their rights can be more fully protected, and they will receive the full benefit of the court experience.

The applicability of s. 577 of the *Code* to all proceedings under the Y.O.A. also provides for the absence of the young person under limited circumstances. Subsection 577(2) gives the youth court authority to exclude the young person where he disrupts the proceedings (para. 577(2)(a)), or during the trial of the issue of whether a young person is unfit on account of insanity to stand trial where his presence might have an adverse effect on his mental health (para. 577(2)(c)). The power to exclude under para. 577(2)(c) cannot be used for any other purpose; see comments concerning s-ss. 13(5) and (6) of the Y.O.A. which provide a broader jurisdiction to exclude the young person during cross-examination concerning a medical or psychological report, in order to prevent detriment to the treatment or recovery of the young person or to prevent harm to a third person.

Under para. 577(2)(b) of the *Code*, the youth court may *permit* the young person to be absent from the court, during the whole or any part of his trial on such conditions as the court considers proper; it is submitted that as a rule, this should occur only when the young person is represented by counsel or assisted by an adult. Paragraph 577(2)(b) applies only when the young person himself expresses a wish to be absent: see *R. v. Page*, [1969] 1 C.C.C. 90, 64 W.W.R. 637 (B.C.C.A.).

Limitation period: subsection 52(4)

Subsection 721(2) of the *Code* limits the institution of proceedings (the laying of an information) under Part XXIV of the *Code* (summary convictions) to six months after the occurrence of the offence. Subsection 52(4) of the Y.O.A. provides that although indictable offences are generally to be dealt with under the Y.O.A. pursuant to Part XXIV of the *Code*, the limitation of s-s. 721(2) does not apply to indictable offences.

Based on the common law principle, *nullum tempus occurrit regi* — "time does not run against the Crown" — there is generally no limitation on the prosecution of indictable offences under the Y.O.A. There are a few specific statutory exceptions, such as treason, s. 48 of the *Code*, and an array of sexual offences listed in ss. 141 and 195 of the *Code*, these exceptions also apply in proceedings under the Y.O.A. In regard to summary conviction offences dealt with under the Y.O.A., the six-month limitation of s-s. 721(2) of the *Code* continues to apply.

Costs: subsection 52(5)

Section 744 of the *Code* allows a summary conviction court to award a successful party costs to compensate for legal expenses; by virtue of s-s. 52(5) of the Y.O.A., this provision of the *Code* does *not* apply in respect of any proceedings under the Y.O.A. Subsection 52(5) does not in any way limit the youth court's authority to order the young person to pay compensation by way of a restitution order under paras. 20(1)(c), (d), (e) or (f). In such situations the youth court is awarding compensation for losses arising out of the commission of the offence, whereas s. 744 involves compensation for the costs of the prosecution or of the defence.

SECTION 53

53. *Counts charged in information.*—Indictable offences and offences punishable on summary conviction may under this Act be charged in the same information and tried jointly.

Joinder of summary and indictable offences: section 53

In adult court, it is clear that an accused person cannot be tried on an indictable offence and a summary offence together, there must be separate trials. Further, there has been some conflict in the jurisprudence as to whether it is even possible to charge an adult with an indictable offence and a summary conviction offence on the same information, though this practice now seems acceptable (see Salhany, *Canadian Criminal Procedure*, 3rd ed. (1978), p. 158). Section 53 of the Y.O.A. alters the law in regard to this matter for proceedings under the Act.

Section 53 makes clear that a young person can be charged on a single information with indictable and summary offences, and further alters practices applicable in adult proceedings by allowing the charges to be tried jointly. The Y.O.A. contemplates situations where it is practicable and non-prejudicial to proceed with summary conviction and indictable offences together, and where expediency supports dealing with them together.

Thus, in proceedings under the Y.O.A., it is acceptable for a single information to contain:

(1) more than one alleged offence, provided that each offence is set out in a separate count (paragraph), para. 724(1)(b) of the *Code*; and

(2) both summary conviction and indictable offences, provided each is set out in a separate count, s. 53 of the Y.O.A.

However, the fact that two or more counts are contained in the same information, or that an indictable offence and an offence punishable on summary conviction are contained on the same information, does not mean they must necessarily be tried together. Subsection 736(4) of the *Code* provides that a youth court "may, before or during a trial, where it is satisfied that ends of justice require it, direct that the [young person] be tried separately upon one or more of the counts in the information." This provides protection for the young person in that he can apply for separate trials where it is either impracticable or prejudicial to proceed with both or all at the same time. Since s-ss. 736(4) and 520(3) of the *Code* contain similar provisions, the jurisprudence under both of these subsections would apply to motions to a youth court under s-s. 736(4) (see Salhany, *Canadian Criminal Procedure*, 3rd ed. (1978), pp. 159-61).

Procuring the attendance of witnesses: section 54

SECTION 54

54. (1) *Issue of subpoena.*—Where a person is required to attend to give evidence before a youth court, the subpoena directed to that person may be issued by a youth court judge, whether or not the person whose attendance is required is within the same province as the youth court.

(2) *Service of subpoena.*—A subpoena issued by a youth court and directed to a person who is not within the same province as the youth court shall be served personally on the person to whom it is directed.

Issue of a subpoena: subsection 54(1)

Part XIX of the *Criminal Code*, ss. 625 to 643, governs procuring the attendance of witnesses, through the issue of and execution of a subpoena. A "subpoena" (Latin for "under punishment") is issued by a court, and orders a person to attend and give testimony; if a witness fails to attend court, he may be arrested under warrant, and if necessary detained until he gives evidence. Pursuant to para. 52(1)(b) of the Y.O.A., the provisions of Part XIX of the *Code* apply to proceedings under the Y.O.A., except as modified by s. 54.

In proceedings in adult court, by virtue of s-s. 630(2) of the *Code*, a subpoena issued by a justice or magistrate has effect only in the province in which it is issued. However, s-s. 54(1) of the Y.O.A. extends the authority of a youth court judge so that a subpoena issued by a youth court judge has effect throughout Canada. A subpoena in a proceeding under the Y.O.A. may be issued by a youth court judge, or by a justice acting under s. 6 of the Y.O.A.. The provisions of s-s. 54(1) do not apply to a subpoena issued by a justice in regard to Y.O.A. proceedings, and it has effect only in the province in which it is issued.

Service of a subpoena: subsection 54(2)

Subsection 629(1) of the *Code* normally allows a subpoena to be served personally on a potential witness by a peace officer, or to be left for the potential witness at his last or usual place of residence with a person who appears to be at least 16 years of age.

Subsection 54(2) of the Y.O.A. provides that if a subpoena is issued by a youth court judge and pursuant to s-s. 54(1) of the Act is directed to a person outside the province of issue, it must be served personally on the person to whom it is directed. Subsection 54(2) of the Y.O.A. is consistent with s-s. 629(2) of the Code, as both require personal service of a subpoena on a person outside the province of issue.

SECTION 55

55. *Warrant.*—**A warrant that is issued out of a youth court may be executed anywhere in Canada.**

Warrant: section 55

Generally under the *Criminal Code*, a warrant for the arrest of an accused person, or for the arrest of a witness who has failed to comply with a subpoena, can only be enforced in the province in which it is issued (s. 456.3 and s-s. 631(2) of the *Code*). In regard to adult proceedings there are procedures which can be used to render a warrant effective in other provinces (see s. 461 and s-ss. 631(1) an 633(3) of the *Code*). By virtue of s. 55 of the Y.O.A. any warrant issued by a youth court judge has effect throughout Canada. A warrant issued by a justice acting pursuant to the Y.O.A., under s. 6 of the Act, has effect only in the province in which it is issued, unless by virtue of the *Code* it has wider effect (see s. 461 and s-ss. 631(1) and 633(3) of the *Code*).

EVIDENCE
(Sections 56 to 63)

Statements of the young person: section 56

Introduction

At common law, the fundamental rule governing the admissibility of statements is that they must be made "voluntarily"; it is important to note that in this context, "voluntary" has a specific legal meaning. The classic statement of this rule was made in the English case of *Ibrahim v. The King*, [1914] A.C. 599 at p. 609 (P.C.):

> It has long been established as a positive rule of English criminal law, that no statement by an accused is admissible in evidence against him unless it is shewn by the prosecution to have been a voluntary statement, in the sense that it has not been obtained from him either by fear of prejudice or hope of advantage exercised or held out by a person in authority.

This statement has found judicial approval in Canada, and the numerous court decisions interpreting and applying this statement are incorporated into the Y.O.A. by way of reference in para. 56(2)(a).

In Canada, the ascertainment of truth, forms the basis for the admissibility of statements. A voluntary confession is admissible because, if voluntary, common sense dictates that it is likely to be true. A confession which is induced by some promise or threat is involuntary, and may be untrue, and therefore is excluded from evidence. Hence, the reliability or truthfulness of the statement is the primary concern when excluding involuntary statements.

In the United States, the principle of fairness to the accused — the protection of his constitutional right to remain silent and the privilege against self-incrimination — has been used as a basis for excluding statements. In addition, some American cases have excluded confessions because they were obtained in circumstances which would place the due administration of justice into disrepute. In these cases, truth or trustworthiness of the particular confession has not been the primary consideration of the court, and this is in direct contrast with the prevailing decisions of the Canadian courts.

The *Canadian Charter of Rights and Freedoms* will undoubtedly have an effect on the existing law relating to the admissibility of statements. In particular, the following rights granted by the *Charter* are likely to have evidentiary implications: the right not to be deprived of "life, liberty and security of the person" except in accordance with the principles of fundamental justice (s. 7); the right to be secure against unreasonable search or seizure (s. 8); the right to be informed promptly upon arrest or detention of the reasons therefor and to retain and instruct counsel without delay (paras. 10(a) and (b)); the right not to be compelled to be a witness against oneself (para. 11(c)); and the right to be tried according to law in a fair and public hearing (para. 11(d)). It may take some time before the application of the *Charter* is clarified by the higher courts.

When a statement is made by an accused person to a person in authority, it is now clear that a *voir dire* must be held by the judge to determine whether the statement is to be admissible in the trial of that person. A *voir dire* has been called a "trial within a trial", during which the judge hears evidence about the circumstances surrounding the making of the statement, for the sole purpose of deciding whether the statement was "voluntarily" made and hence, admissible. The burden of proving that such statements were made voluntarily lies upon the prosecution. In the case of adult trials with a jury, the jury is excluded from the courtroom during the *voir dire*. Although the judge hears the evidence at a *voir dire*, if he subsequently rules the statement to be "involuntary", he must exclude from his mind all the evidence received at the *voir dire*.

It has long been recognized that the confessions of children should not be treated in the same manner as adult confessions: see *R. v. Jacques* (1958), 29 C.R. 249 (Que. S.W.C.) and *R. v. Yensen* (1961), 36 C.R. 339, 130 C.C.C. 353, 29 D.L.R. (2d) 314, [1961] O.R. 703 (H.C.). This judicial attitude is reflected in the following quotation from *Regina v. R. (No. 1)* (1972), 9 C.C.C. (2d) 274 (Ont. Prov. Ct.) at p. 275:

> Recognition of the child's reduced capability of understanding his rights and his reduced capacity to protect himself in his contacts with the adult world has led the Courts to be particularly diligent

when deciding whether a juvenile's statements meet the required test of voluntariness.

In particular, it is recognized that children and young persons are especially susceptible to being influenced by authority figures such as a police officer in uniform, a probation officer, a social worker or school principal; young persons are open to suggestion and may easily adopt a statement offered by a person in authority as their own. A young person who is arrested and placed in detention without being able to talk to his parents or a friend may be induced to confess merely to relieve his anxiety. In such circumstances, a police warning is unlikely to be fully understood and appreciated: see A. B. Ferguson and A. C. Douglas, "A Study of Juvenile Waiver" (1970), 7 San Diego Law Rev. 38. As a result, the truthfulness or reliability of a young person's statement may become an issue and the statement may be excluded.

A number of judicial guidelines have been developed in relation to police questioning in the many cases decided pursuant to the J.D.A., and these will continue to apply under the Y.O.A. In Re A, [1975] 5 W.W.R. 425 at p. 428, 23 C.C.C. (2d) 537 sub nom. R. v. A. (Alta. S.C.) the following guidelines were set out:

(1) Require that a relative, preferably of the same sex as the child to be questioned, accompany the child to the place of interrogation;

(2) Give the child, at the place or room of the interrogation, in the presence of the relative who accompanies him, the choice of deciding whether he wishes his relative to stay in the same room during the questioning;

(3) Carry out the questioning as soon as the child and his relative arrive at headquarters;

(4) Ask the child, as soon as the caution is given, whether he understands it and if not, give him an explanation which he understands and which points out to the child the consequences that may flow from making the statement;

(5) Detain the child, if it is impossible to proceed according to (3) above, in a place designated by the competent authorities as a place for the detention of children;

(6) Explain to a child over the age of 14 years that, while the only charge that can be laid against him is that of being a juvenile delinquent, there is a chance that the juvenile court judge may send him to trial in the higher court, and that he may there be

charged with an offence as an adult, and that offence should be explained to him.

The general law relating to the admissibility of statements made by accused persons (which at the present time consists solely of case law) is made applicable to young persons by virtue of s-s. 56(1) of the Y.O.A. Consequently, reference should be made not only to the cases decided under the former Act, but also to the jurisprudence, articles and relevant texts dealing with this subject-matter generally.

The Y.O.A. goes further, however, in that it establishes certain minimum safeguards which must be met before any statement made by a young person to a person who is, in law, a person in authority, is admissible. These safeguards contained in s-s. 56(2) provide that oral and written statements would be admissible only if:

— the statement was "voluntary" (as defined by the existing jurisprudence);

— before any statement was made, it was clearly explained to the young person that

  • there is no obligation to make a statement,

  • the statement could be used in evidence in proceedings against the young person,

  • the young person has a right to consult counsel, a parent, a relative or appropriate adult, and

  • any statement to be made must be made in the presence of the person consulted unless the young person desires otherwise;

— before any statement was made, a reasonable opportunity was given to consult counsel, a parent, a relative or another appropriate adult person; and

— where a person is consulted, the young person was given a reasonable opportunity to make the statement in the presence of such person.

Subsection 56(4) provides that the young person may waive those rights specified in paras. 56(2)(c) and (d) (right to consult with counsel, parents, relative or adult person), provided such waiver is in writing. The waiver must also contain a statement by the young person that he has been apprised of the rights being waived.

An exception relating to "spontaneous statements" is set out in s-s. 56(3). Thus, a statement made spontaneously to a person in authority before that person had a reasonable opportunity to comply with the s. 56 safeguards, will be admissible provided it is otherwise voluntary.

Subsection 56(2) establishes a number of minimum safeguards, each of which must be present in order for a young person's statement to be admissible against him. It is important to note that these safeguards apply only where a statement is made to a person in authority. Subsection 56(5) extends the protection offered to young persons under the Act by providing that where a young person satisfies the judge that his statement was given under duress imposed by a person not in law "a person in authority", the statement will be inadmissible.

SECTION 56

56. (1) *General law on admissibility of statements to apply.*— Subject to this section, the law relating to the admissibility of statements made by persons accused of committing offences applies in respect of young persons.

(2) *When statements are admissible.*—No oral or written statement given by a young person to a peace officer or other person who is, in law, a person in authority is admissible against the young person unless

(a) the statement was voluntary;

(b) the person to whom the statement was given has, before the statement was made, clearly explained to the young person, in language appropriate to his age and understanding, that

(i) the young person is under no obligation to give a statement,

(ii) any statement given by him may be used as evidence in proceedings against him,

(iii) the young person has the right to consult another person in accordance with paragraph (c), and

(iv) any statement made by the young person is required to be made in the presence of the person consulted, unless the young person desires otherwise;

(c) the young person has, before the statement was made, been given a reasonable opportunity to consult with counsel or a parent, or in the absence of a parent, an adult relative, or in the absence of a parent and an adult relative, any other appropriate adult chosen by the young person; and

(d) where the young person consults any person pursuant to paragraph (c), the young person has been given a reasonable opportunity to make the statement in the presence of that person.

(3) *Exception in certain cases for oral statements.*—The requirements set out in paragraphs (2)(b), (c) and (d) do not apply in respect of oral statements which are made spontaneously by the young person to a peace officer or other person in authority before that person has had a reasonable opportunity to comply with those requirements.

(4) *Waiver of right to consult.*—A young person may waive his rights under paragraph (2)(c) or (d) but any such waiver shall be made in writing and shall contain a statement signed by the young person that he has been apprised of the right that he is waiving.

(5) *Statements given under duress are inadmissible.*—A youth court judge may rule inadmissible in any proceedings under this Act a statement given by a young person in respect of whom the proceedings are taken if the young person satisfies the judge that the statement was given under duress imposed by any person who is not, in law, a person in authority.

Common law applies: subsection 56(1)

Subsection 56(1) makes applicable to the young person the general law on the admissibility of statements, which consists of a large body of Canadian and English judicial decisions. It includes not only those decisions relating to statements made by adults, but also the relevant jurisprudence contained in cases decided under the *J.D.A.* American court decisions are of limited relevance on the issue of the admissibiltiy of statements because the primary purpose of the exclusionary rule in the United States is to protect the constitutional rights of the accused. It is expected that the enactment of the *Canadian Charter of Rights and Freedoms*, however, may give these American decisions a greater significance in Canada.

The basic requirement governing the admissibility of statements at common law is that they must be made "voluntarily" — without "fear of prejudice or hope of advantage exercised or held out by a person in authority." (See the discussion in reference to

Ibrahim v. The King, supra, at p. 367). Although the legal definition of "voluntary" is a complex one, it focusses primarily on reliability and truthfulness. It is only when a statement has been "induced" and thus the reliability or truthfulness of the statement has been cast in doubt, that this evidence will be excluded. The application of the rule, however, is not straightforward as it goes beyond mere threats or inducements and often focusses on police practices. If an atmosphere of compulsion has been created during the arrest, detention or interrogation, the statement may be held to be "induced" and thus "involuntary". In such circumstances, there may be some doubt as to whether the statement is true, and hence it is inadmissible.

The admissibility of a statement is determined during a *voir dire* — a trial within a trial — during which the prosecution attempts to prove, beyond a reasonable doubt, that the statement was "voluntary" in a legal sense. During the *voir dire*, the Crown must call as witnesses all persons who were present during the questioning, or make them available to the defence for cross-examination. In the event that any witness is absent, this absence must be explained to the satisfaction of the court. A *voir dire* must be held, even if the statement appeared to be exculpatory at the time it was made, as such statements may also be made involuntarily. The accused is entitled to call witnesses and to cross-examine on the issues raised in the *voir dire*. He may also give evidence himself, and if he does so, the cross-examination must be confined to those matters in issue in the *voir dire*; he may, however, be cross-examined on his conviction record for the purpose of testing his credibility. In *DeClercq v. The Queen*, [1968] S.C.R. 902, [1969] 1 C.C.C. 197, 70 D.L.R. (2d) 530, 4 C.R.N.S. 205, the Supreme Court of Canada held that an accused testifying on a *voir dire* may be questioned as to the truth or falsity of the statement as that question is relevant to the issue of credibility. The law on this point is different in England: see *R. v. Brophy*, [1981] 3 W.L.R. 103. Both the prosecution and defence counsel are entitled to make submissions relating to the voluntariness of the statement at the conclusion of the *voir dire*.

It is now well established that the court must consider all of the surrounding circumstances, what was said, where it was said, who was present and other factors including the mental state of the accused person.

In Canada, there are no Judges' Rules as in England, to guide the court as to proper and improper police investigative tactics of questioning. These rules have, however, found judicial favour as rules of common sense (*R. v. Fitton*, [1956] S.C.R. 958, 116 C.C.C. 1, 6 D.L.R. (2d) 529, 24 C.R. 371) and are set out in R. *v. Voisin*, [1918] 1 K.B. 53; Schiff, *Evidence in the Litigation Process* (1978), Vol. 2, at p. 88; P. K. McWilliams, *Canadian Criminal Evidence* (Aurora: Canada Law Book Inc., 1974), at p. 657.

The English Judges' Rules confirm that a police officer is entitled to question a person, but require the police to warn the person of his right not to give a statement at the point when the police officer has evidence which would afford reasonable grounds for suspecting that the person has committed an offence. Recent versions of the English Judges' Rules (1964) outline procedures for the taking of statements by police and provide guidelines for police in respect of recording the interview and offering comfort and refreshment to persons interviewed. Procedures applicable to children and young persons are also set out in Appendix B of the English Judges' Rules:

> As far as practicable children (whether suspected of a crime or not) should only be interviewed in the presence of a parent or guardian, or, in their absence, some person who is not a police officer and is of the same sex as the child. A child or young person should not be arrested, nor even interviewed, at school if such an action can possibly be avoided. Where it is found essential to conduct the interview at school, this should only be done with the consent, and in the presence, of the head teacher, or his nominee.

The law as to the use of physical pieces of evidence obtained as a result of a statement is quite different from that applicable to statements, but is totally consistent with the "reliability" or "truthfulness" principle. The basic rule is that physical evidence is admissible, regardless of how it was obtained, whether by force, fraud, trickery, promise or threat. McWilliams in *Canadian Criminal Evidence* at p. 278 discusses the so-called *St. Lawrence* rule:

> Where articles are found as a result of information contained in a confession which is inadmissible as being involuntary, the finding of the articles and such part of the confession as is confirmed by the finding of the articles are admissible. Thus the Crown may prove that the accused told the police where to find stolen goods

and how he knew of their location but the Crown cannot prove that the accused said he put them there because that is not confirmed by the finding ...

See *R. v. St. Lawrence*, [1949] O.R. 215, 93 C.C.C. 376, 7 C.R. 464 (H.C.).

While those involved in obtaining physical evidence in an illegal or unlawful manner may be subject to criminal prosecution or civil suit, the evidence is admissible in the trial of the accused. This situation can be contrasted with that in the United States, where constitutional requirements provide that illegally obtained evidence is normally inadmissible in criminal trials. Subsection 24(2) of the *Canadian Charter of Rights and Freedoms* now provides that if a "court concludes that evidence was obtained in a manner that infringed or denied any rights or freedoms guaranteed by this Charter, the evidence shall be excluded if it is established that, having regard to all the circumstances, the admission of it in the proceedings would bring the administration of justice into disrepute."

On a *voir dire*, the judge must also consider whether the statement was made to "a person in authority" — see *Ibrahim v. The King*, [1914] A.C. 599 (P.C.). As this concept is also referred to in s-s. 56(2) of the Y.O.A., it will be discussed separately.

Person in authority: subsection 56(2)

According to the rule in *Ibrahim v. The King*, *supra*, mere evidence of inducement is insufficient to render a statement inadmissible; it must be shown, in addition, that the promise or threat was made by a "person in authority". Similarly, the Y.O.A., s-s. 56(2), provides that only those statements made to peace officers or other persons who are, in law, persons in authority, are inadmissible unless the safeguards listed in that subsection have been met. If the person to whom the statement is made is not such a person in authority, s-s. 56(5) may be applicable; this subsection places the onus on the young person to prove the existence of duress. Obviously, the definition of "a person in authority" is of great importance.

According to *Cross on Evidence*, 5th ed. (1979), at p. 541, a person in authority is "anyone whom the prisoner might reasonably suppose to be capable of influencing the course of the prosecution." Another definition which has found judicial favour can be found in R. v. *Todd* (1901), 13 Man. R. 364 at p. 376, 4 C.C.C. 514 (C.A.): "A person in authority means, generally speaking, anyone who has authority or control over the accused or over the proceedings or the prosecution against him."

McWilliams in *Canadian Criminal Evidence* (1974), at pp. 248-49 presents the following list of persons in authority:

(i) a master in relation to his servants,

(ii) an employer,

(iii) the complainant,

(iv) the informant,

(v) the prosecutor,

(vi) the police,

(vii) a gaoler,

(viii) a magistrate,

(ix) others including a ship's captain, an insurance adjuster, licence or building inspector and an attorney engaged in investigation.

Until recently it was not established whether the test is an objective or a subjective one; more recently, the Supreme Court of Canada in *Rothman v. The Queen* (1981), 59 C.C.C. (2d) 30, held that the test was subjective, that is, whether the *accused* regarded the person to be a person in authority. This suggests that the issue must be determined upon the facts of each case, and opens up the possibility of a parent being held a "person in authority". In *The Queen v. Midkiff* (1980), 3 Can. J. Fam. L. 307 (Ont. H.C.), the court left open the issue whether a parent can be a person in authority, but did state that the parent or relative present at the taking of the confession *must* be called by the Crown during the *voir dire*.

As the test is a subjective one, at the *voir dire* the court must consider the inducement on the mind of the young person and whether it was reasonable for him to believe that the person making the promise or threat had the authority to follow through on it. Thus, if a person dresses up like a policeman and the accused falsely believes him to be one, that person is a person in authority. Conversely, if a policeman dresses up like a prisoner, and occupies the cell with the accused, the policeman will not be a person in authority: see *Rothman v. The Queen, supra*.

It is now generally accepted that one who makes a threat or inducement to an accused in the presence of a person in authority is himself considered to be a person in authority: see McWilliams, *Canadian Criminal Evidence* (1974) at p. 248. Similarly, a statement made in the presence of but not to a person in authority, must be considered made to a person in authority and must be proved voluntary.

It is unclear whether a teacher or a youth worker as defined under the Act would be a person in authority. However, s-s. 14(10) of the Y.O.A. provides protection for the young person in respect of statements made in the course of the preparation of a pre-disposition report, by prohibiting admission of such statements in any proceedings except those under ss. 16, 20 or 28 to 32. This means that the protection against self-incrimination, in its broadest sense, does not extend to any transfer, disposition or review hearing.

Restrictions on admissibility: subsection 56(2)

The common law governing the admissibility of statements made by young persons to persons who are, in law, persons in authority, is restricted by s-s. 56(2) and in particular, by paras. 56(2)(b), (c) and (d). While para. 56(2)(a) merely restates the common law requirement of voluntariness, the remaining paragraphs impose additional safeguards as prerequisites to admissibility. Before any statement would be admissible, it must be clearly explained to the young person that:

— there is no obligation to make a statement (subpara. 56(2)(b)(i));

— the statement can be used in proceedings against the young person (subpara. 56(2)(b)(ii));

— the young person has the right to consult another person (subpara. 56(2)(b)(iii)); and

— any statement to be made must be made in the presence of the person consulted unless the young person desires otherwise (subpara. 56(2)(b)(iv)).

In addition, the young person must be given a reasonable opportunity to consult with counsel, a parent, adult relative or other adult chosen by the young person (para. 56(2)(c)). Where such a person is consulted, the young person must be given a reasonable opportunity to make the statement in the presence of the person consulted (para. 56(2)(d)).

These safeguards are consistent with the special guarantee of rights and freedoms and with the young person's right to be informed as to what his rights and freedoms are, as set out in the Declaration of Principle, paras. 3(1)(e) and (f) of the Y.O.A. It is clear that these safeguards go beyond the minimum prescribed in the *Canadian Charter of Rights and Freedoms* and in the *Canadian Bill of Rights*.

Where the Crown proposes to enter into evidence the statement of an accused young person, a *voir dire* must be held and the Crown must demonstrate compliance with the safeguards to the court. This obligation is subject to the exception relating to spontaneous oral statements (s-s. 56(3)) and to any waiver of the right to consult with counsel or other persons (s-s. 56(4)).

Voluntary statement: paragraph 56(2)(a)

Paragraph 56(2)(a) restates the requirement that statements made by a young person to a person who, in law, is a person in authority, must be voluntary. It has already been observed that the adoption of the common law relating to the admissibility of statements by s-s. 56(1) include the requirement of voluntariness. Voluntariness is a legal concept and should be distinguished from the ordinary meaning of the word. It has already been pointed out that the obligation to prove that a statement is voluntary lies on the Crown and that the standard of proof is "beyond a reasonable doubt" (see discussion in the *Introduction* to s. 56).

The determination of whether a particular statement is "voluntary" or has been improperly induced is often a difficult question, dependent on all the facts and circumstances. In *Boudreau v. The King*, [1949] S.C.R. 262 at p. 267, 94 C.C.C. 1, [1949] 3 D.L.R. 81, 7 C.R. 427, the Supreme Court of Canada stated:

> The fundamental question is whether a confession of an accused offered in evidence is voluntary. The mere fact that a warning was given is not necessarily decisive in favour of admissibility but, on the othr hand, the absence of a warning should not bind the hands of the Court so as to compel it to rule out a statement. All the surrounding circumstances must be investigated and, if upon their review the Court is not satisfied of the voluntary nature of the admission, the statement will be rejected. Accordingly, the pres-

ence or absence of a warning will be a factor, and in many cases, an important one.

In determining whether a particular statement is "voluntary", the court will consider all the surrounding circumstances: what was said, where it was said, who was present, time of day, period of time over which questioning took place, and the physical state and mental capacity of the accused person. Police must be allowed to ask questions but, in particular circumstances, a question prefaced by an admonition that a youth "better tell the truth" may be construed as an inducement or threat resulting in the inadmissibility of the statement.

Caution: paragraph 56(2)(b)

Paragraph 56(2)(b) provides that no statement made to a person in authority is admissible against a young person unless a caution is given. The person to whom the statement is to be given must clearly explain to the young person, in language appropriate to his age and understanding, that:

(i) the young person is under no obligation to give a statement;

(ii) any statement given by him may be used as evidence in proceedings against him;

(iii) the young person has the right to consult a lawyer or other person referred to in para. 56(2)(c); and

(iv) any statement made by the young person is required to be made in the presence of the person consulted, unless the young person desires otherwise.

It is essential, therefore, for a police investigator to explain each of the rights listed in subparas. 56(2)(b)(i) to (iv) to the young person, or else the statement is not admissible against the young person.

The requirement that the young person be given a clear explanation in "language appropriate to his age and understanding" confirms that a mere recital of words is not sufficient under para. 56(2)(b). It would also appear that the duty on the police under s-s. 56(2) is greater than the duty to advise the young person of his right to be represented by counsel pursuant to s-s. 11(2). The object of s-s. 56(2) is not merely to comply with the statutory requirement but rather to ensure that a young person understands his rights. This means that the person taking the statement must take time using simple language to go over the rights listed in para. 56(2)(b). He must, if necessary, repeat the warning using whatever approach is necessary to ensure comprehension. He must also be prepared to testify in court as to the steps he took to ensure compliance with this subsection; the exact words used should be recorded as they will normally be of particular importance in the case of a younger "young person".

In order to properly explain subpara. 56(2)(b)(iii) to a young person, the person taking the statement must indicate that the consultation can be with a lawyer or a parent, or in the absence of a parent, with an adult relative or adult person. The obligation to clearly explain to the young person in language appropriate to his age and understanding that the young person has a right to consult with counsel suggests that some reference to the availability of legal services should be made.

Opportunity to consult: paragraph 56(2)(c)

Subparagraph 56(2)(b)(iii) requires that the person, to whom the statement is made, explain to the young person that he has a right to consult with another person in accordance with para. 56(2)(c). Paragraph 56(2)(c) goes further by requiring that the young person be given "a reasonable opportunity to consult with counsel or a parent, or in the absence of a parent, an adult relative, or in the absence of a parent or an adult relative, any other appropriate adult chosen by the young person."

A discussion of reasonable opportunity to consult with counsel is included in the comments above on s. 11. The police have an obligation to facilitate contact with counsel and with other persons mentioned in para. 56(2)(c) (*Brownridge v. The Queen*, [1972] S.C.R. 926, 18 C.R.N.S. 308, 7 C.C.C. (2d) 417, 28 D.L.R. (3d) 1) and to allow a young person as many phone calls as required over a reasonable length of time (*R. v. Giesbrecht*, [1975] 5 W.W.R. 630 (Man. Co. Ct.). Should the young person so request, consultation with counsel and other persons in para. 56(2)(c) should be in private (*R. v. Penner*, [1973] 6 W.W.R. 94, 39 D.L.R. (3d) 246, 22 C.R.N.S. 35, 12 C.C.C. (2d) 468 (Man. C.A.) and *R. v. Paterson* (1978), 39 C.C.C. (2d) 355 (Ont. H.C.)).

The young person is given the choice of consulting either with counsel or a parent, it should be emphasized that the young person is given the right to make this choice. The right to consult an adult relative or other adult person is given only in the absence of a parent. Thus, where a parent attends at the police station and the young person does not wish to consult him, it may be argued that as the parent is present, there is no further right to consult an adult relative or other adult person. It could also be argued, however, that a parent whom the young person does not wish to consult, is unavailable for consultation, and therefore the young person is entitled to consult with counsel, an adult relative or other adult person. Such an interpretation is consistent with the increased rights and responsibilities given to young persons by the Act. In any event, the young person is entitled to consult with counsel, whether or not the parent is present, pursuant to s-s. 11(1) of the Act and s.10 of the *Charter*. In determining the admissibility of a statement made by a young person, the youth court judge will evidently have to address these issues.

Presence of the person consulted: paragraph 56(2)(d)

Subparagraph 56(2)(b)(iv) requires that the young person be advised of his right to have the person consulted under para. 56(2)(c) present during the time when the statement is made, unless he desires otherwise. Where the young person exercises his right to consult with another person, he must be given a reasonable opportunity to make his statement in the presence of that person (para. 56(2)(d)). Both of these requirements are preconditions to the admissibility of any subsequent statement; the young person may, however, waive the right under para. 56(2)(d) pursuant to s-s. 56(4). What constitutes a "reasonable opportunity" to make the statement in the presence of the person consulted will ultimately be decided by the court; where the young person asks for the presence of such person and his request is denied, there will be a heavy onus on the person taking the statement to demonstrate why it was unreasonable to accede to the young person's wishes.

Spontaneously made oral statements: subsection 56(3)

Subsection 56(3), which applies only to oral statements, recognizes the common law doctrine relating to "spontaneous confessions"; since this term is not defined in the Y.O.A., the existing case law will be applicable. *Dupuis v. The Queen* (1952), 104 C.C.C. 290, 15 C.R. 309, [1952] 2 S.C.R. 516, states that a spontaneous confession to police in response to a casual question, made voluntarily and without any inducement, before the accused is apprehended or warned, is admissible in evidence. Thus, a statement blurted out by a suspect during the arrest, or upon being questioned about some unrelated matters, before the young person can be cautioned and advised of his rights pursuant to s-s. 56(2), may be admissible. Furthermore, the statement may be made after the para. 56(2)(b) warnings have been given, but prior to consultation with an adult (para. 56(2)(c)), or prior to the statement being taken in the presence of the person consulted (para. 56(2)(d)), and still qualify as being "spontaneous". Presumably a spontaneous statement is one which is volunteered, and not made in response to a direct question or as a result of interrogation. Although a statement is made spontaneously and falls within the s-s. 56(3) exception, it may still be ruled involuntary and inadmissible due to the presence of other circumstances, such as the mental or physical state of the accused or the circumstances of his environment.

It is important to note that the s-s. 56(3) exception is narrower than the corresponding common law rule. The Y.O.A. requires both that the statement be spontaneous *and* that it be made before a person in authority had a reasonable opportunity to comply with the statutory requirements. Failure to meet both requirements would result in the statement being ruled inadmissible. In similar circumstances, the common law rule would give the judge a discretion as to whether to admit the statement, depending on whether it was "voluntary."

An important issue which arises for investigating police officers is at what point must an officer give the warnings provided for by s-s. 56(2). In questioning adults, this decision is not a critical one because the courts have considered the absence of a warning as only one of the factors to consider in determining whether a statement was voluntary. Moreover, the courts have recognized that police questioning must be flexible and that police should not be placed in a strait-jacket of artificial rules (see *Boudreau v. The King*, [1949] S.C.R. 262, 7 C.R. 427, 94 C.C.C. 1, [1949] 3 D.L.R. 81, 7 C.R. 427). In the case of the Y.O.A. the decision as to when to caution a young person is extremely important, because the failure to adhere to the s-s. 56(2) requirements would render the statement inadmissible. It is submitted that the English Judges' Rules should be followed in this regard:

II. As soon as a police officer has evidence which would afford reasonable grounds for suspecting that a person has committed an offence, he shall caution that person or cause him to be cautioned before putting to him any questions, or further questions, relating to that offence.

Waiver of rights: subsection 56(4)

Subsection 56(4) provides that any waiver of rights to consult or to make a statement in the presence of the person consulted must:

— be in writing, and

— contain a statement by the young person that he has been apprised of the right being waived.

The use of the word "apprised" indicates that there must be an adequate explanation and therefore that rights under paras. 56(2)(c) and (d) cannot be waived if the young person doesn't understand the rights and his access to them. An American study (A. B. Ferguson and A. C. Douglas, "A Study of Juvenile Waiver" (1970), 7 San Diego Law Rev. 39) concluded that a large majority of juveniles who were cautioned as to their rights to remain silent and to consult counsel, waived these rights without fully understanding them. This study emphasizes the need to explain such rights to a young person carefully and in language he can understand. Defence counsel would be well advised to examine carefully all the circumstances surrounding an alleged waiver in order to determine whether a challenge should be made; similarly, judges should be aware of the frailties of waivers given by young persons. The young person must have the mental capacity to understand and to waive his rights pursuant to s-s. 56(4); in addition, American cases such as *United States v. Indian Boy X*, 565 F. 2d 585 (1977) state that such a waiver must be a "voluntary" one, in the same sense as a statement must be voluntary in order to be admissible.

It should be noted that the obligation to caution the young person pursuant to para. 56(2)(b) cannot be waived; moreover, a waiver does not affect the requirement that the statement be voluntary (para. 56(2)(a)), or otherwise admissible according to the general law relating to the admissibility of statements (s-s. 56(1)).

Duress: subsection 56(5)

Subsection 56(5) deals with statements given to persons who are not, in law, persons in authority and to which the provisions of s-s. 56(2) do not apply. Where a young person is able to satisfy the judge that a statement was made under duress, the judge may rule the statement inadmissible.

The *Encylopedia of Words and Phrases: Legal Maxims (Canada)*, 3rd ed., Vol. 1, p. 564, states, citing *Rogers v. Rogers*, [1938] 1 D.L.R. 99, 12 M.P.R. 321: "By 'duress' is meant the compulsion under which a person acts through fear of personal suffering, as from injury to the body or from confinement [whether] actual or threatened." Although duress would include psychological and emotional trauma, it contemplates a degree of compulsion which would be fairly difficult to prove in these instances, except in exceptional circumstances. Moreover, even when it is proved, the statement is not automatically inadmissible; rather, the court has a discretion whether to exclude such a statement. The legislation does not provide any guidelines for the exercise of this discretion. Clearly, a statement given under duress should be excluded if its truthfulness or reliability has been cast in doubt. Thus, if a parent (assuming that a parent is *not* a person in authority) physically threatens a young person "to own up" and a statement is given, the judge may rule it inadmissible if he concludes that the threat by the parent constituted "duress". The young person who is threatened in such a way may prefer the strong arm of justice to the wrath of his parent, and confess to something he did not do; therefore, the statement runs a high risk of being unreliable and may be excluded pursuant to s-s. 56(5).

It is clear that a young person's rights and protections in relation to oral or written statements are largely dependent on the person to whom the statements are made. If a statement is given to a person who is, in law, a person in authority, a *voir dire* must be held and the Crown must prove that the statement was voluntarily given, according to common law principles; in addition, the protections provided by s-s. 56(2) apply. However, if the person is not a person in authority, the onus lies on the young person to satisfy the court that the statement was given under duress. The existing jurisprudence substantially narrows the scope of application of s-s. 56(5). For example, one who makes a threat or inducement to an accused in the presence of a person in authority may himself be considered to be a person in authority; moreover, if a statement is made in the presence of, but not to, a person in authority, it must be proved voluntary by the Crown (McWilliams, *Canadian Criminal Evidence* (1974), at p. 248). Thus, as a general rule, s-s. 56(5) will be applicable only in limited circumstances where no person in authority was present either at the time of making the threat or when the actual statement was made.

Proof of age: section 57

The jurisdiction of the youth court is dependent on establishing that the accused is a "young person" within the meaning of the definition found in s-s. 2(1) (see earlier discussion of this definition under s. 2). The purpose of s. 57 is to expand and clarify the ways by which the age of the young person can be proven.

The case law under the *J.D.A.* has not definitively resolved the issue whether proof of age is an essential element of the Crown's case. Some authorities suggest that failure to prove age results in proceedings that are merely a nullity and that a new trial may be ordered: *R. v. Sorenson*, [1965] 2 C.C.C. 242, 46 C.R. 251, 50 W.W.R. 116 (B.C.S.C.). Other cases have held that age is an essential element of the case to be proven by the Crown and that failure to prove age results in an acquittal: *R. v. Crossley* (1950), 10 C.R. 348, [1950] 2 W.W.R. 768, 98 C.C.C. 160 (B.C.S.C.); *R. v. P.* (1979), 48 C.C.C. (2d) 390 (Ont. Prov. Ct.); *R. v. L.* (1981), 59 C.C.C. (2d) 160 (Ont. Prov. Ct.). The view expressed in the more recent cases is that age is an essential ingredient of the offence and a finding that the accused is a young person must be made by the trial court.

Proof of the actual age of a juvenile accused pursuant to the *J.D.A.* has created some problems because of the hearsay evidence objection. Strictly speaking, the evidence of the child as to his age, or the evidence of a father who did not attend the birth could be objected to as being "hearsay", as the person giving the evidence must necessarily rely on information told to him. Situations where there has been a failure to properly prove age by evidence normally considered admissible have often occurred when the Crown is represented by a police officer who may not be fully aware of the intricacies of the law of criminal evidence. The reluctance to see a case dismissed on such a "technicality" often results in the practice of the judge "rescuing" the Crown by asking the child his age; this procedure, however, would be considered improper if one accepts that age is an ingredient of the offence which must be proven by the Crown.

In the absence of proof of actual age, some courts have relied on the physical appearance and demeanour of the juvenile accused in order to establish that the child is "apparently" under the age of 16 (or such other age directed by the province) pursuant to s. 2 of the *J.D.A.* (*R. v. Pilkington* (1968), 5 C.R.N.S. 275, 67 W.W.R. 159, [1969] 3 C.C.C. 327 (B.C.C.A.); *R. v. D.* (1976), 27 R.F.L. 298 (Ont. Prov. Ct.)). By relying on apparent age, some of the problems associated with proving actual age may be avoided, although in many cases it may not be "apparent" whether the person charged falls within the upper age limit — many 15-year-old children look 17 years old and many 17-year-old children may be several years younger in appearance.

Section 57 of the Y.O.A. facilitates the proof of age by allowing into evidence a parent's testimony, a birth certificate or other record and any other reliable information relating to age. As well, inferences may be drawn from the young person's appearance or from statements made by the young person. The definition of "young person" in s-s. 2(1) of the Y.O.A. has continued the concept of findings of age based on appearance, although the wording has been changed to suggest that "appearance" should only be relied upon in the absence of evidence to the contrary. Subsection 57(4) specifically permits the court to draw inferences as to the age of a person from that person's appearance, and presumably this provision is directed at proving actual age as well as apparent age.

While these provisions make clear how age is to be proven, some question remains as to how the issue of age is brought before the court. As age goes to the jurisdiction of the court, many judges took the view that, under the *Juvenile Delinquents Act*, it was their responsibility to establish jurisdiction at the earliest opportunity and to treat it as a preliminary matter. On the other hand, in *R. v. L.* (1981), 59 C.C.C. (2d) 160 at p. 162 (Ont. Prov. Ct.), the court held that: "the finding of age should be part of the trial process in which the trial judge should stand impartial". In any event, it would seem desirable for the Crown to deal with the issue as part of his case. The definition of "young person" in the Y.O.A. has been changed from the corresponding definition of "child" in the *J.D.A.* and s-s. 57(4) of the Y.O.A.

clearly permits the youth court to draw inferences as to the age of a person from the person's appearance. It was the intention of the drafters, in changing the definition of "young person" and in including s-s. 57(4), to provide that the youth court judge must, in the absence of evidence to the contrary, address the question as to whether or not an inference of age can be drawn, and where feasible, make a finding of age based on appearance.

SECTION 57

57. (1) *Testimony of a parent.*—In any proceedings under this Act, the testimony of a parent as to the age of a person of whom he is a parent is admissible as evidence of the age of that person.

(2) *Evidence of age by certificate or record.*—In any proceedings under this Act,

(a) a birth or baptismal certificate or a copy thereof purporting to be certified under the hand of the person in whose custody such records are held is evidence of the age of the person named in the certificate or copy; and

(b) an entry or record of an incorporated society that has had the control or care of the person alleged to have committed the offence in respect of which the proceedings are taken at or about the time the person came to Canada is evidence of the age of that person, if the entry or record was made before the time when the offence is alleged to have been committed.

(3) *Other evidence.*—In the absence, before the youth court, of any certificate, copy, entry or record mentioned in subsection (2), or in corroboration of any such certificate, copy, entry or record, the youth court may receive and act upon any other information relating to age that it considers reliable.

(4) *When age may be inferred.*—In any proceedings under this Act, the youth court may draw inferences as to the age of a person from the person's appearance or from statements made by the person in direct examination or cross-examination.

Testimony of a parent: subsection 57(1)

Subsection 57(1) makes "the testimony of a parent as to the age of a person of whom he is a parent" admissible as evidence of the age of that person. Thus, any person coming within the wide definition of parent in s-s. 2(1) may give evidence of the age of his child. As the term "parent" is defined very broadly under the

Act, the weight given to the evidence may depend on the relationship of the parent to the young person. For example, it would seem that the evidence of a biological parent who was present at the birth would be difficult, if not impossible, to refute, while evidence of a step-parent, a welfare agency or director of a residential facility might be given less weight or discounted entirely if it is considered unreliable. The evidence of an adoptive parent who had custody of the young person from infancy would obviously have credibility.

This provision for admissibility of a parent's testimony regarding age extends the liberal approach currently taken in some cases under the *J.D.A.* Although the testimony of a biological parent present at birth has been preferred because no hearsay objection can be made to it, the evidence of a natural parent who did not actually witness the birth was admitted in *R. v. D.* (1976), 27 R.F.L. 298 (Ont. Prov. Ct.). In another case, an adoptive parent was permitted to give testimony as to her son's age (*R. v. A.M.P.* (1977), 2 Fam. L. Rev. 58 (Ont. Prov. Ct.)); the judge held that the evidence was trustworthy and represented the best available evidence and that therefore an exception to the hearsay rule was justified. The *Y.O.A.* makes clear that an adoptive parent's testimony would be admissible, although the weight to be given to such evidence will depend on the circumstances of the case.

Birth certificates and records of societies: subsection 57(2)

Proof of age is further facilitated by s-s. 57(2), which permits the admission into evidence of birth or baptismal certificates and records of an incorporated society in certain situations where children have been admitted into Canada in the care or control of that society. These provisions extend the admissibility of documentary evidence as proof of age. Under the *J.D.A.*, birth certificates could only be admitted to prove age in accordance with s. 24 of the *Canada Evidence Act*. However, it will still be necessary to prove that the person named in the document is the person appearing before the court, and this may require additional supportive evidence. In corroboration of any such certificate or document, the youth court may receive any other information that it considers reliable (s-s. 57(3)). Presumably, a similarity of names would be some proof of identity, and this could be supported by the similarity of the names of the parents.

Paragraph 57(2)(b) permits the proof of age by allowing into evidence the records of an incorporated society "that has had the control or care of the person alleged to have committed the offence ... at or about the time the person came to Canada." This provision has limited application as it applies only in the narrow situation where children, often refugees, are brought into Canada for adoption. It is assumed that the incorporated society, relief agency or provincial society such as the Children's Aid Society in Ontario, will record the child's age as accurately as possible, as it would have no reason to do otherwise; so long as the entry or record has been made before the time when the offence is alleged to have been committed, it may be admitted into evidence. Paragraph 57(2)(b) is substantially the same as s-s. 585(1) of the *Criminal Code*.

Other evidence: subsection 57(3)

Subsection 57(3) makes a broad range of information about age admissible, provided the youth court considers it reliable, thus giving the court a great deal of flexibility in receiving proof of age. The court may allow into evidence photocopies of documents, for example, or any other evidence that is technically hearsay. Subsection 57(3) provides for the reception of other evidence "in the absence... of any certificate, copy, entry or record mentioned in subsection (2), or in corroboration [thereof] ...". If evidence has been admitted under s-s. 57(2), the youth court may receive and act upon any other corroborative evidence which it considers reliable, whether or not it is admissible according to the common law rules of evidence.

Although s-s. 57(3) substantially enlarges the scope of admissibility in youth court proceedings, it only applies to evidence relating to the age of the young person. Evidence by a witness that he knew the parent of the young person, and that they had told him the young person's birth date, could be considered admissible as "other information relating to age." Any statement made by the young person himself to a third party may be admissible in the first instance, as an "admission" but also under s-s. 57(3) as reliable other information. Where the third party is a "person in authority", however, it is not clear whether the provisions of s. 56 supersede s-s. 57(3), notwithstanding that the statement relates to age and is considered to be reliable by the youth court. It could be argued that if this statement is "voluntary", and hence "reliable", the statement should be admitted even though the para. 56(2)(b) cautions were not given and the young person was not given an opportunity to consult with or make the statement in the presence of the persons mentioned in para. 56(2)(c). On the other hand, s-s. 56(2) appears to apply to all statements made by the young person, whether relating to guilt or to jurisdiction, and accordingly s-s. 57(3) should not be interpreted so as to create an exception to it.

Apparent age: subsection 57(4)

The Y.O.A., like the J.D.A., permits proof of age by a finding of apparent age. Unlike the J.D.A., however, a finding of apparent age may only be made under the Y.O.A. "in the absence of evidence to the contrary." Therefore, apparent age is not to be relied upon where other evidence of age is before the court (see *R. v. Sorensen*, [1965] 2 C.C.C. 242, 46 C.R. 251, 50 W.W.R. 116 (B.C.S.C.) interpreting a similar provision in the *Criminal Code*). Subsection 57(4) permits inferences to be drawn "as to the age of a person from the person's appearance or from statements made by the person in direct examination or cross-examination." A finding of apparent age may be based on a person's size, demeanour and dress (see *R. v. Pilkington* (1968), 5 C.R.N.S. 275, 67 W.W.R. 159, [1969] 3 C.C.C. 327 (B.C.C.A.)).

It should be noted that s-s. 57(4) is permissive, the court may draw inferences as to age from the person's appearance or from statements made by the person in direct examination or cross-examination. The court may also draw inferences as to age from other reliable information admitted pursuant to s-s. 57(3), or use such evidence to corroborate any inferences made from the young person's appearance or testimony.

If the youth court accepts jurisdiction on the basis of apparent age, a finding of fact must be made to that effect: *Re Kelly*, [1929] 1 D.L.R. 716, 51 C.C.C. 113 (N.B.C.A.); *R. v. Harford*, [1965] 1 C.C.C. 364, 43 C.R. 415, 48 W.W.R. 445 (B.C.S.C.).

Admissions: sections 58 and 59

Sections 58 and 59 allow the parties to dispense with proof of facts or proof of evidence on a consent basis, thus expediting proceedings and avoiding unnecessary costs and delays.

SECTION 58

58. (1) *Admissions.*—A party to any proceedings under this Act may admit any relevant fact or matter for the purpose of dispensing with proof thereof, including any fact or matter the admissibility of which depends on a ruling of law or of mixed law and fact.

(2) *Other party may adduce evidence.*—Nothing in this section precludes a party to a proceeding from adducing evidence to prove a fact or matter admitted by another party.

SECTION 59

59. *Material evidence.*—Any evidence material to proceedings under this Act that would not but for this section be admissible in evidence may, with the consent of the parties to the proceedings and where the young person is represented by counsel, be given in such proceedings.

Admission: subsections 58(1) and (2)

Subsection 58(1) provides that a party may admit "any relevant fact or matter" in order to dispense with proof of the fact or matter. Subsection 58(1) is similar to s. 582 of the *Criminal Code*, which also allows admissions; s. 582 of the *Code* provides that the accused may admit any fact alleged against him. Subsection 58(1) of the Y.O.A. appears to be broader, as it permits "a party to any proceedings" to make an admission. The subsection also specifically includes "any fact or matter the admissibility of which depends on a ruling of law or of mixed law and fact."

Examples of facts that could be admitted are the age of the accused or the fact that stolen property did indeed belong to someone else. The opposing party may choose to prove the fact none the less. Subsection 58(2) provides that evidence may be adduced "to prove a fact or matter admitted by another party."

It is unclear whether s. 582 of the *Code* is authority for permitting the accused to waive a *voir dire* as to the voluntariness of a confession, as its truth or voluntariness is a question of law which must be decided by the trial judge. In *R. v. Le Brun* (1954), 110 C.C.C. 262, 19 C.R. 286, 13 W.W.R. 192 (B.C.S.C.) it was held that a confession could not be admitted. Section 582 of the *Criminal Code* was also given a restricted interpretation in *R. v.*

Dietrich (1970), 1 C.C.C. (2d) 49, 11 C.R.N.S. 22, [1970] 3 O.R. 725 (C.A.); leave to appeal to S.C.C. refused 1 C.C.C. (2d) 68*n*, [1970] 3 O.R 744*n* (S.C.C.), although a right to waive a *voir dire* was held to exist apart from the *Code* provision. In *Park v. The Queen*, [1981] 2 S.C.R. 64, 59 C.C.C. (2d) 385, 122 D.L.R. (3d) 1, it was held that no particular words or formula need be used by defence counsel to waive a *voir dire*, as long as the trial judge is satisfied that counsel understands the matter and has made an informed decision to waive the *voir dire*. It should be noted that s-s. 58(1) of the Y.O.A. is considerably broader than s. 582 of the *Code* and appears to specifically allow for the admission of statements, confessions on consent.

Material evidence: section 59

Section 59 provides that, with consent, any material evidence "that would not but for this section be admissible in evidence" may be given, provided the young person is represented by counsel; an unrepresented young person has no right to consent to the admission of evidence which would not otherwise be admissible.

Examples of evidence that may be admitted pursuant to this section are a letter from a doctor to prove age or a document from the owner of property indicating his ownership. Although it is likely that this section will be employed sparingly in contested cases, it permits material information of a non-controversial nature to be admitted without resorting to the expense of calling witnesses and unnecessarily taking up the time of the court. This section could also be used at dispositional hearings to admit uncontested documentary evidence.

Evidence of children and young persons: sections 60 and 61

At common law, no evidence could be received in criminal proceedings except upon oath. A child, even under the age of seven years, could be sworn provided the court was satisfied that the child possessed a sufficient knowledge of the nature and consequences of an oath (*R. v. Brasier* (1779), 1 Leach 199, 168 E.R. 202). Until *R. v. Bannerman* (1966), 55 W.W.R. 257, 48 C.R. 110 (Man. C.A.); affd [1966] S.C.R. v, 57 W.W.R. 736*n*, 50 C.R. 76*n*, it was generally accepted that this test involved an understanding of the theological significance of telling a lie and of divine retribution as a consequence of lying under oath. More-over, it has been held that the child may be instructed as to the nature and meaning of the oath, and even where this was done only a few days before trial, the child's evidence could be re-ceived under oath (R. v. Armstrong (1907), 12 C.C.C. 544, 15 O.L.R. 47 (C.A.)).

In Canada, the common law has been altered by statute to permit the reception of unsworn evidence of children. The Can-ada Evidence Act, R.S.C. 1970, c. E-10 provides:

> 16. (1) In any legal proceeding where a child of tender years is offered as a witness, and such child does not, in the opinion of the judge, justice or other presiding officer, understand the nature of an oath, the evidence of such child may be received, though not given upon oath, if, in the opinion of the judge, justice or other presiding officer, as the case may be, the child is possessed of sufficient intelligence to justify the reception of the evidence, and understands the duty of speaking the truth.

> (2) No case shall be decided upon such evidence alone, and it must be corroborated by some other material evidence.

Section 19 of the Juvenile Delinquents Act is to the same effect, and a similar provision is found in s. 586 of the Criminal Code.

Consequently, children could give evidence in criminal pro-ceedings by qualifying as a sworn witness and taking an oath (or an affirmation pursuant to s. 14 of the Canada Evidence Act) or, if the child was not competent, the child could give unsworn evidence pursuant to s-s. 16(1). In order to determine whether a minor may be sworn, an inquiry into his capacity to understand the nature of the oath must be held. When the child has not demonstrated an adequate understanding of the nature of the oath, the court may admit the child's testimony unsworn. In this case, a further inquiry must be held to determine whether the child is possessed of sufficient intelligence to justify the reception of the evidence and understands the duty of speaking the truth. If the judge is satisfied that the child has such intelligence and understanding, the unsworn evidence of the child may be heard. If the unsworn evidence of the child is received, it must be cor-roborated in some material respect.

Where a child is not of "tender years", there is a presumption that he understands the nature of the oath, and therefore the court need not inquire into his capacity. The term "tender years", however, has not been defined. In R. v. Horsburgh, [1966] 3 C.C.C. 240 (Ont. C.A.), the court stated that the test was a subjective one, not depending on the precise age of the child, but rather on his intelligence, his appreciation of the duty to tell the truth and on conclusions drawn by the presiding judge from observing the appearance, demeanour, manner of speaking and deportment of the witness. Other cases have referred to the presumption that children of 14 years and over understand the nature of the oath, but this is a rebuttable presumption which can be rebutted by circumstances indicating the contrary. It is clear, however, that before the unsworn evidence of a child can be accepted, there must be a judicial inquiry and the judge must form an opinion (see Sankey v. The King, [1927] S.C.R. 436, 48 C.C.C. 97, [1927] 4 D.L.R. 245). The inquiry, when it is made, must be in open court and not in the judge's chambers. Failure of counsel to object does not relieve the judge from making the inquiry prescribed by statute and from forming an opinion.

There is a further rule of practice which requires a judge to warn a jury (or to instruct himself) of the danger of convicting on the evidence of the child, even where that evidence is given under oath. This caution is based on the mental immaturity of the child from which can be generally inferred a limited capacity of observation, recollection and ability to understand questions and to frame intelligent answers. As well, the child's moral responsibility is often less developed.

The Y.O.A. changes the law with respect to the giving of evidence by minors in several important respects:

— the requirement of the oath is eliminated;
— all young persons are deemed to have the capacity to give evidence;
— the test for the capacity of children (under 12) to give evidence is identical to the statutory requirement permitting the reception of unsworn evidence under the Canada Evidence Act, s-s. 16(1);
— a form of solemn affirmation is specified which must be used in the case of all children or young persons who give evidence (s-s. 60(2));
— all evidence taken under solemn affirmation will have the same effect as if taken under oath (s-s. 60(3));

— all evidence of children must be corroborated by some other material evidence, but evidence of young persons does not require corroboration (s-s. 61(2)); and

— the judge must instruct all child witnesses and young persons, where he deems it necessary, as to the duty of the witness to speak the truth and the consequences of failing to do so (paras. 60(1)(a) and (b)).

The change from oath to affirmation clarifies the existing jurisprudence relating to the test of capacity. One line of cases requires an understanding of the nature and consequences of the oath, thus demanding that a child demonstrate belief in a Supreme Being who will reward and punish. In R. v. Bannerman (1966), 55 W.W.R. 257, 48 C.R. 110 (Man. C.A.); affd [1966] S.C.R. v, 57 W.W.R. 736n, 50 C.R. 76n, the requirement of an understanding of both the nature and consequences of the oath was abandoned in favour of an inquiry into the child's understanding of the nature of the oath alone; the judge must be satisfied that the child understands the moral obligation of telling the truth. This test, although approved, was treated inconsistently in cases following Bannerman. In R. v. Taylor (1970), 1 C.C.C. (2d) 321, 75 W.W.R. 45 (Man. C.A.), it was held unnecessary to examine the child upon his religious beliefs, while in R. v. Budin (1981), 32 O.R. (2d) 1, 20 C.R. (3d) 86, 58 C.C.C. (2d) 352, 120 D.L.R. (3d) 536 (C.A.), the majority held that it is essential to establish whether or not the child believes in God or another Almighty, and that he appreciates that, in taking the oath, he is telling God he will tell the truth. Therefore, by dispensing with the oath, ss. 60 and 61 of the Y.O.A. clarify the law in this area. The test of capacity under the Y.O.A. does not require any religious belief and is based solely on sufficiency of intelligence and an understanding of the duty to speak the truth.

Under the Y.O.A. there is a presumption that a young person is sufficiently intelligent to testify and there is no need for the judge to question a young person about his understanding of the duty to speak the truth unless the judge deems it necessary. On the other hand, s. 60 makes the judge's instruction of a child (under 12) mandatory and s. 61 requires that a judge satisfy himself as to the child's intelligence and his understanding of the duty to speak the truth. Thus, to a limited extent, the case law on the capacity of a child of tender years to give unsworn evidence remains significant. Furthermore, s-s. 61(2) requires the corroboration of a child's evidence and therefore the existing jurisprudence relating to "corroboration" continues to be relevant. No similar requirement of corroboration exists for evidence of young persons, in accordance with the Y.O.A.'s recognition of the increased responsibility of young persons. It would be inconsistent to consider a young person mature enough to be held responsible for his criminal actions but to hold him too immature to testify without corroboration.

SECTION 60

60. (1) *Evidence of a child or young person.*—**In any proceedings under this Act where the evidence of a child or a young person is taken, it shall be taken only after the youth court judge or the justice, as the case may be, has**

(a) in all cases, if the witness is a child, and

(b) where he deems it necessary, if the witness is a young person,

instructed the child or young person as to the duty of the witness to speak the truth and the consequences of failing to do so.

(2) *Solemn affirmation.*—**The evidence of a child or a young person shall be taken under solemn affirmation as follows:**

I solemnly affirm that the evidence to be given by me shall be the truth, the whole truth and nothing but the truth.

(3) *Effect of evidence under solemn affirmation.*—**Evidence of a child or a young person taken under solemn affirmation shall have the same effect as if taken under oath.**

SECTION 61

61. (1) *Evidence of a child.*—**The evidence of a child may not be received in any proceedings under this Act unless, in the opinion of the youth court judge or justice, as the case may be, the child is possessed of sufficient intelligence to justify the reception of the evidence, and understands the duty of speaking the truth.**

(2) *Corroboration.*—**No case shall be decided on the evidence of a child alone, but must be corroborated by some other material evidence.**

Instruction of child or young person by a judge: subsection 60(1)

Subsection 60(1) provides that the judge or justice must instruct a child on the duty to speak the truth and on the consequences of his failure to do so. If the judge considers it necessary, he shall instruct a young person as well, although in many cases young persons will be sufficiently intelligent and mature to render instruction unnecessary.

The nature of the judge's instruction may differ depending on whether the judge is instructing a child or a young person and upon the intelligence and understanding of the person being instructed. The extent to which a judge should instruct a child is not clear, nor is the form of his instruction. The requirements of the Act might be met by merely stating the obligation as set out in s-s. 60(1); on the other hand, a judge may wish to discuss the matter with the child at some length. The instruction could take the form of a series of questions posed by the judge. Where, after instruction, the judge is not satisfied that the child is possessed of sufficient intelligence to justify the reception of the evidence and that he understands the duty of speaking the truth, the evidence may not be received. On the other hand, where the witness is a young person, the evidence must be received regardless of the actual capacity of the witness to understand the obligation to tell the truth; presumably any such lack of capacity can be accounted for in the weight which will be subsequently given to this evidence.

Since s-s. 60(2) requires that children and young persons shall give evidence only under solemn affirmation, there is no longer any need for such witnesses to appreciate the spiritual consequences of not telling the truth. Accordingly, the judge need not instruct the child or young person of these impending consequences, for example, by warning that lying on the stand is a sin and that divine retribution may result.

Solemn affirmation: subsection 60(2)

Subsection 60(2) provides that the evidence of a child or young person shall be taken only under solemn affirmation, the precise wording of which is set out in the subsection. Subsection 60(3) provides that the "evidence of a child or a young person taken under solemn affirmation shall have the same effect as if taken under oath.''

The removal of the oath in favour of the affirmation will substantially simplify the procedure for taking evidence from children and young persons. Furthermore, the affirmation itself will presumably be more easily understood by them. In today's society, the requirement that a child understand the theological implications of taking an oath is meaningless in many cases, and the use of the affirmation is more likely to impress upon the witness his obligation to tell the truth.

As a result of the provisions of ss. 60 and 61, it is clear that the evidence of a young person must be accepted; however, there is some authority at common law that retardation or mental illness may render an otherwise competent person incompetent as a witness. Presumably, this common law rule of general application has not been extinguished, for otherwise the principle of reliability underlying the taking of evidence would be undermined. In cases of mental illness, a person insane on one matter may be competent to give evidence on matters not connected with his insanity, if his delusion does not affect his perception, memory or articulation of the events in question: see R. v. Hill (1851), 5 Cox C.C. 259. A person suffering from a mental disease rendering him incapable of interpreting observed events, or of understanding questions asked of him in court, or of communicating, is incompetent to testify. See J. Sopinka and S. N. Lederman, The Law of Evidence in Civil Cases (Toronto: Butterworths, 1974), p. 450.

It is not obligatory to inquire as to the young person's understanding of the duty to speak the truth, although the power to do so is granted to the judge by s-s. 60(1); nor is corroboration of the young person's evidence required. Defence counsel would be allowed to expose the young person's inability to understand the obligation to tell the truth in cross-examination, and this could be accounted for by the judge's discretion in weighing the evidence.

Evidence of a child: section 61

Section 61 provides that the evidence of a child may not be accepted unless the child is "possessed of sufficient intelligence to justify the reception of the evidence, and understands the duty of speaking the truth." This is the test presently used to determine whether a minor who does not understand the nature of an oath can give unsworn evidence: see s. 16 of the *Canada Evidence Act*, and s. 19 of the *Juvenile Delinquents Act*.

At present an inquiry as to whether a child understands the nature of an oath is a condition precedent to a child giving unsworn testimony, pursuant to s. 16 of the *Canada Evidence Act*: *R. v. McKay* (1975), 23 C.C.C. (2d) 4, 31 C.R.N.S. 224, [1975] 4 W.W.R. 235 (B.C.C.A.).

There is little case law on the meaning of "sufficient intelligence to justify the reception of the evidence." In *Nemeth v. Harvey* (1975), 7 O.R. (2d) 719 (H.C.), the defendant applied for permission to examine the infant plaintiff for discovery. It was held that (at p. 720): "[t]he child must have an awareness of the purpose of the examination, its general meaning, a general understanding of its significance and of the sum insight into the importance of what might be said by him on such an examination." The court concluded that the five-year-old child in question did not meet these requirements.

Corroboration: subsection 61(2)

Subsection 61(2) provides that "no case shall be decided on the evidence of a child alone, but must be corroborated by some other material evidence." Section 16 of the *Canada Evidence Act*, s. 19 of the *J.D.A.*, and s. 586 of the *Criminal Code* all contain similar provisions requiring corroboration of the evidence of children of tender years. This corroboration requirement recognizes the inherent mental and developmental immaturity of the child and states that some additional evidence is necessary to strengthen the evidence of the child witness. A judicial definition of corroboration is found in *R. v. Baskerville*, [1916] 2 K.B. 658 at p. 667, 86 L.J.K.B. 28 (Ct. of Crim. App.), a case involving the evidence of accomplices:

> ... evidence in corroboration must be independent testimony which affects the accused by connecting or tending to connect him with the crime. ... The nature of the corroboration will necessarily vary according to the particular circumstances of the offence charged.

Thus, if a child's evidence is part of the Crown's case, independent evidence confirming the child's testimony in some material particular is required for there to be a conviction. Query whether the unsworn evidence of a child would in itself suffice to raise a reasonable doubt and thereby result in an acquittal: see McGillivray C.J.A. (dissenting) in R. v. Dubois (1979), 49 C.C.C.(2d) 501 (Alta C.A.); see also 52 C.C.C.(2d) 64n, [1980] 2 S.C.R. 21.

Although a sworn child has been permitted to give evidence as corroboration of an unsworn child, unsworn children cannot corroborate each other: *Paige v. The King*, [1948] S.C.R. 349, 92 C.C.C. 32, 6 C.R. 93; *Morris v. A.-G. N.B.* (1975), 12 N.B.R. (2d) 520, 63 D.L.R. (3d) 337 (C.A.)

For a further discussion of the concept of corroboration, and the type of evidence which can constitute corroboration: see *R. v. Vetrovec* (1982), 67 C.C.C. (2d) 1, 27 C.R. (3d) 304, 41 N.R. 606 (S.C.C.), and McWilliams, *Canadian Criminal Evidence* (1974), pp. 406-442.

Proof of service: section 62

SECTION 62

62. (1) *Proof of service.*—**For the purposes of this Act, service of any document may be proved by oral evidence given under oath by, or by the affidavit or statutory declaration of, the person claiming to have personally served it or sent it by mail.**

(2) *Proof of signature and official character unnecessary.*—**Where proof of service of any document is offered by affidavit or statutory declaration, it is not necessary to prove the signature or official character of the person making or taking the affidavit or declaration, if the official character of that person appears on the face thereof.**

Proof of service: section 62

The manner of proof of service of documents is set out in s. 62. Service of documents such as a summons to a young person or a notice to parents under s. 9 of the Y.O.A. may be proved by oral evidence, by affidavit or by statutory declaration of the person claiming to have served it personally or mailed it. This provision is similar to that set out in the *Criminal Code*, s-s. 455.5(3). A person claiming to have served a document by mail, whether by ordinary or registered mail, need only swear that he mailed it — proof of delivery is not required.

Subsection 62(2) provides that, in the case where affidavit evidence or a statutory declaration is offered as proof of service, "it is not necessary to prove the signature or official character of the person making or taking the affidavit or declaration, if the official character of that person appears on the face thereof."

SECTION 63

63. *Seal not required.*—It is not necessary to the validity of any information, summons, warrant, minute, disposition, conviction, order or other process or document laid, issued, filed or entered in any proceedings under this Act that any seal be attached or affixed thereto.

Seal not required: section 63

A seal is not necessary to the validity of any process or document related to proceedings under the Y.O.A., unlike, for example, s-s. 627(4) of the *Criminal Code* which provides that a seal is necessary to the validity of a subpoena or warrant issued by a court under Part XIX of the *Code*.

SUBSTITUTION OF JUDGES
(Section 64)

Introduction

As a general rule, a judge who receives the plea of an accused will proceed to hear the evidence, if any, render an adjudication, and impose a disposition, if any. The judge is said to be "seized" of a case after plea, and will continue to deal with the case until final disposition, this ensures fairness and continuity.

Subsection 725(4) of the *Code*, which by virtue of s. 52 of the Y.O.A. is applicable to proceedings in youth court, provides that if one judge accepts a plea, but does not hear any evidence, any other youth court judge having jurisdiction to try the young person may proceed to hear the case and render an adjudication or disposition, if any.

There may be circumstances where the judge who has commenced to deal with a matter is unable to attend court at the time the case is scheduled to proceed. If the original judge's absence is temporary, under s-s. 725(3) of the *Code*, a second judge may simply adjourn the matter until a date when the original judge will be available. In the absence of the youth court judge seized of the case, the matter may be adjourned by a justice (*Y.O.A.*, s. 6, *Criminal Code*, s. 725) or by a clerk of the youth court (*Y.O.A.*, para. 65(b)). There may also be situations in which a youth court judge proceeds beyond taking a plea, and the judge dies "or is for any reason unable to continue the trial"; this situation is governed by s. 726 of the *Code*, to some extent modified by s. 64 of the Y.O.A. Jurisprudence under s. 726 of the *Code* has held that valid reasons for a judge not continuing include a serious illness or an indication by the trial judge of a conflict of interest (*R. v. Holden* (1974), 15 C.C.C. (2d) 70 (Sask. Q.B.)). It is recognized, however, that once a judge has begun to hear evidence, there must be "weighty reasons" for his not continuing to final disposition. The fact that a judge has a heavy docket is not sufficient cause for him to remand a young person convicted of an offence to another judge for disposition (*R. v. Lochard* (1973), 12 C.C.C (2d) 445, 22 C.R.N.S. 196 (Ont. C.A.)). A trial judge who has heard inadmissible evidence is not for that reason alone unable to continue (*R. v. Huard* (1962), 133 C.C.C 349, 39 C.R. 67, 39 W.W.R. 674 (B.C.S.C.)).

SECTION 64

64. (1) *Powers of substitute youth court judge.*—A youth court judge who acts in the place of another youth court judge pursuant to subsection 726(1) of the *Criminal Code* shall,

(a) if an adjudication has been made, proceed with the disposition of the case or make the order that, in the circumstances, is authorized by law; or

(b) if no adjudication has been made, recommence the trial as if no evidence had been taken.

(2) *Transcript of evidence already given.*—Where a youth court judge recommences a trial under paragraph (1)(b), he may, if the parties consent, admit into evidence a transcript of any evidence already given in the case.

Substitution of youth court judges: section 64

The effect of s. 64 of the Y.O.A. and s. 726 of the *Code* is that where a youth court judge dies or is "for any reason unable to continue" a trial, another youth court judge having jurisdiction in the same territorial jurisdiction may deal with the case. If an adjudication has been made, para. 64(1)(a) provides that the second judge may proceed with the matter. This will usually mean making a disposition under s. 20, though in some cases there may be other action required; for example in a s. 745 recognizance (peace bond) situation, the first judge may be satisfied that a recognizance should be entered into, and the second judge will impose the conditions of the recognizance.

Paragraph 64(1)(b) of the Y.O.A. provides that if the first judge begins to hear evidence, but does not render an adjudication before being unable to continue the trial, a second judge must recommence the trial as if no evidence had been taken. However, s-s. 64(2) provides that in this situation, the second judge may admit into evidence a transcript of any evidence already given in the case before the first judge, provided the parties consent. Subsection 64(2) differs from the provisions of s. 726 of the *Code* which governs in ordinary (adult) court and does not allow for the use of a transcript. Subsection 64(2) is intended to permit witnesses to be saved the time and inconvenience of a second appearance and to expedite proceedings before the second judge. Subsection 64(2) is discretionary, and the second judge may refuse to allow use of a transcript, even if the parties consent.

It should be noted that a dispositional review under s. 28, 29, 31, 32 or 33 of the Y.O.A. need not be conducted by the youth court judge who made the original disposition, though frequently as a matter of practice it may, where feasible, be desirable for the original judge to deal with the matter.

FUNCTIONS OF CLERKS OF COURT
(Section 65)

SECTION 65

65. *Powers of clerks.*—In addition to any powers conferred on a clerk of the court by the *Criminal Code,* a clerk of the youth court may exercise such powers as are ordinarily exercised by a clerk of a court, and, in particular, may

(a) administer oaths or affirmations in all matters relating to the business of the youth court; and

(b) in the absence of a youth court judge, exercise all the powers of a youth court judge relating to adjournment.

Functions of youth court clerks: section 65

Section 65 of the Y.O.A. confers on a clerk of the youth court all the powers conferred by the *Criminal Court* on a clerk of a court. It also provides that a clerk of the youth court may exercise such powers as are ordinarily exercised by a clerk of a court, including powers in regard to the administration of oaths or affirmations and in regard to the adjournment of youth court proceedings in the absence of a judge.

Section 2 of the *Criminal Code* defines the term "clerk of the court" to include a "person, by whatever name or title he may be designated, who from time to time performs the duties of a clerk of the court." A clerk of the court has extensive powers to sign various forms issued pursuant to the *Code,* for example Form 7, a warrant for arrest. A youth court clerk also has the power to sign a number of designated forms under the Y.O.A., such as Form 1, a notice to parent issued under s. 9 of the Act.

Paragraph 65(b) of the Y.O.A. empowers a clerk of the youth court to exercise all the powers of a youth court judge relating to adjournments. The clerk of the youth court may not exercise the power conferred by para. 65(b) if a youth court judge is available. The need to exercise this power of adjournment may arise if a youth court judge scheduled to deal with a matter is ill or otherwise unavailable. A justice may also adjourn pursuant to s.

6 of the Y.O.A. and s-s. 725(3) of the *Code*. (In some places, it is common practice for a clerk of the court to also be a justice of the peace.)

Section 65 of the Y.O.A. authorizes a youth court clerk to generally "exercise such powers as are ordinarily exercised by a clerk of the court"; this might include responsibility for announcing the presence of the judge, marking exhibits, keeping a court calendar, arranging court dockets, ensuring that parties receive notice of hearings, and carrying out a variety of administrative functions.

Section 40 of the Y.O.A. gives the youth court clerk special responsibilities in regard to youth court records. The clerk shall keep, separate from records of cases in ordinary court, a complete record of every case coming before the youth court; the clerk must ensure that access to these records is limited to those individuals named in s-ss. 40(2) and (3) of the Act, and that these records are ultimately destroyed in accordance with s. 45. See the discussion following ss. 40, 45 and 46 for a fuller description of a clerk's responsibilities in this regard.

FORMS, REGULATIONS AND RULES
OF COURT
(Sections 66 to 68)

Introduction

Various sections of the Y.O.A. make specific provision for forms, and these are set out in the Schedule following the Act. However, use of these forms is not mandatory, and they may be modified to meet local needs or circumstances. There are many situations where it may be useful for youth courts and others involved in Y.O.A. proceedings to develop forms not specifically provided for in the Act; this may be done, where appropriate, using forms set out as part of the *Criminal Code*. Nevertheless, these model forms serve to promote uniformity, particularly where documentation is required to give effect to the rights of the young person.

SECTION 66

66. (1) *Forms.*—**The forms set out in the schedule, varied to suit the case, or forms to the like effect, are valid and sufficient in the circumstances for which they are provided.**

(2) *Where forms not provided.*—**In any case for which forms are not set out in the schedule or prescribed under section 67, the forms set out in Part XXV of the *Criminal Code*, with such modifications as the circumstances require, or other appropriate forms, may be used.**

Forms: subsection 66(1)

In order for a form to give legal effect to the purpose for which it is designed, it must be valid and sufficient in law in relation to the statute section which governs its issuance. Subsection 66(1) of the Y.O.A. stipulates that the forms set in the Schedule after the Act are valid and sufficient in the circumstances for which they are provided; thus the forms in the Schedule give legal effect to the purposes for which they are designed. Subsection 66(1) allows for forms to be "varied to suit the case, or forms to the like effect." Obviously, it may be necessary to have minor modifications and changes to suit the details of a particular case or locality, and such variation is specifically permitted by s-s. 66(1). As long as a form is to "the like effect" as a form in the Schedule, it will be valid.

There are specific statutory provisions in the Y.O.A. concerning the contents of documents, some of which are contained in the Schedule. In particular, s-s. 9(6) requires notices to parents and other adults (Forms 1 and 2) to include the name of the young person, the charge against the young person, the time and place of appearance, and a statement that the young person has a right to be represented; further s-s. 11(9) requires that a summons (Form 16), a warrant for arrest (Form 17), and a notice of a dispositional review (Form 11) to include a statement that the young person has the right to be represented by counsel.

The words of s-s. 66(1) of the Y.O.A. are very similar to the words of s-s. 773(1) of the *Code*, which governs the forms in the *Code*; both provide for flexibility in the modification of documents.

Where forms not provided: subsection 66(2)

The Schedule of forms attached to the Y.O.A. will address most of the requirements created by the Act. There are, however, many situations in which documents and notices will be required to give effect to the Y.O.A. and which are not included in the Schedule. Subsection 66(2) allows other forms to be used; these forms may be developed from a number of sources, including:

— the Governor in Council (federal Cabinet) may make regulations prescribing additional forms, or varying existing ones, s. 67 of the Y.O.A.;

— if the Governor in Council does not prescribe forms, this may be done in provincial youth court rules, made pursuant to s. 68 of the Y.O.A.; and

— those responsible may design their own forms, provided they are "appropriate", s-s. 66(2). Subsection 66(2) specifically suggests those designing forms make use of the forms set out in Part XXV, at the end of the *Criminal Code*; these include information (Form 2), summons (Form 6), warrant to arrest (Form 7), appearance notice (Form 8.1), promise to appear (Form 8.2), recognizance (Form 8.3), and subpoena to a witness (Form 11).

Examples of forms which will have to be designed include an undertaking of a responsible person given pursuant to s-s. 7(4), and a youth court order transferring a young person from open to secure custody pursuant to s-s. 24(7).

By virtue of s-s. 11(9) of the Y.O.A., the following forms, whatever their source, must include a statement that a young person has a right to be represented by counsel: any appearance notice or summons issued to the young person, any warrant to arrest the young person, any promise to appear given by the young person, any recognizance entered into by the young person before an officer in charge, and any notice of a review of disposition given to a young person.

SECTION 67

67. *Regulations.*—The Governor in Council may make regulations

(a) varying the forms set out in the schedule or prescribing additional forms;

(b) establishing uniform rules of court for youth courts across Canada, including rules regulating the practice and procedure to be followed by youth courts; and

(c) generally for carrying out the purposes and provisions of this Act.

Regulations: section 67

Section 67 of the Y.O.A. allows the Governor in Council (federal Cabinet) to make regulations:

— varying the forms set out in the Schedule or prescribing additional forms, para. 67(a);

— establishing uniform rules of court for youth courts across Canada, including rules regulating the practice and procedure to be followed by youth courts, para. 67(b); and

— generally for carrying out the purposes of the Y.O.A., para. 67(c).

Section 67 allows the federal government to ensure that an undesirable degree of variation does not develop in practices in youth courts across the country; such variation would be inconsistent with the federal government's exclusive jurisdiction in matters of criminal law and procedure. As well, it permits the federal Cabinet to fill any gaps which may only become apparent upon implementation of the Act.

Section 438 of the *Criminal Code* provides the making of rules in regard to certain proceedings under the *Code*, with the Governor in Council (federal Cabinet) being given the authority to make uniform rules to prevail over any other rules. Paragraph 67(b) grants the Governor in Council a similar rule-making authority in regard to proceedings in youth court. The rules may deal with such matters as the duties of the officers of the youth court, sittings of the court, form of applications to the court, preparation of transcripts and so on (see s. 438 of the *Code*). Paragraph 67(c) of the Y.O.A. also grants a broader authority to make regulations "generally for carrying out the purpose and provisions of this Act." This would, for example, appear to allow for the making of regulations governing the method of destruction of various records as required under s. 45 of the Y.O.A. Although the regulation-making power is broad, it is clear that it does not extend so far as to permit the amendment of the legislative provisions of the Act itself.

Regulations made pursuant to s. 67 of the Y.O.A. must comply with the *Statutory Instruments Act*, S.C. 1970-71-72, c. 38, and in particular s. 6, which requires that regulations be registered with the Clerk of the Privy Council, and s. 11 of that Act requires the publication of any such regulations in the *Canada Gazette*, Part II.

SECTION 68

68. (1) *Youth court may make rules.*—Every youth court for a province may, at any time with the concurrence of a majority of the judges thereof present at a meeting held for the purpose and subject to the approval of the Lieutenant Governor in Council, establish rules of court not inconsistent with this or any other Act of Parliament or with any regulations made pursuant to section 67 regulating proceedings within the jurisdiction of the youth court.

(2) *Rules of court.*—Rules under subsection (1) may be made

(a) generally to regulate the duties of the officers of the youth court and any other matter considered expedient to attain the ends of justice and carry into effect the provisions of this Act;

(b) subject to any regulations made under paragraph 67(b), to regulate the practice and procedure in the youth court; and

(c) to prescribe forms to be used in the youth court where not otherwise provided for by or pursuant to this Act.

(3) *Publication of rules.*—Rules of court that are made under the authority of this section shall be published in the appropriate provincial gazette.

Youth court rules: section 68

Section 68 allows for the formulation of rules of court on a provincial basis to govern the practice and procedure of the youth courts in a province. Rules established under s. 68 require the approval of a majority of the youth court judges of a province and of the Lieutenant Governor in Council (provincial Cabinet); the rules are to be published in the appropriate provincial gazette, s-s. 68(3).

Any rules formulated under s. 68 of the Y.O.A. must be consistent with the provisions of the Y.O.A. and other federal legislation, such as the *Criminal Code*. Any regulations or rules made under s. 67 will prevail over rules made under s. 68.

The rules of court made under s. 68 may deal with the duties of the officers of the youth court, hours of sitting of the court, form of applications to the court, preparation of transcripts and similar matters (see s. 438 of the *Code*); the rules may also prescribe forms for use in the youth courts.

YOUTH JUSTICE COMMITTEES
(Section 69)

SECTION 69

69. *Youth Justice Committees.*—The Attorney General of a province or such other Minister as the Lieutenant Governor in Council of the province may designate, or a delegate thereof, may establish one or more committees of citizens, to be known as youth justice committees, to assist without remuneration in any aspect of the administration of this Act or in any programs or services for young offenders and may specify the method of appointment of committee members and the functions of the committees.

Youth justice committees: section 69

Section 69 of the Y.O.A. empowers the Attorney General of a province, or such other Minister of a province as the Lieutenant Governor in Council (Cabinet) of the province may designate, to establish one or more committees of citizens to be known as "youth justice committees". A youth justice committee is to assist, without remuneration, in any aspect of the administration of the Y.O.A. or in any program or service for young offenders. The power to create youth justice committees is permissive, and it is not necessary that they be established. It is within the discretion of the Attorney General or other designated minister to specify the method of appointment of committee members and the functions of the committee.

Section 27 of the *Juvenile Delinquents Act* required a "juvenile court committee" to be established in connection with the juvenile court, and ss. 28 and 29 specified certain duties for the committees. In fact, the appointment of juvenile court committees pursuant to the *J.D.A.* has varied from province to province and in some provinces the practice has been sporadic. Section 69 of the Y.O.A. allows for juvenile court committees which have been serving a useful function to be continued as youth justice committees, provided there is appropriate ministerial authorization.

In addition to carrying out monitoring functions, youth justice committees might, for example, become involved in administering programs of alternative measures, under s. 4 of the Y.O.A., or in supervising the operation of pre-trial detention facilities for young persons.

When s. 27 of the J.D.A. was first enacted in 1908, it was felt necessary to require that juvenile court committees be established to ensure community involvement and promote the objectives of that Act. Since that time, Canada has seen the creation of a highly-trained group of professionals to operate its juvenile justice and corrections systems. The Y.O.A. specifically provides that youth court proceedings will ordinarily be open to the public (contrast s. 39 of the Y.O.A. with s. 12 of the J.D.A.), and for community involvement in alternative measures and certain dispositions. Thus, it was not felt necessary to make mandatory provision in the Y.O.A. for the creation of formal institutions to allow for community involvement, but s. 69 gives the provinces the flexibility to establish such bodies in response to local needs and pressures. As the province may specify the method of appointment of committee members, the method could include a direct appointment or election by the community.

AGREEMENTS WITH PROVINCES
(Section 70)

SECTION 70

70. *Agreements with provinces.*—Any Minister of the Crown may, with the approval of the Governor in Council, enter into an agreement with the government of any province providing for payments by Canada to the province in respect of costs incurred by the province for care of and services provided to young persons dealt with under this Act.

Federal-provincial agreements: section 70

The responsiblity for enacting legislation to deal with young persons who commit violations of criminal law is federal, under the *Constitution Act, 1867*, s-s. 91(27), criminal law and procedure. On the other hand, the responsibility for providing the services necessary to implement the Y.O.A. lies principally with the provinces. These services include judicial, legal and administrative services for youth courts, pre-trial detention facilities, alternative measures programs, youth court workers to prepare reports and supervise probation, and various dispositional services, including custodial facilities. The provincial jurisdiction arises out of the power given provinces under the *Constitution Act, 1867*, s-s. 92(6) , public reformatories, and s-s. 92(14), the administration of justice.

Section 70 of the Y.O.A. authorizes the federal government to enter into agreements with the provinces to provide payments in respect of the care of young persons and for services provided pursuant to the Act. Such payments may allow adequate funding to ensure an appropriate level of services to young persons in all parts of Canada, and will generally assist the provinces with the financial impact of implementing the *Young Offenders Act*.

Section 70 provides flexibility by allowing any federal minister to be involved in the process of negotiating agreements with provincial governments. Thus the Minister of Justice may be involved in an agreement concerning payments to cover increased costs for legal aid services resulting from s. 11 of the

Y.O.A., while the Solicitor General might negotiate an agreement concerning payments for pre-trial detention facilities. It is also possible for there to be a single agreement, covering all payments arising out of the Y.O.A., perhaps negotiated jointly by the Ministers of two or more government departments. Any agreement requires the approval of the Governor in Council (federal Cabinet).

CONSEQUENTIAL AMENDMENTS
(Sections 71 to 78)

Introduction

Sections 71 to 78 of the Y.O.A. contain a number of amendments to different pieces of federal legislation which are a consequence of the enactment of various provisions of the *Young Offenders Act*.

SECTION 71

71. Subsection 4(2) of the *Canada Evidence Act* is repealed and the following substituted therefor:

"(2) *Idem.*—The wife or husband of a person charged with an offence against subsection 50(1) of the *Young Offenders Act* or with an offence against any of sections 143 to 146, 148, 150 to 155, 157, 166 to 169, 175, 195, 197, 200, 248 to 250, 255 to 258, 289, paragraph 423(1)(c) or an attempt to commit an offence under section 146 or 155 of the *Criminal Code*, is a competent and compellable witness for the prosecution without the consent of the person charged."

Testimony of spouse, Canada Evidence Act subsection 4(2): section 71

Section 71 of the Y.O.A. amends s-s. 4(2) of the *Canada Evidence Act*, R.S.C. 1970, c. E-10 (C.E.A.) by repealing it and substituting a new s-s. 4(2) in its place.

Subsection 4(2) of the C.E.A. deals with the competence and compellability of one spouse to give testimony in a case in which the other spouse is accused of a criminal offence. At common law, various rules developed to limit the extent to which one spouse could testify for or against the other in a criminal case. This was in part based on concerns about undermining a marital relationship by allowing such testimony, and also on the views about "unity of legal personality" of a husband and wife. These rules have been modified by statute. Subsection 4(1) of the

C.E.A. makes a spouse a competent witness for the defence in any criminal case. Subsection 4(2) of the C.E.A. makes one spouse a competent and compellable witness for the prosecution in a charge against the other spouse, if the offence is one listed in s-s. 4(2); the offences listed involve sexual crimes, crimes of violence, and crimes by one spouse against the other or against children. The effect of s-s. 4(2) of the C.E.A. is that if one spouse is charged with a listed offence, the prosecution can require the other to testify against the accused spouse. The rationale for s-s. 4(2) of the C.E.A. is to ensure that a person, accused of crimes of violence involving the other spouse or children, cannot be protected against conviction by notions of spousal privilege.

The effect of s. 71 of the Y.O.A. is to delete the reference in s-s. 4(2) of the C.E.A. to offences under ss. 33 and 34 of the *Juvenile Delinquents Act*, and to include charges under s. 50 of the Y.O.A. in the list of offences with which one spouse may be charged and the other spouse may be a competent and compellable witness for the prosecution. Section 80 of the Y.O.A. repeals all of the *J.D.A.*, including s. 33, contributing to delinquency, and s. 34, interfering with a juvenile disposition. Section 50 of the Y.O.A. creates offences for interfering with a disposition of a young person, imposed under the Y.O.A.; it roughly replaces s. 34 of the *J.D.A.*

Nothing in s-s. 4(2) of the *Canada Evidence Act*, as amended, makes one spouse compellable by the prosecution if the spouses are jointly charged under s. 50 of the Y.O.A.; that is, if spouses are jointly charged with interfering with the disposition of a young person, the prosecution cannot require one spouse to testify against the other.

Amendments to the Criminal Code: sections 72 to 75

SECTION 72

72. Sections 12 and 13 of the *Criminal Code* are repealed and the following substituted therefor:

"12. *Child under twelve.*—No person shall be convicted of an offence in respect of an act or omission on his part while he was under the age of twelve years."

Children under twelve: section 72

Section 72 of the Y.O.A. repeals the sections of the *Criminal Code* dealing with the minimum age of criminal liability, and replaces them with a section setting the age of 12 as the minimum age for criminal responsibility. Children under 12 who engage in illegal behaviour may be dealt with under provincial legislation.

To understand the full significance of s. 72, it is necessary to consider the common law defence of *doli incapax* (incapacity to form criminal intent), which came to be codified in ss. 12 and 13 of the *Code*.

The common law rule of *doli incapax* was comprised of two parts. First, it established a rebuttable presumption that a child under 14 did not have capacity to know the moral significance of his actions. As a result, a child under 14 unless it was proved that he was competent, could not be held criminally responsible for any act that formed the basis for an alleged criminal offence. Secondly, the common law rule provided that a child under seven lacked the necessary capacity and, thus could not be convicted of an offence.

In 1892 the common law rule of *doli incapax* was codified, and apart from inconsequential changes, remains the same today in the *Criminal Code* as it did in its original statutory form. Sections 12 and 13 presently found in the *Code* provide that:

> 12. No person shall be convicted of an offence in respect of an act or omission on his part while he was under the age of seven years.

> 13. No person shall be convicted of an offence in respect of an act or omission on his part done while he was seven years of age or more, but under the age of fourteen years, unless he was competent to know the nature and consequences of his conduct and to appreciate that it was wrong.

Under s. 13 of the *Code*, therefore, there is a rebuttable presumption that a child between seven and 14 is incompetent to commit a crime, while under s. 12 a child under seven is absolutely deemed incompetent. Therefore, in cases under the *J.D.A.*, the prosecutor has the onus of proving beyond a reasonable doubt that a juvenile between the ages of seven and 14 is not incompetent; see *R. v. M.S. and C.S.* (1979), 2 Fam. L. Rev. 66 (Ont. Prov. Ct., Fam. Div.). As a juvenile approaches the age of

14, other things being equal, the presumption against capacity weakens.

Section 72 of the Y.O.A. repeals ss. 12 and 13 of the *Criminal Code*. In their place, it substitutes the new provision as s. 12 of the *Code* that: "No person shall be convicted of an offence in respect of an act or ommission on his part while he was under the age of twelve years." The purpose of s. 72 of the Y.O.A. is to raise the minimum age of criminal responsibility from seven to 12, and to totally remove the rebuttable presumption of *doli incapax*. The repeal and substitution provided by s. 72 of the Y.O.A. was intended to effect a state of full criminal responsibility, within the overall philosophy of the Y.O.A., for young persons 12 and older.

Although not expressly stated, it is submitted that the effect of the rules of statutory interpretation is such that young persons between the ages of 12 and 14 can no longer rely on the common law rule of *doli incapax*. Section 72 repeals that portion of the *doli incapax* rule which creates a rebuttable presumption of incapacity for children aged seven to 11 years inclusive. Thus, it could be argued that, by not expressly repealing the common law rule of *doli incapax* along with ss. 12 and 13 of the *Code*, that part of the rule dealing with the rebuttable presumption of incompetence from age 12 to 14 has somehow "survived" or perhaps more accurately "revived".

It is, however, submitted that the common law rule of *doli incapax* was supplanted by the original codification in 1892 and, hence, does not exist as common law at the present time. Paragraph 35(a) of the *Interpretation Act* provides that "where an enactment is repealed in whole or in part, the repeal does not revive any enactment or anything not in force or existing at the time when the repeal takes effect." The defence of *doli incapax*, although based on a prior common law rule is, under the *Criminal Code*, a statutory defence and its repeal will not revive a historic rule that was "not in force or existing when the repeal takes place."

Further, the manifest purpose of the repeal of ss. 12 and 13, when read in conjunction with the overall scheme of the Y.O.A. is to raise the minimum age of criminal responsibility from seven to 12 and to remove the *doli incapax* rule. (For analogous examples of repeal of statutory provisions superseding common law, see *R. v. Firkins* (1977), 37 C.C.C. (2d) 227, 80 D.L.R. (3d) 63, 39 C.R.N.S. 178 (B.C.C.A.), leave to appeal to S.C.C. refused, 37 C.C.C. (2d) 227n, 80 D.L.R. (3d) 63n, 17 N.R. 119n (S.C.C.), and *R. v. Camp* (1977), 17 O.R. (2d) 99, 39 C.R.N.S. 164, 36 C.C.C. (2d) 511, 79 D.L.R. (3d) 462 (C.A.).)

Although a young person cannot rely on the old statutory or common law rule of *doli incapax*, a young person who truly lacks mental capacity may be found not guilty by reason of insanity, or unfit on account of insanity to stand trial: see discussion under s.13 of the Y.O.A. Further, alternative measures may be invoked in circumstances where the young person, although competent, is very young and immature, and the alternative measures program appears to be a good response to the young person's situation.

SECTION 73

73. Section 441 of the said Act is repealed.

Repeal of section 441 of the Criminal Code: section 73

Section 441 of the *Criminal Code* at present provides that where an accused is under the age of 16, and as a result of transfer is dealt with in adult court, his trial in adult court is to "take place without publicity." Section 441 accords with the general philosophy of private trials for juveniles, found in s. 12 of the *J.D.A.* The repeal of s. 441 of the *Code* is consistent with the new open court provisions of the Y.O.A.

Subsection 17(1) of the Y.O.A. provides for a court ordered ban on the publication of any information presented at a transfer hearing, until such time as the trial has ended in ordinary court.

SECTION 74

74. Subsection 442(1) of the said Act is repealed and the following substituted therefor:

"442. (1) *Exclusion of public in certain cases.*—Any proceedings against an accused shall be held in open court, but where the presiding judge, magistrate or justice, as the case may be, is of the opinion that it is in the interest of public morals, the maintenance of order or the proper administration of justice to exclude all or any members of the public from the court room for all or part of the proceedings, he may so order."

Amendment to subsection 442(1) of the Criminal Code: section 74

Subsection 442(1) of the *Code* presently provides for trials in "open court" when the accused is 16 years of age or more, unless the court is of the opinion that it "is in the interest of public morals, the maintenance of order or the proper administration of justice" to exclude all or any members of the public. Section 74 of the Y.O.A. amends s-s. 442(1) by providing that all trials in the ordinary criminal courts will be in open court, unless the court is of the opinion that it "is in the interest of public morals, the maintenance of order or the proper administration of justice" to exclude all or any members of the public. The amendment of s-s. 442(1) of the *Code* accords with the repeal of s. 441 of the *Code* by s. 73 of the Y.O.A., and is also consistent with the requirement of the Y.O.A. that proceedings be generally open to the public.

The provisions of s-s. 442(1) of the *Code*, as amended, will apply to all young persons transferred to the ordinary courts under s. 16 of the Y.O.A., as well as to adults who normally appear in those courts.

SECTION 75

75. The said Act is further amended by adding thereto, immediately after section 660 thereof, the following section:

"660.1 (1) *Transfer of young persons to place of custody.*— Where a young person is sentenced to imprisonment under this or any other Act of Parliament, the young person may, with the consent of the provincial director, be transferred to a place of custody for any portion of his term of imprisonment that expires before two years after the young person becomes an adult.

(2) *Removal of young person from place of custody.*— Where the provincial director certifies that a young person transferred to a place of custody under subsection (1) can no longer be held therein without significant danger of escape or detrimentally affecting the rehabilitation or reformation of other young persons held therein, the young person may be imprisoned during the remainder of his term of imprisonment in any place where he might, but for subsection (1), have been imprisoned.

(3) *Definitions.*—**For the purposes of this section, the expressions "young person", "provincial director" and "adult" have the meanings assigned to them by subsection 2(1) of the *Young Offenders Act* and the expression "place of custody" means "open custody" or "secure custody" within the meaning assigned by subsection 24(1) of that Act."**

Young persons sentenced in ordinary court after transfer: section 75

Section 75 of the Y.O.A. adds a section to the *Criminal Code* which will allow correctional authorities to place a young person who was transferred to ordinary (adult) court under s. 16 of the Y.O.A. in facilities for young persons, rather than in adult facilities. Subsection 660.1(1) of the *Code* will allow the correctional authorities to transfer a young person sentenced to imprisonment in ordinary court to a "place of custody" (open or secure custody facility for young persons); the transfer may be for any portion of the term of imprisonment that "expires before two years after the young person becomes an adult" (where the maximum age is under 18, the transfer can last until the person is 20).

The purpose of s. 660.1 of the *Code* is to allow a person who has been transferred to ordinary court, and convicted and sentenced in that court, to still benefit from programs geared to specific age groups at a place of custody reserved for young persons, and at the same time be segregated from adult offenders.

The procedure created by s. 660.1 of the *Code* is strictly administrative. The young person has no right to seek such a transfer. Nor can the sentencing judge in ordinary court order such a transfer as part of the sentence; he can merely make a recommendation in this regard and it is for the correctional authorities to make a decision (see *R. v. Deans* (1977), 39 C.R.N.S. 338, 37 C.C.C. (2d) 221 (Ont.C.A.)).

A transfer under s-s. 660.1(1) of the *Code* requires the approval of the adult correctional authorities, and the consent of the "provincial director" (defined by s-s. 2(1) of the Y.O.A.).

Subsection 660.1(2) of the *Code* provides that where a provincial director certifies that a young person who has been transferred to facilties for young persons pursuant to s-s. 660.1(1) can "no longer be held therein without significant danger of escape", he may be transferred back to any place of imprisonment which could have contained him prior to transfer under s-s. 660.1(1). Similarly, the young person may be transferred back to an adult facility on a provincial director's certificate, if the young person is "detrimentally affecting the rehabilitation or reformation of other young persons" held in a youth facility. This latter power to transfer those who interfere with the reformation of other young persons provides an avenue to correct a situation whereby under s-s. 660.1(1) of the *Code* an offender has grown too old for detention in an youth facility. The discretion provided by s-s. 660.1(2) allows the juvenile correctional authorities the flexibility to alter custodial arrangements in accordance with changes in the circumstances of the case.

Subsection 660.1(3) of the *Code* provides that the terms "young person", "adult" and "provincial director", used in s. 660.1, will have the same meaning as defined by s-s. 2(1) of the Y.O.A. A young person is transferred under s-s. 660.1(1) to a "place of custody", as defined in s-s. 24(1) of the Y.O.A.

It should be noted that a person transferred to a youth facility under s. 660.1 of the *Code* continues to be dealt with under the legislative provisions governing adults, for such matters as temporary absence and parole. The various provisions of the Y.O.A., such as review of dispositions, will *not* apply to such young persons.

SECTION 76

76. Section 120 of the *Indian Act* is repealed.

Repeal of section 120 of the Indian Act: section 76

Section 76 of the Y.O.A. repeals s. 120 of the *Indian Act*, R.S.C. 1970, c. I-6. This section of the *Indian Act* provides that an Indian child who is expelled or suspended from school or who refuses or fails to attend school regularly shall be deemed to be a "juvenile delinquent" within the meaning of the *J.D.A.* Section 120 of the *Indian Act* is repealed since it is highly discriminatory. A non-Indian child is not deemed to be a juvenile delinquent under the same circumstances. Consequently the section impinges on the provisions of the *Canadian Bill of Rights*: see *Re B. (F.J.)*, [1982] W.D.F.L. 364 (Ont. Prov. Ct.); it would also violate s. 15 of the *Canadian Charter of Rights and Freedoms*, dealing with "equality rights", when that provision comes into force (April, 1985). Further, as s. 120 of the *Indian Act* appears tantamount to conviction without a trial, it may violate ss. 7 and 11 of the *Charter*.

SECTION 77

77. The definition "inmate" in section 2 of the *Parole Act* is repealed and the following substituted therefor:

" 'inmate' means a person who is under a sentence of imprisonment pursuant to an Act of Parliament or imposed for criminal contempt of court but does not include

(a) a child within the meaning of the *Juvenile Delinquents Act*, as it read immediately prior to the coming into force of the *Young Offenders Act*, who is under sentence of imprisonment for an offence known as a delinquency under the *Juvenile Delinquents Act*,

(b) a young person within the meaning of the *Young Offenders Act* who has been committed to custody under that Act, or

(c) a person in custody solely by reason of imprisonment that has been ordered to be served intermittently pursuant to section 663 of the *Criminal Code*."

Definition of "inmate" in the Parole Act: section 77

Section 77 of the Y.O.A. changes the definition of "inmate" in the *Parole Act*, R.S.C. 1970, c. P-2, as amended by S.C. 1976-77, c. 53, s-s. 17(1), so that a young person receiving a custodial disposition under the Y.O.A. is *not* governed by the provisions of the *Parole Act*. At present, the definition of "inmate" under the *Parole Act* provides that a delinquent dealt with under the *J.D.A.* is *not* subject to the *Parole Act*, so this amendment to the definition simply has the effect of continuing the present system of restricting the applicability of the *Parole Act* to those sentenced to imprisonment in adult proceedings. Paragraph (a) of the definition makes clear that delinquents dealt with under the *J.D.A.* will not be caught within the definition of "inmate" during the transitional stage — after repeal of the *J.D.A.* and replacement of it with the Y.O.A. (see also s. 79 of the Y.O.A.).

Young persons placed in custody under the Y.O.A. will not be subject to the provisions of the *Parole Act*. However, their dispositions will be subject to review under the more flexible provisions of ss. 28 to 31 of the Y.O.A. Similarly, where a young person placed in custody under the Y.O.A. is transferred to a provincial correctional facility for adults pursuant to a court order under s-s. 24(14) of the Y.O.A., the review procedures of the Y.O.A. continue to apply. If, however, a young person is transferred to ordinary court under s. 16 of the Y.O.A., convicted, and sentenced to a term of imprisonment in that court, he may still be transferred to a youth facility pursuant to s. 660.1 of the *Criminal Code* (see s. 75 of the Y.O.A.); in this case he would continue to be dealt with under the *Parole Act*, and not under the Y.O.A.

SECTION 78

78. The definition "prisoner" in section 2 of the *Prisons and Reformatories Act* is repealed and the following substituted therefor:

" 'prisoner' means a person, other than

(a) a child within the meaning of the *Juvenile Delinquents Act*, as it read immediately prior to the coming into force of the *Young Offenders Act*, with respect to whom no order pursuant to section 9 of that Act has been made, or

(b) a young person within the meaning of the *Young Offenders Act* with respect to whom no order pursuant to section 16 of that Act has been made,

who is confined in a prison pursuant to a sentence for an offence under an Act of Parliament or any regulations made thereunder."

Definition of "prisoner" in the Prisons and Reformatories Act: section 78

Section 78 of the Y.O.A. amends the definition of "prisoner" in the *Prisons and Reformatories Act*, R.S.C. 1970, c. P-21, as amended by S.C. 1976-77, c. 53, s. 45 so that a young person receiving a custodial dispositionis *not* governed by the *Prisons and Reformatories Act*. At present, the definition of "prisoner" under the *Prisons and Reformatories Act* provides that a delinquent child under the J.D.A. is *not* subject to the *Prisons and Reformatories Act*, so that this amendment to the definition simply has the effect of continuing the present system of restricting the applicability of the *Prisons and Reformatories Act* to those sentenced to imprisonment in adult proceedings. Paragraph (a) of the definition makes clear that delinquents dealt with under the *J.D.A.* will not be caught within the definition of "prisoner" during the transitional stage after repeal of the *J.D.A.* and replacement of it with the Y.O.A. (see also s. 79 of the Y.O.A.).

Young persons placed in custody under the Y.O.A. will not be subject to the provisions of the *Prisons and Reformatories Act.* Even if a young person placed in custody under the Y.O.A. is transferred to a provincial correctional facility for adults pursuant to a youth court order under s-s. 24(14) of the Y.O.A., he will continue to be dealt with under the Y.O.A. If, however, a young person is transferred to ordinary court under s. 16 of the Y.O.A., convicted and sentenced to a term of imprisonment in that court, he will be subject to the *Prisons and Reformatories Act*; he will continue to be subject to the *Prisons and Reformatories Act* for such matters as temporary absence, even if transferred to a youth facility pursuant to s. 660.1 of the *Code* (see s. 75 of the Y.O.A.).

TRANSITIONAL
(Section 79)

Introduction

Section 79 deals with a variety of transitional problems arising out of the repeal of the *Juvenile Delinquents Act* and the proclaiming into force of the *Young Offenders Act*. See s. 80 concerning repeal of the *J.D.A.* and s. 81 for proclaiming into force of the Y.O.A.

If a young person commits an offence on or after the day the Y.O.A. comes into force, he is dealt with solely under the Y.O.A. or complementary provincial legislation. The *J.D.A.* clearly has no applicability.

If a young person commits a delinquency while the *J.D.A.* is in force, but proceedings are not commenced before the Y.O.A. is proclaimed in force, s-ss. 79(1), (3) and (4) provide he will not be dealt with under the *J.D.A.*, but rather under the new legislation.

If a young person commits a delinquency while the *J.D.A.* is in force and proceedings are commenced under the *J.D.A.*, the effect of s-s. 79(2) of the Y.O.A. is essentially to continue the proceedings under the *J.D.A.*, but to apply some of the provisions of the Y.O.A., particularly in regard to disposition.

It should be noted that by virtue of s-s. 45(8) of the Y.O.A., the destruction of records provisions of the Y.O.A. apply "with such modifications as the circumstances require, in respect of records relating to the offence of delinquency under the *Juvenile Delinquents Act*"; this applies regardless of when the adjudication of delinquency occurs.

SECTION 79

79. (1) *Transitional.*—**On and after the coming into force of this Act, no proceedings may be commenced under the *Juvenile Delinquents Act* in respect of a delinquency as defined in that Act.**

(2) *Idem.*—Where, before the coming into force of this Act, proceedings are commenced under the *Juvenile Delinquents Act* in respect of a delinquency as described in that Act alleged to have been committed by a person who was at the time of the delinquency a child as defined in that Act, the proceedings and all matters consequent thereon may be dealt with in all respects as if this Act had not come into force except that

(a) no court may, after the coming into force of this Act, make an order under section 9 of the *Juvenile Delinquents Act* in respect of a person who in any such proceedings has been adjudged a juvenile delinquent;

(b) where an adjudication of delinquency is made under the *Juvenile Delinquents Act,* all subsequent proceedings shall be taken under this Act as if the adjudication were a finding of guilt under section 19; and

(c) where a disposition is made under section 20 of the *Juvenile Delinquents Act,* sections 28 to 33 of this Act apply in respect of the disposition as if it were made under section 20 of this Act unless the young person may, pursuant to subsection 21(1) of the *Juvenile Delinquents Act,* be dealt with under the laws of a province.

(3) *Idem.*—Any person who, before the coming into force of this Act, commits an offence under a provincial statute or a by-law or ordinance of a municipality in respect of which proceedings are not commenced under the *Juvenile Delinquents Act* may be dealt with under provincial law as if the *Juvenile Delinquents Act* had not been in force when the person committed the offence.

(4) *Idem.*—Any person who, before the coming into force of this Act, while he was a young person committed an offence in respect of which no proceedings were commenced before the coming into force of this Act may be dealt with under this Act as if the offence occurred after the coming into force of this Act.

(5) *Proceedings commence with information.*—For the purposes of this section, proceedings are commenced by the laying of an information.

Where proceedings NOT commenced under the J.D.A.: subsections 79(1), (3), (4) and (5)

Subsection 79(1) of the Y.O.A. provides that where a youth is alleged to have committed an act which is defined under the J.D.A. to be a "delinquency" and no proceedings are commenced until the Y.O.A. comes into force, no proceedings may be commenced thereafter under the J.D.A. The definition of "delinquency" found in s-s. 2(1) of the J.D.A. is much broader than the definition of "offence" in the Y.O.A. Part of the J.D.A. definition includes violations of federal statutes which roughly corresponds to "offences" under the Y.O.A., but also includes violations of provincial statutes, municipal by-laws and "status offences" such as "sexual immorality and any similar form of vice."

Subsection 79(5) stipulates that for the purposes of s. 79, proceedings are commenced by the laying of an information, and thus, no information can be laid under the J.D.A. once the Y.O.A. comes into force.

Subsection 79(4) provides that if a "young person" is alleged to have committed an "offence" (i.e. violation of federal law) while the J.D.A. was in force, and no proceedings were commenced under the J.D.A. (no information laid), the young person may be dealt with under the Y.O.A., as if the Y.O.A. had been in force when the act was alleged to have occurred. The young person is entitled to all the benefits of the Y.O.A., and subject to all the rigours of the Act.

The definition of "juvenile delinquent" in s-s. 2(1) of the J.D.A. includes a juvenile who violates any "provincial statute, or any by-law or ordinance of a municipality." Such violations are not, however, "offences" under the Y.O.A., and the provinces will have to enact complementary legislation, to take effect upon the repeal of the J.D.A., to deal with "children" (under 12) and young persons (12 to 15, 16 or 17, inclusive) who violate provincial and municipal laws. This legislation may be "quasi-criminal", or take a child welfare approach. Subsection 79(3) of the Y.O.A. provides that "any person" who is alleged to have committed an offence under a provincial statute, or a by-law or ordinance of a municipality in respect of which no proceedings were commenced under the J.D.A. (no information laid), that person may be dealt with under "provincial law as if the *Juvenile Delinquents Act* had not been in force when the person committed the offence."

The effect of s-s. 79(3) will be to allow children and young persons to be dealt with under provincial law for violations of provincial or municipal law committed while the J.D.A. was in force.

It may be asked whether s-s. 79(4) of the Y.O.A. or similar provincial legislation might violate para. 11(g) of the *Charter of Rights*, which provides that:

> 11. Any person charged with an offence has the right
>
> . . . . .
>
> (g) not to be found guilty on account of any act or omission unless, at the time of the act or omission, it constituted an offence under Canadian . . . law . . .

It is submitted that s-s. 79(4) of the Y.O.A. does not violate the *Charter*. This is because s-s. 79(4) does not retroactively penalize a young person for conduct which was not criminal when it occurred; rather it simply changes the manner in which a particular offence is dealt with by the courts. As Pratte J. stated in *Morris v. The Queen*, [1979] 1 S.C.R. 405 at p. 426, 43 C.C.C. (2d) 129, 91 D.L.R. (3d) 161, 6 C.R.(3d) 36, 23 N.R. 109:

> . . . the *Juvenile Delinquents* Act does not prescribe any special rule of human conduct for juveniles; the *Criminal Code*, and other statutes . . . are applicable to juveniles and non-juveniles alike. Essentially, the *Juvenile Delinquents* Act does not create any offence; the offence results from the violation of another statute . . . But, when the offence is committed by a juvenile, a particular method of enforcement is prescribed . . .

This makes clear that neither the J.D.A. nor the Y.O.A. create an offence, and thus, para. 11(g) of the *Charter* is not violated by s-s. 79(4) of the Y.O.A.

Paragraph 11(i) of the *Charter* may have applicability in transitional situations, however. It provides that:

> 11. Any person charged with an offence has the right
>
> . . . . .
>
> (i) if found guilty of the offence and if the punishment for the offence has been varied between the time of commission and the time of sentencing, to the benefit of the lesser punishment.

Paragraph 11(i) thus requires that in rendering a disposition in proceedings regarding offences committed while the J.D.A. was in force, courts cannot, pursuant to the Y.O.A., impose a greater penalty than would have been possible under the J.D.A. For any given offence under the J.D.A., the court has the discretion to impose any measure listed in s. 20 thereof, which could include a committal to custody of indefinite duration or in excess of that allowed under the Y.O.A. By way of contrast, the Y.O.A. limits the duration of custodial dispositions to two or three years, depending on the offence. However, whether a disposition under the Y.O.A. is "lesser punishment" than a disposition under the J.D.A., is to be determined in the circumstances of each case.

Special problems arise in regard to status offences ("sexual immorality or any similar form of vice") and delinquencies committed by children under 12 which occurred while the J.D.A. was in force but in respect of which proceedings were not commenced — these problems are considered further below.

Where proceedings commenced under the J.D.A.: subsection 79(2)

Subsection 79(2) of the Y.O.A. creates a procedure to deal with delinquencies alleged to have been committed while the J.D.A. was in force, in respect of which proceedings were commenced under the J.D.A. Subsection 79(2) provides that, subject to specified exceptions, proceedings shall continue to be dealt with "in all respects" as if the Y.O.A. had not come into force. This means that all of the provisions of the J.D.A. apply, and further that the various laws and practices applicable to proceedings under the J.D.A., for example, in regard to the provision of counsel and the admissibility of evidence, continue to apply.

Paragraph 79(2)(a) prohibits a transfer to adult court being ordered under s. 9 of the J.D.A., after the Y.O.A. comes into force, in respect of a youth who has been adjudged a juvenile delinquent. The effect of para. 79(2)(a) is to prevent a J.D.A. transfer from occuring after adjudication. Under s. 9 of the J.D.A., a transfer can occur before or after adjudication. Subsection 20(3) of the J.D.A. allows a transfer to be ordered in the context of a disposition review, which can occur at any time before a juvenile reaches 21. Section 16 of the Y.O.A. allows a transfer order to be made only before adjudication; hence, para. 79(2)(a) gives a young person the benefit of the Y.O.A. in this regard. If a proceeding is commenced under the J.D.A. and continued after the Y.O.A. comes into force, a transfer order can still be made prior to adjudication. Such a transfer is only to be made if the criteria of s. 9 of the J.D.A. are satisfied; the "good of the child and the interest of the community" must "demand it".

Paragraph 79(2)(b) provides that if proceedings commenced under the J.D.A. are continued when the Y.O.A. is in force, "where an adjudication of delinquency is made under the *Juvenile Delinquents Act*, all subsequent proceedings shall be under this Act as if the adjudication [of delinquency] were a finding of guilt under section 19 of the Y.O.A.". Thus, pre-trial detention, and all evidentiary, procedural and substantive matters leading up to adjudication are dealt with under the *J.D.A.*, but if a finding of guilty is made, disposition, disposition review, the effect of disposition and all other matters after disposition are dealt with under the Y.O.A. The effect of para. 79(2)(b) may be modified by para. 11(i) of the *Charter of Rights*, which provides that:

11. Any person charged with an offence has the right

. . . . .

(i) if found guilty of the offence and if the punishment has been varied between the time of commission and the time of sentencing, to the benefit of the lesser punishment.

Thus, at a disposition hearing held under the Y.O.A. in regard to an offence committed while the *J.D.A.* was in force, all of the procedural aspects of the disposition hearing will be determined by the Y.O.A., but in rendering a disposition, the judge must not assess a greater penalty than would have been possible under the *J.D.A.* The young person must be given the benefit of the "lesser punishment". However, whether a disposition made under the *J.D.A.* actually constitutes a "lesser punishment" than one under the Y.O.A., is to be determined in the circumstances of each case.

Paragraph 79(2)(c) of the Y.O.A. provides that where a disposition has been made under s. 20 of the *J.D.A.*, once the Y.O.A. comes into force, disposition review will occur pursuant to ss. 28 to 33 of the Y.O.A. rather than under s-s. 20(3) of the *J.D.A.* Paragraph 79(2)(c) does not, however, apply when the youth is dealt with under provincial law pursuant to s-s. 21(1) of the *J.D.A.* Subsection 21(1) of the *J.D.A.* provides that if a juvenile has been committed to the care of a Children's Aid Society or to an industrial school pursuant to s. 20 of the *J.D.A.*, he shall, if so ordered by the provincial secretary, thereafter be dealt with under provincial law, and not by way of dispositional review under s-s. 20(3) of the *J.D.A.* Thus, the dispositional review provisions of the Y.O.A. will only be applied in regard to the review of dispositions made under the *J.D.A.* where there has not been a transfer of jurisdiction by the provincial secretary.

The remarks made above with respect to the effect of para. 11(i) of the *Charter* on para. 79(2)(b) of the Y.O.A. apply equally to para. 79(2)(c). In any disposition review under the Y.O.A., occurring in accordance with para. 79(2)(c), the youth is entitled to the benefit of the "lesser punishment" under the Y.O.A. or the J.D.A.

Status offences in the transitional period

As well as dealing with violations of federal, provincial or municipal laws, the definition of "juvenile delinquent" in s-s. 2(1) of the J.D.A. includes a youth who is "guilty of sexual immorality or any similar form of vice, or who is liable by reason of any other act to be committed to an industrial school." For the sake of compendious reference in this text, this will be referred to as the "status offence" provision of the J.D.A., as it creates an offence for which a juvenile may be adjudged delinquent but for which an adult may not suffer sanction; those in a particular "status", childhood, are subject to particular sanction. The Y.O.A. abolishes "status offences"; a young person can only be charged with an offence for which an adult may be charged.

If a juvenile commits a "status offence" under the J.D.A., but proceedings are not commenced under the J.D.A. before the Y.O.A. comes into force, no charges can be laid under the J.D.A. by virtue of s-s. 79(1) of the Y.O.A.; further, no charges can be laid pursuant to the Y.O.A. under s-s. 79(4), as a status offence is not an " offence" under the Y.O.A. Accordingly, unless a province has enacted legislation continuing to make "status offence" conduct a provincial offence, no proceedings can be taken against the young person. Where provincial legislation makes the "status offence" conduct an offence, s-s. 79(3) of the Y.O.A. would apply.

Where proceedings have been started under the J.D.A. respecting a status offence, the *Charter of Rights* may affect how a status offence is dealt with after the Y.O.A. comes into force. Paragraph 11(i) of the *Charter* provides that where a person is convicted of an offence for which the punishment has varied between its occurrence and the time of sentencing, the person is entitled to the "lesser punishment". As status offences are eliminated under the Y.O.A., there is of course no punishment provided for the commission of such an offence. It may therefore be argued that no sanction can be imposed at the time of disposition, and it follows that proceedings commenced under the

J.D.A. concerning status offences will be withdrawn if no disposition has been made before the *Y.O.A.* comes into force.

Where a disposition has been made in regard to a status offence under the *J.D.A.* while that Act is still in force, but the disposition continues to be in effect when the *Y.O.A.* is in force, there may be grounds for a disposition review under ss. 28 to 33 of the *Y.O.A..* The review provisions of the *Y.O.A.* are applicable due to para. 79(2)(c) of the *Y.O.A.*

It should be noted that it may be possible to argue that a charge of "sexual immorality or any similar form of vice" under the *J.D.A.* may be subject to direct challenge under the *Charter.* It may be argued that such charge is so vague that it contravenes the "principles of fundamental justice", and hence violates s. 7 of the *Charter.*

Offences committed by a child

A person between the ages of seven and 11 may be charged under the *J.D.A.*, subject to raising a defence under s. 13 of the *Criminal Code* of *doli incapax* — incapacity due to age to form an intent to do wrong. Under the *Y.O.A.*, a "child", being a person under the age of 12, is not subject to prosecution. Thus, it will be up to each province to enact legislation to deal with the illegal conduct of "children".

In regard to dealing with conduct by children under 12 which would constitute a violation of federal or provincial law if it involved an older person, a province may choose one of two approaches: an offence oriented approach or a child welfare approach.

An offence oriented approach would involve the enactment of some form of provincial "Child Offender Act" applicable to matters within the purview of provincial jurisdiction. This approach would involve focussing on the misconduct of children. There may be some constitutional problem with provinces taking an offence approach in regard to conduct otherwise dealt with by federal criminal law, particularly in the light of s. 12 of the *Criminal Code*, as amended by s. 72 of the *Y.O.A.*, which provides that: "No person shall be convicted of an offence [under any federal statute] in respect of an act or omission on his part while he was under the age of twelve years." In any event, if a province creates a certain class of offences for children under 12, s-ss. 79(2) and (3) of the Y.O.A. are available to deal with transitional problems.

A child welfare approach would have offences committed by children under 12 dealt with in the context of provincial welfare legislation. The fact that a child committed an act which would be an offence if he were 12 years or older would be a ground for finding him in "need of protection", but a disposition would involve a consideration of all aspects of a child's life and would be based primarily on his "best interests". Legislation taking a welfare approach might well provide for greater involvement of parents and child welfare authorities than is required under the Y.O.A.

If a province adopts a child welfare approach in regard to the misconduct of children under 12, upon the repeal of the J.D.A. it will not be possible to say that a child who commits an act which would be an offence if he were older is committing an "offence under a provincial statute". This raises certain transitional issues similar to those arising in regard to status offences under the J.D.A., as s-s. 79(3) is not applicable. If proceedings regarding an offence committed by a child under 12 while the J.D.A. was in force have not been commenced prior to the Y.O.A. coming into force, they cannot be commenced under the Y.O.A.: s-ss. 79(1), (3) and (4). If proceedings have been commenced and no disposition has been made, para. 11(i) of the *Charter* would probably require their discontinuance, as the child is entitled to the benefit of the lesser punishment available at the time of sentencing, and "no punishment" is available after the repeal of the J.D.A. It would seem that if a child were already subject to a disposition under the J.D.A. when the Y.O.A. comes into force, this would be a factor which would be considered by the youth court on reviewing the disposition.

Another transitional problem may occur when a child under 12 commits an offence under the J.D.A. prior to the coming into force of the Y.O.A. In this instance, the Y.O.A. will not apply to the child; however, reference should be made to any relevant provincial legislation for possible retroactive effect.

REPEAL
(Section 80)

SECTION 80

80. The *Juvenile Delinquents* Act is repealed.

Section 80 repeals the *Juvenile Delinquents Act*, effective the date that the *Young Offenders Act* is proclaimed in force. Section 79 of the Y.O.A. deals with a variety of transitional issues which may arise.

COMMENCEMENT
(Section 81)

SECTION 81

81. *Commencement*.—This Act shall come into force on a day to be fixed by proclamation.

The *Young Offenders Act* received Royal Assent on July 7, 1982 and was proclaimed in force on April 2, 1984.

The uniform maximum age provisions do not become manadatory until April 1, 1985, and accordingly the maximum age in individual provinces may by proclamation of the Governor in Council, at the request of a province, remain at 16, 17 or 18 as the case may be; thereafter, it will be under 18 in all provinces. The timing of the uniform maximum age provision will coincide with the coming into force of s. 15 of the *Canadian Charter of Rights and Freedoms*, governing equality rights.

A delay in proclamation is required to allow the provinces time to enact complementary legislation, and establish various programs to implement the Act. It may also give the federal and provincial governments time to make financial arrangements for the implementation of the Act.

Finally, the delay will give those who must work with the Act an opportunity to study and understand it. Hopefully, the preceding materials have been of assistance in this regard.

CANADIAN CHARTER OF RIGHTS AND FREEDOMS

CANADIAN BILL OF RIGHTS

Introduction

All of the provisions of the Y.O.A. and all proceedings involving young persons, are subject to the *Canadian Charter of Rights and Freedoms* and the *Canadian Bill of Rights*. This is clear from a reading of these constitutional documents, and confirmed by para. 3(1)(e) of the Y.O.A., which recognizes the principle that "young persons have rights and freedoms in their own right, including those stated in the *Canadian Charter of Rights and Freedoms* or in the *Canadian Bill of Rights*."

Reference has been made in the discussion of various sections of the Y.O.A. to situations in which the *Charter* or the *Bill of Rights* may appear particularly applicable to proceedings under the Y.O.A. Of course, if the *Charter* or the *Bill of Rights* is held by the courts to affect more general criminal legislation, this may also affect proceedings under the Y.O.A.

All of those involved in the administration of juvenile justice will have to keep abreast of judicial developments in regard to the *Charter* and *Bill of Rights*. Useful reference tools in this regard are such looseleaf services as *The Canadian Charter of Rights Annotated*, edited by J. B. Laskin, E. L. Greenspan *et al.* (Aurora: Canada Law Book), and *Canadian Rights Reporter*, edited by C. Ruby and Edward (Toronto: Butterworths).

Some of the provisions of the *Charter* and *Bill of Rights* which are most applicable to proceedings under the Y.O.A. are set out here.

CANADIAN CHARTER OF RIGHTS AND FREEDOMS

Guarantee of Rights and Freedoms

1. *Rights and freedoms in Canada.*—The *Canadian Charter of Rights and Freedoms* guarantees the rights and freedoms set out in it subject only to such reasonable limits prescribed by law as can be demonstrably justified in a free and democratic society.

Fundamental Freedoms

2. *Fundamental freedoms.*—Everyone has the following fundamental freedoms:

(a) freedom of conscience and religion;

(b) freedom of thought, belief, opinion and expression, including freedom of the press and other media of communication;

(c) freedom of peaceful assembly; and

(d) freedom of association.

. . . . .

Legal Rights

7. *Life, liberty, and security of person.*—Everyone has the right to life, liberty and security of the person and the right not to be deprived thereof except in accordance with the principles of fundamental justice.

8. *Search or seizure.*—Everyone has the right to be secure against unreasonable search or seizure.

9. *Detention or imprisonment.*—Everyone has the right not to be arbitrarily detained or imprisoned.

10. *Arrest or detention.*—Everyone has the right on arrest or detention

(a) to be informed promptly of the reasons therefor;

(b) to retain and instruct counsel without delay and to be informed of that right; and

(c) to have the validity of the detention determined by way of *habeas corpus* and to be released if the detention is not lawful.

11. *Proceedings in criminal and penal matters.*—Any person charged with an offence has the right

(a) to be informed without unreasonable delay of the specific offence;

(b) to be tried within a reasonable time;

(c) not to be compelled to be a witness in proceedings against that person in respect of the offence;

(d) to be presumed innocent until proven guilty according to law in a fair and public hearing by an independent and impartial tribunal;

(e) not to be denied reasonable bail without just cause;

(f) except in the case of an offence under military law tried before a military tribunal, to the benefit of trial by jury where the maximum punishment for the offence is imprisonment for five years or a more severe punishment;

(g) not to be found guilty on account of any act or omission unless, at the time of the act or omission, it constituted an offence under Canadian or international law or was criminal according to the general principles of law recognized by the community of nations;

(h) if finally acquitted of the offence, not to be tried for it again and, if finally found guilty and punished for the offence, not to be tried or punished for it again; and

(i) if found guilty of the offence and if the punishment for the offence has been varied between the time of commission and the time of sentencing, to the benefit of the lesser punishment.

12. *Treatment or punishment.*—Everyone has the right not be subjected to any cruel and unusual treatment or punishment.

13. *Self-incrimination.*—A witness who testifies in any proceedings has the right not to have any incriminating evidence so given used to incriminate that witness in any other proceedings, except in a prosecution for perjury or for the giving of contradictory evidence.

14. *Interpreter.*—A party or witness in any proceedings who does not understand or speak the language in which the proceedings are conducted or who is deaf has the right to the assistance of an interpreter.

Equality Rights

15. (1) *Equality before and under law and equal protection and benefit of law.*—Every individual is equal before and under the law and has the right to the equal protection and equal benefit of the law without discrimination and, in particular, without discrimination based on race, national or ethnic origin, colour, religion, sex, age or mental or physical disability.

(2) *Affirmative action programs.*—Subsection (1) does not preclude any law, program or activity that has as its object the amelioration of conditions of disadvantaged individuals or groups including those that are disadvantaged because of race, national or ethnic origin, colour, religion, sex, age or mental or physical disability.

[Note: Due to s-s. 32(2) of the *Charter*, s. 15 of the *Charter* will not come into force until April 17, 1985.]

. . . . .

Enforcement

24. (1) *Enforcement of guaranteed rights and freedoms.*— Anyone whose rights or freedoms, as guaranteed by this Charter, have been infringed or denied may apply to a court of competent jurisdiction to obtain such remedy as the court considers appropriate and just in the circumstances.

(2) *Exclusion of evidence bringing administration of justice into disrepute.*—Where, in proceedings under subsection (1), a court concludes that evidence was obtained in a manner that infringed or denied any rights or freedoms guaranteed by this Charter, the evidence shall be excluded if it is established that, having regard to all the circumstances, the admission of it in the proceedings would bring the administration of justice into disrepute.

CANADIAN BILL OF RIGHTS

1. *Recognition and declaration of rights and freedoms.*—It is hereby recognized and declared that in Canada there have existed and shall continue to exist without discrimination by reason of race, national origin, colour, religion or sex, the following human rights and fundamental freedoms, namely,

(a) the right of the individual to life, liberty, security of the person and enjoyment of property, and the right not to be deprived thereof except by due process of law;

(b) the right of the individual to equality before the law and the protection of the law;

(c) freedom of religion;

(d) freedom of speech;

(e) freedom of assembly and association; and

(f) freedom of the press.

2. *Construction of law.*—Every law of Canada shall, unless it is expressly declared by an Act of Parliament that it shall operate notwithstanding the *Canadian Bill of Rights*, be so construed and applied as not to abrogate, abridge or infringe or to authorize the abrogation, abridgment or infringement of any of the rights or freedoms herein recognized and declared, and in particular, no law of Canada shall be construed or applied so as to

(a) authorize or effect the arbitrary detention, imprisonment or exile of any person;

(b) impose or authorize the imposition of cruel and unusual treatment or punishment;

(c) deprive a person who has been arrested or detained

(i) of the right to be informed promptly of the reason for his arrest or detention,

(ii) of the right to retain and instruct counsel without delay, or

(iii) of the remedy by way of *habeas corpus* for the determination of the validity of his detention and for his release if the detention is not lawful;

(d) authorize a court, tribunal, commission, board or other authority to compel a person to give evidence if he is denied counsel, protection against self incrimination or other constitution safeguards;

(e) deprive a person of the right to a fair hearing in accordance with the principles of fundamental justice for the determination of his rights and obligations;

(f) deprive a person charged with a criminal offence of the right to be presumed innocent until proved guilty according to law in a fair and public hearing by an independent and impartial tribunal, or of the right to reasonable bail without just cause; or

(g) deprive a person of the right to the assistance of an interpreter in any proceedings in which he is involved or in which he is a party or witness, before a court, commission, board or other tribunal, if he does not understand or speak the language in which such proceedings are conducted.

INDEX